D1027482

Human Personality

and Its Survival of Bodily Death

F. W. H. MYERS

Edited by
SUSY SMITH

Foreword by
ALDOUS HUXLEY

DOVER PUBLICATIONS, INC.
Mineola, New York

Bibliographical Note

This Dover edition, first published in 2005, is an unabridged republication of the edition originally published by University Books, Inc., New Hyde Park, New York, in 1961. The University Books edition, as Susy Smith notes in her Preface, was restructured and abbreviated from the original 1,360-page, two-volume edition, which was published by Longmans, Green, and Company, New York, in 1903.

Library of Congress Cataloging-in-Publication Data

Myers, Frederic William Henry, 1843-1901.
    Human personality and its survival of bodily death / F.W.H. Myers ; edited by Susy Smith ; foreword by Aldous Huxley.
       p. cm.
    Originally published: New Hyde Park, N.Y. : University Books, 1961.
    Includes bibliographical references and index.
    ISBN 0-486-43818-X (pbk.)
    1. Parapsychology. 2. Personality. 3. Immortality. I. Smith, Susy. II. Title.

BF1031.M85 2004
133.9'01'3—dc22

                        2004056237

Manufactured in the United States of America
Dover Publications, Inc., 31 East 2nd Street, Mineola, N.Y. 11501

CONTENTS

FOREWORD

Is the house of the soul a mere bungalow with a cellar? Or does it have an upstairs above the ground floor of consciousness as well as a garbage-littered basement beneath? Freud, the most popular and influential of modern psychologists, inclined to the bungalow-with-basement view of human nature. It was only to be expected; for Freud was a doctor and, like most doctors, paid more attention to sickness than to health. His primary concern was with the subterranean rats and black beetles, and with all the ways in which a conscious ego may be disturbed by the bad smells and the vermin below stairs.

F.W.H. Myers, who was born fifteen years before Freud and predeceased him by forty, was not a doctor and so had no vested interest in sickness. As a classical scholar, a minor poet, a conscientious observer and a platonic philosopher, he was free to pay more attention to the positive aspects of the subliminal self than to its negative and destructive aspects. He knew, of course, that the cellar stinks and is alive with vermin; but he was more interested in what goes on in the rooms (ordinarily locked) above street level—in the treasures of the *piano nobile,* in the far-ranging birds (and perhaps even angels) that come and go between the rafters of a roofless attic that is open to the sky.

In this great book Myers brought together an immense store of information about the always strange and often wonderful goings-on in the upper stories of a man's soul-house. And this information he presents within a theoretical frame of reference that takes account not only of the rats and beetles in the cellarage, but also of those treasures, birds and angels so largely ignored by Freud and his followers.

For some tastes, Myers' theoretical framework may seem excessively "spiritual." But at least it has the merit of "saving the appearances," of covering all the facts. His account of the unconscious is superior to Freud's in at least one respect; it is more comprehensive and truer to the data of experience. It is also, it seems to me, superior to Jung's account in being more richly documented with concrete facts and less encumbered with those psycho-anthropologico-pseudo-genetic speculations which becloud the writings of the sage of Zurich. Jung is like those classical German scholars of whom Porson once said that "they dive deeper and come up muddier than any others." Myers dives no less deeply into that impersonal spiritual world which transcends and interpenetrates our bodies, our conscious minds and our personal unconscious—dives no less deeply but comes up with a minimum of mud on him.

How strange and how unfortunate it is that this amazingly rich, profound and stimulating book should have been neglected in favor of descriptions of human nature less complete and of explanations less adequate to the given facts! The editor and the publisher of this new, one-volume edition of Myers' forgotten classic deserve all our gratitude.

ALDOUS HUXLEY

PREFACE

For six decades, since its original publication in 1903, HUMAN PERSON-
ALITY AND ITS SURVIVAL OF BODILY DEATH has been the most highly
esteemed work in the field of psychical research. During the brief history
of scholarly writing on this subject, Frederic W. H. Myers' monumental
study has often, and with justification, been referred to as a classic. Unfortunately, voluminous classics are widely praised but rarely read. The
present edition is an abridgement of the original two-volume 1,360 page
work, prepared to make its major content more readily accessible to the
modern reader.

This volume would not be complete without an introductory appraisal
of F. W. H. Myers, the man. In an evaluation of his character, Professor
Gardner Murphy,[1] Director of Research at the Menninger Foundation, in
the Introduction to a previous edition, referred to Myers as "an encyclo-
pedic student of the new wisdom." Murphy added that Myers "had the
courage, the range and the depth to take into account findings in a vast
area still looked upon askance by science."

Although schooled primarily in languages and the classics, and
thinking of himself as a "minor poet and amateur savant," Myers became
expert in many fields in order to write this book. Murphy refers to his
"colossal scope" of inquiry and "unflagging intensity," as he not only
made himself familiar with modern medicine and psychology, but en-
compassed most of the literature of psychiatry, as well as the new psychical
field—learning all "those techniques of investigation of human personality which were just beginning to take shape in the late nineteenth century."

Speaking of Myers' service to psychology by writing HUMAN PERSON-
ALITY, William James[2] has stated that "for half a century now, psychologists have fully admitted the existence of a subliminal mental region,
under the name either of unconscious cerebration or of the involuntary
life; but they have never definitely taken up the question of the extent of

[1] HUMAN PERSONALITY AND ITS SURVIVAL OF BODILY DEATH, 2 vols., with
Introduction by Gardner Murphy, New York, Longmans, Green and Co., printed by
arrangement with Garrett Publications, 1954.
[2] "Frederic Myers' Service to Psychology," *Proceedings* of the Society for Psychical
Research, Vol. XVII, 1901.

this region, never sought explicitly to map it out. Myers definitely attacks this problem, which, after him, it will be impossible to ignore."

But Myers did more than this, according to James:[3] "Anyone with a healthy sense of evidence, a sense not methodically blunted by the sectarianism of 'science,' ought now ... to feel that exalted sensibilities and memories, veridical phantasms, haunted houses, trances with supernormal faculty, and even experimental thought-transference, are natural kinds of phenomena which ought, just like other natural events, to be followed up with scientific curiosity."

James added that "the existence all about us of thousands and tens of thousands of persons, not perceptibly hysteric or unhealthy, who are mediumistic ... is a phenomenon of human life which [psychologists] do not even attempt to connect with any of the other facts of nature. Add the fact that the mediumship often gives supernormal information, and it becomes evident that the phenomenon cannot consist of pure eccentricity and isolation ... It cries aloud for serious investigation."

William James was thus "disposed to think it a probability that Frederic Myers will always be remembered in psychology as the pioneer who staked out a vast tract of mental wilderness and planted the flag of genuine science upon it."

Frederic William Henry Myers was born in Keswick, Cumberland, England on February 6, 1843, the son of a clergyman. From early boyhood he was a devoted student of classical literature. He attended Cheltenham School, and at the age of 17 entered Trinity College, Cambridge. Between the ages of 16 and 23 there was, in his own words, "no influence in my life comparable to Hellenism in the fullest sense of the word." Then, for a time, he rediscovered the Christianity of his youth "in its emotional fullness." But later, because of "increased knowledge of history and science, from a wider outlook of the world," began a process of disillusionment with religion as he had comprehended it in earlier years.

This disillusionment left him, he stated, with "an agnosticism or virtual materialism which sometimes was a dull pain borne with joyless doggedness, sometimes ... a shock of nightmare-panic amid the glaring dreariness of the day. It was the hope of the world which was vanishing, not mine alone."

Once, "in a starlight walk I shall not forget," he asked his favorite teacher, Henry Sidgwick, "as his only hope in his perplexities," whether he thought that observable psychic phenomena might solve the riddle of

---

[3] "Review of HUMAN PERSONALITY AND ITS SURVIVAL OF BODILY DEATH," *Proceedings* of the Society for Psychical Research, Vol. XVIII, 1903.

the universe when other methods had failed. Upon Sidgwick's cautious encouragement, an informal association was formed, with the addition of Mrs. Sidgwick and Edmund Gurney, for the investigation of these phenomena. This ultimately led to the foundation of the Society for Psychical Research.

Myers received his degree in 1864, became a classical lecturer at Cambridge, and a fellow of Trinity in 1865; but in 1872 he abandoned this for the post of inspector of schools at Cambridge. There seems to have been a purpose in this move, for during the thirty years he held this position, he had ample leisure to write and to spend many hours in psychical research.

In 1873, when he was thirty years old, Myers fell in love with Annie Hill Marshall, the wife of his cousin Walter James Marshall, who lived at Hallsteads, Cumberland. Her marriage was reasonably happy, but, for her, unromantic. The proud, sensual, and emotional young Myers experienced for her a passionate love; but to judge from what he has written about her, she returned his love only as far as was compatible with complete loyalty to her husband. They walked together, and talked ardently, in the valley at Hallsteads. She died suddenly on August 29, 1876.

According to W. H. Salter,[4] member of the Council of the Society for Psychical Research, in his biographical sketch, Annie Marshall was for Myers "a woman with whom marriage was impossible and an irregular union unthinkable." Her sudden death was a shattering blow to him, but the intensity of his feelings convinced him that they and their love could survive the death of the body. Salter states that from then on he had "a faith that satisfied his emotions, his intelligence and his moral sense in a way that he had not found possible in any of the phases of belief through which he had previously passed."

Before his faith was thus assured, he and Sidgwick had begun their psychical researches. "I had at first," Myers wrote, "a great repugnance to studying the phenomena alleged by the spiritualists." The personal second-rateness of many of the mediums with whom he sat was distasteful to what Salter calls "his socially exclusive nature." He saw many physical (telekinetic) phenomena, but was never enthusiastic about them. His main interest lay in mental mediumship and communications tending to prove survival of bodily death. Myers wrote that it was in the autumn of 1873 that "I came across my first personal experience of forces unknown to science." It was some years later that a communication from Annie Marshall, through a medium, finally confirmed his belief in survival.

[4] "Our Pioneers," *Journal* of the Society for Psychical Research, Vol. 39, September, 1958.

In 1882, on the initiative of the Dublin physicist, Sir William F. Barrett, the Society for Psychical Research was established in London; the Rev. W. Stainton Moses, Henry Sidgwick, Edmund Gurney, and Myers himself were among its distinguished founders. Myers played a large part in the first twenty years' work of the Society. Salter[5] notes that he could speak "eloquently and wittily on all aspects of psychical research. During his life the Society never ran short of good discussion meetings. If Myers had no paper to contribute, without notes and with little preparation he could be trusted to give an interesting account of current inquiries. A sociable man, he talked psychical research to everyone he met, and in this and other ways became the best publicist the Society and its work have ever enjoyed."

William James[6] said of him that "never by nature a philosopher in the technical sense . . . not crammed with science at college, or trained to scientific method by any passage through a laboratory; Myers had as it were to re-create his personality before he became the wary critic of evidence, the skillful handler of hypothesis, the learned neurologist and omnivorous reader of biological and cosmological matter, with whom in later years we were acquainted. The transformation came about because he needed to be all these things in order to work successfully at the problem that lay near his heart; and the ardor of his will and the richness of his intellect are proved by the success with which he underwent so unusual a transformation."

James[7] also stated: "When I hear good people say . . . that dabbling in such phenomena reduces us to a sort of jelly, disintegrates the critical faculties, liquefies the character, and makes of one a gullible fool generally, I console myself by thinking of my friends Frederic Myers and Richard Hodgson. These men lived exclusively for psychical research, and it converted both to spiritism . . . Myers' character . . . grew stronger in every particular for his devotion to these inquiries. Brought up on literature and sentiment, something of a courtier, passionate, disdainful, and impatient naturally, he was made over again from the day when he took up psychical research seriously. He became learned in science, circumspect, democratic in sympathy, endlessly patient, and above all, happy. The fortitude of his last hours touched the heroic, so completely were the atrocious sufferings of his body cast into insignificance by his interest in

5 *Op. cit.*, footnote 4.
6 *Op. cit.*, footnote 2.
7 "The Final Impressions of a Psychical Researcher," in MEMORIES AND STUDIES, New York, Longmans, Green and Co., 1911.

the cause he lived for. When a man's pursuit gradually makes his face shine and grow handsome, you may be sure it is a worthy one."

Myers died on a visit to Rome at the age of 58, on January 17, 1901, during his year as President of the Society for Psychical Research. He was buried in Keswick. He left his widow, Eveleen Tennant, whom he had married in 1880, and three children.

His great work, HUMAN PERSONALITY AND ITS SURVIVAL OF BODILY DEATH, left unfinished at his death, was prepared for publication two years later by his friend Richard Hodgson and Miss Alice Johnson.

Frederic Myers, after his death, is credited with giving what some consider to be the strongest evidence yet obtained for survival and communication. The "cross correspondence" method is attributed to him.

Raynor C. Johnson,[8] Master of Queen's College, University of Melbourne, writes: "The idea underlying [the cross correspondences] is this. Suppose an incident or a theme characteristic, let us say, of the deceased F. W. H. Myers appeared in an automatic script, it might be claimed by the critic that it had been drawn from the medium's own subliminal mind or derived by her telepathically from the minds of other living persons who knew Myers. Suppose, however, that Myers (whom we will postulate as surviving) divided his message into phrases and fragments, sending some of these through the script of one automatist and some through the script of a second and of a third. These fragments, which to the automatist would seem meaningless and incoherent, if placed together skillfully by an independent person would show purpose and planning by a mind independent of the automatists. Evidence that such experiments were being attempted began to appear in scripts from 1907 onward."

At about this time, four women who were deeply interested in psychical research began to develop considerable facility in automatic writing. These were Mrs. A. W. Verrall, her daughter Helen (the future Mrs. Salter), Mrs. Holland (a pseudonym for Rudyard Kipling's sister) who lived in India, and Mrs. Leonore Piper in the United States. They began to receive a great deal of material reflecting considerable classical knowledge on the part of the sender. Those who studied the scripts, seeking to interpret them, were inevitably led to the thought that it might be Myers who was making an effort to prove his survival. As Gardner Murphy[9] says: "Often a message developed from these scattered scripts from various automatists would have a peculiarly Myers-like ring; would appear

[8] THE IMPRISONED SPLENDOUR, New York, Harper & Brothers, 1953.
[9] Footnote 1.

to be the sort of thing which a surviving Myers would have delighted in developing and planting in the subliminal minds of the automatists who were concerned with him ... It is of some interest that he whose volume is the classical statement of an ordered scientific effort to cope with the problem of human survival should be the individual for whose own continuity the largest amount of empirical material has been secured."

Aside from the cross correspondences attributed to him, there is some evidence that Myers may have given another indication of his continued existence by his posthumous message. He had left a sealed envelope with the hope that a medium might give a veridical report of its contents before is was opened, as proof that the information came from a surviving Myers. Shortly after his death a message was received through Mrs. Verrall which read: "I have long told you of the contents of the envelope. Myers' sealed envelope left with Lodge. You have not understood. It has in it the words from the SYMPOSIUM—about Love bridging the chasm."

The envelope was then opened and the message Myers had left read: "If I can revisit any earthly scene, I should choose the *Valley* in the grounds of Hallsteads, Cumberland."

It was then reported that this experiment had completely failed. But several leaders of the Society for Psychical Research, including Mrs. Sidgwick, Miss Alice Johnson, Sir Oliver Lodge, G. W. Balfour, and J. G. Piddington, after study of other documents came to the conclusion that, although the test had been formally and literally a failure, there was a definite connection, and that a paranormal one, between the communication and the message.

Myers in 1893 had privately printed a booklet of 43 pages which he called FRAGMENTS OF INNER LIFE. Copies were sent to certain old friends in sealed packets to be opened after his death. A large part of this booklet was republished posthumously by Mrs. Myers in 1904.[10] The references to Plato in the last chapter of the first booklet, references then for the first time made public, show that there was an association in Myers' mind between the valley at Hallsteads and the view of love described in Plato's SYMPOSIUM.

Thus there seems to be more than coincidence between the message which refers to Myers's desire to visit the scene of his first great love and the message which refers to love as described in the SYMPOSIUM.

"Taking all the matters discussed together," W. H. Salter[11] says, "I am definitely of the opinion that Mrs. Verrall's scripts ... make allusions,

---

[10] FRAGMENTS OF PROSE AND POETRY, London, Longmans, Green and Co., 1904.
[11] "F. W. H. Myers' Posthumous Message," *Proceedings* of the Society for Psychical Research, Vol. LII, 1958.

for which no normal explanation is sufficient, to Myers' love for Annie Marshall, to his account of it in unpublished writings which Mrs. Verrall had not seen, and to this posthumous message."

While Myers was writing HUMAN PERSONALITY AND ITS SURVIVAL OF BODILY DEATH, the question of man's soul-less descent from the apes was the center of intellectual controversy. It showed great daring, at that time, to express a belief that man has a soul, and to attempt to show that this soul can survive death. Myers was a pioneer in the field of psychical research in an era when scientific pioneering all around him proceeded in the opposite direction, toward philosophical materialism and determinism.

At the present unsettled point in world history, science has grown less dogmatic. This would seem to be particularly true in the field of physics, which views its ever-changing scene with ever more precise instruments, its philosophical horizons widening as its physical horizons grow increasingly boundless. This was brought out by Dr. Henry Margenau,[12] Professor of Physics and Natural Philosophy at Yale University, who observed that:

"This decline of materialism occurred first because various discoveries, culminating in the demonstration of the Relativity Principle, made untenable the notion of a continuous material medium upon whose postulation materialism was dependent. Next, the atom, which had been conceived as a solid pellet of stuff, turned out to be wholly empty, containing nothing that could be called 'matter' at all. It had degenerated into a series of singularities haunting space. This rather disposed of matter.

"Furthermore," Dr. Margenau added, "there has been a change in the old-style dogmatism that imbued the whole of physical science."

This, then, a time when dogmatism and philosophical materialism are in decline, is a period in which Myers' work may well be viewed with new appreciation, especially since world conditions now arouse in us a need to think seriously about the question of survival of bodily death. Dr. J. B. Rhine,[13] Director of the Parapsychology Laboratory at Duke University, feels that if we are to prevent man from "going down in the rubble of the crash of his physical world which his increasingly ingenious weapons threaten to produce, he must discover (and learn how to direct) the forces of his own fundamental nature. Only through a better science of

[12] Layman's Movement for a Christian World: SEMINAR ON THE DECLINE OF MATERIALISM, Wainwright House, Rye, New York, 1957.
[13] "The Question of Spirit Survival," Journal of the American Society for Psychical Research, Vol. XLIII, April, 1949.

personality, one broad enough to include such a problem as that of survival, can [man] save himself." The challenge is there, Dr. Rhine says, adding that, "in the question of spirit survival scientific method has both a problem and something real to attack, and parapsychology has a mandate."

Indeed, the goals of this book written in the last century are even more urgent today.

Building upon the foundation laid by Myers, both psychology and psychical research have advanced since his death; but neither has actually outdated his findings. There are new ways of stating concepts now, new terminologies, new testing procedures. But even stated in more modern vocabulary, the basic premises of HUMAN PERSONALITY can still be summed up as simply as this:

1. Myers' object was to recognize what we now call extrasensory perception as something natural, not unnatural. And he sought to describe the "soul" as an actual, definable component of the organism, which could survive the body at death.

2. As Myers saw it, even the most emotionally stable mind gives occasional indications of paranormal experiences. From his vast supply of case histories he reported instances when sleeping people were seen somewhere else by others, or, having dreamed of the dead, they had awakened with previously unknown information. He pointed out that geniuses sometimes have "subliminal uprushes" of unusual talents and aptitudes which are difficult to explain.

3. To prove the normal by the abnormal, Myers described split or dissociated personalities. It is often evident that these "sick" people have access to telepathic or precognitive information, or they may claim to talk with spirits. Similar phenomena may be induced in some perfectly well subjects by hypnosis.

4. Myers cited occasions when the dead have been seen and described by persons who had never seen them in life. There are instances where those who have died appear in dreams or visions or as apparitions and give information which was not previously known to the one who saw them. And there is a considerable volume of material which has been received through mediums ostensibly from the deceased.

5. Myers carefully indicated that many supposedly psychic phenomena are doubtless only manifestations from the subconscious mind of the individual. However, he found in each category certain well-documented instances which could only be regarded as paranormal. He

assembled a vast amount of illustrative material[14] in support of his statements.

6. After his arguments and their illustrations, Myers drew the conclusion that if sleeping, hypnotized, abnormal, and normal people communicate telepathically and have "out of the body" experiences, then there is something in the organism which can leave it, or appear to leave it; and this, he believed, could be called the "soul" or "spirit."

7. If living persons receive information known only to the deceased entity which purports to be communicating, then, Myers concluded, this indicates that the personality of the communicator has survived bodily death. And to Frederic Myers it was a glorious achievement to have been able to apply scientific methods of analysis and discussion to the question of survival, to him the most crucial of all human problems.

This volume has been prepared with the support of the Parapsychology Foundation, Inc.; among those whose help has been invaluable are: Professor C. J. Ducasse, Brown University, and also Professor C. D. Broad, Cambridge University, Mrs. Rosalind Heywood, London, Mr. G. W. Lambert, London, Professor H. H. Price, Oxford University, and Professor F. J. M. Stratton, Cambridge University.

It is hoped that the reader will find HUMAN PERSONALITY AND ITS SURVIVAL OF BODILY DEATH in this new simplified form to be the challenge and stimulation it has been to past generations of psychical researchers.

SUSY SMITH

New York
1961

[14] In the original two-volume edition, the illustrative and case material was scattered in appendices which had to be referred to constantly. In the present volume much of this material has been deleted; the rest has been shortened, incorporated into the text, and set off by use of an ornament § to make for easier reading. Corroborative statements are not as a rule given here since only case histories which were thoroughly documented in the original have been used in this edition.

Human Personality

and Its Survival of Bodily Death

Chapter One

INTRODUCTION

In the long story of man's endeavors to understand his own environment and to govern his own fate, there is one gap or omission so singular that its simple statement has the air of a paradox. Yet it is strictly true to say that man has never yet applied the methods of modern science to the problem which most profoundly concerns him—whether or not his personality involves any element which can survive bodily death.

Nor is this strange omission due to any general belief that the problem is incapable of solution by any observation whatever which mankind could make. Although the resolutely agnostic view is no doubt held by many learned minds, it has never been the creed of the human race generally. In most civilized countries there has been for nearly two thousand years a distinct belief that survival has actually been proved by certain phenomena observed at a given date in Palestine. And beyond the Christian pale—whether through reason, instinct, or superstition—it has ever been commonly held that ghostly phenomena of one kind or another exist to testify to a life beyond the life we know.

But nevertheless, neither those who believe on vague grounds nor those who believe on definite grounds that the question might possibly be solved by human observation of objective fact have made any serious attempt in this direction. They have not sought for fresh corroborative instances, for analogies, for explanations; rather they have kept their convictions on these fundamental matters in a separate and sealed compartment of their minds, a compartment consecrated to religion or to superstition, but not to observation or experiment.

It is my object in the present work—as it has from the first been the object of the Society for Psychical Research, on whose behalf most of the evidence here set forth has been collected—to do what can be done to break down that artificial wall between science and superstition. My one contention is that in the discussion of the deeper problems of man's nature and destiny there ought to be exactly the same openness of mind, diligence in the search for objective evidence of any kind, and critical analysis of results as is habitually shown, for instance, in the discussion of the nature and destiny of the planet upon which man now moves.

To the phenomenon of the Resurrection it would be illegitimate for me to refer in defense of my argument. I have appealed to Science and

21

to Science I must go. Yet this one great tradition, as we know, has won the adhesion and reverence of the great majority of Western minds. The Christian religion, the Christian Church, became for them the accredited representative and guardian of all phenomena bearing upon the World Unseen. So long as Christianity stood dominant, all phenomena which seemed to transcend experience were absorbed in her realm—were accounted as minor indications of the activity of her angels or of her fiends. And when Christianity was seriously attacked, these minor manifestations passed unconsidered. The priests thought it safest to defend their own traditions without going afield in search of independent evidence of a spiritual world. Their assailants kept their powder and shot for the orthodox ramparts, ignoring any isolated strongholds which formed no part of the main line of defense.

Meantime, indeed, the laws of Nature held their wonted way. As ever, that which the years had once brought they brought again; and every here and there some marvel, liker to the old stories than any one cared to assert, cropped up between superstition on the one hand and contemptuous indifference on the other. Witchcraft, Mesmerism, Swedenborgianism, Spiritism—these especially, amid many minor phenomena, stood out in turn as precursory of the inevitable wider inquiry.

A large group of persons have founded upon these and similar facts a scheme of belief known as Modern Spiritualism. Later chapters in this book will show how much I owe to certain observations made by members of this group—how often my own conclusions concur with conclusions at which they have previously arrived. And yet this work of mine is in large measure a critical attack upon the main Spiritist position—the belief that all or almost all supernormal phenomena are due to the action of spirits of the dead. By far the larger proportion, I hold, are due to the action of the still embodied spirit of the agent or percipient himself. Apart from speculative differences, moreover, I altogether dissent from the conversion into a sectarian creed of what I hold should be a branch of scientific inquiry, growing naturally out of our existing knowledge. It is, I believe, largely to this temper of uncritical acceptance, degenerating often into blind credulity, that we must refer the lack of progress in Spiritualistic literature, and the encouragement which has often been bestowed upon manifest fraud—so often, indeed, as to create among scientific men a strong indisposition to the study of phenomena recorded or advocated in a tone so alien from Science.

In about 1873—at the crest of perhaps the highest wave of materialism which has ever swept over these shores—it became the conviction of a small group of Cambridge friends (from which the Society for Psychical

Research developed) that the deep questions thus at issue must be fought out in a way more thorough than the champions either of religion or of materialism had yet suggested. Our attitudes of mind were in some ways different; but to myself, at least, it seemed that no adequate attempt had yet been made to determine whether anything could be learnt as to an unseen world or no. I felt that if anything were knowable it must be discovered by simple experiment and observation, using precisely the same methods of deliberate, dispassionate, exact inquiry which have built up our actual knowledge about the world which we can touch and see. It must be an inquiry resting primarily upon objective facts actually observable, upon experiments which we can repeat today, and which we may hope to carry further tomorrow. It must be an inquiry based on the presumption that if a spiritual world exists, and if that world has at any epoch been manifest or even discoverable, then it ought to be manifest or discoverable now.

It was from these general considerations that the group with which I have worked approached the subject. In those early days we were more devoid of precedents, of guidance, even of criticism that went beyond mere expressions of contempt, than is now readily conceived. Seeking evidence as best we could, we were at last fortunate enough to discover a convergence of experimental and of spontaneous evidence upon one definite and important point. We were led to believe that there was truth in a thesis which at least since Swedenborg and the early mesmerists had been repeatedly but cursorily and ineffectually presented to mankind— the thesis that a communication can take place from mind to mind by some agency not that of the recognized organs of sense. We found that this agency, discernible even on trivial occasions by suitable experiment, seemed to connect itself with an agency more intense, or at any rate more recognizable, which operated at moments of crisis or at the hour of death. Edmund Gurney—the invaluable collaborator and friend whose loss in 1888 was our heaviest discouragement—set forth this evidence in a large work, *Phantasms of the Living,* in whose preparation Mr. Frank Podmore and I took a minor part.

In the course of this present work it will be my task to show in many connections how far-reaching are the implications of this direct and supersensory communion of mind with mind. Among those implications none can be more momentous than the light thrown by this discovery upon man's intimate nature and possible survival of death.

We gradually discovered that the accounts of apparitions at the moment of death—testifying to a supersensory communication between the dying man and the friend who sees him—led on without perceptible break to apparitions occurring after the death of the person seen, but while that death was yet unknown to the percipient, and thus apparently due not to mere brooding memory but to a continued action of that departed spirit. The task next incumbent on us therefore seemed plainly to be the collection and analysis of evidence of this and other types, pointing directly to the survival of man's spirit. But after pursuing this task for some years I felt that in reality the step from the action of embodied to the action of disembodied spirits would still seem too sudden if taken in this direct way. So far, indeed, as the evidence from apparitions went, the series seemed continuous from phantasms of the living to phantasms of the dead. But the whole mass of evidence pointing to man's survival was of a much more complex kind. It consisted largely, for example, in written or spoken utterances, coming through the hand or voice of living men, but claiming to proceed from a disembodied source. To these utterances no satisfactory criterion had ever been applied.

In considering cases of this kind, then, it became gradually plain to me that before we could safely mark off any group of manifestations as definitely implying an influence from beyond the grave, there was need of a more searching review of the capacities of man's incarnate personality than psychologists unfamiliar with this new evidence had thought it worth their while to undertake.

Let me then without further preamble embark upon that somewhat detailed survey of human faculty, as manifested during various phases of human personality, which is needful in order to throw fresh light on these unfamiliar themes. My discussion, I may say at once, will avoid metaphysics as carefully as it will avoid theology. For somewhat similar reasons I do not desire to introduce the philosophical opinions which have been held by various thinkers in the past, nor myself to speculate on matters lying beyond the possible field of objective proof. I shall merely for the sake of clearness begin by the briefest possible statement of two views of human personality which cannot be ignored.

The following passage, taken from a work once of much note, Reid's "Essay on the Intellectual Powers of Man," gives the old-fashioned, common sense view of human personality:

§ . . . My personal identity . . . implies the continued existence of that indivisible thing which I call myself. Whatever this self may be, it is something which thinks, and deliberates, and resolves, and acts, and suffers. I am not thought, I am not action, I am not feeling; I am something that thinks, and acts, and suffers. My thoughts and actions and feelings change every moment: they have no continued, but a successive existence; but that *self* or *I*, to which they belong, is permanent, and has the same relation to all succeeding thoughts, actions, and feelings which I call mine.... §

Contrast with this the newer view of experimental psychology in the passage with which M. Ribot concludes his essay on "Les Maladies de la Personnalité."

§ It is the organism, with the brain, its supreme representative, which constitutes the real personality; comprising in itself the remains of all that we have been and the possibilities of all that we shall be. The whole individual character is there inscribed, with its active and passive aptitudes, its sympathies and antipathies, its genius, its talent or its stupidity, its virtues and its vices, its torpor or its activity. The part thereof which emerges into consciousness is little compared with what remains buried, but operative nevertheless. The conscious personality is never more than a small fraction of the psychical personality. The unity of the Ego is not therefore the unity of a single entity diffusing itself among multiple phenomena; it is the co-ordination of a certain number of states perpetually renascent, and having for their sole common basis the vague feeling of our body ... *the Self is a co-ordination.* It oscillates between two extremes at each of which it ceases to exist—absolute unity and absolute incoherence. §

Here, then, we have two clear and definite views, apparently incompatible the one with the other. The supporters of the view that "The Self is a co-ordination"—and this is now the view prevalent among experimental psychologists—have frankly given up any notion of an underlying unity—of a life independent of the organism—in a word, of a human soul. The supporters of the unity of the Ego, on the other hand, if they have not been able to be equally explicit in *denying* the opposite view, have made up for this by the thorough-going way in which they have *ignored* it. Yet certain fresh evidence can now be adduced which has the effect of showing the case on each side in a novel light; nay, even of closing the immediate controversy by a judgment more decisively in favor of *both* parties than either could have expected. On the one side, and in favor of the co-ordinators—all their analysis of the Self into its constituent elements, all that they urge of positive observation, of objective experiment, must—as I shall maintain on the strength of the new facts which I shall adduce—be unreservedly conceded. It is on the negative side that the conclusions of this school need a complete overhauling. Deeper, bolder inquiry along their own line shows that they have erred when they asserted that analysis showed no trace of faculty beyond such as the life of earth—as they conceive it—could foster, or the environment of earth employ. For in reality analysis shows traces of faculty which this material or planetary life could not have called into being, and whose exercise even here and now involves and necessitates the existence of a spiritual world.

On the other side, and in favor of the partisans of the unity of the Ego, the effect of the new evidence is to raise their claim to a far higher ground, and to substantiate it for the first time with the strongest presumptive proof which can be imagined for it; a proof, namely, that the Ego can and does survive—not only the minor disintegrations which affect it during earth-life—but the crowning disintegration of bodily death. In view of this unhoped-for ratification of their highest dream, they may be more than content to surrender as untenable the far narrower conception of the unitary Self which was all that "common-sense philosophies" had ventured to claim. The " conscious Self" of each of us—the empirical, the supraliminal Self, as I should prefer to say—does not comprise the whole of the consciousness, or of the faculty within us. There exists a more comprehensive consciousness, a profounder faculty, which for the most part remains potential only so far as regards the life of earth, but which reasserts itself in its plenitude after the liberating change of death.

Towards this conclusion, which assumed for me something like its present shape some fourteen years since, a long series of tentative speculations, based on gradually accruing evidence, has slowly conducted me. The conception is one which has hitherto been regarded as purely mystical; and if I endeavor to plant it upon a scientific basis I certainly shall not succeed in stating it in its final terms or in the best arguments which longer experience will suggest. Its validity, indeed, will be impressed upon the reader only by the successive study of the various kinds of evidence which this book will set forth.

The idea of a *threshold* of consciousness—of a level above which sensation or thought must rise before it can enter into our conscious life—is a simple and familiar one. The word *subliminal,* meaning "beneath that threshold," has already been used to define those sensations which are too feeble to be individually recognized. I propose to extend the meaning of the term, so as to make it cover *all* that takes place beneath the ordinary threshold, or outside the ordinary margin of consciousness. This includes not only those faint stimulations whose very faintness keeps them submerged, but much else which psychology as yet scarcely recognizes; sensations, thoughts, emotions, which may be strong, definite, and independent, but which seldom emerge into that *supraliminal* current of consciousness which we habitually identify with *ourselves*. Perceiving that these submerged thoughts and emotions possess the characteristics which we associate with conscious life, I feel bound to speak of a *subliminal* or *ultramarginal consciousness*. Perceiving further that this conscious life beneath the threshold or beyond the margin seems to be no discontinuous or intermittent thing; that not only are these isolated subliminal processes comparable with isolated supraliminal processes (as when a problem is solved by some unknown procedure in a dream), but that there also is a continuous subliminal chain of memory (or more chains than one) involving just that kind of individual and persistent revival of old impressions, and response to new ones, which we commonly call a Self—I find it permissible and convenient to speak of subliminal Selves, or more briefly of a subliminal Self. I do not by using this term assume that there are two correlative and parallel selves existing always within each of us. Rather I mean by the subliminal Self that part of the Self which is commonly subliminal; and I conceive that there may be, not only *co-operations* between these quasi-independent trains of thought, but also upheavals and alternations of personality of many kinds, so that what was once below the surface may for a time, or permanently, rise above it. And I conceive also that no Self of which we can here have cognizance is in reality more than a fragment of a larger Self.

We find that the subliminal uprushes—the impulses or communications which reach our emergent from our submerged selves—are often characteristically different in quality from any element known to our ordinary supraliminal life. They are different in a way which implies faculty of which we have had no previous knowledge, operating in an environment of which hitherto we have been wholly unaware. This broad statement it is of course the purpose of my whole work to justify. Assuming its truth here for argument's sake, we see at once that the problem of the hidden self entirely changes its aspect. Telepathy and clairvoyance—the perception of distant thoughts and of distant scenes without the agency of the recognized organs of sense—suggest either incalculable extension of our own mental powers, or else the influence upon us of minds freer and less trammeled than our own.

Now there are those who would explain this supernormal phenomenon altogether as the agency of discarnate minds, or spirits. And if the subliminal faculties for which I argue are denied to man, some such hypothesis as this, of almost continuous spirit-intervention and spirit-guidance, is at once rendered necessary.

However, I explain this by the action of man's own spirit, without invoking spirits external to himself. Yet the one view still gives support to the other. For these faculties of distant communication exist none the less, even though we should refer them to our own subliminal selves. We can affect each other at a distance, telepathically; and if our incarnate spirits can act thus in at least apparent independence of the fleshly body, the presumption is strong that other spirits may exist independently of the body, and may affect us in similar manner.

It will be my object in this book to lead by transitions as varied and as gradual as possible from phenomena held as normal to phenomena held as supernormal, and it may be useful to conclude this introductory chapter by a brief sketch of the main tracts across which our winding road must lie.

Our inquiry will naturally begin by discussing the subliminal structure, in disease or health, of those two familiar phases of human personality, ordinary waking and ordinary sleep. I shall go on to consider in what way the disintegration of personality by disease is met by its reintegration and purposive modification by hypnotism and self-suggestion. I shall go on then to *sensory automatism* which is the basis of hallucination. This includes phenomena claiming an origin outside the automatist's own mind. It will be found that that origin is often to be sought in the minds of other living men; and various forms of *telepathy* will be brought under review. The conception of telepathy is not one that needs be confined to spirits still incarnate; and we shall find evidence that intercourse of similarly direct type can take place between discarnate and incarnate spirits. The remainder of the book will discuss the methods and results of this supernormal intercourse.

My second chapter may at first sight appear to stray somewhat far from my main purport. It is of the *evolution* of human personality that this work proposes to treat; of faculties newly dawning, and of a destiny greater than we know. Yet I must begin with a detailed discussion of certain modes of that personality's disintegration and decay. Alternations of personality and hysterical phenomena generally are in fact spontaneous experiments of precisely the type most instructive to us. For my own argument, indeed, I urgently need some true conception of the psychological meaning of *hysteria,* and when that conception has been reached, the support which is given by analogy to my own principal thesis will be found to be of the most striking kind.

Continuing this inquiry in my third chapter, I shall consider what kind of man he is to whom the epithet of *normal* may be most fitly applied. I shall at least claim that that man shall be regarded as normal who has the fullest grasp of faculties which inhere in the whole race. Among these faculties I shall venture to count subliminal as well as supraliminal powers; the mental processes which take place below the conscious threshold as well as those which take place above it. What class of men, then, can we regard as reaping most advantage from this submerged mentation? Men of *genius,* I shall reply, describing an "inspiration of genius" as a *subliminal uprush,* an emergence into ordinary consciousness of ideas matured below the threshold.

In the fourth chapter I shall deal with the alternating phase through which man's personality is constructed habitually to pass. I speak of *sleep,* which I regard as a phase of personality, adapted to maintain our existence in the spiritual environment, and to draw from thence the vitality of our physical organisms. Those faculties which form man's link with the spiritual world—telepathy and clairvoyance—are apt (as dreams obscurely show us) to make in sleep their first rudimentary appearance.

For I hold that telepathy and clairvoyance do in fact exist—telepathy, a communication between incarnate mind and incarnate mind, and perhaps between incarnate minds and minds unembodied; clairvoyance, a knowledge of things terrene which overpasses the limits of ordinary perception, and which perhaps also achieves an insight into some other than terrene world.

Thus far I shall have been dealing with conditions or phases of personality which, whether for good or evil, appear spontaneously and without artificial induction. We are able to mix therewith an element of experiment which, although yet in its infancy, has already, in my view, given us an insight into much of man's nature which no mere speculation or introspection could ever have reached. First among our experimental methods I must speak of hypnotism. We see here the influence exercised by suggestion and self-suggestion on higher types of faculty, supernormal as well as normal, on character, on personality. It is on this side, indeed, that the outlook is the most deeply interesting. Man is in course of evolution; and the most pregnant hint which these nascent experiments have yet given him is that it may be in his power to hasten his own evolution in ways previously unknown.

In the following chapter on Sensory Automatism (Chapter Six) I shall proceed to describe certain other experiments, less familiar to the public than those classed as hypnotic, but which give a still further insight into our subliminal faculty. With those experiments will be intermingled many spontaneous phenomena. The chapter's theme will be the messages which the subliminal self sends up to the supraliminal in sensory form; the visions fashioned internally, but manifested not to the inward eye alone; the voices which repeat as though in audible tones the utterance of the self within. In this way we shall be in continued connection with the phenomena of Chapter Two also; but instead of the morbid hallucinations which were there described we shall be dealing with hallucinations which not only are consistent with health and sanity, but also resemble and in a sense surpass the inspirations of genius in their manifestation of important faculty, habitually screened from our view. Even so long as these subliminal messages convey to us knowledge of no new kind—they are nevertheless full of instruction as regards the extent of subliminal faculty.

But at this point, and amid these subjective hallucinations which, although they *extend,* do not fundamentally *modify* previous conceptions, we come face to face with a class of perceptions which, although in one sense hallucinatory, are in another sense the messengers of a truth deeper and more direct from the source than any which our ordinary senses convey to us. We come upon experiments which prove *telepathy;* the transference of ideas and sensations from one mind to another without the agency of the recognized organs of sense. We shall already have encountered some telepathic and clairvoyant incidents among the phenomena of dreams and of hypnosis. But we shall now find that telepathy and clairvoyance occur in waking moments also; occur sometimes as the result of direct experiment; oftener as the spontaneous and apparently casual convergence of forces which we may be led to suppose to be normally operative between all of us. I at least can see no logical halting-place between the first admission of supersensory faculty and the conclusion that such faculty is exercised by something within us which is not generated from material elements, nor confined by mechanical limitations, but which may survive and operate uninjured in a spiritual world.

There is one particular line of telepathic experiment and observation which seems to lead us by an almost continuous pathway across the hitherto impassable gulf. Among telepathic *experiments,* to begin with, none is more remarkable than the occasional power of some agent to project himself phantasmally; to make himself manifest, as though in actual presence, to some percipient at a distance. The mechanism of such projection is entirely unknown to the agent himself; nor is the act always preceded by any effort of the supraliminal will. But our records of such cases do assuredly suggest a quite novel disengagement of some informing spirit from the restraint of the organism; a form of distant operation in which we cannot say whether the body in its apparent passivity co-operates or no.

With these experiments in mind, let us turn to the spontaneous telepathic phenomena of apparitions of a distant person mainly at moments of crisis, and at the moment of death. Here we come face to face with the supreme problem: The question of the existence or nonexistence of a spiritual world. To prove that telepathy implies a spiritual environment would be at once to lift our knowledge of the Cosmos to a higher level. To prove that man survives death would also be to transform and transfigure his whole life here and now. Before us, as of old, is that all-embracing problem; but before us also, for the first time, is some hint and indication as to the track which may be pursued towards its solution.

The old conception of the *ghost*—a conception which seemed to belong only to primitive animism and to modern folklore—has received a new meaning from observations of phenomena occurring between living men. We realize that a phantasmal figure may bear a true relation to some distant person whose semblance is thus shown; we learn by instances of directly provable coincidence that wraiths of this kind correspond with death too often to leave the correspondence attributable to chance alone. The vague question of former times narrows down, then, to the more precise question: Is there still evidence of some such definite type as this, showing that a phantasm can appear not only at but *after* a man's bodily death, and can still indicate connection with a persistent and individual life?

To this distinct question there can now be given a distinct and affirmative answer. There is evidence that the self-same living spirit is still operating, and it may be in the self-same way. And thus my general dogma receives its specific confirmation. Telepathy, I have said, looks like a law prevailing in the spiritual as well as in the material world. And that it does so prevail, I now add, is proved by the fact that those who communicated with us telepathically in this world communicate with us telepathically from the other. At first, the mere observation of these phantasms does not seem as though it could lead us far. It is like the observation of shooting stars— of meteors which appear without warning and vanish in a flash of fire. Yet systematic observation has learnt much as to these meteors; has learnt the point in heaven from which they issue; their orbital relation to earth and sun. Somewhat similarly, continuous observation of these brief phantasmal appearances may tell us much of them at last; much, for instance, as to their relative frequency at different epochs after death; something as to their apparent knowledge of what has happened on earth since they left it.

Much more, indeed, than would at first seem likely can be learnt by mere prolonged observation of spontaneous phantasms of the dead. Yet here as everywhere, here more than anywhere, the need of actual experiment is felt. And in fact such experiment turns out to be actually feasible. It is feasible in connection with each of the four forms of communication, of verbalization, with which human life is familiar. There is a possibility of inducing a spiritual hearing and a spiritual picture-seeing or reading; and also a spiritually-guided writing and speech. Both our sensory automatism and our motor automatism may be initiated and directed by intelligence outside our own.

In Chapter Six, on Sensory Automatism, we shall already have discussed the passive methods in which communications of this kind may be awaited. We have now (in Chapter Seven) to consider in what ways Motor Automatism—the unwilled activity of hand or voice—may be used to convey messages which come to the automatist as though from without himself.

As though from without himself, I say; but of course their apparent externality does not prove that they have not originated in submerged strata of his own mind. In most cases, indeed, with motor as with sensory automatism, this is probably what really occurs. We find that a tendency to automatic writing is by no means uncommon among sane and healthy persons. But we also find that the messages thus given do not generally rise above the level of an incoherent dream. They seem to emerge from a region where scraps of thought and feeling exist confusedly, with no adequate central control. Yet sometimes the vague scrawling changes its character. It becomes veridical; it begins to convey a knowledge of actual facts of which the automatist has no previous information; it indicates some subliminal activity of his own, or some telepathic access to an external mind. There will often be great difficulty of interpretation; great perplexity as to the true relation between a message and its alleged source. But every year of late has added both to the mass of matter and to the feasibility of interpretation. These are not the hieroglyphs of the dead but the hieroglyphs of the living.

Side by side with the automatism of arm and hand we must place the automatism of throat and tongue (Chapter Nine). Automatic utterance parallels automatic script throughout the scale of degrees by this time familiar. It begins with mere incoherence; but it assumes in some cases a veridical character; with knowledge delivered from some subliminal stratum or some external mind. And in some cases the special knowledge displayed in the utterances lends probability to their claim to proceed from a departed spirit.

When this occurs, when the utterance reaches this point of veracity and intensity, it is sometimes accompanied by certain other phenomena which for those who have witnessed them carry a sense of reality which description can hardly reproduce. The ordinary consciousness of the automatist appears to be suspended; he passes into a state of trance which in its turn seems but the preparation for an occupation by an invading intelligence—by the surviving spirit, let us boldly say, of some recognizable departed friend. This friend then disposes of voice and hand almost as freely as though he were their legitimate owner.

And here we reach a point which has become, without my anticipation, and as a matter (so to say) of mere scientific policy even against my will, the principal difficulty of the present work. This book has been forced unexpectedly forward by the sheer force of evidence until it must now dwell largely on the extreme branch of the subject, far beyond the reserves and cautious approaches originally designed.

For in truth during the last ten years our evidence has shifted profoundly. When this work was first contemplated there was *most* evidence for telepathy between the living; *next most* for phantasms of the dead; *least*, perhaps, for actual possession and control of human organisms by departed spirits.

With the recent development of trance-phenomena, however, this semblance of logical proportion has been quickly altered. We seem suddenly to have arrived, by a kind of short cut, at a direct solution of problems which we had till then been approaching by difficult inference or laborious calculation of chances. What need of computing coincidental death-wraiths, of analyzing the evidential details of post-mortem apparitions, if here we have the departed ready to hear and answer questions, and to tell us frankly of the fate of souls?

Following on the first revelation of Mrs. Piper's[1] trance-phenomena came the permission accorded to me by the executors of Mr. Stainton Moses to read and analyze his private records after his death. The strong impression which his phenomena had made upon me during his life was increased by this posthumous and intimate study; and his history was seen to be in many respects analogous to Mrs. Piper's. Further parallels have been afforded since by more than one other medium; and it seems to me now that the evidence for communication with the spirits of identified deceased persons through the trance-utterances and writings of sensitives apparently controlled by those spirits is established beyond serious attack.

I do not of course mean that we ought to accept the messages unquestioningly as being in all cases literally what they claim to be. We are bound to regard conscious or unconscious fraud, self-suggestion, telepathy between the living, and the like, as possibly operative. But I mean that where we get beyond these simpler causes, where we are forced to accept the messages as representing in some way the continued identity of a

---

[1] Mrs. Leonore E. Piper of Boston, one of the earliest and best trance mediums (see pp. 379 ff.)

former denizen of earth, I do not think that either tradition or philosophy affords us any solid standpoint from which to criticize those messages.

Closely allied to speculations such as these is another speculation, more capable of being subjected to experimental test, yet which remains still inconclusively tested, and which has become for many reasons a stumbling-block rather than a corroboration in the spiritual inquiry. I refer to the question whether any influence is exercised by spirits upon the gross material world otherwise than through ordinary organic structures. We know that the spirit of a living man controls his own organism, and we shall see reason to think that discarnate spirits may also control, by some form of "possession," the organisms of living persons, may affect directly some portions of matter which we call living, namely, the brain of the entranced sensitive. There seems to me, then, no paradox in the supposition that some effect should be produced by spiritual agency—possibly through the mediation of some kind of energy derived from living human beings—upon inanimate matter as well. And I believe that as a fact such effects have been observed and recorded in a trustworthy manner by Sir William Crookes, the late Dr. Carleton Speer and others in the cases especially of D. D. Home and of W. Stainton Moses. If I call these and certain other records still inconclusive it is mainly on account of the mass of worthless narratives with which they have been smothered; the long history of so-called investigations which have consisted merely in an interchange of credulity and fraud. For the present the evidence of this kind which has real value is better presented, I think, in separate records than collected or discussed in any generalized form. All that I purpose in this work, therefore, is briefly to indicate the relation which these "physical phenomena" hold to the psychical phenomena with which my book is concerned. Alongside of the faculty or achievement of man's ordinary self I shall demarcate the faculty or achievement which I ascribe to his subliminal self; and alongside of this again I shall arrange such few well-attested phenomena as seem to demand the physical intervention of discarnate intelligences.

The reader who may feel disposed to give his adhesion to the long series of evidences which have pointed with more and more clearness to the survival of human personality, and to the possibility for men on earth of actual contact with a world beyond, may feel perhaps that the intimate and universal hope of every generation of men has never until this day approached so near to fulfillment. There has never been so fair a prospect for Life and Love. Deep in this spiritual environment the cosmic secret lies. Can we, for instance, learn anything—to begin with fundamental problems—of the relation of spiritual phenomena to Space, to

Time, to the material world? The subject-matter has not yet been exhausted of half its significance. The conclusions to which our evidence points are not such as can be discussed or dismissed as a mere matter of speculative curiosity. They affect every belief, every faculty, every hope and aim of man; and they affect him the more intimately as his interests grow more profound. Whatever meaning be applied to ethics, to philosophy, to religion, the concern of all these is here.

Who can think that either Science or Revelation has spoken as yet more than a first half-comprehended word? But if in truth souls departed call to us it is to them that we shall listen most of all.

Chapter Two

DISINTEGRATIONS OF PERSONALITY

Of the race of man we know for certain that it has been evolved through many ages and through countless forms of change. We know for certain that its changes continue still; we may reasonably conjecture that it will continue to change with increasing rapidity, and through a period in comparison with which our range of recorded history shrinks into a moment.

The actual nature of these coming changes lies beyond our imagination. Many of them are probably as inconceivable to us now as eyesight would have been to our eyeless ancestors. All that we can do is to note so far as possible the structural laws of our personality as deduced from its changes thus far; inferring that for some time to come its further changes will proceed upon similar lines.

I have already indicated my general view of the nature of human personality. I regard each man as at once profoundly unitary and almost infinitely composite, as inheriting from earthly ancestors a multiplex organism but also as ruling and unifying that organism by a soul or spirit absolutely beyond our present analysis—a soul which has originated in a spiritual environment; which even while embodied subsists in that environment; and which will still subsist therein after the body's decay.

In the organism as we can observe it in common life we have no complete or unchanging unity, but rather a complex hierarchy of groups of cells exercising vaguely limited functions, and working together with rough precision, tolerable harmony, fair success. That these powers ever work *perfectly* together we have no evidence. Our feeling of health is but a rough haphazard register of what is passing within us.

Many disturbances and disintegrations of the personality must presently be described. But the reader who may follow me must remember the point of view from which I am writing. The aim of my analysis is not to destroy but to fulfill; my hope is that observation of the ways in which the personality tends to disintegrate may suggest methods which may tend to its more complete integration.

I begin, then, with the obvious remark that when we conceive any act other than our own as a conscious act, we do so either because we regard it as *complex,* and therefore *purposive,* or because we perceive that it has been *remembered.* Thus we call the fencer or the chess-player fully conscious; we say, "The man who seemed stunned after that blow on the

36

head must really have been conscious all the time; for he afterwards recalled every incident." The *memorability* of an act is, in fact, a better proof of consciousness than its complexity.

This being so, I cannot see how we can phrase our definition more simply than by saying that any act or condition must be regarded as conscious if it is *potentially memorable;* if it can be recollected by the subject concerned. It does not seem needful that the circumstances under which such recollection may occur should arise while the subject is still incarnated on this planet. We shall never on this planet remember the great majority of our dreams but those dreams were presumably no less conscious than the dreams which a sudden awakening allowed us to keep in memory. Certain hypnotic subjects who can be made to remember their dreams by suggestion, apparently remember dreams previously latent just as easily as dreams previously remembered. And we shall have various other examples of the unexpected recollection of experiences supposed to have been entirely devoid of consciousness.

We are bound, I think, to draw at least this negative conclusion: that we must not take for granted that our apparently central consciousness is something wholly different in kind from the minor consciousnesses out of which it is in some sense elaborated. I do indeed believe it to be in an important sense different; but this difference must not be assumed on the basis of our subjective sensations alone. We must approach the whole subject of split or duplicated personalities with no prepossession against the possibility of any given arrangement or division of the total mass of consciousness which exists within us.

The process of disintegration begins with something which is to the psychical organism no more than a boil or a corn is to the physical. In consequence of some suggestion from without, or of some inherited tendency, a small group of psychical units sets up a process of exaggerated growth which shuts them off from free and healthy interchange with the rest of the personality.

The first symptom of disaggregation is thus the *idée fixe,* the persistence of an uncontrolled and unmodifiable group of thoughts or emotions, which from their brooding isolation, from the very fact of deficient interchange with the general current of thought, become alien and intrusive, so that some special idea or image presses into consciousness with undue and painful frequency. We may perhaps suppose that the fixed idea here represents the psychological aspect of some definite, although ultra-microscopic, cerebral lesion. One may look for analogy to a corn, to a boil, to an encysted tumor, to a cancer. The *idée fixe* may be little more than an indurated prejudice which hurts when pressed upon. Or it may be like a hypertrophied center of inflammation, which sends its smart and ache abroad through the organism. Or for certain hysterical fixed ideas we shall find our best parallel if, accepting a well-known hypothesis, we suppose that a tumor may originate in the isolated and extravagant growth of some fragment of embryonic matter, accidentally nipped off or extruded from the embryo's concordant development. Such tumors may be encysted or encapsuled, so that they injure surrounding tissues by pressure, while yet their own contents can only be discovered by incision. Just such, one may say, are the forgotten and irrecoverable terrors which give rise to hysterical attacks. Such tumors of the mind may sometimes be psychologically cut down upon and removed by free discussion; "talked out," as it were. Worst of all, of course, are the cancer-like cases, where the degeneration, beginning it hardly matters where, invades with rapid incoherence the whole compass of the mind.

Let us dwell for a few moments on the nature of these fixed or insistent ideas. They are not generally or at the first outset extravagant fancies, as that one is made of glass, or the like. Rather will "fixed ideas" come to seem a mere expression for something in a minor degree common to most of us. Hardly any mind, I suppose, is wholly free from tendencies to certain types of thought or emotion for which we cannot summon any adequate check—useless recurrent broodings over the past or anxieties for the future, perhaps traces of old childish experience which have become too firmly fixed ever wholly to disappear. Nay, it may well be that we must look even further back than our own childhood for the origin of many haunting troubles. Inherited tendencies to terror seem to reach back far into a prehistoric past.

At any rate, we have actually on record a great series of *idée fixes,* of various degrees of intensity, cured by suggestion; cured, that is to say, by a subliminal setting in action of minute nervous movements which our supraliminal consciousness cannot in even the blindest manner manage to set to work. Some such difference as exists on a gross scale between striped and unstriped muscle seems to exist on a minute scale among these smallest involved cells and fibers, or whatever they be. Some of them obey our conscious will, but most of them are capable of being governed only by subliminal strata of the self.

If, however, it be the subliminal self which can reduce these elements to order, it is often probably the subliminal self to which their disorder is originally due. If a fixed idea, say agoraphobia, grows up in me, this may probably be because the proper controlling co-ordinations of thought, which I ought to be able to summon up at will, have sunk below the level at which will can reach them. I am no longer able to convince myself by reasoning that there is no danger in crossing the open square. And this may be the fault of my subliminal self, whose business it is to keep the ideas which I need for common life within my reach, and which has failed to do this, owing to some enfeeblement of its grasp of my organism.

Now we shall find, I think, that all the phenomena of hysteria are reducible to the same general conception. Or in some cases we may go a step further, and say that these fixed ideas show us, not merely an ordinary supraliminal instinct functioning without due check, but rather a submerged and primitive instinct rising with a subliminal uprush into undesired prominence, and functioning wildly instead of remaining hidden and quiescent.

Speaking broadly, we may say that the symptoms of hysteria form, in the first place, a series of phantom copies of real maladies of the nervous system; and, in the second place, a series of fantasies played upon that system—of unreal, dreamlike ailments, often such as no physiological mechanism can be shown to have determined.

Let us briefly review some common types of hysterical disability, taking as our first guide Dr. Pierre Janet's admirable work, *L'Etat Mental des Hystériques* (Paris, 1893).

It is in the assimilation of the elementary sensations or affective states with the *perception personnelle,* as Janet terms it, that the advanced hysteric fails. His field of consciousness is so far narrowed that it can only take in the minimum of sensations necessary for the support of life. "One must needs have consciousness of what one sees and hears, and so the patient neglects to perceive the tactile and muscular sensations with which he thinks that he can manage to dispense. At first he could perhaps turn his attention to them, and recover them at least momentarily within the field of personal perception. But the occasion does not present itself, and the *psychological bad habit* is formed. . . . One day the patient— for he is now veritably a patient—is examined by the doctor. His left arm is pinched, and he is asked whether he feels the pinch. To his surprise the patient realizes that he can no longer feel consciously, can no longer bring back into his personal perception sensations which he has neglected too long—he has become anæsthetic. . . . Hysterical anæsthesia is thus a fixed and perpetual distraction, which renders its subjects incapable of attaching certain sensations to their personality; it is a restriction of the conscious field."

The proof of these assertions depends on a number of observations, all of which point in the same direction, and show that hysterical anæsthesia does not descend so deep into the personality as true anæsthesia caused by nervous decay, or by the section of a nerve.

We regard the fragments of perceptive power over which the hysteric has lost control as being by no means really extinguished, but rather as existing immediately beneath the threshold, in the custody of a dream-like or hypnotic stratum of the subliminal self, which has selected them for reasons sometimes explicable as the result of past suggestions, sometimes inexplicable. If this be so, we may expect that the same kind of suggestions which originally cut off these perceptions from the main body of perception may stimulate them again to action either below or above the conscious threshold.

What has been said of hysterical defects of sensation might be repeated for motor defects. There, too, the powers of which the supraliminal self has lost control continue to act in obedience to subliminal promptings.

§ "I cannot in the least understand what is going on," said Maria, when she entered the hospital [I quote Dr. Janet again]; "for some time past I have been working in an odd way; it is no longer I who am working, but only my hands. They get on pretty well, but I have no part in what they do. When it is over I do not recognize my work at all. I see that it is all right; but I feel that I am quite incapable of having accomplished it. If any one said, 'It is not *you* who did that!' I would answer, 'True enough, it is not I.' When I want to sing it is impossible to me; yet at other times I hear my voice singing the song very well. It is certainly not I who walk; I feel like a balloon which jumps up and down of itself. When I want to write I find nothing to say, my head is empty, and I must let my hand write what it chooses, and it fills four pages, and if the stuff is silly I cannot help it."

The curious point is [continues M. Janet] that in this fashion she produces some really good things. If she makes up a dress or writes a letter she sometimes shows real talent, but it is all done in a bizarre way. She looks absorbed in her work, but yet unconscious of it; when she lifts her head she seems dazed as if she was coming out of a dream, and does not recollect what she has been doing. §

To this side of the study of hysteria Drs. Breuer and Freud (in their *Studien über Hysterie*, Leipsig, 1895) have made valuable contribution. Drawing their patients not from hospital wards but from private practice, they have had the good fortune to encounter, and the penetration to understand, some remarkable cases where unselfish but powerful passions have proved too much for the equilibrium of minds previously well-fortified both by principle and by education.

Miss Lucy R., the heroine of the first case, was an English governess in the family of a German manufacturer.

The symptom for which Miss R. consulted Dr. Freud was, in fact, a persistent hallucinatory smell of *burnt pudding*. Careful inquiry traced the origin of this smell to a scene when the children under her charge, affectionately sporting with her, had allowed some pudding which was on the schoolroom fire to burn. It was not obvious why this incident should have carried so much emotional import. Gradually the truth came out, a truth which Miss R.—and this is an essential point—had *concealed from herself* with all the resolution of which she was capable. She had unconsciously fallen in love with her employer, a widower, whose children she had promised their dying mother to care for always. The scene of the burnt pudding represented a moment at which an obscure scruple of conscience urged her to quit her trust, to leave these children, who were now devoted to her, on account of something dimly felt to be unsuitable in her own attitude of mind towards their father. When once this confession had been made—a confession new to herself as well as to the physician—the hallucinatory smell of burnt pudding disappeared. Its persistence had indicated that the emotional memory on which it was based had not, so to say, been absorbed into the general psychical circulation, but had remained encysted in the personality, a cause of pressure and distress.

Still more remarkable was the case of Fräulein Anna O. who was greatly above the average standard in character, education, and physical vigor. Fräulein O. led an active and happy life; her strongest attachment was to her father. Her thoughts did not dwell on love or marriage (in the whole range of her hallucinations and delirium there was no trace of this), but she had great imaginative activity in day-dreams, the invention of stories and the like.

The cause of her breakdown lay in a long, distressing, and ultimately fatal illness of her father when she was twenty-one years old. She nursed him with a passionate devotion which was no doubt unwise but which can hardly be called *morbid*. Her nervous system gave way and a quantity of hysterical affections set in. There were headaches, strabismus, disturbances of sight and of speech, positive and negative hallucinations, the influence of *idées fixes,* contractions, anæsthesiæ, etc. The condition of extreme instability thus induced, varying from hour to hour, gave rise at times to a secondary personality which lay outside the primary memory. We thus have a very direct transition from isolated disturbances to a cleavage of the whole personality.

Disturbances of *speech* may give very delicate indications of internal turmoil of the personality; and Fräulein O.'s great linguistic gift made her perhaps the most interesting example on record of hysterical aphasia and paraphasia. Sometimes she was altogether speechless. Sometimes she talked German in ungrammatical fashion. Sometimes she spoke English, apparently believing it to be German, but understood German; sometimes she spoke English and could not understand German. Sometimes she spoke French or Italian; and in French or Italian states she had no memory of English states, and *vice versâ.* Sometimes, however, in an English state she could understand French or Italian books; but if she read them aloud she read them in English, apparently unaware that they were not in that language.

We may now pass from the first to the second of the categories of disintegration of personality. The cases which I have thus far described have been mainly cases of *isolation* of elements of personality. We have not dealt as yet with *secondary personalities* as such. There is, however, a close connection between these two classes. This second class starts from sleep-wakings of all kinds, and includes all stages of alternation of personality, from brief somnambulisms up to those permanent and thorough changes which deserve the name of dimorphisms.

In the first place, it should be borne in mind that the dreaming state, though I will not call it the normal form of mentation, is nevertheless the form which our mentation most readily and habitually assumes. Dreams of a kind are probably going on within us both by night and by day, unchecked by any degree of tension of waking thought. This view seems to me to be supported by one's own actual experience in momentary dozes or even momentary lapses of attention. The condition of which one then becomes conscious is that of swarming fragments of thought or imagery, which have apparently been going on continuously, though one may become aware of them and then unaware at momentary intervals—while one tries, for instance, to listen to a speech or to read a book aloud between sleep and waking.

This, then, is the kind of mentation from which our clearer and more coherent states may be supposed to develop. Waking life implies a fixation of attention on one thread of thought running through a tangled skein. In hysterical patients we see some cases where no such fixation is possible, and other cases where the fixation is involuntary, or follows a thread which it is not desirable to pursue.

First we deal with a class of secondary personalities consisting of elements *emotionally selected* from the total or primary personality. We see some special group of feelings grow to morbid intensity, until at last it dominates the sufferer's mental being, either fitfully or continuously, but to such an extent that he is "a changed person," not precisely insane, but quite other than he was when in normal mental health. In such cases the new personality is of course dyed in the morbid emotion. In other respects the severance between the new and the old self is not very profound. Dissociations of memory, for instance, are seldom beyond the reach of hypnotic suggestion. The cleavage has not gone down to the depths of the psychical being.

We must now go on to cases where the origin of the cleavage seems to us quite arbitrary, but where the cleavage itself seems even for that very reason to be more profound. It is no longer a question of some one morbidly exaggerated emotion, but rather of a scrap of the personality taken at random and developing apart from the rest. To recur to our physical simile, we are dealing no longer with a corn, a boil, a cancer, but with a tumor starting apparently from some scrap of embryonic tissue which has become excluded from the general development of the organism.

The commonest mode of origin for such secondary personalities is from sleep-waking which, instead of merging into sleep again, repeats and consolidates itself, until it acquires a chain of memories of its own, alternating with the primary chain.

An old case of Dr. Dyce's forms a simple example of this type. In this instance the secondary state is manifestly a degeneration of the primary state, even when certain traces of supernormal faculty are discernible in the narrowed psychical field.

This account is taken from a paper by Dr. Elliotson on "Instances of Double States of Consciousness independent of Mesmerism" in the *Zoist,* vol. iv p. 158, being quoted by him from the *Edinburgh Philosophical Transactions* of 1822.

§ Dr. Devan read to the Royal Society of Edinburgh in February, 1822 the history of a case observed by Dr. Dyce of Aberdeen, in a girl sixteen years old, which lasted from March 2nd to June 11th, 1815. The first symptom was an uncommon propensity to fall asleep in the evenings. This was followed by the habit of talking in her sleep on these occasions. One evening she fell asleep in this manner: imagining herself an Episcopal clergyman, she went through the ceremony of baptizing three children, and gave an appropriate prayer.

She sometimes dressed herself and the children while in this state, answered questions put to her in such a manner as to show that she understood the question. . . . One day, in this state, she sat at breakfast, with perfect correctness, with her eyes shut. She afterwards awoke with the child on her knees, and wondered how she got on her clothes. . . . [One] Sunday she was taken to church by her mistress while the paroxysm was on her. She shed tears during the sermon, particularly during the account given of the execution of three young men at Edinburgh. When she returned home she recovered in a quarter of an hour, was quite amazed at the questions put to her about the church sermon, and denied that she had been to any such place; but next night on being taken ill she mentioned that she had been at church, repeated the words of the text, and in Dr. Dyce's hearing gave an accurate account of the tragical narrative of the three young men by which her feelings had been so powerfully affected. §

And here, as an illustration of a secondary condition purely degenerative, I may first mention *post-epileptic* states, although they belong too definitely to pathology for full discussion here. Post-epileptic conditions may run parallel to almost all the secondary phases which we have described. They may to all outward semblance closely resemble normality, differing mainly by a lack of rational *purpose,* and perhaps by a recurrence to the habits and ideas of some earlier moment in the patient's history. Such a condition resembles some hypnotic trances, and some factitious personalities as developed by automatic writing. Or, again, the post-epileptic state may resemble a suddenly developed *idée fixe* triumphing over all restraint, and may prompt to serious crime, abhorrent to the normal, but premeditated in the morbid state.

The following case of involuntary crime committed by a boy named Sörgel, in a state of secondary consciousness, is summarized from an account given in the paper by Dr. Elliotson.

§ Sörgel (says Dr. Elliotson) was a poor, innocent, industrious youth, subject first to violent epilepsy, and then to paroxysms of second consciousness, in which he had delusions and ungovernable criminal propensities, the whole of which he was ignorant of upon returning to his ordinary state of consciousness, though in his morbid state he remembered the occurrences of his natural state. On September 7th, 1824, in a state of post-epileptic consciousness, Sörgel murdered an old woodcutter in a forest, chopping off his head and both his feet with one of his own axes. Returning from the forest, Sörgel told several people what he had done. He said that he had drunk a felon's blood, and that he was now quite well, as a felon's blood was supposed to be a cure for the falling sickness.

The next day Sörgel was examined by the criminal court, and repeated the same story; he was taken to see the body, and recognized it without the slightest air of embarrassment or remorse. As an excuse for the murder, he repeatedly said that he killed the man in order to drink his blood and be cured by it.

This state of consciousness lasted a week. He then returned spontaneously to his natural state. On September 15th the judges found him quiet: his conversation was coherent; his appearance and manner totally changed. He did not remember anything about the murder, but supposed he must have committed it, since every one told him he had. Of the period between September 7th and 15th, he only knew that "his head was very confused, and that he dreamt all manner of nonsense." He was acquitted of the crime, as not being responsible for his action at the time, and died a few months later in a lunatic asylum. §

A full account of the well-known case of Ansel Bourne was first published in the *Proceedings* S.P.R., vol. vii., 1891–92, in a paper by Dr. Richard Hodgson entitled "A Case of Double Consciousness." The report below is condensed from Hodgson's personal interviews with Bourne, as compared with the records of Dr. S. Weir Mitchell, who also investigated the case, and from contemporary newspaper accounts.

§ January 17, 1887, Ansel Bourne went from his home in Coventry, R.I. to Providence, expecting to return home the same afternoon. In Providence he drew out of the bank $551, paid several small bills, and then disappeared. No tidings whatever were received of him till March 14th, eight weeks later.

Two weeks after his disappearance from Providence, Mr. Bourne arrived in Norristown, Pa. Under the name of A. J. Brown he rented a store room, dividing it into two by means of curtains. He slept and prepared his meals in the rear, and stocked the front portion of the room with notions, toys, confectionery, etc. He put a sign in the window and opened up for business, nothing in his manner in any way suggesting anything peculiar. He was quiet in behavior, precise and regular in his habits, and paid his bills promptly.

Mr. Bourne (as Brown) attended the Methodist Church on Sunday, and on one occasion, at a religious meeting, he related an incident which he said he had witnessed years previously about a boy who had kneeled down and prayed in the midst of the passengers on a steamboat between Albany and New York City.

On the morning of Monday, March 14th, about 5 o'clock, he heard an explosion like the report of a gun or pistol, and waking, he noticed that there was a ridge in his bed not like the bed he had been accustomed to sleep in. He rose in a strange room and pulled away the curtains and looked out on a strange street. He felt very weak, and thought that he had been drugged. His next sensation was that of fear, knowing that he was in a place where he had no business to be. The last thing he could remember was being at the corner of Dorrance and Broad Streets in Providence.

He waited to hear someone move, and for two hours he suffered great mental distress. Finally he opened his door and met Mr. Earle, the landlord, who said, "Good morning, Mr. Brown." When "Mr. Brown" declared that he was Ansel Bourne, that he was in Providence, R.I., that it was January instead of March, Mr. Earle thought he was out of his mind and sent for a doctor. After that Bourne was reunited with his home and family, still a much puzzled man.

Early in 1890 Professor William James heard of the case and became interested. He conceived the idea that if Mr. Bourne could be hypnotized they might obtain from him the complete history of the whole incident, and at the same time, by post-hypnotic suggestion, prevent the recurrence of any such episode.

Mr. Bourne was anxious to have any light possible thrown upon his experience, and he acquiesced in the proposals made for hypnotism.

James endeavored to obtain from him, when he was under hypnosis, a detailed account of his doings during the eight weeks, January 17th to March 13, 1887. The following statements were elicited from him while he was in a deep sleep:

He said that his name was Albert John Brown, that on January 17th he went from Providence to Pawtucket in a horse-car, thence by train to Boston, and thence to New York, where he registered as A. J. Brown at the Grand Union Hotel. He left New York on the following morning and went to Philadelphia, where he spent a week or so in a boarding-house on Filbert Street near the depot. (It has since been determined that an A. J. Brown did board for a week or more during that time at "The Kellogg House" on Filbert Street, in Philadelphia.) He thought of taking a store in a small town, and after looking around at several places, chose Norristown, where he started a little business of five cent goods.

He stated under hypnosis that he was born in Newton, New Hampshire, July 8, 1826 (Ansel Bourne was born in New York City, July 8, 1826), had passed through a great deal of trouble, loss of wife, friends, and property, but that everything was confused prior to his finding himself in the horse-car on the way to Pawtucket; and that the last thing he remembered about his keeping store in Norristown was going to bed on Sunday night, March 13th.

The statements made by Mr. Bourne in trance concerning his doings in Norristown agreed with those made by his landlord and other persons there.

Taken altogether, the case is not a little perplexing. In the Brown state, while forgetting some of the most important events in his past life, including his own name and his second marriage, and the place of his birth, he remembered the *date* of his birth correctly, the date of his first wife's death, etc., and curiously enough, on one occasion related in the church an incident that occurred on a steamboat between Albany and New York, which in his Bourne state he also well remembered. In induced trance another time, he recalled that he had children living, but on a different date when hypnotized, he had no recollection of them. It is difficult to see along what definite channels the temporary obliteration of Bourne's memories proceeded, with, as consequence, his transformation into Brown. Neither Mr. Bourne nor his wife could suggest any clue which might lead to any explanation of his adopting A. J. Brown as his name, or Newton, New Hampshire, as his birthplace. §

Dr. Hodgson concluded that the facts suggest a post-epileptic partial loss of memory.

The following case of "Automatisme Somnambulique avec dédoublement de la personnalité" was reported by J. M. Boeteau, Interne des Asiles de la Seine, in the *Annales Médico-psychologiques* for January, 1892. It has some resemblance to the Ansel Bourne case, insomuch as the lost memory of an escapade is recovered under hypnotization, but differs from it in the presence of marked hysteria. There seemed to be no suspicion of epilepsy. I abbreviate M. Boeteau's very full and clear account:

§ Marie M., aged twenty-two, has been subject to hysterical attacks since she was twelve years old. She became an out-patient at the Hôpital Andral for these attacks; and on April 24th, 1891, the house physician there advised her to enter the surgical ward at the Hôtel Dieu, as she would probably need an operation for an internal trouble. Greatly shocked by this news, she left the hospital at 10 A.M., and lost consciousness. When she recovered consciousness she found herself in quite another hospital— that of Ste. Anne—at 6 A.M. on April 27th. She had been found wandering in the streets of Paris, with haggard aspect, worn-out boots, and lacerated feet, in the evening of the day on which she left the Hôpital Andral, under the shock of painful apprehension. On returning to herself, she could recollect absolutely nothing of what had passed in the interval. While she was thus perplexed at her unexplained fatigue and footsoreness, and at the gap in her memory, M. Boeteau hypnotized her. Like Ansel Bourne, she passed with ease into the hypnotic state, although she had never before been hypnotized, and like him she at once remembered the events which filled at least the earlier part of the gap in her primary consciousness. . . . She had walked to Chaville, and then on to Versailles, and walked back to Paris. During this long walk, which wore out her boots and wounded her feet, she was insensible to fatigue or hunger. But on regaining Paris she began to be haunted by spectral surgeons, endeavoring to perform operations on her. She was found in an increasing state of maniacal excitation, and was taken to a police infirmary on the 25th and to the Hospital of Ste. Anne on the 26th April.

The patient's account of her adventures was found to be correct. §

The next case is taken from an article entitled "Duplex Personality: Report of a Case," by William F. Drewry, M.D., of Petersburg, Virginia, in the *Medico-Legal Journal* for June, 1896:

§ Mr. K was 50 years old, in good health, sober, moral and industrious, affable, with a large circle of friends. One day he went to a northern city to purchase goods for his store. Starting homeward on a steamer, he felt tired and went to his stateroom. When tickets were collected he was missing. He had suddenly and mysteriously disappeared, leaving his valise and its contents behind him. No one had seen him leave the boat, jump or fall overboard. A vigorous search was made to find him, detectives were employed, and the newspapers were full of accounts of his strange disappearance.

Six months later he suddenly appeared at the home of a relative in a distant southern city. He was brought home in a partially dazed condition, able to recognize but few of his friends. He was an entirely changed man, having lost weight from 250 to 150 lbs., and was very feeble.

He was at once put under treatment, and in four weeks he recovered his previous bodily and mental health. A day or two after his return home an abscess, deep down in the auditory canal, broke and discharged a large quantity of sanguino-purulent matter. Immediately thereupon improvement began and went on rapidly.

He said that he remembered nothing after he went to his stateroom on the boat until six months later when he suddenly came to himself in a distant city in the South, where he found himself driving a fruit-wagon on the street. He started at once for Virginia, but on the way again lost consciousness a time or two, finally managing to get to the town where his relative lived. §

I may next cite a case in which the secondary state seems to owe its origination to a kind of tidal exhaustion of vitality, as though the repose of sleep were not enough to sustain the weakened personality, which lapsed on alternate days into exhaustion and incoherence. It is taken from the paper by Dr. Elliotson in *Zoist*, vol. iv. p. 185, being quoted by him from the *Northern Journal of Medicine* for June, 1845. The case was there reported by Dr. David Skae.

The patient was an unmarried man, in the prime of life, connected with the legal profession, regular and temperate in his habits. His complaint began with the usual symptoms of dyspepsia, passing into hypochondria and ultimately into a state between hypochondria and mental alienation. Feelings of gloom and despondency were at the same time developed; the most trifling errors were magnified into unpardonable crimes. He began a system of reading the Bible with great zeal and rapidity; by quickly scanning the pages and turning over the leaves, he grew to believe that he read through the whole Bible once or twice daily. He sat up most of the night and lay in bed all day, surrounded with Bibles and Psalm-books.

Dr. Skae writes:

§ It was observed that the symptoms displayed an aggravation *every alternate day*. On each alternate day the patient will neither eat, sleep, nor walk, but continues incessantly turning over the leaves of a Bible and complaining piteously of his misery. On the intermediate days he is, comparatively speaking, quite well, enters into the domestic duties of his family, eats heartily, walks out, transacts business, assures every one he is quite well, and appears to entertain no apprehension of a return of his complaints. What is chiefly remarkable is the sort of double existence which the individual appears to have. On those days on which he is affected with his malady he appears to have no remembrance whatever of the previous or of any former day on which he was comparatively well, nor of any of the engagements of those days. On the intermediate days he distinctly remembers the transactions of previous days on which he was well, but appears to have little or no recollection of the occurrences of the days on which he was ill. He appears in short to have a sort of two-fold existence, one half of which he spends in the rational enjoyment of life and discharge of its duties, and the other in a state of hopeless hypochondriacism, amounting almost to complete mental aberration. §

Up to this point the secondary states which we have considered, however startling to old-fashioned ideas of personality, may, at any rate, be regarded as forms of mental derangement or decay—varieties on a theme already known. Now, however, we approach a group of cases to which it is difficult to make any such definition apply. They are cases where the secondary state is *not* obviously a degeneration; where it may even appear to be in some ways an *improvement* on the primary; so that one is left wondering how it came about that the man either originally was what he was or—being what he was—suddenly became something so very different.

I give here the case of Dr. Azam's often quoted patient, Félida X.[1]

In this the somnambulic life finally became the normal life. But the point on which I wish to dwell is this: that Félida's second state was altogether *superior* to the first—physically superior, since the nervous pains which had troubled her from childhood disappeared; and morally superior, inasmuch as her morose, self-centered disposition was exchanged for a cheerful activity which enabled her to attend to her children and her shop much more effectively than when she was in the "état bête," as she called what was once the only personality that she knew. In this case, then, which at the time Dr. Azam wrote—1887—was of nearly thirty years standing, the spontaneous readjustment of nervous activities—the second state, no memory of which remained in the first state—resulted in an improvement profounder than could have been anticipated from any moral or medical treatment that we know. The case shows us how often the word "normal" means nothing more than "what happens to exist."

A very complete account of the case is given in Dr. A. Binet's *Altérations de la Personnalité* (pp. 6–20), and I briefly summarize this:

§ Félida was born at Bordeaux in 1843 of healthy parents. Towards the age of thirteen years she began to exhibit symptoms of hysteria. When about fourteen and a half she used suddenly to feel a pain in her forehead and then fall into a profound sleep for some ten minutes, after which she woke spontaneously in her secondary condition. This lasted an hour or two; then the sleep came on again, and she awoke in her normal state. The change at first occurred every five or six days. As the hysterical symptoms increased, Dr. Azam was called in to attend her in 1858.

His report of that time states that in the primary state she appears very intelligent and fairly well educated; of a melancholy disposition, talking little, very industrious; constantly thinking of her maladies and suffering acute pains in various parts of the body, especially the head, all her actions, ideas, and words being perfectly rational. Almost every day what she calls her *crise* comes on spontaneously—often while she is sitting at her needlework—preceded by a brief interval of profound sleep, from which no external stimulus can rouse her. On waking into the secondary state she appears like an entirely different person, smiling and gay; she continues her work cheerfully or walks about briskly, no longer feeling all the pains she

[1] For the fullest account of Félida, see *Hypnotisme, Double Conscience,* etc., par le Dr. Azam. Paris, 1887.

has just before been complaining of. The condition, in fact, is much superior to her ordinary one, as shown by the disappearance of her physical pains, and especially by the state of her memory.

In this condition she remembers perfectly all that has happened on previous occasions when she was in the same state, and also all the events of her normal life; whereas during her normal life she forgets absolutely the occurrences of the secondary state. She declares whatever state she is in at the moment is the normal one; the other one is always her *crise*. . . . .

She married early, and her *crises* became more frequent. The secondary state gradually encroached more and more on the primary state, till the latter began to appear only at intervals and for a brief space of time. These alternations were excessively inconvenient, since she forgot in them all the events of what was now her ordinary life, all the arrangements of her business, etc.; for instance, in going to a funeral, she had a *crise,* and consequently found it impossible to remember who the deceased person was. She had a great dread of these occurrences, though, by long practice, she had become very skillful at concealing them from every one but her husband. A peculiar feeling of pressure in the head warned her that the *crise* was coming, and she would then, for fear of making mistakes in her business, hastily write down whatever facts she most needed to keep in mind. §

The following is another case in which the faculties appeared to be heightened in the secondary condition. The account is taken from the *Proceedings* S.P.R., vol. iv. pp. 230–32. The case was sent to Professor Barrett, in 1876, by a clergyman, then vicar of a London parish, and father of the subject. He did not choose to give further particulars, or to allow his name to be published.

§ My son was in his seventeenth year attacked by what was said to be cataleptic hysteria. At their first commencement they were little more than prolonged fainting fits; afterwards, each attack began by his passing in an instant into a state of complete rigidity. After a time he would rise with a sigh, move about, and speak without the slightest hesitation or incoherency, and thence continue for hours or days, leading an entirely separate existence, not recognizing friends or relations or even the way to his own bedroom, and taking no notice if addressed by his own name, writing letters with another signature, always imagining himself to have arrived at middle-age, and alluding to incidents of his imaginary youth, which teemed with echoes of his past reading; he was most courteous and pleasant in his manner, excepting when any doubt was implied as to the accuracy of any statement which he made.

At times all his faculties were in a most excited state. He would continue for hours playing games of skill with almost preternatural dexterity; he would repeat to the air pages of poetry; and he would play and sing in a wild and original manner, of which he was incapable at other times, quite unconscious of the presence of others and impervious to any interruptions. In this state he has continued for a week at a time, going out with us to dine with old friends whom, however, he never recognized but treated as new acquaintances. He always spoke of his parents as far off in some distant Eastern country, in which he himself had been born, and spoke to us (his father and mother) as kind hosts and friends whom he was soon to leave. Suddenly he would fall to the ground, roll about in convulsive agony with loud groans, and, a little water being poured into his lips, would get up and go on talking upon the subject of conversation on which he had been engaged at the time of his seizure, and without the slightest remembrance of anything that had passed meanwhile. These attacks continued every few days for more than two years, during which he was forbidden all kinds of study. At the age of nineteen we were advised to send him on a voyage, and accordingly he paid a visit to an uncle, a military officer at Madras; from thence he returned in six or seven months quite cured, went up to the University of Cambridge, where he went out in honors; and is now at the bar. §

The old case of Mary Reynolds, which I next cite, is again remarkable in respect of the change of character involved. Observe, also, the tendency of the two states gradually to *coalesce* apparently in a third phase likely to be preferable to either of the two already known. It is taken from Professor W. James' "Principles of Psychology," vol. i. pp. 381–84, being there quoted from Dr. Weir Mitchell's report in the *Transactions of the College of Physicians of Philadelphia,* April 4th, 1888.

§ This dull and melancholy young woman, inhabiting the Pennsylvania wilderness in 1811, was found one morning, long after her habitual time for rising, in a profound sleep from which it was impossible to arouse her. After eighteen or twenty hours of sleeping she awakened, but in a state of unnatural consciousness. Memory had fled. To all intents and purposes she was as a being for the first time ushered into the world.

Her eyes were virtually for the first time opened upon the world. Her parents, brothers, sisters, friends, were not recognized or acknowledged as such by her. She had never seen them before—never known them. To the scenes by which she was surrounded she was a perfect stranger. The house, the fields, the forest, the hills, the vales, the streams—all were novelties.

She had not the slightest consciousness that she had ever existed previous to the moment in which she awoke from that mysterious slumber. In a word, she was an infant, just born, yet born in a state of maturity.

The first lesson in her education was to teach her by what ties she was bound to those by whom she was surrounded.

The next lesson was to re-teach her the arts of reading and writing. She was apt enough, and made such rapid progress in both, that *in a few weeks* she had readily re-learned to read and write.

The next thing that is noteworthy is the change which took place in her disposition. Instead of being melancholy, she was now cheerful to extremity. Instead of being reserved, she was buoyant and social. Formerly taciturn and retiring, she was now merry and jocose. While she was, in this second state, extravagantly fond of company, she was much more enamored of nature's works, as exhibited in the forests, hills, vales, and watercourses. She used to start in the morning, either on foot or horseback, and ramble until nightfall over the whole country; nor was she at all particular whether she were on a path or in the trackless forest.

She knew no fear, and as bears and panthers were numerous in the woods, and rattlesnakes and copperheads abounded everywhere, her friends told her of the danger to which she exposed herself; but it produced no other effect than to draw forth a contemptuous laugh, as she said, "I know you only want to frighten me and keep me at home, but you miss it, for I often see your bears, and I am perfectly convinced that they are nothing more than black hogs."

One evening, after her return from her daily excursion, she told the following incident: "As I was riding today along a narrow path a great black hog came out of the woods and stopped before me. I never saw such an impudent black hog before. It stood up on its hind feet and grinned and gnashed its teeth at me. I could not make the horse go on. I told him he was a fool to be frightened at a hog, and tried to whip him past, but he would not go and wanted to turn back. I told the hog to get out of the way, but he did not mind me. 'Well,' said I, 'if you won't for words, I'll try blows;' so I got off and took a stick, and walked up toward it. When I got pretty close by, it got down on all fours and walked away slowly and sullenly, stopping every few steps and looking back and grinning and growling. Then I got on my horse and rode on."

Thus it continued for five weeks, when one morning after a protracted sleep, she awoke and was herself again. She recognized the parental, the brotherly, and sisterly ties as though nothing had happened, and immediately went about the performance of duties incumbent upon her, and which she had planned five weeks previously. Great was her surprise at the change which one night (as she supposed) had produced. Nature bore a different aspect. Not a trace was left in her mind of the giddy scenes through which she had passed. Her ramblings through the forest, her tricks and humor, all were faded from her memory, and not a shadow left behind. Of course her natural disposition returned; her melancholy was deepened by the information of what had occurred. All went on in the old-fashioned way. After the lapse of a few weeks she fell into a profound sleep, and awoke in her second state, taking up her new life again precisely where she had left it when she before passed from that state. All the knowledge she possessed was that acquired during the few weeks of her former period of second consciousness. She knew nothing of the intervening time. In this state she came to understand perfectly the facts of her case, not from memory, but from information. Yet her buoyancy of spirits was so great that no depression was produced. On the contrary, it added to her cheerfulness, and was made the foundation, as was everything else, of mirth.

These alternations from one state to another continued at intervals of varying length for fifteen or sixteen years, but finally ceased when she attained the age of thirty-five or thirty-six, leaving her *permanently in her second state.* In this she remained without change for the last quarter of a century of her life. [The emotional opposition of the two states seems, however, to have become gradually effaced in Mary Reynolds.] The change from a gay, hysterical, mischievous woman, fond of jests and subject to absurd beliefs or delusive convictions, to one retaining the joyousness and love of society, but sobered down to levels of practical usefulness, was gradual. The most of the twenty-five years which followed she was as different from her melancholy, morbid self as from the hilarious condition of the early years of her second state. Some of her family spoke of it as her third state. She is described as becoming rational, industrious, and very cheerful, yet reasonably serious; possessed of a well-balanced temperament, and not having the slightest indication of an injured or disturbed mind. For some years she taught school, and in that capacity was both useful and acceptable, being a general favorite with old and young.

During these last twenty-five years she lived in the same house with the Rev. Dr. John V. Reynolds, her nephew, part of that time keeping house for him, showing a sound judgment and a thorough acquaintance with the duties of her position.

"Dr. Reynolds, who is still living in Meadville," says Dr. Mitchell, "and who has most kindly placed the facts at my disposal, states in his letter to me of January 4th, 1888, that at a later period of her life she said she did sometimes seem to have a dim, dreamy idea of a shadowy past, which she could not fully grasp, and could not be certain whether it originated in a partially restored memory or in the statements of the events by others during her abnormal state.

"Miss Reynolds died in January, 1854, at the age of sixty-one. On the morning of the day of her death she rose in her usual health, ate her breakfast, and superintended household duties. While thus employed she suddenly raised her hands to her head and exclaimed: 'Oh! I wonder what is the matter with my head!' and immediately fell to the floor. When carried to a sofa she gasped once or twice and died." §

For another and more detailed account, see "Mary Reynolds: a Case of Double Consciousness," by the Rev. W. S. Plummer, D.D., in *Harper's Magazine* for May 1860. The most important additional details in this account are: The first time she was in the secondary state, she recovered through *dreams* some of the knowledge that she had lost while awake. She dreamt that she heard a man preach and explain passages in the Bible to her, and after the dream seemed to regain all her knowledge of the Bible, though at the time unable to read it. In the same dream she saw and talked with a woman whom she did not recognize but described minutely on waking; and the description was said to correspond exactly to a dead sister, whose existence while awake she had forgotten. After this she often dreamt of the same sister and also of another dead friend.

We now come to spontaneous cases of *multiplex* personality, of which Louis Vivé's is one of the best known:

§ Louis Vivé began life (in 1863) as the neglected child of a turbulent mother. He was sent to a reformatory at ten years old, and there showed himself quiet, well-behaved, and obedient. Then at fourteen years old he had a great fright from a viper—a fright which threw him off his balance and started the series of psychical oscillations on which he has been tossed ever since. At first the symptoms were only physical, epilepsy and hysterical paralysis of the legs; and at the asylum of Bonneval, whither he was next sent, he worked at tailoring steadily for a couple of months. Then suddenly he had a hystero-epileptic attack—fifty hours of convulsions and ecstasy—and when he awoke from it he was no longer paralyzed, no longer acquainted with tailoring, and no longer virtuous. His memory was set back to the moment of the viper's appearance and he could remember nothing since. His character had become violent, greedy, and quarrelsome, and his tastes were radically changed. For instance, though he had before the attack been a total abstainer, he now not only drank his own wine but stole the wine of the other patients. He escaped from Bonneval, and after a few turbulent years, tracked by his occasional relapses into hospital or madhouse, he turned up once more at the Rochefort asylum in the character of a private of marines, convicted of theft, but considered to be of unsound mind. And at Rochefort and La Rochelle, by great good fortune, he fell into the hands of three physicians who tried experiments on him.

The state into which he has gravitated is a very unpleasing one. There is paralysis and insensibility of the right side, and (as is often the case in right hemiplegia) the speech is indistinct and difficult. Nevertheless, he is constantly haranguing any one who will listen to him, abusing his physicians, or preaching, with a monkey-like impudence rather than with reasoned clearness, radicalism in politics and atheism in religion. He makes bad jokes and if any one pleases him he endeavors to caress him. He remembers recent events during his residence at Rochefort asylum, but only two scraps of his life before that date, namely, his vicious period at Bonneval and a part of his stay at Bicêtre.

But the physicians of Rochefort had faith in the efficacy of the contact of metals in provoking transfer of hysterical hemiplegia from one side to the other. They tried various metals in turn on Louis Vivé. Lead, silver, and zinc had no effect. Copper produced a slight return of sensibility in the paralyzed arm. But steel, applied to the right arm, transferred the whole insensibility to the left side of the body.

Such phenomena are now, of course, generally attributed to suggestion. What puzzled the doctors was the change of character which accompanied the change of sensibility. When Louis Vivé issued from the crisis of transfer, with its minute of anxious expression and panting breath, he was what might fairly be called a new man. The restless insolence, the savage impulsiveness, have wholly disappeared. The patient is now gentle, respectful, and modest. He can speak clearly now, but he only speaks when he is spoken to. If he is asked his views on religion and politics, he prefers to leave such matters to wiser heads than his own. It might seem that morally and intellectually the patient's cure had been complete.

But now ask him what he thinks of Rochefort; how he liked his regiment of marines. He will blankly answer that he knows nothing of Rochefort, and was never a soldier in his life. "Where are you, then, and what is the date of to-day?" "I am at Bicêtre; it is January 2nd, 1884; and I hope to see M. Voisin to-day, as I did yesterday."

It is found, in fact, that he has now the memory of two short periods of life (different from those which he remembers when his *right* side is paralyzed), periods during which, so far as can now be ascertained, his character was of the same decorous type and his paralysis was on the left side.

If he is placed in an electric bath, or if a magnet be placed on his head, it looks at first sight as though a complete physical cure had been effected. All paralysis, all defect of sensibility, has disappeared. His movements are light and active, his expression gentle and timid. But ask him where he is, and you find that he has gone back to a boy of fourteen, that he is at St. Urbain, his first reformatory, and that his memory embraces his years of childhood and stops short on the very day when he had the fright with the viper. If he is pressed to recollect the incident of the viper a violent epileptiform crisis puts a sudden end to this phase of his personality. §

Yet, if Louis Vivé's case thus strangely intensifies the already puzzling notion of *ecmnesia*—as though the whole organism could be tricked into forgetting the events which had most deeply stamped it—what are we to say to Dr. Morton Prince's case of "Sally Beauchamp," with its grotesque exaggeration of a subliminal self—a kind of hostile bedfellow which knows everything and remembers everything—which mocks the emotions and thwarts the projects of the ordinary reasonable self which can be seen and known?

The following account of this interesting case is abridged from Dr. Prince's report to the International Congress of Psychology, Paris, August, 1900, which was published in the *Proceedings* S.P.R., vol. xv. pp. 466–83.

§ ... This case has been the subject of a continuous study for at least three years, and has occupied hundreds of hours of time. . . .

When Miss Beauchamp first came under observation she was a neurasthenic of a very severe type. She was a student in one of our colleges, and there received a very good education. But in consequence of her neurasthenic condition it was simply impossible for her to go on with her work. She was a wreck, I might say, in body. In temperament she is a person of extreme idealism, with a very morbid New England conscientiousness, and a great deal of pride and reserve, so that she is very unwilling to expose herself or her life to anybody's scrutiny.

The usual methods were employed with no result and it seemed as if her case was hopeless. Finally I concluded to try hypnotic suggestions. She proved a very good subject, and the suggestions produced at the time rather brilliant results. In hypnosis she went easily into the somnambulistic state. This somnambulistic state came later to be known as B. II., while the first personality with whom I became acquainted, Miss Beauchamp herself, was known as B. I. Now I used to notice that as B. II. she was continually rubbing her eyes; her hands were in constant motion, always trying to get at her eyes. Still I paid very little attention to it, or placed very little significance in this fact, merely attributing it to nervousness. One day when I hypnotized her and referred to something that she had done in a previous hypnotic state—that is to say, something that she had said or done in a previous state when I supposed she was B. II.—she denied all knowledge of it, and said it was not so. This surprised me, and I attributed the denial at first to an attempt at deception. Finally it turned out that when she went into the state of which she later denied the facts, she was an entirely distinct and separate person. This third personality, which then developed, came to be known as B. III. We had then three mental states, B. I., B. II., and B. III. . . .

Now B. III has proved to be one of the most interesting of all the personalities that have developed in the case. In one respect it is one of the most remarkable personalities, I think, that has ever been exhibited in any of these cases of multiple personality, as will, I think, presently appear. B. III., like B. II., was constantly rubbing her eyes, so that I was frequently compelled to hold her hands by force to prevent her from doing so. One day, some time after this, when she was at home, owing to some nervous excitement she was thrown into the condition of B. III., and then, I not being there to prevent it, she rubbed her eyes until she got them opened, and from that time to this she (B. III.) has had a spontaneous and independent existence, and she always refers to events as being "before" or "after she got her eyes opened."

Now this personality came afterwards to be known as Sally. . . . In character she differs very remarkably from B. I. . . . B. I. is a very serious-minded person, fond of books and study, of a religious turn of mind, and possesses a very morbid conscientiousness. Sally, on the other hand, is full of fun, does not worry about anything; all life is one great joke to her, she hates books, loves fun and amusement, does not like serious things, hates church, in fact is thoroughly childlike in every way. She is a child of nature. She insists, although of this I have no absolute proof, that she never sleeps, and that she is always awake while Miss Beauchamp is asleep. I believe it to be true. Then Miss B. is a neurasthenic, Sally is perfectly well. She is never fatigued and never suffers pain. During the first year Sally and Miss Beauchamp used to come and go in succession. At first whenever B. I. became fatigued or upset from any cause, Sally was likely to come. The periods during which Sally was in existence might be any time from a few minutes to several hours. Later these periods became prolonged to several days. It must not be forgotten that though Miss Beauchamp knows nothing of Sally, Sally, when not in the flesh, is conscious of all Miss Beauchamp's thoughts and doings, and the latter could hide nothing from her. Curiously enough, Sally took an intense dislike to B. I. She actually hated her and there was no length to which she would not go to cause her annoyance. She would play every kind of prank on her to make her miserable. She tormented her to a degree almost incredible. While Sally would never do anything to make any one else unhappy, she was absolutely remorseless in the way she tormented Miss Beauchamp by practical jokes and by playing upon her sensibilities. I will give a few illustrations. If there is one thing which Miss Beauchamp has a perfect horror of, it is snakes and spiders. They throw her into a condition of terror. One day Sally went out into the country and collected some snakes and spiders and put them into a little box. She brought them home and did them up in a little package, and addressed them to Miss Beauchamp, and when B. I. opened the package they ran out and about the room and nearly sent her into fits. In order to get rid of them she had to handle them, which added to her terror.

A great friend of Miss Beauchamp, to whom she felt under strong obligations, had asked her to knit a baby's blanket. She worked on that blanket for nearly a year; as fast as she would get it near completion, Sally would unravel it, and then she would have to begin the task again, and regularly every time Sally would pull the whole thing to pieces. Finally she came to herself one day and found herself standing in the middle of the room tied up in a perfect network and snarl of worsted yarn; it was wound round the pictures and then round and round the furniture, the bed, the chairs, herself, and she had to cut it to get out of the snarl. Miss Beauchamp is a person with a great sense of dignity, and dislikes anything that smacks of a lack of decorum or of familiarity. Sally had a way of punishing her by making her sit on a chair with her feet upon the mantelpiece. B. I. could not take her feet down, and was mortified to think she had to sit that way. Sally carries on a correspondence with Miss Beauchamp, writes letters to her pointing out all the weak points of her character, dwelling on all the little slips and foibles of her mind, telling her all the reckless acts and secret thoughts, indeed, everything she has done that won't bear criticism. . . .

One of the most interesting problems is, who is Sally? . . . Sally as an individuality goes back to early infancy, and has grown with the growth of Miss Beauchamp. The theory which finally, I think, has been demonstrated, is that Sally represents the *subliminal consciousness.*

Although B. I. knows nothing of Sally, Sally not only is conscious of Miss Beauchamp's thoughts at the moment they arise, but she is capable, as I have said, of controlling her thoughts and her arms and legs and tongue to a certain extent. . . . During the times when Sally is in existence, B. I. is —as Sally puts it—"dead," and these times represent complete gaps in Miss Beauchamp's memory, and she has no knowledge of them whatever. "What becomes of her?" Sally frequently asks. Sally is never "dead." Her memory is continuous; there are no gaps in it. She not only knows all B. I.'s thoughts and emotions and sensations, but will have a train of thought at the same time with B. I., of an entirely different nature. The most remarkable part of Sally's personality, I think, is that she has been able to write out for me her autobiography, beginning with the time when she was in her cradle, which she remembers. She actually describes her own thoughts and feelings as distinct from B. I.'s, all through her childhood, up to and including the present time; although, as she says, she never got an independent existence until she "got her eyes open." She remembers her cradle, draws a picture of the bars in its sides, and remembers what she, as distinct from Miss Beauchamp, thought at the time when she was learning to walk. Then B. I. was frightened and wanted to go back, but Sally was not at all frightened and wanted to go ahead. She describes B. I. as having had a butterfly mind as contrasted with her own. She, as a small child, disliked the things that B. I. liked, and *vice versâ.* She describes her school life, her own feelings when B. I. did things, and the different sensations of the two selves when, for example, B. I. was punished and felt badly, and she herself was entirely indifferent and without remorse. Thus I have been able to get *an actual autobiography of a subliminal consciousness, in which are described the contemporaneous and contrasted mental lives of two consciousnesses, the subliminal and the dominant, from early infancy to adult life.* In this Sally has described for me various scenes and incidents which occurred and which she saw during her early life, but of which Miss Beauchamp is entirely ignorant. These usually represent scenes which occurred while B. I. was absorbed in thought, but which Sally as a subliminal noticed. Taking all this into consideration—taking the present relations of Sally's thoughts to Miss Beauchamp's thought, and many other facts, like automatic writing, which Sally performs with ease, and uses for purposes of correspondence—I think we are safe in saying that *Sally is the subliminal consciousness,* which has become highly developed and organized and obtained finally an independent existence, and led an individual life of its own. §

Later another personality became evident. This was called B. IV. She was of a very different character from either Sally or Miss Beauchamp, being irritable, quick-tempered, and often quite unpleasant.

Although Sally's mental life was also continuous during that of B. IV., and although she knew everything B. IV. did at the time she did it, heard what she said, read what she wrote, and saw what she did, nevertheless *Sally did not know B. IV.'s thoughts.* . .

For this reason Sally had great contempt for B. IV. and dubbed her the "Idiot." From this time on, Sally transferred her hatred from B. I. to the "Idiot."

Dr. Prince particularly stressed one point—namely, that however normal each of the personalities appeared, none was quite normal, as in each were missing some of the attributes of the original Miss Beauchamp.

Through suggestion given during hypnosis Dr. Prince was finally able to synchronize the various personalities into what was to all appearances the original Miss Beauchamp—the one who existed before she underwent the various nervewracking experiences which had made her personality split. Sally called her "that new thing," and when she was present Sally was unable to make herself evident. Eventually, when this synthesis—the new or whole Miss Beauchamp—took over entirely, Sally went back, as she put it, "to where I came from." Dr. Prince concludes:

§ This final synthesis—the construction of what appears to be the original self—seems to me akin to a proof of the correctness of the diagnosis. §

The case of Mollie Fancher, of which I quote such brief and imperfect account as is accessible, might have been one of the most instructive of all, had it been observed and recorded with scientific accuracy—nay, even with the most ordinary diligence and care. It is true that at the remote date when Miss Fancher's phenomena were at their best an observer both willing and capable would have been as hard to find among professed *savants* as among professed spiritualists. And there is at least this good point in the case, that the *probity* of the whole group has always been held above suspicion.

The case of "Mollie Fancher" was recorded in a book by Judge Abram H. Dailey, entitled "Mollie Fancher: the Brooklyn Enigma. An Authentic Statement of Facts in the Life of Mary J. Fancher, the Psychological Marvel of the Nineteenth Century" (Brooklyn, N. Y.). This book consists of a rather disconnected narrative by Judge Dailey, abstracts of a diary kept by Miss Fancher's aunt, a series of signed statements made by friends, and a number of reprints of articles which had originally appeared in the daily papers.

§ Miss Fancher was born August 16, 1848. As a child her health was good, but in March of 1864 it began to fail. Later she was thrown from a horse and severely injured. In the course of the following summer the lower part of her body suddenly became paralyzed. As she was recovering from this she was injured in a fall from a street car. This was followed by serious illness, and convulsions. Soon afterwards she lost, in rapid succession, sight, speech and hearing. Her history was that of a hysteric of the worst type, anæsthesias, paralyses, contractures, and convulsions succeeding each other in bewildering variety. Her sight was never restored, although in later years she seemed to be recovering some portion of it. Throughout this period normal sleep seemed to be replaced by "trance," in which the whole body became rigid.

During her years of blindness Miss Fancher convinced her friends that she possessed supernormal powers of vision. It is claimed that she repeatedly read sealed letters, described events at a distance, and found lost articles. She also believed that she saw the world of spirits, but was extremely reticent upon that topic.

Judge Dailey adduces little evidence of value in support of these claims. He has, indeed, recorded the narratives of many witnesses whose truthfulness no one would question, but in not one of these narratives are the facts given with that attention to details and that care to avoid misdescription which the nature of the case demands. Many are vague in the extreme, and very few tell us how much time elapsed between the event and its committal to writing. To glance at only the best of these: Professor Parkhurst submitted to Miss Fancher a sealed envelope containing a slip of printed paper, the contents of which he did not himself know. She told him it contained the words "court," "jurisdiction," and the numerals 6, 2, 3, 4. These he wrote in his notebook, took the envelope away still sealed, read Miss Fancher's statement to two friends, and in their presence opened the envelope. Miss Fancher's statements were found to be correct.

Dr. Speir states that Miss Fancher once wrote for him upon a slate the contents of a letter which had just been brought to her by the postman, and was as yet unopened.

In brief, the evidence which Judge Dailey has collected will seem satisfactory only to those who are already satisfied of the possibility of clairvoyance. It will do little towards establishing that possibility. §

The case of Anna Winsor, next to be cited, goes so far further in its suggestion of interference from without, that it presents to us, at any rate, a contrast and even conflict between positive insanity on the part of the organism generally with wise and watchful sanity on the part of a *single limb,* with which that organism professes to have no longer any concern.

Perhaps, indeed, the conception which this case suggests is not so much that of an external spirit intervening on the sufferer's behalf, as of her own spirit, coexisting in gentleness and wisdom alongside of all that wild organic excitement and decay. Of course I do not press so strange a notion; yet to myself, I must in fairness add, it is by no means ludicrous. Indeed, I think that all these sudden changes and recuperations should teach us our inability to say *how deep* even the severest psychical lesion goes—whether there may not at the worst be *that* within us which persists unmutilated and untarnished through all confusion of the flesh.

The case of Anna Winsor represents an extreme form of hystero-epilepsy, with very violent and frequent convulsions, and intervals of insane delusions. Much relief was given by hypnotism (called by Dr. Barrows "magnetism," or "animal magnetism"), but no cure was effected. The detailed record extends over two and a half years, from May 9th, 1860, to January, 1863, but some of Dr. Barrows' comments were made at a later date. Miss Winsor died in 1873.

§ *May 9th*—First visit . . . Treated her for what appeared to be typhoid fever. At the end of about seventeen days she became convalescent, and I anticipated a speedy recovery. Now, suddenly and without apparent cause, about June 1st, a relapse of fever . . . delirium . . . convulsions . . . loss of consciousness . . .

No change worthy of notice until June 15th. Apparently unconscious of everything around her; emaciated, haggard, and seemingly about to die; we noticed her toes moving as if trying to form letters on the sheet. Since we didn't give any particular attention to this, she began, with her forefinger, to form letters on the sheet as if trying to spell some word. It was suggested that paper and a pencil be given to her. She began to write names of persons long since dead. Then followed directions about her sickness, and predictions as to her future, saying: "It (always using the third person singular) will be a long time sick; lose her sense of smell; be blind many months; doubtful if she ever walks again. Her sickness will develop many phases and strange phenomena." Continues to be very sick. Spasms increase in frequency and severity.

August 9th.—Tried animal magnetism. Succeeded in putting her to sleep; slept a short time, but more quiet through the day.

September 8th.—She has not been able to utter a word for ten weeks. All communications are made by writing.

September 13th.—Complains that the room is dark; cannot see. Tells what is going on in an adjoining room. Tells the time by a clock in another room. 14th and 15th.—"Balls" of pain in back and head. 16th, A.M.—Some delirium; in the evening a raving maniac. Tore her hair out by handfuls; fought and bit all who came near her. Rubbed with Tinct. Bell.: magnetism. Succeeded at 12:50 in getting her quiet. 17th and 18th.—

Wild with delirium. Tears her hair, bed-clothes, pillow-cases, both sheets, night-dress all to pieces. Her right hand prevents her left hand, by seizing and holding it, from tearing out her hair, but tears her clothes with her left hand and teeth.

[This appears to be the first distinctly noted usurpation of the right arm by the secondary personality.]

September 24th.—Writes the time of day; motions for a book; holds it upside down. Right hand predicts the number of spasms she will have a day: some days more, some less. . . . 29th.—Complains of great pain in right arm, more and more intense, when suddenly it falls down by her side. She looks at it in amazement. Thinks it belongs to some one else; positive it is not hers. Sees her right arm drawn around upon her spine. Cut it, prick it, do what you please to it, she takes no notice of it. Complains of great pain in the neck and back, which she now calls her shoulder and arm; no process of reasoning can convince her of the contrary. [To the present time (1866, when the Report was read at a Medical Society in Boston), now nearly five years, the hallucination remains firm. She believes her spine is her right arm, and that her right arm is a foreign object and a nuisance. She believes it to be an arm and hand, but treats it as if it had intelligence and might keep away from her. She bites it, pounds it, pricks it, and in many ways seeks to drive it from her. She calls it "Stump; old Stump." Sometimes she is in great excitement and tears, pounding "Old Stump." Says "Stump" has got this, that, or the other that belongs to her.]. . . . 13th.—Spasms as usual. In the evening, while sleeping, personates "Aunt Chloe"; writes for flour, mixes and makes some biscuits; pares an apple and makes a pie; *uses both hands when asleep, when awake has no power to move the right.* . . .

January 1st, 1861.—From November 20th up to this time, raving delirium; pulls her hair nearly all out from the top of her head. If she can get a pin, plunges it into whoever comes near her. Tears her clothes sadly. *The right hand protects her against the left as much as possible.* She now becomes more rational; talks again; first loud words uttered since November 6th. Calls for a book; reads with it upside down. January 4th.—Becomes blind. From this time to February 1st, constant delirium; frequent spasms.

February 1st to 11th.—No particular change. Swallows water when in the magnetic sleep, and personates sundry persons; personates a Quaker; speaks loud and rapidly; gives an amusing lecture. When the magnetism passes off, remembers nothing of the past; can hardly speak in whispers, and is much prostrated. . . . More or less spasms nearly every day. Under the influence of magnetism writes poetry; personates different persons, mostly those who have long since passed away. Whenever in the magnetic state, whatever she does or says is not remembered when she comes out of it. Commences a series of drawings with her right (paralyzed) hand, "Old Stump." Also writes poetry with it. Whatever "Stump" writes or draws, or does, she appears to take no interest in; says it is none of hers, and that she wants nothing to do with "Stump" or "Stump's."

April 9th.—Becomes deaf; great pain in head; is conscious of her suffering most of the time. Commences bead work; makes three bead baskets; does it all with her left hand; threads her needle, strings her beads, makes her baskets; works alike by daylight, gaslight, twilight, and in the dark. I have sat by her in the evening and witnessed her work. I lowered the gas to almost total darkness, and asked her to thread her needle and proceed with her work, which she did at once, not seeming to notice that the room was darkened. She selected a small needle from her needlebook, stuck it perpendicularly into a cushion lying by her, bit off the end of the thread, rolled it between her thumb and finger and passed it through the needle's eye as easily and readily as I would have passed it through a finger ring, and proceeded at once to string her beads; eyes closed.

May 15th.—Delirious, imagining herself Queen Anne. . . . May 19th.—Three spasms in the A.M.; at 2 P.M. a fourth. Her head is drawn downward and rests upon her knees; but suddenly her body elevates and she balances upon her head; remains in this position a few moments, falls over upon her right side; her body forms an arch while she rests upon the right side of her right foot and upon her right hand, and remains in this position half-an-hour. The spasm passes off; she sinks down prostrate, still delirious.

During the last two and a half years I have been obliged to be absent three or four times for a week or more, and although she has been attended and magnetized by either my friend Dr. C., or Dr. S.—who both have the power of magnetizing—she has lost sleep and become raving crazy, tearing her hair, pounding her head; giving herself the name "Queen Victoria," "Queen Anne," Mary, etc., and calling her mother "Queen of Sheba," "Bloody Mary," etc. myself "Dr. Kane," the "Old Giant," "God Almighty," and so on. . . . After going into the magnetic sleep at night she is very patient, pleasant, modest. Is pleased to see friends; converses pleasantly and rationally upon all subjects but one; upon this she is monomaniac. Her right hand and arm is not hers. Attempt to reason with her and she holds up her left arm and says, "This is my left arm. I see and feel my right arm drawn behind me. You say this 'stump' is my right arm. Then I have three arms and hands." In this arm the nerves of sensation are paralyzed, but the nerves of motion preserved. *She* has no will to move it. *She* has no knowledge of its motion. *This arm appears to have a separate intelligence. When she sleeps it writes or converses by signs. It never sleeps;* watches over her when she sleeps; endeavors to prevent her from injuring herself or her clothing when she is raving. It seems to possess an independent life, and, to some extent, foreknowledge. §

The case which I place last in this series, the "Watseka Wonder," must plainly be presented to the reader as a duplication of personality—a pseudo-possession, if you will—determined in a hysterical child by the suggestion of friends. Thus, I repeat, the story must for the present be offered and received. At a later stage, and when some other wonders have become to us more familiar—not less wonderful—than now, we may perhaps consider once more what further lessons this singular narrative may have to teach us.

A detailed record of the case of Mary Lurancy Vennum was originally given in the *Religio-Philosophical Journal* in 1879, and shortly afterwards published in pamphlet form under the title "The Watseka Wonder," by E. W. Stevens. Some additional evidence was obtained by Dr. Hodgson in personal interviews with some of the chief witnesses. This was published in the *Religio-Philosophical Journal* for December 20th, 1890. Colonel J. C. Bundy, who was Editor of the *Religio-Philosophical Journal* when the record was first published, and was himself well known as a skilful and scrupulously honest investigator of spiritistic phenomena, speaks in the highest terms of Dr. Stevens (who died in 1885), and adds: "We took great pains before and during publication to obtain full corroboration of the astounding facts from unimpeachable and competent witnesses."

§ Mary Lurancy Vennum, a girl nearly fourteen years old, living at Watseka, Illinois, became apparently controlled by the spirit of Mary Roff, a neighbor's daughter who had died at the age of eighteen years and nine months, when Lurancy Vennum was a child of about fifteen months old. The "control" by Mary Roff lasted almost continuously for a period of nearly four months, from February 1st till May 21st, 1878. The narrative by Dr. Stevens was prepared shortly afterwards.

On July 11th, 1877, Lurancy had a sort of fit, and was unconscious for five hours. Next day the fit recurred, but while lying as if dead she described her sensations to her family, declaring that she could see heaven and the angels, and a little brother and sister and others who had died.

The fits or trances, occasionally passing into ecstasy, when she claimed to be in heaven, occurred several times a day up to the end of January, 1878; she was generally believed to be insane, and most friends of the family urged that she should be sent to an insane asylum.

At this stage Mr. and Mrs. Asa B. Roff, whose daughter, Mary Roff had had periods of insanity, persuaded Mr. Vennum to allow him to bring Dr. E. W. Stevens of Janesville, Wisconsin, to investigate the case.

Dr. Stevens, an entire stranger to the family, was introduced by Mr. Roff at four o'clock P.M.; no other persons present but the family. The girl sat near the stove, in a common chair, her elbows on her knees, her hands under her chin, feet curled up on the chair, eyes staring, looking every way like an "old hag." She sat for a time in silence, until Dr. Stevens moved his chair, when she savagely warned him not to come nearer. She appeared sullen and crabbed, calling her father "Old Black Dick" and her mother "Old Granny." She refused to be touched, even to shake hands, and was reticent and sullen with all save the doctor, with whom she entered freely into conversation, giving her reasons for doing so; she said he was a spiritual doctor, and would understand her.

She described herself first as an old woman named Katrina Hogan, and then as a young man named Willie Canning, and after some insane conversation had another fit, which Dr. Stevens relieved by hypnotizing her. She then became calm, and said that she had been controlled by evil spirits. Dr. Stevens suggested that she should try to have a better control, and encouraged her to try and find one. She then mentioned the names of several deceased persons, saying there was one who wanted to come, named Mary Roff.

Mr. Roff being present, said: "That is my daughter; Mary Roff is my girl. Why, she has been in heaven twelve years. Yes, let her come, we'll be glad to have her come." Mr. Roff assured Lurancy that Mary was good and intelligent, and would help her all she could; stating further that Mary used to be subject to conditions like herself. Lurancy, after due deliberation and counsel with spirits, said that Mary would take the place of the former wild and unreasonable influence.

On the following morning, Mr. Vennum called at the office of Mr. Roff and informed him that the girl claimed to be Mary Roff, and wanted to go home. He said, "She seems like a child real homesick, wanting to see her pa and ma and her brothers."

Mary had had fits frequently from the age of six months, which gradually increased in violence. She also had periods of despondency, in one of which she cut her arm with a knife until she fainted. Five days of raving mania followed, after which she recognized no one, and seemed to lose all her natural senses, but when blindfolded could read and do everything as if she saw. After a few days she returned to her normal condition, but the fits became still worse, and she died in one of them in July, 1865. Her mysterious illness had made her notorious in the neighborhood during her lifetime, and her alleged clairvoyant powers are said to have been carefully investigated "by all the prominent citizens of Watseka," including newspaper editors and clergymen.

It was in February, 1878 that her supposed "control" of Lurancy began. The girl then became "mild, docile, polite, and timid, knowing none of the family, but constantly pleading to go home."

Mrs. A. B. Roff and her daughter, Mrs. Minerva Alter, Mary's sister, hearing of the remarkable change, went to see the girl. As they came in sight, far down the street, Mary, looking out of the window, exclaimed exultingly, "There comes my ma and sister Nervie!"—the name by which Mary used to call Mrs. Alter in girlhood. As they came into the house she caught them around their necks, wept and cried for joy, and seemed so happy to meet them. From this time on she seemed more homesick than before.

On the 11th day of February, 1878, they sent the girl to Mr. Roff's, where she met her "pa and ma," and each member of the family, with the most gratifying expressions of love and affection, by words and embraces. On being asked how long she would stay, she said, "The angels will let me stay till some time in May;" and she made it her home there till May 21st, three months and ten days, a happy, contented daughter and sister in a borrowed body.

The girl seemed to know every person and everything that Mary knew when in her original body, twelve to twenty-five years ago, recognizing and calling by name those who were friends and neighbors of the family from 1852 to 1865, when Mary died, calling attention to scores, yes, hundreds of incidents that transpired during her natural life.

Mrs. Parker, who lived neighbor to the Roffs in Middleport in 1852, and next door to them in Watseka in 1860, came in with her daughter-in-law, Nellie Parker. Mary immediately recognized both of the ladies, calling Mrs. Parker "Auntie Parker," and the other "Nellie," as in the acquaintance of eighteen years ago. In conversation with Mrs. Parker Mary asked, "Do you remember how Nervie and I used to come to your house and sing?" Mrs. Parker says that was the first allusion made to that matter, nothing having been said by any one on that subject, and says that Mary and Minerva used to come to their house and sit and sing "Mary had a little lamb," etc. Mrs. Dr. Alter (Minerva) says she remembers it well.

One evening Mr. Roff was sitting in the room waiting for tea, and reading the paper, Mary being out in the yard. He asked Mrs. Roff if she could find a certain velvet head-dress that Mary used to wear the last year before she died. If so, to lay it on the stand and say nothing about it, to see if Mary would recognize it. Mrs. Roff readily found and laid it on the stand. The girl soon came in, and immediately exclaimed as she approached the stand, "Oh, there is my head-dress I wore when my hair was short!" She then asked, "Ma, where is my box of letters? Have you got them yet?" Mrs. Roff replied, "Yes, Mary, I have some of them." She at once got the box with many letters in it. As Mary began to examine them she said, "Oh, ma, here is a collar I tatted! Ma, why did you not show to me my letters and things before?" The collar had been preserved among the relics of the lamented child as one of the beautiful things her fingers had wrought before Lurancy was born.

In conversation with Dr. Stevens about her former life, she spoke of cutting her arm as hereinbefore stated, and asked if he ever saw where she did it. On receiving a negative answer, she proceeded to slip up her sleeve as if to exhibit the scar, but suddenly arrested the movement, as if by a sudden thought, and quickly said, "Oh, this is not the arm; that one is in the ground," and proceeded to tell where it was buried, and how she saw it done, and who stood around, how they felt, etc., but she did not feel bad. I heard her tell Mr. Roff and the friends present, how she wrote to him a message some years ago through the hand of a medium, giving name, time, and place. Also of rapping and of spelling out a message by another medium, giving time, name, place, etc., etc. which the parents admitted to be all true. I heard her relate a story of her going into the country with the men, some twenty odd years ago, after a load of hay, naming incidents that occurred on the road, which two of the gentlemen distinctly remembered.

Mary often spoke of seeing the children of Dr. Stevens in heaven, who were about her age and of longer residence there than herself. She said she was with them much, and went to his home with him. She correctly described his home and gave the names and ages of his children.

During her stay at Mr. Roff's her physical condition continually improved, being under the care and treatment of her supposed parents and the advice and help of her physician. She was ever obedient to the government and rules of the family, like a careful and wise child, always keeping in the company of some of the family, unless to go in to the nearest neighbors across the street. She was often invited and went with Mrs. Roff to visit the first families of the city, who soon became satisfied that the girl was not crazy, but a fine, well-mannered child.

On the morning of May 21st Mr. Roff writes as follows:

"Mary is to leave the body of Rancy today, about eleven o'clock, so she says. She is bidding neighbors and friends good-bye. Rancy to return home all right today. Mary came from her room upstairs, where she was sleeping with Lottie, at ten o'clock last night, lay down by us, hugged and kissed us, and cried because she must bid us good-bye, telling us to give all her pictures, marbles, and cards, and twenty-five cents Mrs. Vennum had given her to Rancy, and had us promise to visit Rancy often."

The girl was returned home that day. There was some alternation of the control on the way, but the normal Lurancy Vennum on arriving at her own home recognized all the members of her own family, and was perfectly well and happy in her own surroundings.

A letter from Mr. Roff, dated December 4th, 1886, published in the *Religio-Philosophical Journal,* states that Lurancy Vennum continued to live with her parents until January 1st, 1882, when she married a farmer, George Binning. The Roffs saw her often both before and after her marriage, until she moved further west in 1884, "and then," Mr. Roff says, "Mary would take control of Lurancy just as she did during the time she was at our house in 1878. Aside from this, she had little opportunity of using her mediumship, her parents being afraid to converse with her on the subject lest it should cause a return of the 'spells' (as they called them), and her husband never having made himself acquainted with spiritualism. Lurancy has what might be called, perhaps, a remembrance of her old experience while controlled by the spirit. She always speaks of it thus: 'Mary told me,' or 'Mary made me acquainted,' etc. She became acquainted with several persons while Mary controlled her, and when the control left her, she continued the acquaintance thus formed. She has never had any occasion for a physician since she left us, never having been sick since then."

[Dr. Hodgson visited Watseka on April 12th, 1890, and cross-examined the principal witnesses of the case who were still living in the neighborhood.]

Mrs. Roff stated that Lurancy Vennum had never been in her house until she came there as Mary Roff. After looking round the house she said, "Why, there's our old piano, and there's the same old piano cover." This piano and cover had been familiar to Mary Roff in another house. Lurancy referred to some peculiar incidents in Mary Roff's life almost every day, and she spoke once in detail about her stay at a water-cure place in Peoria where Mary Roff had been. Mrs. Roff once said to her, "Mary, do you remember when the stove pipe fell down and Frank was burned?" "Yes." "Do you know where he was burned?" "Yes; I'll show you," and she showed the exact spot on the arm where Frank was burned.

Mrs. Minerva Alter said that the mannerisms and behavior of Lurancy when under the control resembled those of her sister Mary. Lurancy Vennum knew Mrs. Alter previously as Mrs. Alter, having met her at the school, but when under the control of Mary she embraced Mrs. Alter affectionately and called her "Nervie"—a name by which Mrs. Alter had not been called for many years, but which was Mary's special pet name for her. Lurancy, as Mary Roff, stayed at Mrs. Alter's home for some time, and almost every hour of the day some trifling incident of Mary Roff's life was recalled by Lurancy. One morning she said, "Right over there by the currant bushes is where Allie greased the chicken's eye." This incident happened several years before the death of Mary Roff. Mrs. Alter remembered it very well, and recalled their bringing the chicken into the house for treatment. Lurancy had never met Allie, who is now Mrs. H——, living in Peoria, Ill. One morning Mrs. Alter asked her if she remembered the old dog (a dog which died during the lifetime of Mary Roff). Lurancy replied, "Yes; he died just there," and she pointed out the exact spot where the dog had breathed his last.

When Lurancy was being taken to Mr. Roff's house she tried to get to another house on the way, insisting that it was her home. They had to take her past it almost forcibly. This house was the house where Mr. Roff was living at the time of Mary Roff's death, and was also the house in which Mary Roff died.

Mrs. Wagner stated that she knew Lurancy Vennum very well both before, and during, and after the remarkable circumstances of her connection with Mary Roff. When Mary Roff died Mrs. Wagner's name was Mrs. Lord, and Mary Roff had been in her class at Sunday School. She had known Mary Roff for several years before her death. Mary Roff died in 1865, and Mrs. Lord married a second time in 1866. When she called upon the Roffs after Lurancy had gone there she was greeted very affectionately by the child who said "Oh Mary Lord, you look so very natural and have changed the least of anyone I have seen since I came back."

[Dr. Hodgson tried in vain to get some direct statements from Mrs. George Binning (formerly Lurancy Vennum), but received no answer to his inquiries. He writes:]

I have no doubt that the incidents occurred substantially as described in the narrative by Dr. Stevens, and in my view the only other interpretation of the case—besides the spiritistic—that seems at all plausible is that which has been put forward as the alternative to the spiritistic theory to account for the trance-communications of Mrs. Piper and similar cases, viz., secondary personality with supernormal powers. It would be difficult to disprove this hypothesis in the case of the Watseka Wonder, owing to the comparative meagerness of the record and the probable abundance of "suggestion" in the environment, and any conclusion that we may reach would probably be determined largely by our convictions concerning other cases. My personal opinion is that the "Watseka Wonder" case belongs in the main manifestations to the spiritistic category. §

We have now briefly surveyed a series of disintegrations of personality ranging from the most trifling *idée fixe* to actual alternations or permanent changes of the whole type of character. All these form a kind of continuous series, and illustrate the structure of the personality in concordant ways.

And from this point it is that our inquiries must now take their fresh departure. We in this work are concerned with changes which are the *converse* of hysterical changes. We are looking for integrations in lieu of disintegrations; for intensifications of control, widenings of faculty, instead of relaxation, scattering, or decay.

When we shall have completed the survey here indicated, we shall see, I think, how significant are the phenomena of hysteria in any psychological scheme which aims at including the hidden powers of man. For much as the hysteric stands in comparison with us ordinary men, so perhaps do we ordinary men stand in comparison with a not impossible ideal of faculty and of self-control.

It will surely have become evident, as we have studied the evidence in this chapter that human personality is a much more *modifiable* complex of forces than is commonly assumed, and is a complex, moreover, which has hitherto been dealt with only in crude, empirical fashion. Each stage, each method of disintegration, suggests a corresponding possibility of integration. Two points have been especially noticeable throughout the chapter. In the first place, we observe in many of the narratives some rudiment of supernormal perceptivity cropping up; probably something in itself useless, yet enough to indicate to us how great a reserve of untapped faculty is latent at no great depth beneath our conscious level. In the second place, we observe that in the more recent cases, where it has been possible to appeal, mainly through hypnotic suggestion, to the deeper strata of the personality, that appeal has seldom been made in vain. In almost every case something more has been thus learned of the actual mischief which was going on, something effected towards the reestablishment of psychical stability. These disturbances of personality are no longer for us—as they were even for the last generation—mere empty marvels, which the old-fashioned skeptic would often plume himself on refusing to believe. On the contrary, they are beginning to be recognized as psycho-pathological problems of the utmost interest; no one of them exactly like another, and no one of them without some possible insight into the intimate structure of man.

Chapter Three

GENIUS

Genius—if that vaguely used word is to receive anything like a psychological definition—should be regarded as a power of utilizing a wider range than other men can utilize of faculties in some degree innate in all. It is a power of appropriating the results of subliminal mentation to subserve the supraliminal stream of thought. An "inspiration of Genius" will be in truth a *subliminal uprush*, an emergence into the current of ideas which the man is consciously manipulating of other ideas which he has not consciously originated, but which have shaped themselves beyond his will, in profounder regions of his being. I shall urge that there is here no real departure from normality; no abnormality, at least in the sense of degeneration; but rather a fulfillment of the true norm of man, with suggestions, it may be, of something *supernormal*—of something which transcends existing normality as an advanced stage of evolutionary progress transcends an earlier stage.

I am not assuming that the faculty which is at the service of the man of genius is of a kind different from that of common men. Genius seems at present attainable rather by fortunate sports of heredity than by any systematic training; but it is, nevertheless, important to realize that a level thus definitely higher than our own has already often been reached in the normal progress of the race.

When I say "The differentia of genius lies in an increased control over subliminal mentation," I express, I think, a well-evidenced thesis, and I suggest an important inference, namely, that the man of genius is for us the best type of the normal man, in so far as he effects a successful co-operation of an unusually large number of elements of his personality —reaching a stage of integration slightly in advance of our own. Thus much I wish to say: but my thesis is not to be pushed further: as though I claimed that all our best thought was subliminal, or that all that was subliminal was potentially "inspiration."

Hidden in the deep of our being is a rubbish-heap as well as a treasure-house; degenerations and insanities as well as beginnings of higher development. The range of our subliminal mentation is more extended than the range of our supraliminal. At one end of the scale we find *dreams,* a normal subliminal product, but of less practical value than any form of sane supraliminal thought. At the other end of the scale we find that the

74

rarest, most precious knowledge comes to us from outside the ordinary field, through the eminently subliminal processes of telepathy, clairvoyance, and ecstasy. And between these two extremes lie many subliminal products, varying in value according to the dignity and trustworthiness of the subliminal mentation concerned.

For the purpose of present illustration of the workings of genius it seems well to choose a kind of ability which is quite indisputable and which also admits of some degree of quantitative measurement. I would choose the higher mathematical processes, were data available. Meantime there is a lower class of mathematical gift which by its very specialization and isolation seems likely to throw light on our present inquiry.

The public has been from time to time surprised and diverted by some so-called "calculating boy" or "arithmetical prodigy," generally of tender years and capable of performing "in his head" and almost instantaneously problems for which ordinary workers would require pencil and paper and a much longer time. In some few cases, indeed, the ordinary student would have no means whatever of solving the problem which the calculating boy unriddled with ease and exactness.

In almost every point where comparison is possible, we shall find this computative gift resembling other manifestations of subliminal faculty, such as the power of seeing hallucinatory figures, rather than the results of steady supraliminal effort such as the power of logical analysis. In the first place, this faculty, in spite of its obvious connection with general mathematical grasp and insight, is found almost at random, among non-mathematical and even quite stupid persons, as well as among mathematicians of mark. In the second place, it shows itself mostly in early childhood, and tends to disappear in later life; in this resembling visualizing power in general and the power of seeing hallucinatory figures in particular; which powers are habitually stronger in childhood and youth than in later years. Again, it is noticeable that when the power disappears early in life it is apt to leave behind it no memory whatever of the processes involved. And even when, by long persistence in a reflective mind, the power has become adopted into the supraliminal consciousness, there nevertheless may still be flashes of pure "inspiration," when the answer "comes into the mind" with absolutely no perception of intermediate steps.

It may be of interest to quote a passage about his brother from an autobiographical statement kindly furnished to me by Mr. Edward L. I. Blyth, of Edinburgh, the well-known civil engineer.

From *Proceedings* S.P.R., vol. viii. p. 352.

§ I shall now endeavor, in response to your request, to give some account of my late brother Benjamin's faculty of arithmetical calculation. My brother very early manifested a marvelous power of mental calculation. When almost exactly six years of age Benjamin was walking with his father before breakfast, when he said, "Papa, at what hour was I born?" He was told four A.M.

Ben.—"What o'clock is it at present?"

Ans.—"Seven fifty A.M."

The child walked on a few hundred yards, then turned to his father and stated the number of seconds he had lived. My father noted down the figures, made the calculation when he got home, and told Ben he was 172,800 seconds wrong, to which he got a ready reply: "No, papa, you have left out two days for the leap years—1820 and 1824," which was the case. §

Passing on to two other men of high ability known to have possessed this gift, Professor Safford and Archbishop Whately, we are struck with the evanescence of the power after early youth, or even before the end of childhood. I quote from Dr. Scripture Archbishop Whately's account of his powers:

§ There was certainly something peculiar in my calculating faculty. It began to show itself at between five and six and lasted about three years. . . . I soon got to do the most difficult sums, always in my head, for I knew nothing of figures beyond numeration. I did these sums much quicker than any one could upon paper and I never remember committing the smallest error. *When I went to school, at which time the passion wore off, I was a perfect dunce at ciphering, and have continued so ever since.* §

Still more remarkable, perhaps, was Professor Safford's loss of power. Professor Safford's whole bent was mathematical; his boyish gift of calculation raised him into notice; and he is now a Professor of Astronomy. He had therefore every motive and every opportunity to retain the gift, if thought and practice could have retained it. But whereas at ten years old he worked correctly in his head, in one minute, a multiplication sum whose answer consisted of 36 figures, he is now, I believe, neither more nor less capable of such calculation than his neighbors.

In the case of Mangiamele, there may have been real ingenuity subliminally at work. Our account of this prodigy is authentic, but tantalizing from its brevity.

§ In the year 1837 Vito Mangiamele, who gave his age as 10 years and 4 months, presented himself before Arago in Paris. He was the son of a shepherd of Sicily, who was not able to give his son any instruction. By chance it was discovered that by methods peculiar to himself he resolved problems that seemed at the first view to require extended mathematical knowledge. In the presence of the Academy Arago proposed the following questions: "What is the cubic root of 3,796,416?" In the space of about half a minute the child responded 156, which is correct. "What satisfies the condition that its cube plus five times its square is equal to 42 times itself increased by 40?" Everybody understands that this is a demand for the root of the equation $x^3 + 5x^2 - 42x - 40 = 0$. In less than a minute Vito responded that 5 satisfied the condition; which is correct. The third question related to the solution of the equation $x^5 - 4x - 16779 = 0$. This time the child remained four to five minutes without answering: finally he demanded with some hesitation if 3 would not be the solution desired. The secretary having informed him that he was wrong, Vito, a few moments afterwards, gave the number 7 as the true solution. Having finally been requested to extract the 10th root of 282,475,249 Vito found in a short time that the root is 7.

At a later date a committee, composed of Arago, Cauchy, and others, complains that "the masters of Mangiamele have always kept secret the methods of calculation which he made use of." §

Let us see whether we can find traces of subliminal intensification of those perceptions of a less specialized kind which underlie our more elaborate modes of cognizing the world around us. The sense of the *efflux of time,* and the sense of *weight,* or of muscular resistance, are amongst the profoundest elements in our organic being. And the sense of time is indicated in several ways as a largely subliminal faculty. There is much evidence to show that it is often more exact in men sleeping than in men awake, and in men hypnotized than in men sleeping. The records of spontaneous somnambulism are full of predictions made by the subject as to his own case, and accomplished, presumably by self-suggestion, but without help from clocks, at the precise minute foretold. Or this hidden knowledge may take shape in the imagery of dream, as in a case published by Professor Royce, of Harvard, where his correspondent describes "a dream in which I saw an enormous flaming clock-dial with the hands standing at 2:20. Awaking immediately, I struck a match, and upon looking at my watch found it was a few seconds past 2:20."

I must pass on into a much trodden field—the records, namely, left by eminent men as to the element of subconscious mentation, which was involved in their best work. I prefer to direct my readers' attention to a modest volume, in which a young physician has put together the results of a direct inquiry addressed to some Frenchmen of distinction as to their methods especially of imaginative work.[1] I quote a few of the replies addressed to him, beginning with some words from M. Sully Prudhomme —at once psychologist and poet—who is here speaking of the subconscious clarification of a chain of abstract reasoning. "I have sometimes suddenly understood a geometrical demonstration made to me a year previously without having in any way directed thereto my attention or will. It seemed that the mere spontaneous ripening of the conceptions which the lectures had implanted in my brain had brought about within me this novel grasp of the proof."

With this we may compare a statement of Arago's—"Instead of obstinately endeavoring to understand a proposition at once, I would admit its truth provisionally; and next day I would be astonished at understanding thoroughly that which seemed all dark before."

Condillac similarly speaks of finding an incomplete piece of work finished next day in his head.

Somewhat similarly, though in another field, M. Retté, a poet, tells Dr. Chabaneix that he falls asleep in the middle of an unfinished stanza, and when thinking of it again in the morning finds it completed. And M. Vincent d'Indy, a musical composer, says that he often has on waking a fugitive glimpse of a musical effect which (like the memory of a dream) needs a strong immediate concentration of mind to keep it from vanishing.

Rémy de Gourmont: "My conceptions rise into the field of consciousness like a flash of lightning or like the flight of a bird."

M. S. writes: "In writing these dramas I seemed to be a spectator at the play; I gazed at what was passing on the scene in an eager, wondering expectation . . . I felt that this came from the depth of my own being."

Saint-Saens had only to listen, as Socrates to his Dæmon; and M. Ribot, summing up a number of similar cases, says: "It is the unconscious which produces what is vulgarly called inspiration. This condition is a positive fact, accompanied with physical and psychical characteristics peculiar to itself. Above all, it is impersonal and involuntary, it acts like an instinct, when and how it chooses; it may be wooed, but cannot be compelled. Neither reflection nor will can supply its place in original creation. . . . The bizarre habits of artists when composing tend to create a special physiological condition, to augment the cerebral circulation in order to provoke or to maintain the unconscious activity."

[1] "Le Subconscient chez les Artistes, les Savants, et les Ecrivains," par le Dr. Paul Chabaneix, Paris, 1897.

The subjective sensations of the musician accord with the view of the essentially subliminal character of the gift with which he deals. In no direction is "genius" or "inspiration" more essential to true success. It is not from careful poring over the mutual relations of musical notes that the masterpieces of melody have been born. They have come as they came to Mozart— in an uprush of unsummoned audition, of unpremeditated and self-revealing joy. They have come, as to Browning's Abt Vogler, with a sense of irrecoverable commingling of depths of soul and heights of heaven.[1] Translating the phrases of poetry into such terms as we here employ, we may say that we have reached a point where the subliminal uprush is felt by the supraliminal personality to be deeper, truer, more permanent than the products of voluntary thought.

We note that a very brief and shallow submergence beneath the conscious level is enough to infuse fresh vigor into supraliminal trains of thought. Ideas left to mature unnoticed for a few days, or for a single night, seem to pass but a very little way beneath the threshold. They represent, one may say, the sustenance of the supraliminal life by impulse or guidance from below.

And in some of these instances we see the man of genius achieving spontaneously, and unawares, much the same result as that which is achieved for the hypnotic subject by deliberate artifice. He is in fact co-ordinating the waking and the sleeping phases of his existence. He is carrying into sleep the knowledge and the purpose of waking hours; and he is carrying back into waking hours again the benefit of those profound assimilations which are the privilege of sleep. Hypnotic suggestion aims at co-operations of just this kind between the waking state in which the suggestion, say, of some functional change, is planned and the sleeping state in which that change is carried out—with benefit persisting anew into waking life. The hypnotic trance, which is a *developed* sleep, thus accomplishes for the ordinary man what ordinary sleep accomplishes for the man of genius.

The coming chapters on Sleep and Hypnotism will illustrate this point more fully. But I may here anticipate my discussion of *dreams* by quoting one instance where dreams, self-suggested by waking will, formed, as one may say, an integral element in distinguished genius.

[1] More definite than most of the descriptions of this type in musical literature are the following words of Schumann (*Robert Schumann's Early Letters*, p. 268): "The piano is getting too limited for me. It is most extraordinary how I write almost everything in canon, and then only detect the imitation afterwards—and often find inversions, rhythms in contrary motion." And again, p. 271: "I do not realize all this while I am composing; it only comes to me afterwards; you who are at the top of the tree will understand what I mean."

Robert Louis Stevenson, being in many ways a typical man of genius, was in no way more markedly gifted with that integrating faculty—that increased power over all strata of the personality—which I have ascribed to genius, than in his relation to his dreams (see "A Chapter on Dreams" in his volume *Across the Plains*). Seldom has the essential analogy between dreams and inspiration been exhibited in such a striking way. His dreams had always (he tells us) been of great vividness, and often of markedly *recurrent* type. But the point of interest is that, when he began to write stories for publication, the "little people who managed man's internal theatre" understood the change as well as he.

§ When he lay down to prepare himself for sleep, he no longer sought amusement, but printable and profitable tales; and after he had dozed off in his box-seat, his little people continued their evolutions with the same mercantile designs. . . . For the most part, whether awake or asleep, he is simply occupied—he or his little people—in consciously making stories for the market. . . .

The more I think of it, the more I am moved to press upon the world my question: "Who are the Little People?" They are near connections of the dreamer's, beyond doubt; they share in his financial worries and have an eye to the bank-book; they share plainly in his training; . . . they have plainly learned like him to build the scheme of a considerate story and to arrange emotion in progressive order; only I think they have more talent; and one thing is beyond doubt—they can tell him a story piece by piece, like a serial, and keep him all the while in ignorance of where they aim.

That part [of my work] which is done while I am sleeping is the Brownies' part beyond contention; but that which is done when I am up and about is by no means necessarily mine, since all goes to show the Brownies have a hand in it even then. §

Slight and imperfect as the above statistics and observations admittedly are, they seem to me to point in a more useful direction than do some of the facts collected by that modern group of anthropologists who hold that genius is in itself a kind of nervous malady, a disturbance of mental balance, akin to criminality or even to madness.

Were any charge of degeneracy or "nervosity" made out against all these eminent men as a body, it would merely seem to prove the paradox that degeneracy makes for success. But in truth many of the cases alleged admit of a much simpler explanation. There are in most of us some traits of human nature which we are not very anxious to reveal. If the great world looks at us too closely these traits tend to come out. The case is the same with those who are born great as with those who achieve greatness. But it is scarcely worth while to go to history for what any *valet de chambre* will maintain of any hero. What you have to prove is rather that the average man is any less degenerate than his betters. And this is not easy; for we must reckon in our account abnormalities of defect as well as of exaggeration; bluntness and opacities must be set against irritabilities and illusions; and hardly a good easy man among us but might be analyzed into half neuropath and half Philistine, if it would serve a theory.

George Sand's career was not without moral faults; but they were the faults, not of a morbid, but of a prepotent organization; and they belonged, moreover, almost wholly to her early life. Throughout long years of healthy maturity and age she formed a striking example of the combination of enormous imaginative productiveness with inward tranquility and meditative calm. What George Sand felt in the act of composition was a continuous and effortless flow of ideas, sometimes with and sometimes without an apparent *externalization* of the characters who spoke in her romances. Turning now to another author, as sane and almost as potent as George Sand herself, we find a phenomenon which would have suggested to us actual insanity if observed in a mind less robust and efficient. If the allusions to the apparent independence of Dickens' characters which are scattered through his letters be read with our related facts in view, it will no longer be thought that they are intended as a mystification. Mrs. Gamp, his greatest creation, spoke to him, he tells us, generally in church, as with an inward monitory voice.

And note further that as scientific introspection develops we are likely to receive fuller accounts of these concurrent mental processes, these partial externalizations of the creatures of the romancer's brain. One such account, both definite and elaborate, has been published by M. Binet in *L'Année Psychologique* for 1894, and I summarize it here.[1]

M. de Curel, a French dramatist of distinction, while apparently quite unaware of the phenomena described either by Dickens or by Stevenson, does nevertheless carry the waking experiences of the one to a point where they closely approach the dream-experiences of the other. M. de Curel's personages, after a period of painful incubation, seem to assume an independent type; they carry on their conversations independently of his will, nor neeed he even keep his attention fixed on them. The process of invention thus continues without conscious fatigue. We are here reminded of certain performances under hypnotic suggestion, where mental or bodily feats, as play-acting, are accomplished without effort or exhaustion.

It will be seen that this account is thoroughly concordant with several

---

[1] *L'Année Psychologique*, i. 1894, p. 124, F. de Curel, par A. Binet.

other cases already known to us. It comes midway between Stevenson's dreams and the hysteric's *idées fixes*.

Let us proceed to push the inquiry a step further. It has been claimed in this work for subliminal uprushes generally that they often contain knowledge which no ordinary method of research could acquire. Is this supernormal knowledge—we ought now to ask—ever represented in the uprushes to which we give the name of Genius?

What is the relation, in short, of the man of Genius to the sensitive?[1]

If the man of Genius be, as I have urged, on the whole the completest type of humanity, and if the sensitive's special gift be in itself one of the most advanced forms of human faculty, ought not the inspirations of genius to bring with them flashes of supernormal knowledge as intimate as those which the sensitive—perhaps in other respects a commonplace person—from time to time is privileged to receive?

Some remarkable instances of this kind undoubtedly do exist. The most conspicuous and most important of all cannot, from motives of reverence, be here discussed. Nor will I dwell upon other founders of religions, or on certain traditional saints or sages. But among historical characters of the first mark the names of Socrates and of Joan of Arc are enough to cite. The monitions of the Dæmon of Socrates—the subliminal self of a man of transcendent genius—have in all probability been described to us with literal truth; and did in fact convey to that great philosopher precisely the kind of clairvoyant or precognitive information which forms the sensitive's privilege today. We have thus in Socrates the ideal unification of human powers.

It must, however, be admitted that such complete unification is not the general rule for men of genius; that their inspirations generally stop short of telepathy or of clairvoyance. I think we may explain this limitation somewhat as follows. The man of genius is what he is by virtue of possessing a readier communication than most men possess between his supraliminal and his subliminal self. From his subliminal self, he can only draw what it already possesses; and we must not assume as a matter of course that the subliminal region of any one of us possesses that particular sensitivity—that specific transparency—which can receive and register *definite facts* from the unseen. *That* may be a gift which stands as much alone—in independence of other gifts or faculties—in the subliminal region, as, say, a perfect musical ear in the supraliminal. The man of genius may draw much from those hidden wells of being without seeing reflected therein any actual physical scene in the universe beyond his ordinary ken.

---

[1] A sensitive is a medium or automatist—a person through whom communication is deemed to be carried on between living men and spirits of the departed.

I believe, however, that true, though vague, impressions of a world beyond the range of sense are actually received—I do not say by all men of genius, but by men of genius of certain types. It would seem, then, that for any valid appreciation of what I may call the *vague supernormal content* of moments of inspiration, we shall have to examine a very limited group of men of genius. Chiefly, perhaps, of the philosopher and the poet must we needs feel that if any genius reaches out into an interpenetrating spiritual world, *theirs* must do so; that *they* ought to have some message corroborating, even though but in vague general fashion, the results to which sensitives have been led by a plainer, if a narrower, way.

For our present purposes, however, one single poet—almost one single poem—will practically suffice. In whatever rank Wordsworth may be placed as an artist in language, there can be no doubt as to his conscientious veracity as an introspective psychologist. "The Prelude, or Growth of a Poet's Mind" is, for our present purposes, unique. For it is a deliberate, persistent attempt to tell the truth, the whole truth, and nothing but the truth, about exactly those emotions and intuitions which differentiate the poet from common men.

> "In a world of life they live,
> By sensible impressions not enthralled,
> But by their quickening impulse made more prompt
> To hold fit converse with the spiritual world."

Chapter Four

SLEEP

It is obvious that in my review of phases or alternations of personality I have left out of sight the most constant, the most important alternation of all. I have thus far said nothing of *sleep*. Yet *that* change of personality, at least, has been borne in on every one's notice as an essential part of life.

Sleep must assuredly now be studied, and from two points of view.

Regarding sleep as an alternating phase of personality, we must consider what are its special characteristics and faculties. Regarding it as an integral factor in our earthly existence, and on an equal footing with the waking state, we must consider how the faculties of sleep, as of waking, can be improved and concentrated in the course of the physical and psychical evolution of man. Such improvement or concentration, however, presupposes a comprehension of the true nature of sleep which we are by no means entitled to take for granted.

First, then, let us consider the specific characteristics of sleep.

The definition of sleep is an acknowledged puzzle in physiology. And I would point out that the increased experience of hypnotic sleep which recent years have afforded has made this difficulty even more striking than before. A physiological explanation must needs assume that some special bodily condition—such, for instance, as the clogging of the brain by waste-products—is at least the usual antecedent of sound sleep. But it is certain, on the other hand, that with a large percentage of persons profound and prolonged sleep can be induced, in *any* bodily condition, by simple suggestion. Hypnosis, indeed, may be prolonged, with actual benefit to the sleeper, far beyond the point which the spontaneous sleep of a healthy subject ever reaches. A good subject can be awakened and thrown into hypnosis again almost at pleasure, and independently of any state either of nutrition or of fatigue. Such sleep belongs to those phenomena which we may call nervous if we will, but which we can observe or influence from the psychological side alone.

We can hardly hope, from the ordinary data, to arrive at a definition of sleep more satisfactory than others have reached. We must defer that attempt until we have collected something more than the ordinary evidence as to what occurs or does not occur during the abeyance of waking life. One point, however, is plain at once. We cannot treat sleep—as it has generally been treated—in its purely *negative* aspect. We cannot be content merely to dwell, with the common text-books, on the mere *absence* of waking faculties—on the diminution of external perception, the absence of controlling intelligence. We must treat sleep *positively,* so far as we can, as a definite phase of our personality, co-ordinate with the waking phase.

Assuredly in sleep some agency is at work which far surpasses waking efficacy. The regenerative quality of healthy sleep is something which no completeness of waking quiescence can rival or approach. A few moments of sleep—a mere blur across the field of consciousness—will sometimes bring a renovation which hours of lying down in darkness and silence would not yield. A mere bowing of the head on the breast, if consciousness ceases for a second or two, may change a man's outlook on the world. The break of consciousness is associated in some way with a potent physiological change. That is to say, even in the case of a moment of ordinary sleep we already note the appearance of that special recuperative energy which is familiar in longer periods of sleep, and which, as we shall presently see, reaches a still higher level in hypnotic trance.

Sleep is capable of strange developments, and night can sometimes suddenly outdo the most complex achievements of day. Take first the degree of control over the voluntary muscles. In ordinary sleep this is neither possessed nor desired; in nightmare its loss is exaggerated into an appalling fear; while in somnambulism—a kind of new personality developed—the sleeper walks on perilous ridges with steady feet. Morbid somnambulism bears to sound sleep a relation something like that which hysteria bears to normal life. But between the healthy somnambulist and the subject of nightmare we find from another point of view a contrast resembling that between the man of genius and the hysteric. The somnambulist, like the man of genius, brings into play resources which are beyond ordinary reach.

The permanent result of a dream is sometimes such as to show that the dream has not been a mere superficial confusion of past waking experiences, but has had an unexplained potency of its own—drawn, like the potency of hypnotic suggestion, from some depth in our being which the waking self cannot reach. Two main classes of this kind are conspicuous enough to be easily recognized—those, namely, where the dream has led to a "conversion" or marked religious change, and those where it has been the starting-point of an "insistent idea" or of a fit of actual insanity.[1] The dreams which convert, reform, change character and creed, have of course a claim to be considered as something other than ordinary dreams. Those, on the other hand, which suddenly generate an insistent idea of an irrational type are closely and obviously analogous to post-hypnotic self-sug-

[1] See Dr. Féré in *Brain* for January, 1887.

gestions, which the self that inspired them cannot be induced to counter-mand. Such is the dream related by M. Taine,[1] where a gendarme, im-pressed by an execution at which he has assisted, dreams that he himself is to be guillotined, and is afterwards so influenced by the dream that he at-tempts suicide.

Two cases illustrative of self-suggestion in dreams follow. I quote the first from a paper by Dr. Faure in the *Archives de Médecine*, vol. i., 1876, p. 554, as a sample, showing that in an apparently healthy subject an ap-parently causeless dream may leave traces quite as persistent as any hyp-notic suggestion could implant from without. The dream is in fact a self-suggestion of the most potent kind.

§ A shop assistant, strongly built and regular in habits, awoke one morn-ing in a state of fever and agitation, perspiring copiously, anxious and un-easy. He announced that all his savings were gone; he was ruined, done for. He said that on the previous day, while driving a van, he had got into a quarrel with a coachman; and that, in the confusion, his van had broken in the front window of a mirror-maker. He would have to pay for the dam-age. His wife assured us that when he had returned home the evening be-fore he was in his usual condition; that he had seen to his business, passed the evening at home, and gone to bed with no trouble upon him.

For three days he continued in this state of mind, unable to calm him-self for a moment, although he was taken to the actual place where the imaginary accident had occurred. It was some days later before he thor-oughly understood that it had been a dream. And for a whole month he would fall daily into the same confusion of memory—would sit down in despair, crying and repeating "We are ruined!" Even seven years after-wards he still had occasional crises of this nature, when he forgot the truth, and lived for several days under the shock of this imaginary disaster. §

We may compare with this the next case, where "the touch of a van-ished hand" appeared to bring physical relief to the dreamer—the re-covery being more rapid than ordinary conditions could explain.

From *Proceedings* S.P.R., vol. viii. p. 374. The account is given by M. L. Holbrook, M.D., Editor of the *Herald of Health,* 13 and 15 Laight Street, New York, and is dated July 30, 1884.

§ Dr. Holbrook had been quite ill with acute bronchitis which occurred every winter and spring for several years. As he was young and newly em-barked on a career which was of great interest to him, he was despondent

---

[1] *De l'Intelligence,* vol. i. p. 119.

for fear it would ultimately become chronic, and perhaps terminate his life. In this depressed condition he fell into a light sleep and seemed to see his sister, who had been dead more than twenty years. She said: "Do not worry about your health, we have come to cure you; there is much yet for you to do in the world." Then she vanished, and his brain seemed to be electrified as if by a shock from a battery, not painful, but delicious. It spread downward over his entire body. He awoke and found himself well, and never again had an attack of the disease. §

Ordinary sleep is roughly intermediate between waking life and deep hypnotic trance; and it seems probable that its memory will have links of almost equal strength with the memory which belongs to waking life and the memory which belongs to the hypnotic trance. And this is in fact the case; the fragments of dream-memory are interlinked with both these other chains. Thus, for example, without any suggestion to that effect, acts accomplished in the hypnotic trance may be remembered in dream; and remembered under the illusion which was thrown round them by the hypnotizer. Thus Dr. Auguste Voisin suggested to a hypnotized subject to stab a patient—really a stuffed figure—in the neighboring bed.[1] The subject did so; and of course knew nothing of it on waking. But three days afterwards he returned to the hospital complaining that his dreams were haunted by the figure of a woman, who accused him of having stabbed and killed her. Appropriate suggestion laid this ghost of a doll.

Conversely, dreams forgotten in waking life may be remembered in the hypnotic trance.

Dream-memory will occasionally be found to fill up gaps in waking memory, other than those due to hypnotic trance; such so-called "ecmnesic" periods, for instance, as sometimes succeed a violent shock to the system, and may even embrace some space of time *anterior* to the shock. These periods themselves resemble prolonged and unremembered dreams. Such accidents, however, are so rare, and such dream-memory so hard to detect, that I mention the point mainly for the sake of theoretical completeness; and must think myself fortunate in being able to cite a case of M. Charcot's which affords an interesting confirmation of the suggested view.[2]

§ A certain Madame D., a healthy and sensible woman of thirty-four, was subjected, on August 28th, 1891, to a terrible shock. Some scoundrel told

[1] *Revue de l'Hypnotisme,* June, 1891, p. 302.
[2] *Revue de Médecine,* February, 1892. A full account and discussion of the case of Madame D. is contained in Dr. P. Janet's *Névroses et Idées fixes,* vol. i. pp. 116 *et seq.*

her brusquely that her husband was dead, and that his corpse was being brought home. This was absolutely false; but the news threw her into a state of profound agitation; and when some indiscreet friend, seeing the husband approach, cried out *Le voilà!* the poor woman, supposing that the *corpse* was thus announced, fell into a prolonged hysterical attack. After two days of raving she came to herself; but had lost the memory of all events since a date six weeks before the shock. This kind of retroactive ecmnesia—inexplicable as it is—is known to occur sometimes after a physical concussion. In Madame D.'s case the shock had been wholly a mental one; yet the forgetfulness continued. Madame D. was possessed of full recollection of her life up to July 14th, 1891; but she could recall no event whatever which had occurred since that date. She endeavored to continue her domestic duties; but if she wished to recollect anything she had to write it down instantly in a note-book to which she constantly referred. For instance, she was bitten by a dog believed to be mad. She instantly made a written note of the fact; but except when actually referring to her note-book she retained no recollection whatever of the bite or of her subsequent treatment in M. Pasteur's laboratory.

Here, surely, was a case where it might have seemed that there had been some absolute evanescence, absolute abolition of whatsoever traces or tendencies may be held to constitute memory.

But one fact was observed which threw a decisive light upon this puzzling case. The patients in the two beds adjoining Madame D.'s were told to observe her at night. They reported that she was in the habit of talking in her sleep; and that in the fragments of dreams thus revealed she made frequent allusions to the mad dog's bite, and to other events which had occurred during her ecmnesic period. This hint, of course, was enough for M. Charcot. Classing her ecmnesia as a kind of prolongation of a hystero-epileptic attack, he hypnotized the patient, and found that in the hypnotic trance her memory for the ecmnesic period was absolutely intact. Post-hypnotic suggestions to remember the lost days slowly restored the poor woman to the possession of her whole past. §

The fact which interests us here is the accidentally discovered persistence in dream of memories which had vanished from the supraliminal consciousness. This shows that in dream Madame D. had got down—not merely to a stratum of confusion—but to a state so far deeper than the waking state that the memories of which shock or hysteria had robbed the waking state were there found to be uninjured. This well-observed case may here stand as representative of the gap-filling dream-memory which I ventured to anticipate. Other cases will be noticeable when spontaneous somnambulism comes under review, in its complex relations with common dreams, hypnotism, hysteria, and even epilepsy.

I pass on to the still more novel and curious questions involved in the apparent existence of a dream-memory which, while accompanying the memory of ordinary life, seems also to have a wider purview, and to indicate that the record of external events which is kept within us is far fuller than we know.

Let us consider what stages such a memory may show.

I. It may include events once known to the waking self, but now definitely forgotten.

II. It may include facts which have fallen within the sensory field, but which have never been supraliminally cognized in any way. It is plain that inferences of this kind will be liable to be mistaken for direct retrocognition, direct premonition, direct clairvoyance; while yet they need not actually prove anything more than a perception on the part of the subliminal self more far-reaching than is the perception or the memory of the supraliminal self which we know.

As to the *first* of the above-mentioned categories no one will raise any doubt. It is a familiar fact—or a fact only sufficiently unfamiliar to be noted with slight surprise—that we occasionally recover in sleep a memory which has wholly dropped out of waking consciousness. As an example, we may take the dream of M. Delbœuf's, discussed in his interesting book, *Le Sommeil et les Rêves.* In that dream the name of the "Asplenium Ruta Muralis" figured as a familiar phrase. On waking, he puzzled himself in vain to think where he could have learnt that botanical appellation. Long afterwards he discovered the name "Asplenium Ruta Muraria" in his own handwriting—in a little collection of flowers and ferns to which he had added their designations, under the dictation of a botanical friend.

In this and similar cases the original piece of knowledge had at the time made a definite impress on the mind, had come well within the span of apprehension of the supraliminal consciousness. Its reappearance after however long an interval is a fact to which there are already plenty of parallels. But the conclusion to which the cases about to be cited seem to me to point is one of a much stranger character. I think that there is evidence to show that many facts or pictures which have never even for a moment come within the apprehension of the supraliminal consciousness are nevertheless retained by the subliminal memory, and are occasionally presented in dreams with what seems a definite purpose.

The following is a case of a lost object, where waking effort soon after the loss fails to recall any supraliminal knowledge of the place of deposit. The account is quoted from *Journal* S.P.R., vol. iv., 1889, p. 142:

§ On reaching Morley's Hotel, at five o'clock on Tuesday, 29th January, 1889, I missed a gold brooch, which I supposed I had left in a fitting-room at Swan & Edgar's. I sent there at once, but was very disappointed to hear that after a diligent search they could not find the brooch. I was very vexed, and worried about the brooch, and that night dreamed that I should find it shut up in a number of the *Queen* newspaper that had been on the table, and in my dream I saw the very page where it would be. I had noticed one of the plates on that page. Directly after breakfast I went to Swan & Edgar's and asked to see the papers, at the same time telling the young ladies about the dream, and where I had seen the brooch. The papers had been moved from that room, but were found, and, to the astonishment of the young ladies, I said, "This is the one that contains my brooch"; and there, at the very page I expected, I found it.

A. M. BICKFORD-SMITH §

The next case was given in the *Proceedings* of the American S.P.R. (vol. i. No. 4, p. 363) on the authority of Professor Royce of Harvard. The narrator was Colonel A. v. S. of Texas (whose full name was known to Professor Royce). This case is more complicated than that last given, inasmuch as the missing article was apparently revealed to the percipient by her dead brother in a dream—and revealed in a place where it had been previously looked for in vain. The "orthodox" explanation, however, would be that the position of the knife was first perceived by the subliminal self, which only succeeded in informing the supraliminal self through a dramatic dream.

§ Colonel A. v. S. of Texas wrote that he would pledge his word of honor as to the truth of the dream he reported. He said that one day he bought for each of his three daughters a very small lady's knife. The youngest girl, age 8 or 9 at the time, was so delighted with her present that she carried it with her all the time. A few days later while playing with other children in a large barn, she lost her knife. Everyone looked diligently for it, but it could not be found, and she went to bed weeping. She dreamed that her dead brother took her by the hand and showed her where it was, on top of a hay mow. Although the whole party had looked there many times the day before, the knife was found just where the dream indicated. §

I quote another case which raises a somewhat curious point as to the relation of what I may call the subliminal gaze to defects of ordinary vision.

From *Proceedings* S.P.R., vol. viii. p. 389:

§ In September, 1880, I lost the landing order of a large steamer containing a cargo of iron ore, which had arrived in the port of Cardiff. She had to commence discharging at six o'clock the next morning. I received the landing order at four o'clock in the afternoon, and when I arrived at the office at six I found that I had lost it. I came home in a great degree of trouble about the matter, as I feared that I should lose my situation in consequence.

That night I dreamed that I saw the lost landing order lying in a crack in the wall under a desk in the Long Room of the Custom House.

At five the next morning I went down to the Custom House and got the keeper to get up and open it. I went to the spot of which I had dreamed, and found the paper in the very place.

HERBERT J. LEWIS

(Mr. Lewis does not believe it was there when he searched previously.) §

In the cases which I have thus far quoted the dream-self has presented a significant scene—has chosen from its gallery of photographs the special picture which the waking mind desired—but has not needed to draw any more complex inference from the facts presumably at its disposal. I have now to deal with a small group of dreams which reason as well as remember, which indicate something which overpasses the scheme prescribed for the present chapter.

The first case is of old date but was reported by the dreamer to Dr. Davey, a physician well known in his day, and was published in the *Zoist* as a case of clairvoyance.

§ Mr. C. J. E. says that he had been bothered since September with an error in his cash account, and despite many hours' examination, it defied all his efforts. It had been the subject of his waking thoughts for many nights, and had occupied a large portion of his leisure hours. On the night of December 11th he dreamed of his cash-book, and without any apparent trouble he discovered the cause of the mistake, which had arisen out of a complicated cross-entry. He dreamed that he picked up a slip of paper and made such a memorandum as would enable him to correct the error. When he awoke the next morning he did not remember the dream, and it didn't occur to him until evening when he was shaving. He took up a piece of paper from his dressing table to wipe his razor and discovered on it the memorandum he had dreamed he'd written the night before. He rushed to the office with it and found that it was the correct solution to his problem. §

Some striking cases in which, during sleep, complex inferences have been drawn from data presumably present to the waking mind, with more than waking intelligence, were recorded by Professor W. Romaine Newbold, of the University of Pennsylvania, in a paper entitled "Sub-conscious Reasoning," in the *Proceedings* S.P.R., vol. xii. pp. 11–20, from which I give the following extracts:

§ The first case (says Professor Newbold) was given me by my friend and colleague, William A. Lamberton, Professor of Greek in the University of Pennsylvania, and I transcribe his own written statement.

"I went to the Lehigh University in the fall of 1869 as instructor in Latin and Greek. My spare time, however, came to be given almost entirely to mathematics.

"Somewhere in the spring, I think it was, of 1870, I attacked this problem: Given an ellipse, to find the locus of the foot of the perpendicular let fall from either focus upon a tangent to this ellipse at any point. I endeavored to solve this analytically, starting from the well-known equations of the tangent to an ellipse, and of a perpendicular to a given line from a given point. No thought of attempting a geometrical solution ever entered my head. After battling with these equations for a considerable time—it was over a week and may have been two weeks—I came to the natural conclusion that I was bogged, and that all my efforts, if continued, would only sink me deeper in the bog; the proper thing to do was to call a halt, dismissing the problem as far as possible from my thoughts, and after some time, when my mind had got completely free from it, to return to it afresh, when, I had no doubt, a few minutes would put me in possession of the solution. This I did absolutely and with success. After about a week, I woke one morning and found myself in possession of the desired solution under circumstances to me strange and interesting, so much so that the impression of them has never died away, or even, so far as I can say, become dim or altered in any way. First: the solution was entirely geometrical, whereas I had been laboring for it analytically without drawing or attempting to draw a single figure. Second: it presented itself by means of a figure objectively pictured at a considerable distance from me on the opposite wall.

"I sprang from bed and drew the figure on paper; needless to say, perhaps, that the geometrical solution being thus given, only a few minutes were needed to get the analytical one."

W. A. LAMBERTON §

The following account is also taken from Professor Romaine New-bold's paper, just quoted. He states that for this case he is indebted to an-other friend and colleague, Dr. Herman V. Hilprecht, Professor of As-syrian in the University of Pennsylvania, who writes:

§ One Saturday evening, about the middle of March, 1893, I had been wearying myself, as I had done so often in the weeks preceding, in the vain attempt to decipher two small fragments of agate which were supposed to belong to the finger-rings of some Babylonian. The labor was much in-creased by the fact that the fragments presented remnants only of charac-ters and lines, that dozens of similar small fragments had been found in the ruins of the temple of Bel at Nippur with which nothing could be done, that in this case furthermore I had never had the originals before me, but only a hasty sketch made by one of the members of the expedition sent by the University of Pennsylvania to Babylonia. I could not say more than that the fragments, taking into consideration the place in which they were found and the peculiar characteristics of the cuneiform characters pre-served upon them, sprang from the Cassite period of Babylonian history (*circa* 1700–1140 B.C.); moreover, as the first character of the third line of the first fragment seemed to be KU, I ascribed this fragment, with an interrogation point, to King Kurigalzu, while I placed the other fragment, as unclassifiable, with other Cassite fragments upon a page of my book where I published the unclassifiable fragments. The proofs already lay be-fore me, but I was not satisfied. The whole problem passed again through my mind that evening before I placed my mark of approval under the last correction in the book. Even then I had come to no conclusion.

About midnight, weary and exhausted, I went to bed and was soon in deep sleep. Then I dreamed the following remarkable dream. A tall, thin priest of the old pre-Christian Nippur, about forty years of age and clad in a simple abba, led me to the treasure-chamber of the temple, on its south-east side. He went with me into a small, low-ceiled room, without win-dows, in which there was a large wooden chest, while scraps of agate and lapis-lazuli lay scattered on the floor. Here he addressed me as follows: "The two fragments which you have published separately upon pages 22 and 26, belong together, are not finger-rings, and their history is as fol-lows: King Kurigalzu (*circa* 1300 B.C.) once sent to the temple of Bel, among other articles of agate and lapis-lazuli, an inscribed votive cylinder of agate. Then we priests suddenly received the command to make for the statue of the god Ninib a pair of earrings of agate. We were in great dis-may, since there was no agate as raw material at hand. In order to execute the command there was nothing for us to do but cut the votive cylinder into three parts, thus making three rings, each of which contained a portion of the original inscription. The first two rings served as earrings for the statue of the god; the two fragments which have given you so much trouble are portions of them. If you will put the two together you will have confirmation of my words. But the third ring you have not yet found in the course of your excavations, and you never will find it." With this, the priest disappeared.

I awoke at once and immediately told my wife the dream that I might not forget it. Next morning—Sunday—I examined the fragments once more in the light of these disclosures, and to my astonishment found all the details of the dream precisely verified in so far as the means of verification were in my hands. The original inscription on the votive cylinder read: "To the god Ninib, son of Bel, his lord, has Kurigalzu, pontifex of Bel, presented this."

The problem was thus at last solved. I stated in the preface that I had unfortunately discovered too late that the two fragments belonged together, made the corresponding changes in the Table of Contents, pp. 50 and 52, and, it being not possible to transpose the fragments, as the plates were already made, I put in each plate a brief reference to the other.

H. V. HILPRECHT §

Professor Newbold is well versed in the analysis of evidence making for supernormal powers, and his explanation of the vision as the result of "processes of associative reasoning analogous to those of the upper consciousness" must, I think, be taken as correct. But had the incident occurred in a less critical age of the world—in any generation, one may say, but *this*—how majestic a proof would the phantasmal Babylonian's message be held to have afforded of his veritable co-operation with the modern *savant* in the reconstruction of his remote past!

With this case of Professor Hilprecht's we seem to have reached the utmost intensity of sleep-faculty, which shows scattered signs of at least a potential equality with the faculty of waking hours.

We have already seen this as regards muscular movements, inward vision and audition, and memory; and these last records complete the series by showing us the achievement in sleep of intellectual work of the severest order. Coleridge's *Kubla Khan* had long ago shown the world that a great poet might owe his masterpiece to the obscuration of waking sense. And the very imperfection of *Kubla Khan*—the memory truncated by an interruption—may again remind us how partial must ever be our waking knowledge of the achievements of sleep.

May I not, then, claim a real analogy between certain of the achievements of *sleep* and the achievements of *genius?* In both there is the same triumphant spontaneity, the same sense of drawing no longer upon the narrow and brief endurance of nerves and brain, but upon some unknown source exempt from those limitations.

Thus far, indeed, the sleep-faculties which we have been considering, however strangely intensified, have belonged to the same class as the normal faculties of waking life. We have now to consider whether we can detect in sleep any manifestation of *supernormal* faculty—any experience which seems to suggest that man is a cosmical spirit as well as terrestrial, and is in some way in relation with a spiritual as well as with a material world. It will seem to be natural that this commerce with a spiritual environment should be more perceptible in sleep than in waking.

What can approach the antiquity, the ubiquity, the unanimity of man's belief in the wanderings of the spirit in dream? In the Stone Age, the skeptic would have been rash indeed who ventured to contradict it. And though I grant that this "palæolithic psychology" has gone out of fashion for the last few centuries, I do not think that (in view of the evidence now collected) we can any longer dismiss as mere dream-imagery the constant recurrence of the idea of visiting in sleep some distant scene— with the acquisition thereby of new facts not otherwise accessible.

Starting, then, not from savage authority, but from the evidential scrutiny of modern facts, we shall find that there are coincidences of dream with truth which neither pure chance nor any subconscious mentation of an ordinary kind will adequately explain. We shall find that there is a perception of concealed material objects or of distant scenes, and also perception of or communion with the thoughts and emotions of other minds. I ventured in 1882 to suggest the wider terms *telepathy* (the communication of impressions of any kind from one mind to another, independently of the recognized channels of sense) and *clairvoyance* (any direct sensation or perception of objects or conditions independently of the recognized channels of sense). I shall use these words in the present work. But I am far from assuming that these terms comprise the whole field of supernormal faculty.

On the contrary, I think it probable that the facts of the spiritual world are far more complex than the facts of the material world; and that the ways in which spirits perceive and communicate, apart from fleshly organisms, are subtler and more varied than any perception or communication which we know. Specially manifest is this when we deal with *premonitions,* which seem even further away from ordinary processes of perception than the phenomena of telepathy or clairvoyance.

For the present I must confine myself to a brief sketch of some of the main types of supernormal dreams, arranged in a kind of ascending order. I shall begin with such dreams as primarily suggest a kind of heightening or extension of the dreamer's own innate perceptive powers, as exercised on the world around him. And I shall end with dreams which suggest his entrance into a spiritual world, where commerce with incarnate or discarnate spirits is subject no longer to the conditions of earthly thought.

I begin, then, with some dreams which seem to carry perceptive faculty beyond the point at which some unusual form of common vision can be plausibly suggested in explanation.

A young man sees in a dream the place where his friend's watch has fallen in a field. It might be suggested that the loser's subliminal self had seen the watch fall and afterwards communicated that knowledge telepathically to his sleeping friend. The analogy of other cases, however, would seem rather to point to an excursion or extension of the dreamer's perception, so as to include the field where the watch was found. The account was originally sent to Professor W. James, and I quote it from the *Proceedings* S.P.R., vol. xi. p. 397.

§ A young man of this place, J. L. Squires by name, was at work on the farm of T. L. Johnson, with another young man, Wesley Davis, who was one day far from the buildings mending fence around a large pasture. Squires was not with him, nor had he ever been far into the pasture. At some time during the day Davis lost his watch and chain from the vest pocket, and although he searched diligently, could not find it, as he had no idea as to the probable locality of the watch. Although only a silver watch, Davis worked for a living and could hardly afford its loss.

In his sympathy for his friend, Squires could not keep his mind off the watch, and after two or three days' thinking of it, went to bed one night still thinking of it. During the night he had a dream, or vision, as we may call it, and saw the watch lying on the ground with the chain coiled in a peculiar position; rocks, trees, and all the surroundings were perfectly plain to him. Telling his story at the breakfast table, he was, of course, well laughed at, but being so convinced that he could go straight to the watch, he saddled a horse and found it exactly as he expected to.

All the parties concerned are wholly honest and reliable. I will have a detailed statement sworn to if you would like it.

JOHN E. GALE, Guilford, Vermont §

The following case, from *Proceedings* S.P.R., vol. xi. p. 375, was borrowed originally from the *Religio-Philosophical Journal,* which described it as follows:

§ A prominent Chicago journalist states [in the Chicago *Times*] that his wife asked him one morning while still dressing, and before either of them had left their sleeping-room, if he knew any one named Edsale or Esdale. A negative reply was given, and then a "Why do you ask?" She replied: "During the night I dreamed that I was on the lake shore, and found a coffin there with the name of Edsale or Esdale on it, and I am confident that some one of that name has recently been drowned there." On opening the morning paper, the first item that attracted his attention was the report of the mysterious disappearance from his home in Hyde Park of a young man named Esdale. A few days afterwards the body of a young man was found on the lake shore. §

The next case is again explicable on the supposition that the subliminal self of the dreamer perceived the positions of the vessels and gave the warning. Mr. Brighten is known to Mr. Frank Podmore, member of the S.P.R., who concurs in what appears to be the estimate generally formed of that gentleman, namely, that he is a shrewd, unimaginative, practical man. The account is taken from *Proceedings* S.P.R., vol. viii. p. 400. Mr. Brighten writes:

§ I owned a 35-ton schooner, and in August, 1876, in very calm weather, I dropped anchor in the Thames. The current being exceedingly swift at that part we let out plenty of chain cable before going to bed. Towards morning I found myself awake in my cabin with the words ringing in my ears, "Wake, awake, you'll be run down." I waited a few moments, then dropped off to sleep, but was again awakened by the same words ringing in my ears. Upon this I leisurely put on some clothes and went on deck and found the tide rushing past very swiftly, and that we were enveloped in a dense fog, and all was calm and quiet in the early morning, and there was already some daylight. I paced the deck once or twice, then went below, undressed, got into my berth, and fell asleep, only to be again awakened by the same words. I then somewhat more hastily dressed, went on deck, and climbed some way up the rigging to get above the fog, and was soon in a bright, clear atmosphere, with the fog like a sea at my feet, when looking round I saw a large vessel bearing down directly upon us. I fell, rather than scrambled, out of the rigging, rushed to the forecastle, shouted to the captain, who rushed on deck, explained all in a word or two; he ran to the tiller, unlashed it, put it hard aport: the swift current acting upon the rudder caused the boat to slew across and upward in the current, when on came the large vessel passing our side, and it would have cleared us, but her anchor which she was carrying caught in our chain, when she swung round and came alongside, fortunately, however, doing us very little damage.

WM. E. BRIGHTEN §

From the *Journal* S.P.R., vol. viii. p. 140. The following statement of experiences by Miss Luke was sent to us by Dr. R. Osgood Mason, of New York, author of *Telepathy and the Subliminal Self.*

§ Miss Mary Luke, New York City, age 40 has been very well known to me for more than fifteen years, I having been the attending physician in the family during that time. Her own health, however, has been almost perfect; she is free from all hysterical or nervous symptoms. Miss Luke rents the second floor of her home to lodgers. The second floor front, at the time of the dream I am to relate, was occupied by a man and his wife who had been with her six months; they seemed very pleasant people, and she had no occasion to mistrust their honesty. However, she dreamed they had left, taken everything belonging to them and also everything of hers of value. She told her sister of this dream the next morning. Then they investigated and found the lodgers gone, everything in disorder, and her jewelry and trinkets stolen. §

I will next refer to certain cases where the sleeper by clairvoyant vision discerns a scene of direct interest to a mind other than his own—as the danger or death of some near friend. Sometimes there is a flash of vision, which seems to represent correctly the critical scene. Sometimes there is what seems like a longer gaze, accompanied, perhaps, by some sense of *communion* with the invaded person. And in some few cases—the most interesting of all—the circumstances of a death seem to be symbolically *shown* to a dreamer, as though by the deceased person, or by some intelligence connected with him.

The following account (taken from *Phantasms of the Living*, vol. i. p. 202) comes from Mrs. West, of Hildegarde, Furness Road, Eastbourne. It was written in 1883.

§ My father, Sir John Crowe, who was Consul-General for Norway, and my brother were on a journey to Norway during the winter of 1871–72.

I was expecting them home, without knowing the exact day of their return. One night I dreamed I was looking out of a window, when I saw father driving in a sledge, followed in another by my brother.

They had to pass a cross-road, on which another traveller was driving very fast, also in a sledge with one horse. Father seemed to drive on without observing the other fellow, who would without fail have driven over father if he had not made his horse rear, so that I saw my father drive under the hoofs of the horse. Every moment I expected the horse would fall down and crush him. I called out "Father! father!" and woke in a great fright. The next morning my father and brother returned. I said to him, "I am so glad to see you arrive quite safely, as I had such a dreadful dream about you last night," and then I told them my dream. My brother then related to me what had actually happened. It tallied exactly with my dream. My brother in his fright, when he saw the feet of the horse over father's head, had called out, "Oh, father, father!"

HILDA WEST §

One of the best instances of the flash of vision is Canon Warburton's, which I quote from *Phantasms of the Living*, vol. i. p. 338—a case whose remoteness is rendered less of a drawback than usual by the character of the narrator and the simplicity and definiteness of the fact attested.

The following is his account:

§ Somewhere about the year 1848 I went up from Oxford to stay a day or two with my brother, Acton Warburton. When I got to his chambers I found a note on the table apologizing for his absence, and saying that he had gone to a dance somewhere in the West End, and intended to be home soon after 1 o'clock. Instead of going to bed, I dozed in an armchair, but started up wide awake exactly at 1, ejaculating "By Jove! he's down!" and seeing him coming out of a drawing room into a brightly illuminated landing, catching his foot in the edge of the top stair, and falling headlong, just saving himself by his elbows and hands. (The house was one which I had never seen, nor did I know where it was.) Thinking very little of the matter, I fell a-doze again for half-an-hour, and was awakened by my brother suddenly coming in and saying, "Oh, there you are! I have just had as narrow an escape of breaking my neck as I ever had in my life. Coming out of the ballroom, I caught my foot, and tumbled full length down the stairs."

That is all. It may have been "only a dream," but I always thought it must have been something more.

W. WARBURTON §

The impression here produced is as though a jerk were given to some delicate link connecting the two brothers. The brother suffering the crisis thinks vividly of the other; and one can of course explain the incident, as we did on its first publication, as the endangered man's projection of the scene upon his brother's mind. The passive dozing brother, on the other hand, feels as though he were suddenly *present* in the scene—say in response to some sudden call from the brother in danger—and I am here bringing into relief *that* aspect of the incident, on account of its analogy with cases soon to be quoted. But the main lesson no doubt may be that no hard and fast line can be drawn between the two explanations.

From the *Journal* S.P.R., vol. v. p. 40. The following narrative was sent to us by the Right Hon. Sir John Drummond Hay, K.C.B., G.C.M.G., who was for many years H. M.'s Minister in Morocco and resided at Tangier.

§ In the year 1879 my son Robert Drummond Hay resided at Mogodor with his family, where he was at that time Consul. It was in the month of February. I had lately received good accounts of my son and his family; I was also in perfect health. About 1 A.M. (I forget the exact day in February), whilst sleeping soundly [at Tangier], I was woke by hearing distinctly the voice of my daughter-in-law, who was with her husband at Mogodor, saying in a clear, but distressed tone of voice, "Oh, I wish papa only knew that Robert is ill." There was a night lamp in the room. I sat up and listened, looking around the room, but there was no one except my wife, sleeping quietly in bed. I listened for some seconds, expecting to hear footsteps outside, but complete stillness prevailed, so I lay down again, thanking God that the voice which woke me was a hallucination. I had hardly closed my eyes when I heard the same voice and words, upon which I woke Lady Drummond Hay, and told her what had occurred, and got up and went into my study, adjoining the bedroom, and noted it in my diary. Next morning I related what had happened to my daughter, saying that, though I did not believe in dreams, I felt anxious for tidings from Mogodor. That port, as you will see in the map, is about 300 miles south of Tangier. A few days after this incident a letter arrived from my daughter-in-law, Mrs. R. Drummond Hay, telling us that my son was seriously ill with typhoid fever and mentioning the night during which he had been delirious. Much struck by the coincidence that it was the same night I had heard her voice, I wrote to tell her what had happened. She replied, the following post, that in her distress at seeing her husband so dangerously ill, and from being alone in a distant land, she had made use of the precise words which had startled me from sleep, and had repeated them. As it may be of interest for you to receive a corroboration of what I have related from the persons I have mentioned, who happen to be with me at this date, they also sign to affirm the accuracy of all I have related.

Signed
{
J. H. DRUMMOND HAY
ANNETTE DRUMMOND HAY
EUPHEMIA DRUMMOND HAY
ALICE DRUMMOND HAY §
}

From the *Journal* S.P.R., vol. v. p. 61. Mr. Edward Crewdson, Jr. of Tuckerville, Chester County, Nebraska, U.S.A. writes that he owned two ranches. He and his family lived on the East ranch and every week he went to the West ranch with one or two of his three sons to stay a night or two. He continues:

§ My wife expected to have a baby towards the end of April. March 20th (as nearly as I can remember), I was leaving the East Ranch as usual, with blankets, food, etc., for the two eldest boys and myself, when the youngest boy Hugh came running out crying and begged to be taken. Mrs. Crewdson was standing by the buckboard, bidding us goodbye, and said, "Oh yes, do take Hughie, and I will have a thorough rest till you come back." So Hughie jumped up and we left. The West Ranch is fifteen miles from the East, and we got there about 6:30. I cooked our supper, had a pipe, and I suppose by 9:30 or 10 we were all sound asleep.

How long I slept I could not tell, but I was awakened by Hughie, who was sleeping with me, sitting up and crying, "Oh, pa! pa!" "What is it, Hughie?" "Oh, pa, there is a little baby in bed with mamma." Now the child had no idea there was one expected—could have had none, for our children are absurdly innocent, even the older ones—awkwardly innocent at times. It was so strange, and I was so thoroughly awake that I did not go to sleep for some time, and was on the point of getting up and driving home, but felt that if there was nothing I should look so very foolish.

In the morning I hurried through my business, telling the last man my reason for cutting him short. Before I was five miles away from the ranch a cowboy met me with the news that a baby had been born in the night.

The farmer's name to whom I told the incident, before leaving the West Ranch, is James Whitehead; his testimony is appended.

EDW. CREWDSON, JR. §

And here I feel bound to introduce some samples of a certain class of dreams—more interesting, perhaps, and certainly more perplexing than any others—but belonging to a category of phenomena which at present I can make no attempt to explain. I mean precognitive dreams—pictures or visions in which future events are foretold or depicted.

I give below a thoroughly characteristic example—characteristic alike in its definiteness, its purposelessness, its isolated unintelligibility.

From *Proceedings* S.P.R., vol. xi. p. 505.

§ In 1882 the Duchess of Hamilton experienced what she said was a most extraordinary vision, not a dream. She was not yet asleep and saw a scene as if in a play before her. The actors in it were Lord L... (whom she knew only by sight), as if in a fit, with a man wearing a red beard standing over him. He was by the side of a bath, over which a red lamp was distinctly shown. The Duchess told her doctor, Mr. Alfred Cooper (who reports this story), about her vision. About a week later Mr. Cooper was called because of Lord L...'s illness. When he walked in he saw the scene duplicated. The male nurse taking care of Lord L... had a red beard, and there was a red lamp (which was very unusual) over the bath beside which he found them. §

The next account taken from *Proceedings* S.P.R., vol. xi. p. 509 was addressed to Professor James.

§ Mr. T. F. Ivey of Forney, Texas was in perfect health, not superstitious, nor subject to hallucinations. His 21 year old son Walter had been working away from home for three years, but he had never had a moment's worry about him until a few months before the premonition. Then he began to feel increasingly uneasy, and finally his depression, centered about his son, became intense. The night of December 19th the oppression which weighted him was unusually heavy.

His wife awoke at 7 A.M. and told him her waking dream, which had strangely impressed her. She had thought her husband was in a strange place, among a large family of people she had never seen before, but with whom he was very intimate. She came to this place in a wagon, but her husband was already there, and a grown-up daughter of the family was sitting on his lap and kissing him. "While I was wondering where you had met these people to become so intimate with them, you suddenly dropped over and died," she said. Her husband told her he was so troubled about Walter that life had become a burden.

About noon that day they received a dispatch to the effect that Walter had been fatally injured. Mr. Ivey went by freight train, but his wife and daughter had to go by wagon across country to the place where he was. When they arrived they learned he had been taken to the home of the family whose daughter he had been courting. Mrs. Ivey recognized it at once as the house and people of her dream. They had all loved her son and were grieving, for he had died. "With the single exception of putting my husband in place of my son, the dream was a real and vivid anticipation of the actual," Mrs. Ivey writes. §

Even this great inaccuracy—the substitution of the husband for the son —does not, I think, destroy the impression of a true relation between the actual and the visionary scene.

In some cases the premonitory dream, although it may have made a vivid impression, and perhaps have even been narrated to others, is then apparently clean forgotten until the moment of its fulfillment.

The following case, from a lady known to me, is interesting in this connection; since a dream revives in memory just in time to enable the dreamer to avert its complete fulfillment. From *Proceedings* S.P.R., vol. xi. p. 497.

§ The lady had dreamed that she saw her old coachman falling from the top of the carriage to the road, landing on his head. Later that day after a long drive during which she had forgotten completely about her dream, the dream would have been fulfilled if she hadn't suddenly recalled it in time. Looking through the glass front of the brougham she saw the coachman leaning back in his seat, as if he were not well. She called to him to stop the carriage, jumped out, and motioned to a nearby police-man. Just then the coachman swayed and fell off the box. The po-liceman was by then near enough to catch him and keep him from land-ing on his head and being severely injured, as the dream had foretold. §

The *aversion* of the fulfillment, by reasonable precaution, is here an important feature.

Here again is a case where a somewhat complex scene, involving the action of several persons, is dreamt and narrated beforehand. It is quoted from *Proceedings* S.P.R., vol. xi. p. 491, the account being given by Mr. Haggard, of the British Consulate, Trieste, Austria.

§ A few months ago I had an extraordinarily vivid dream, and waking up repeated it to my wife at once. All I dreamt actually occurred about six weeks afterwards, the details of my dream falling out exactly.

There seems to have been no purpose whatsoever in the dream; and one cannot help thinking, what was the good of it?

I dreamt that I was asked to dinner by the German Consul-General, and accepting, was ushered into a large room with trophies of East African arms on shields against the walls. (*N.B.*—I have myself been a great deal in East Africa.)

After dinner I went to inspect the arms, and amongst them saw a beautifully gold-mounted sword which I pointed out to the French Vice-Consul—who at that moment joined me—as having probably been a present from the Sultan of Zanzibar to my host the German Consul-General.

At that moment the Russian Consul came up too. He pointed out how small was the hilt of the sword and how impossible in consequence it would be for a European to use the weapon, and whilst talking he waved his arm in an excited manner over his head as if he was wielding the sword, and to illustrate what he was saying.

At that moment I woke up and marvelled so at the vividness of the dream that I woke my wife up too and told it to her.

About six weeks afterwards my wife and myself were asked to dine with the German Consul-General; but the dream had long been forgotten by us both.

We were shown into a large withdrawing room which I had never been in before, but which somehow seemed familiar to me. Against the walls were some beautiful trophies of East African arms, amongst which was a gold-hilted sword, a gift to my host from the Sultan of Zanzibar.

To make a long story short, everything happened exactly as I had dreamt—but I never remembered the dream until the Russian Consul began to wave his arm over his head, when it came back to me like a flash.

Without saying a word to the Russian Consul and French Vice-Consul (whom I left standing before the trophy), I walked quickly across to my wife, who was standing at the entrance of a boudoir opening out of the withdrawing room, and said to her: "Do you remember my dream about the Zanzibar arms?" She remembered everything perfectly, and was a witness to its realization. On the spot we informed all the persons concerned of the dream, which naturally much interested them. §

I shall conclude this group with a case quoted from *Proceedings* S.P.R., vol. xi. p. 577 where there is a suggestion of personal guardianship and care.

§ Lady Q. relates a dream which came to her three times at long intervals, and which was at last fulfilled. It was of her beloved uncle, who had raised her. She dreamed he had been found dead by a certain bridle-path along which he occasionally rode. When he was carried home and upstairs, his left hand hung down and was bruised striking against the banisters. This occurred some six or more years later just as she had dreamed it. §

I shall quote Mrs. Storie's narrative in more detail because the case is both evidentially very strong, and also in the naïveté of its confusion, extremely suggestive of the way in which these psychical communications are made. Mrs. Storie, who is now dead, was, by the testimony of Edmund Gurney, Professor Sidgwick, and others, a witness eminently deserving of trust; and, besides a corroboration from her husband of the manifestation of a troubled dream, before the event was known, we have the actual notes written down by her the day, or the day after, the news of the fatal accident arrived, solely for her own use, and unmistakably reflecting the incoherent impressiveness of the broken vision. These notes form the narrative given in *Phantasms of the Living* vol. i. p. 370 which I reproduce here. The fact that the deceased brother was a *twin* of Mrs. Storie's adds interest to the case, since one clue (a vague one as yet) to the causes directing and determining telepathic communications lies in what seems their exceptional frequency between *twins*—the closest of all relations.

§ HOBART TOWN, Australia, *July,* 1874.

On the evening of the 18th July, I felt unusually nervous. At 2 o'clock I woke from the following dream. It seemed like in dissolving views. In a twinkle of light I saw a railway, and the puff of the engine. I thought, "What's going on up there? Traveling? I wonder if any of us are traveling and I dreaming of it." *Some one* unseen by me answered, "No; something quite different—something wrong." "I don't like to look at these things," I said. Then I saw behind and above my head William's upper half reclining, eyes and mouth half shut; his chest moved forward convulsively, and he raised his right arm. Then he bent forward, saying, "I suppose I should move out of this." Then I saw him lying, eyes shut, on the ground, flat. The chimney of an engine at his head. I called in excitement, "That will strike him!" The "some one" answered "Yes—well, here's what it was" and immediately I saw William sitting in the open air—faint moonlight—on a raised place sideways. He raised his right arm, shuddered, and said, "I can't go on, or back, *No.*" Then he seemed lying flat. I cried out, "Oh! Oh!" and others seemed to echo, "Oh! Oh!" He seemed then upon his elbow, saying, "Now it comes." Then as if struggling to rise, turned twice round quickly, saying, "Is it the train? *the train, the train,*" his right shoulder reverberating as if struck from behind. He fell back like fainting; his eyes rolled. A large dark object came between us like panelling of wood, and rather in the dark something rolled over, and like an arm was thrown up, and the whole thing went away with a *swish.* Close beside me on the ground there seemed a long dark object. I called out, "They've left something behind; it's like a man." It then raised its shoulders and head, and fell down again. The same *some one* answered, "*Yes*" *sadly.* After a moment I seemed called on to look up, and said, "Is that *thing* not away yet?" Answered, "*No.*" And in front, in light, there was a railway compartment in which sat Rev. Mr. Johnstone, of Echuca. I said, "What's he doing there?" Answered, "He's there."

The news reached me one week afterwards. The accident had happened to my brother on the same night about half past 9 o'clock. Rev. Mr. Johnstone and his wife were actually in the train which struck him. He was walking along the line, which is raised two feet on a level country. He seemed to have gone 16 miles—must have been tired and sat down to take off his boot, which was beside him, dozed off and was very likely roused by the sound of the train; 76 sheep-trucks had passed without touching him, but some wooden projection, likely the step, had touched the *right* side of his head, bruised his right shoulder, and killed him instantaneously. . . .

Mrs. Storie reported later that the engine she saw behind him had a chimney of peculiar shape, such as she had not at that time seen; and she remembers that Mr. Storie thought her foolish about insisting on the chimney—unlike (he said) any which existed; but he informed her when he came back from Victoria, where her brother was, that engines of this kind had just been introduced there. §

I propose as an explanation—for reasons which I endeavor to justify in later chapters—that the deceased brother, aided by some other dimly discerned spirit, was endeavoring to present to Mrs. Storie a series of pictures representing his death—as realized *after* his death. I add this last clause, because one of the marked points in the dream was the presence in the train of Mr. Johnstone of Echuca—a fact which the dying man could not possibly know.

The following is quoted from the *Journal* S.P.R., vol. vii. p. 100. Mrs. Manning writes to Professor James as follows:

§ When I was a child at my home in Rochester, N.Y., my elder sister Jessie had almost entire care of me. In 1875 I was living at Fort Hartsuff,

Nebraska, a military post, the station of my husband. My sister then lived in Omaha.

One night in November I awoke from a dreamless sleep, wide awake, and yet to my own consciousness the little child of years ago, in my own room in the old home; the sister had gone and I was alone in the darkness. I sat up in bed, and called with all my voice, "Jessie! Jessie!" This aroused my husband, who spoke to me.

I wrote to my sister the next day, telling her of the strange experience. In a few days I received a letter from her, dated the same as my letter, having passed mine on the way. In it she said that such a strange thing had happened the night before: she had been awakened by my voice calling her name twice. She said the impression was so strong that she made her husband go to the door to see if it could possibly be I. No one else had called her; she had not been dreaming of me. She recognized my voice.

MARY M. CLARKSON MANNING §

The following cases tell strongly for "psychical invasion"—a conception which we shall have to discuss more fully in a later chapter.

From *Phantasms of the Living*, vol. i. p. 225. The narrator of the following case is the late Rev. P. H. Newnham, who described himself as "an utter skeptic, in the true sense of the word."

§ In March, 1854, I was up at Oxford, keeping my last term, in lodgings. I was subject to violent neuralgic headaches, which always culminated in sleep. One evening, about 8 P.M., I had an unusually violent one; when it became unendurable, about 9 P.M., I went into my bedroom, and flung myself, without undressing, on the bed, and soon fell asleep.

I then had a singularly clear and vivid dream, all the incidents of which are still as clear to my memory as ever. I dreamed that I was stopping with the family of the lady who subsequently became my wife. As I bid members of the family good night I perceived that my *fiancée* was near the top of the staircase. I rushed upstairs, overtook her on the top step, and passed my two arms round her waist, under her arms, from behind.

On this I woke, and a clock in the house struck ten almost immediately afterwards. So strong was the impression of the dream that I wrote a detailed account of it next morning to my *fiancée*.

Crossing my letter, not in answer to it, I received a letter from the lady in question: "Were you thinking about me, very specially, last night, just about ten o'clock? For, as I was going upstairs to bed, I distinctly heard your footsteps on the stairs, and felt you put your arms round my waist."

P. H. NEWNHAM §

From *Proceedings* S.P.R., vol. xi. p. 444.

§ *Statement of Mrs. Shagren regarding Appearance of Mr. Hendrickson*

This happened one day after I had finished my morning's work, house-work. It was about 10 o'clock. I stood before the mirror doing my hair, when I suddenly saw Mr. Hendrickson coming from behind, as if approaching on tip-toe. His hands were outstretched, and I had an impression that he would place them on my shoulders; I could even hear his last step, like the squeak of a boot, as he put his foot down. I turned in surprise, and faced him, consequently seeing him out of the glass and in the glass. As I turned I exclaimed, "Is that you?" At least I felt that I said that, but as I spoke he vanished. He was perfectly natural in appearance, and fully dressed, just as I had always seen him.

The next day a young lady friend of mine, and also a friend of Mr. Hendrickson's family, came to visit me, and knowing of her friendship with Mr. Hendrickson, I asked her if she knew anything of the family, or where they were living, as I had heard nothing from them for about four years, I having been south during that time, and they in the meantime having left the city.

I asked if she knew if Mr. Hendrickson was still living, as I knew he had consumption. She replied that he was living the last time she had heard from them. And then I said, "I saw him yesterday morning."

My friend was not surprised, and regarded the appearance as a warning of death. "Let us write," she suggested, "and find out if he is living or dead." Then we wrote we both felt uneasy, and I told of seeing him. In a few days we received a reply saying that he was not dead, but the doctors had said he could not live, and then Mrs. H. related his experience of seeing me in a dream, while asleep on the morning he had appeared to me. Although he had never been in the house, he described my room, and said to his wife, concerning his dream, "she looked stouter than she used to," which was true, as I had grown much stouter in the four years since they had seen me.

Mrs. Hendrickson and myself were friends from childhood. I had only known Mr. Hendrickson since his marriage. We were just good friends. Mr. Hendrickson once told his wife that I had appeared to him. That was long before my experience of seeing him.

[MRS.] C. M. SHAGREN §

These cases of invasion by the spirits of living persons pass on into cases of invasion by the dying, of which several instances are given. The following case is quoted from *Phantasms of the Living*, vol. i. p. 365. The account is written by Mr. N. T. Menneer, Principal of Torre College, Torquay:

§ My wife, since deceased, had a brother residing at Sarawak, and at the time to which I refer, staying with the Raja, Sir James Brooke.

The following is an extract from the second volume of *The Raja of Sarawak,* by Gertrude L. Jacob, p. 238. "Mr. Wellington" (my wife's brother) "was killed in a brave attempt to defend Mrs. Middleton and her children." The Chinese, it appears, taking Mr. Wellington for the Raja's son, struck off his head.

And now for the dream. I was awoke one night by my wife, who started from her sleep, terrified by the following dream. She saw her *headless* brother standing at the foot of the bed with his head lying on a coffin by his side. I did my best to console my wife, who continued to be much distressed for some considerable time. At length she fell asleep again, to be awoke by a similar dream. In the morning, and for several days after, she constantly referred to her dream, and anticipated sad news of her brother.

And now comes the strangest part of the story. When the news reached England I computed approximately the time, and found *it coincided with the memorable night to which I have referred.*

N. T. MENNEER §

We have since seen a letter from Sir James Brooke (Raja of Sarawak) and an extract from the *Straits Times* of March 21st, 1857, in the (London) *Times* for April 29th, 1857, which make it, I think, quite conceivable that the dream was a reflection of knowledge acquired by Mr. Wellington after death, and that the *head on the coffin* had a distinct meaning. Sir James Brooke says: "Poor Wellington's remains were consumed by the Chinese; his head, borne off in triumph, alone attesting his previous murder." The *Straits Times* says: "The head was given up on the following day." The head, therefore, and the head alone, must undoubtedly have been buried by Mr. Wellington's friends; and its appearance in the dream *on a coffin,* with the headless body standing beside it, is a coincidence even more significant.

The next case quoted from *Phantasms of the Living,* vol. i. p. 453 is from Mrs. Lightfoot, a lady who was none the worse witness because she took not the slightest interest in our work. The names and dates were filled in by Gurney, immediately after a personal interview, January 30th, 1884.

§ In giving the following experience, I may premise that as a child, and since, I have comparatively had but little knowledge (as a personal experience) of fear; and in the existence of ghosts I have always disbelieved. Did I ever see or hear sights or sounds for which, on examination, I could not account, I have always come to the conclusion that they arose from natural causes which were beyond my reach of inquiry—hence I always refused to accept anything without proof, and I may add, that I have rarely been convinced.

On the night of September 21st, 1874, ... a little after midnight I was sound asleep. As I knew afterwards, I must have slept about three hours, when I was suddenly aroused (and was, so far as I know, *perfectly wide awake*) by a violent noise at my door, which was locked. I have some recollection of feeling astonished (of fear I then had none) at seeing or rather hearing within the instant my door thrown violently open, as though by some one in great anger, and I was instantly conscious that some one, something, what shall I call *it*, was in the room. For the hundredth part of a second it seemed to pause just within the room, and then by a movement, which it is impossible for me to describe—but it seemed to move with a rapid push—*it* was at the foot of my bed. Again a pause; for again the hundredth part of a second, and the figure-shape rose. I *heard* it, but as it got higher its movements quieted, and presently *it* was above my bed, lying horizontally, its face downwards, parallel with my face, its feet to my feet, but with a distance of some three or four feet between us. This for a moment, whilst I waited simply in astonishment and curiosity (for I had not the very faintest idea of either who or what it was), but no fear, and then it spoke. In an instant I recognized the voice as that of my friend Mrs. Reed from India. In her familiar imperious way of speaking, my Christian name sounded clear and full through the room. "Frances," it repeated, "I want you; come with me. Come at once." *My* voice responded as instantaneously, "Yes, I'll come. What need for such a hurry?" and then came a quick imperative reply, "But you *must* come *at once;* come instantly, and without a moment's pause or hesitation." I seemed to be drawn upwards by some extraordinary magnetic influence, and then just as suddenly and violently thrown down again.

In one second of time the room was in a deathly stillness, and the words "She is dead," were simply burnt into my mind. I sat up in bed dazed, and *now,* for the first time, frightened beyond measure. ...

That same afternoon, curiously enough, a sister came to see me, who had been abroad with me, and whilst there had known and liked this same friend. During our chat she said, "By the way, have you heard anything lately of Mrs. Reed? when last I heard, she was not very well." *Instantly* came my reply, "Oh, she is dead," and it was only my sister's look of blank horror and astonishment that recalled me to myself. But tell her the dream I *could* not, so I merely answered, "You will see that I am right when you look in the newspapers—*how* I have heard of it I will tell you some other time," and directly I changed the conversation.

And so the matter rested, but within a month from the date of my dream came the news of Mrs. Reed's death, on September 21st.

The bereaved husband returned to England and called upon me. He gave me some details of the last days, and on my asking whether he remembered her last words, he turned to me with quite a look of surprise, and said, "Why, Mrs. Lightfoot, I believe *your* name was the last she mentioned."

For myself I never really recovered from the shock for a long time, and even now the impression is as vivid as though it had only happened yesterday.

FRANCES W. LIGHTFOOT §

From *Proceedings,* S.P.R., vol. vi. p. 341. Communicated by Fräulein Schneller, sister-in-law of the percipient, and known to F. W. H. M., January, 1890.

§ DOBER UND PAUSE, SCHLESIEN, *December 12th,* 1889.

About a year ago there died in a neighboring village a brewer called Wünscher, with whom I stood in friendly relations. His death ensued after a short illness, and as I seldom had an opportunity of visiting him, I knew nothing of his illness nor of his death. On the day of his death I went to bed at nine o'clock. Being of a very healthy constitution, I fell asleep as soon as I lay down. In my dream I heard the deceased call out with a loud voice, "Boy, make haste and give me my boots." This awoke me, and I noticed that, for the sake of our child, my wife had left the light burning. I pondered with pleasure over my dream, thinking in my mind how Wünscher, who was a good-natured, humorous man, would laugh when I told him of this dream. Still thinking on it, I hear Wünscher's voice scolding outside, just under my window. I sit up in my bed at once and listen, but cannot understand his words. What can the brewer want? I thought, much vexed with him, that he should make a disturbance in the night. Suddenly he comes into the room from behind the linen press, steps with long strides past the bed of my wife and the child's bed; wildly gesticulating with his arms all the time, as his habit was, he called out, "What do you say to this, Herr Oberamtmann? This afternoon at five o'clock I have died." Startled by this information, I exclaim, "Oh, that is not true!" He replied: "Truly, as I tell you; and what do you think? They want to bury me already on Tuesday afternoon at two o'clock," accentuating his assertions all the while by his gesticulations. During this long speech of my visitor I examined myself as to whether I was really awake and not dreaming.

I asked myself: Is this a hallucination? Is my mind in full possession of its faculties? Yes, there is the light, there the jug, this is the mirror, and this the brewer; and I came to the conclusion: I am awake. Then the thought occurred to me, What will my wife think if she awakes and sees the brewer in our bedroom? In this fear of her waking up I turn round to my wife, and to my great relief I see from her face, which is turned towards me, that she is still asleep; but she looks very pale. I say to the brewer, "Herr Wünscher, we will speak softly, so that my wife may not wake up, it would be very disagreeable to her to find you here." To which Wünscher answered in a lower and calmer tone: "Don't be afraid, I will do no harm to your wife." Things do happen indeed for which we find no explanation—I thought to myself, and said to Wünscher: "If this be true, that you have died, I am sincerely sorry for it; I will look after your children." Wünscher stepped towards me, stretched out his arms and moved his lips as though he would embrace me; therefore I said in a threatening tone, and looking steadfastly at him with frowning brow: "Don't come so near, it is disagreeable to me," and lifted my right arm to ward him off, but before my arm reached him the apparition had vanished. My first look was to my wife to see if she were still asleep. She was. I got up and looked at my watch, it was seven minutes past twelve. My wife woke up and asked me: "To whom did you speak so loud just now?" "Have you understood anything?" I said. "No," she answered, and went to sleep again.

The next day I learned that the brewer *had* died that afternoon at five o'clock, and was buried on the following Tuesday at two.

With great respect,
KARL DIGNOWITY
(Landed Proprietor) §

From the *Journal* S.P.R., vol. viii. p. 123. The account was sent to Dr. Hodgson by Mr. A. E. Dolbear, Professor of Physics in Tufts College, Mass.

§ Professor Dolbear was lecturing at Greenacre, Me., and he stopped for the night at a summer hotel run by Miss Farmer, daughter of the late Moses G. Farmer. He had met Mr. Farmer on two or three occasions before his death, but knew him only slightly. During the night he dreamed that he had a visit from Mr. Farmer. He asked him, "How shall I know it is you and not some one else?" (for he couldn't see him). Farmer replied, "I'll show you my hand," and his left hand was extended. The professor took hold of it; it was very cold and made him so shudder that he was at once awakened. Directly he slept again he had the same dream. This time Mr. Farmer showed him a trick he could do with the fingers of his left hand, straightening out his first and third fingers while the second and fourth were bent in a very uncommon way.

The next morning Professor Dolbear told Miss Farmer about his dream. She stated that her father had been able to perform this unusual trick with his fingers which nobody else could do. Miss Farmer and others at the hotel were spiritualists and were convinced that Professor Dolbear had really had a visit from her father. §

We have now briefly reviewed certain phenomena of sleep from a standpoint somewhat differing from that which is commonly taken. We have not (as is usual) fixed our attention primarily on the *negative* characteristics of sleep, or the extent to which it lacks the capacities of waking hours. On the contrary, we have regarded sleep as an independent phase of personality, existing with as good a right as the waking phase, and dowered with imperfectly expressed faculties of its own. In investigating those faculties we have been in no wise deterred by the fact of the apparent uselessness of some of them for our waking ends. *Useless* is a pre-scientific, even an anti-scientific term, which has perhaps proved a greater stumbling-block to research in psychology than in any other science. In science the *use* of phenomena is to prove laws, and the more bizarre and trivial the phenomena, the greater the chance of their directing us to some law which has been overlooked till now. In reviewing the phenomena of sleep we were bound to ask whether the self of sleep showed any faculty of a quite different order from that by which waking consciousness maintains the activity of man. We found that this was so indeed; that there was evidence that the sleeping spirit was susceptible of relations unfettered by spatial bonds; of clairvoyant perception of distant scenes; of telepathic communication with distant persons, or even with spirits of whom we can predicate neither distance nor nearness, since they are released from the prison of the flesh.

The inference which all this evidence suggests is entirely in accordance with the hypothesis on which my whole work is based.

I have assumed that man is an organism informed or possessed by a soul. This view obviously involves the hypothesis that we are living a life in two worlds at once; a planetary life in this material world, to which the organism is intended to react; and also a cosmic life in that spiritual world which is the native environment of the soul. From that unseen world the energy of the organism needs to be perpetually replenished.

Admitting, for the sake of argument, these vast assumptions, it will be easy to draw the further inference that it may be needful that the soul's attention should be frequently withdrawn from the business of earthly life, so as to pursue with greater intensity the maintenance of the fundamental, pervading connection between the organism and the spiritual world.

On this view of sleep, be it observed, there will be nothing to surprise us in the possibility of increasing the proportion of the sleeping to the waking phase of life by hypnotic suggestion. We shall begin at once in the next chapter to trace out that great experimental modification of sleep, from which, under the names of mesmerism or of hypnotism, results of such conspicuous practical value have already been won.

Chapter Five

HYPNOTISM

A very complex subject must in this chapter be discussed with as much completeness as brevity will allow. So for my first step I shall endeavor to trace the connection of hypnotism with the subjects of the former chapters, especially with sleep and hysteria, and to indicate what kind of advance in faculty may be expected from such experimental developments of sleep-waking states, and of subliminal activity in general, as those to which the broad general title of hypnotism (or hypnotic suggestion) is now commonly given. Hypnotism is too often presented as though it comprised a quite isolated group of phenomena. Until it is more definitely correlated with other phases of personality, it can hardly occupy the place it merits in any psychological scheme.

Discussing in Chapter Two the various forms of disintegration of personality, we had frequent glimpses of beneficent subliminal powers. We saw the deepest stratum of the self intervening from time to time with a therapeutic object (in the case of Anna Winsor), or we caught it in the act of exercising, even if aimlessly or sporadically, some faculty beyond supraliminal reach. And we observed, moreover, that the agency by which these subliminal powers were invoked was generally the *hypnotic trance.* Of the nature of that trance I then said nothing; it was manifest only that here was some kind of induced or artificial somnambulism, which seemed to systematize that beneficial control of the organism which spontaneous sleep-waking states had exercised in a fitful way. We must try to understand these hypnotic phenomena; to push as far as possible what seems like an experimental evolution of the sleeping phase of personality.

Let us suppose, then, that we are standing at our present point, but with no more knowledge of hypnotic phenomena than existed in the boyhood of Mesmer. We shall know well enough what, as experimental psychologists, we desire to do; but we shall have little notion of how to set about it. We desire to summon at our will, and to subdue to our use, these rarely emergent sleep-waking faculties. On their physical side, we desire to develop their inhibition of pain and their reinforcement of energy; on their intellectual side, their concentration of attention; on their emotional side, their sense of freedom, expansion, joy. Above all, we desire to get hold of those supernormal faculties—telepathy and clairvoyance—of which we have caught fitful glimpses in somnambulism and in dream.

Now, Mesmer's experiment was almost a "fool's experiment," and Mesmer himself was almost a charlatan. Yet Mesmer and his successors, working from many different points of view, and following many divergent theories, have opened an ever-widening way, and have brought us now to a position where we can fairly hope, by experiments made no longer at random, to reproduce and systematize most of those phenomena of spontaneous somnambulism which once seemed to lie so tantalizingly beyond our grasp.

That promise is great indeed; yet it is well to begin by considering precisely how far it extends. We must not suppose that we shall at once be subduing to our experiment a central, integrated, reasonable Self. On the contrary (as has already been explained in Chapter Three), it has been characteristic of hysteria and usually also of somnambulism that the spontaneous changes, although subliminal, have been *piecemeal* changes; that they have involved not *highest-level* but *middle-level* centers; not those centers which determine highest perception and ideation, but centers which control complex co-ordinated movements, such as the synergies necessary for walking or for sight or for dreamlike unintelligent speech.

This metaphor of higher and lower, although it may sound inappropriate, is still of service when we are dealing with stages of faculty all of them below the level of the conscious threshold. For our general evidence as to subliminal processes has by this time obliged us to assume that there exists in that submerged region also a gradation of somewhat similar type. We may reach by artifice (that is to say) some subliminal faculty, and yet we may not be reaching any central or controlling judgment. We may be reaching centers which exercise over those subliminal faculties only a fragmentary sway; so that we shall have no reason for surprise if there be something dreamlike, something of bizarrerie or of incoherence, in the manifestation which our experiment evokes. We must be content (at first at any rate) if we can affect the personality in the same limited way as hysteria and somnambulism have affected it; but yet can act deliberately and usefully where these have acted hurtfully and at random. It is enough to hope that we may inhibit pain, as it is inhibited for the hysteric; or concentrate attention, as it is concentrated for the somnambulist; or change the tastes and passions, as these are changed in alternating personalities; or (best of all) recover and fix something of that supernormal faculty of which we have caught fugitive glimpses in vision and dream. Our proof of the origination of any phenomenon in the deeper strata of our being must lie in the intrinsic nature of the faculty exhibited—not in the wisdom of its actual direction.

We begin by defining hypnotism as the empirical development of the sleeping phase of man's personality. In that sleeping phase the most conspicuous element is the repair of wasted tissues, the physical, and therefore also largely the moral, refreshment and rejuvenation of the tired organism. We find that we have in hypnotism a veritable evolution of those recuperative energies which give its practical value to sleep.

For one form of sleep-waking capacity we are already prepared by what has been said in Chapter Four of the solution of problems in sleep. This is one of the ways in which we can watch the gradual merging of a vivid dream into a definite somnambulic act. The solution of a problem (as we have seen) may present itself merely as a sentence or a diagram, constructed in dream and remembered on waking. Or the sleeper may rise from bed and *write out* the chain of reasoning, or the sermon, or whatever it may be. Or again, in rarer cases ("Rachel Baker" is a curious example) the somnambulic output may take the form of oratory, and edifying discourses may be delivered by a preacher whom no amount of shaking or pinching will silence or, generally, even interrupt.

Rachel Baker,[1] one of the most noted "sleeping preachers," was born at Pelham, in Massachusetts, in 1794. Her parents were Presbyterians of limited means, and the chief element in her education, which was otherwise limited to seven months' regular schooling, was religious instruction. She is said to have been a child "of a serious make, of few words, timorous, and much given to melancholy, . . . [her] mental faculties, in the opinion of all those best acquainted with her, are far from being beyond what is common to females." In June, 1811, at the age of seventeen, she fell into a state of religious melancholy, which gradually became more acute till November of the same year, when the somnambulic condition first appeared; being apparently asleep in a chair in the evening, she talked incoherently of her fears of hell, etc. The fit or trance, with the same kind of talk, constantly recurred till January 27th, 1812, when a mental crisis occurred in the waking state—a climax of terror and despair, succeeded by a kind of "conversion," which produced a happy and calming effect on her mind. From this time onwards the trances continued, but her talk became much more regular and rational, and many persons used to come and listen to it.[2] It consisted of prayers and religious addresses, and those who

---

[1] See "Remarkable Sermons of Rachel Baker, and Pious Ejaculations, delivered during Sleep," by Dr. Mitchill, M.D., Professor of Physic, the late Dr. Priestley, LL.D., and Dr. Douglass (London, 1815).

[2] *"Several hundreds* every evening flock to hear this *most wonderful Preacher,* who is instrumental in converting more persons to Christianity, when *asleep,* than all the other Ministers together, whilst *awake."* (*Op. cit.* title page.)

knew her well declared that her intellectual faculties were increased to an extraordinary degree while in the trance. It was observed "that all that Rachel expresses in her state of somniloquism is the result of preconceived ideas and opinions, but delivered with a readiness and a fluency which is very far above her waking state," and the specimens quoted bear out this view. The so-called "fits," which occurred almost every evening, lasted about forty-five minutes, beginning and ending with slight epileptiform symptoms, and passing off into natural sleep for the rest of the night. In her waking state she knew nothing of what had happened in the "fit," except from the information of others. No other morbid symptoms of any kind were detected in her by the doctors who report on the case; the "fits" ceased during temporary ill-health, and returned as soon as she recovered.

Two other cases of "sleeping preachers" are recorded in the same book —that of Job Cooper, a Pennsylvanian weaver, in 1774, and Joseph Payne, a boy of about sixteen, at Reading in England, in 1759, whose case is described in *The Gentleman's Magazine* for May, 1760. See also the case of "X + Y = Z" in Chapter Nine.

The next stage is a very important one. We come to the manifestation in spontaneous sleep-waking states of manifestly supernormal powers— sometimes of telepathy, but more commonly of clairvoyance. Unfortunately these cases have been, as a rule, very insufficiently observed (see the case of Mollie Fancher). Still, it appears that in spontaneous somnambulism there is frequently some indication of supernormal powers, though the observers—even if competent in other ways—have generally neglected to take account of the hyperæsthesia and heightening of memory and of general intelligence that often accompany the state. I quote, however, from Dr. Dufay a case which does not seem open to these objections. The writer of the account was M. Badaire, formerly director of the École Normale at Guéret, the subject, Théophile Janicaud, having been one of his pupil-teachers. Janicaud had been subject to frequent attacks of somnambulism from about the age of eight to ten; afterwards they ceased almost entirely till he was nineteen. M. Badaire writes:

§ ... During the first year that he was at school we noticed nothing unusual in him; but during the excessive heat in the months of June and July, 1859 the condition of young Janicaud completely changed, and attacks of somnambulism occurred every night, with a frequency which soon gave cause for anxiety as to his health. In a few weeks he was so much altered as to be hardly recognizable even to the members of his family. His eyes were sunken, tired, and haggard, and an extreme thinness took the place of robust health.

Every evening he got up, walked about the dormitory, descended to the study to work in the dark, or wandered about the gardens for hours at a time, after which he went back to bed. . . .

One evening about 11 o'clock Janicaud, having escaped from the dormitory [in spite of all the precautions taken to avoid the risks of his nocturnal expeditions] knocked at the door of my bedroom.

"I have just arrived from Vendôme," he said, "and have come to give you the news of your family. M. and Mme. Arnault are well, and your little son has four teeth."

"As you have seen them at Vendôme, could you go back again and tell me where they are at present?"

"Wait . . . I am there . . . They are sleeping in a room on the first floor; their bed is at the farther end of the room, to the left. The nurse's bed is to the right, and Henry's cradle close to it."

The description of the room and the position of the beds were perfectly exact, and the following day I received a letter from my father-in-law telling me that my child had cut his fourth tooth.

A few days later Janicaud came to me at about the same time, telling me that he had again come from Vendôme, and that an accident had happened to the child during the day. My wife, being much startled, anxiously inquired what the accident was.

"Oh! do not be frightened, Madame, reassure yourself, there will be no serious consequences, whatever the doctor, who is now with the child, may think. If I had known that I should have caused you so much alarm, I should not have spoken of it. It will be nothing."

The next morning I wrote to my father-in-law to tell him what Janicaud had said, and begged for news of the child by return of post. The answer was that he was perfectly well and no accident had occurred.

But in the month of September, when I went home for the holidays, I learnt the whole truth, which my father-in-law, on the advice of the doctor, had hidden from me. He told me that at the time when Janicaud came to tell me that an accident had happened, the doctor did not expect the child to live through the night. During the day the nurse, having got hold of the key of the cellar, had become completely intoxicated, and the child having been fed by her when in this condition, was seized with violent sickness, which endangered his life for several days.

One night Janicaud suddenly jumped up in bed, and turning to one of his companions, said—

"See, Roullet, how careless you are. I certainly told you to shut the door of the bookbinding workshop, but you did not do it, and a cat, in eating the paste, has just knocked over the dish, which is broken into five pieces."

Some one went down at once to the workshop, and it was found that what the somnambulist had said was perfectly correct.

The following night he related how he saw on the Glény road the body of a man, who had been drowned while bathing in the Creuse, and that he was being brought to Guéret in a carriage. Next day I made inquiries, and heard that an inhabitant of the town had really been drowned the previous day at Glény, and that his body had been brought to Guéret during the night. But nobody in the house, not even in the town, had known of the accident the day before. . . .

Once he rose up during the night with the fixed determination of going fishing. M. Simonet decided to accompany him, and before starting succeeded in inducing him to alter the nature of his excursion, and go and visit a relative residing some distance off. This was done, Janicaud being undisturbed from his sleeping condition either by the noise of barking dogs or by the fatigues of the walk. At last he decided upon going home, and on the way, having come to a narrow and dangerous path by the river, his brother-in-law begged him to be careful as to where he put his foot. Janicaud, however, assured him that he could see the better of the two, and as a proof asked his companion whether he saw the match which was under his left foot. M. Simonet at once felt under his foot, and sure enough found a match there. Not only was it very dark, but Janicaud with his night-cap drawn over his face was some thirty paces ahead.

In his natural state Janicaud has an uncertain memory, and retains what he learns with difficulty; but on several occasions when he has been studying his history lessons in bed the assistant master has taken the book from his hand, and the somnambulist has then repeated the five or six pages which he had just read without omitting a syllable. Awakened immediately after, he had no recollection of what he had just read and repeated.

BADAIRE §

Before leaving this subject of spontaneous sleep-waking states, I ought briefly to mention a form of trance with which we shall have to deal more at length in a later chapter. I speak of trance ascribed to *spirit-possession*. As will be seen, I myself fully adopt this explanation in a small number of the cases where it is put forward. Yet I do not think that spirit-agency is necessarily present in all the trances even of a true subject of possession. With all the leading sensitives—with D. D. Home, with Stainton Moses, with Mrs. Piper and others—I think that the depth of the trance has varied greatly on different occasions, and that sometimes the subliminal self of the sensitive is vaguely simulating, probably in an unconscious dream-like way, an external intelligence. This hypothesis suggested itself to several observers in the case especially of D. D. Home, with whom the moments of strong characterization of a departed personality, thought far from rare, were yet scattered among tracts of dreamy improvisation which suggested only the utterance of Home's subliminal self (see Chapter Nine). However we choose to interpret these trances, they should be mentioned in comparison with all the other sleep-waking states. They probably form the best transition between those shallow somnambulisms, on the one hand, which are little more than a vivid dream, and those profound trances, on the other hand, in which the native spirit quits the sensitive's organism, and is for the time replaced by an invading spirit from that unseen world.

This brief review of non-hypnotic somnambulisms has not been without its lessons. It has shown us that the supranormal powers which we have traced in each of the preceding chapters in turn do also show themselves, in much the same fashion, in spontaneous sleep-waking states of various types. We must now inquire how far they occur in sleep-waking states experimentally induced.

Now, we have found nothing but *suggestion* which really induces the phenomena of hypnotic trance. So with some reserves as to telepathic action, I shall assent to the dogma that hypnotic agencies may be simplified into *suggestion* and *self-suggestion*. Yet we cannot possibly regard this as any real answer to the important question of *how* the hypnotic responsiveness is induced, on *what* conditions it depends. These words bring no true solution: they are mere names which disguise our ignorance. We do not know either why a subject obeys any suggestion which may be made to him, or how he obeys it. We do not know this even when the suggestion bears upon some easy, external matter. Still deeper is the mystery when the suggestion is an *organic* or *therapeutic* command—when the subject is told (for instance) not to feel an aching tooth. If he cannot stop feeling the ache by his own strong desire, how can he stop feeling it out of deference to a doctor? Unless there be some supernormal influence or effluence —telepathic or mesmeric—from doctor to patient, we cannot credit the doctor with doing more than set in motion some *self-suggestive* machinery by which the patient cures his toothache himself. Where no such telepathic influence is exercised, suggestion is merely equivalent to self-suggestion. And self-suggestion remains for our solution as an inexplicable and capricious responsiveness—a sudden obedience of subliminal agencies to supraliminal commands, which at certain times will modify both body and mind far more effectively than any exertion of the ordinary will. No serious attempt has yet been made to explain this obedience to control; and before trying to explain it we must review its range and limits from a psychological as well as from a physiological standpoint. In the meantime I define suggestion as *successful appeal to the subliminal self.*

Here, then, we come to an important conclusion which cannot well be denied, yet is seldom looked fully in the face. Suggestion from without must for the most part resolve itself into suggestion from within. Unless there be some telepathic or other supernormal influence at work between hypnotizer and patient (which I shall presently show ground for believing to be sometimes, though not often, the case), the hypnotizer can plainly do nothing by his word of command beyond starting a train of thought which the patient has in most cases started many times for himself with no result; the difference being that now at last the patient starts it again, and it *has* a result. But *why* it thus succeeds on this particular occasion, we simply do not know. We cannot predict when the result will occur; still less can we bring it about at pleasure.

Nay, we do not even know whether it might not be possible to dispense altogether with suggestion from outside in most of the cases now treated in this way, and merely to teach the patient to make the suggestions for himself. If there be no "mesmeric effluence" passing from hypnotizer to patient, the hypnotizer seems little more than a mere personage provided simply to impress the imagination, who must needs become even absurdly useless so soon as it is understood that he has no other function or power.

Self-suggestion, whatever this may really mean, is thus in most cases, whether avowedly or not, at the bottom of the effect produced. It has already been used most successfully, and it will probably become much commoner than it now is. I should rather say (since every one no doubt suggests to himself when he is in pain that he would like the pain to cease), I anticipate that self-suggestion, by being in some way better directed, will become more *effective,* and that the average of voluntary power over the organism will rise to a far higher level than it at present reaches. I believe that this is taking place even now; and that certain *schemes of self-suggestion,* so to call them, are coming into vogue, where patients in large masses are supplied with effective conceptions, which they thus impress repeatedly upon themselves without the need of a hypnotizer's attendance on each occasion. I shall presently explain that the "Miracles of Lourdes" and the cures effected by "Christian Science" fall, in my view, under this category. We have here suggestions given to a quantity of more or less suitable people *en masse,* much as a platform hypnotizer gives suggestions to a mixed audience, some of whom may then be affected without individual attention from himself. The suggestion of the curative power of the Lourdes water, for instance, is thus thrown out, partly in books, partly by oral addresses; and a certain percentage of persons succeed in so persuading themselves of that curative efficacy that when they bathe in the water they are actually cured.

These *schemes of self-suggestion,* as I have termed them, constitute one of the most interesting parts of my subject, and will need careful study at a later point. But here it is important to point out that in order to make self-suggestion operative, no strong belief or enthusiasm, such as those schemes imply, is really necessary.

No recorded cases of self-suggestion, I think, are more instructive than those from a paper on "The Connection of Hypnotism with the Subjective Phenomena of Spiritualism," by Dr. Hugh Wingfield, in the *Proceedings* S.P.R., vol. v. pp. 279 *et seq.* Dr. Wingfield was a Demonstrator in Physiology in the University of Cambridge, and his subjects were mainly candidates for the Natural Sciences Tripos. In these cases there was no excitement of any kind, and no previous belief. The phenomena occurred incidentally during a series of experiments on other points, and were a surprise to every one concerned.

The passage quoted below goes far to prove Dr. Wingfield's general thesis: "It seems probable that . . . all phenomena capable of being produced by the suggestion of the hypnotizer can also be produced by self-suggestion in a self-suggestive subject."

§ The facts of self-suggestion adduced in this paper were not, I would expressly state, the subject of a series of experiments. The cases occurred quite unexpectedly during a series of experiments on other points; but owing to the possible danger of such phenomena if carried too far, I did not feel justified in attempting to work out the subject. Hence the chain of experiments is necessarily very incomplete. The experiments adduced were all made on subjects in the waking state. Muscular rigidity, though the most general form of phenomenon produced by self-suggestion, was not by any means the only one met with. Inhibition of voluntary movements, local anæsthesia, even delusions were produced by it in some cases. No subject however, in whom I could produce delusions was allowed to experiment on himself, as it was considered unsafe, so that the most interesting field of experiment in this direction had to be left untouched. All the subjects referred to were men between the ages of eighteen and twenty-four, and all healthy. In no case, except when specially mentioned, had the hypnotic sleep ever been induced, but merely waking phenomena, *e.g.* susceptibility to inhibitory and imperative suggestions, muscular rigidity, and, in some cases, local anæsthesia.

We will first take the case of muscular rigidity and anæsthesia.

N., by means of stroking his arm and looking at it, could render it rigid. He could not do so, however, if unable to see his arm.

Fi. could make his arm rigid by stroking only; this he could do whether he could see his arm or not.

F. could also make his arm rigid by merely looking at it.

E. could make his arm rigid by an effort of mind without seeing it or stroking it.

In all cases they were able at once to remove the rigidity by reverse strokes. These instances serve to show how the degree in which subjects possess this power varies.

F. when he rendered his arm rigid also made it anæsthetic; the anæsthesia was removed at the same time as the rigidity.

In N. (who had afterwards been sent to sleep), I succeeded eventually in producing anæsthesia. He could then do it himself.

The case of E. was very striking: his power of producing muscular rigidity was astonishing. He was able by an effort of mind to throw his whole body into a state of cataleptic rigidity, so that he could rest with his heels on one chair and head on another, and remain supported in that condition.

Other phenomena of the waking state were also produced by self-suggestion. T. and L. could both close their own eyes so that they were unable to open them. T. used to shut his eyes and stroke the lids downwards. He was then unable to open them. Several other subjects showed the same phenomenon. T. could fix his hand to the table by a few passes; this also was done by several others.

Other subjects could fix their hands together. The following experiment was tried: Five subjects were taken, two of whom had been previously hypnotized; none had been sent to sleep. They were asked to put their hands together, and imagine that they could not part them. They closed their eyes, put their hands together, and tried. One could not part his hands, the others could. They were then told to shut their eyes and imagine the operator gazing at them, and saying, "You cannot part your hands." Not one was able to do so. They were able after this to produce the same phenomena in themselves, quite apart from the operator, in their own rooms. They found at first that they were obliged to imagine the operator giving the suggestion, but afterwards were able to do it without imagining him at all.

As regards delusions I can only give one instance. Doubtless many subjects could produce them in themselves if they tried, but I have never allowed them to do so. In the case of C., however, we have proof that they can be produced by self-suggestion. He could by a simple effort of mind make himself believe almost any delusion, *e.g.* that he was riding on horseback, that he was a dog, or anything else, or that he saw snakes, etc. If left to himself the delusion vanished slowly. Any one else could remove it at once by a counter-suggestion. He made these experiments without my consent, as I consider them unsafe. §

Experiments like these seem to me to open a new inlet into human faculty, as surprising in its way as those first wild experiments of Mesmer himself. Who would have supposed that a healthy undergraduate could "by an effort of mind throw his whole body into a state of cataleptic rigidity, so that he could rest with his heels on one chair and head on another, and remain supported in that condition"? or that other healthy young men could "close their own eyes so that they were unable to open them," and the like? The trivial character of these laboratory experiments makes them physiologically the more remarkable. There is the very minimum of predisposing conditions, of excited expectation, or of external motive prompting to extraordinary effort. And the results are not subjective merely—relief of pain and so on—but are definite neuro-muscular changes, capable of unmistakable test.

Yet, important though these and similar experiments in self-suggestion may be, they do not solve our problem as to the ultimate origin and distribution of the faculty thus displayed. We know no better with self-suggestion than with suggestion from outside *why* it is that one man succeeds where others fail, or why a man who succeeds once fails in his next attempt. Within the ordinary range of physiological explanations nothing (I repeat) has as yet been discovered which can guide us to the true nature or exciting causes of this characteristic responsiveness of hypnosis. If we are to find any light, it must be in some direction which has as yet been little explored.

The hint which I have to offer here involves, I hope, something more than a mere change of appellation. I define suggestion as "successful appeal to the subliminal self"—not necessarily to that self in its most central, most unitary aspect; but to some one at least of these strata of subliminal faculty which I have in an earlier chapter described.

I do not indeed pretend that my explanation can enable us to reduce hypnotic success to a certainty. I cannot say why the process should be so irregular and capricious; so that now and then we seem to touch a spring which gives instant access to profound recesses; then all is closed and inaccessible again. But I can show that this puzzle is part of a wider problem, which meets us in all departments of subliminal operation. In split personalities, in genius, in dreams, in sensory and motor automatisms, we find the same fitfulness, the same apparent caprice. The answer to the problem of the uncertainty of hypnotism must be involved in the answer to all these other problems too. Hypnotic success or failure cannot depend, as some have fancied, on some superficial difference in the kind of suggestion given. It is part and parcel of a wider mystery—of the obscure relationships and interdependencies of the supraliminal and the subliminal self.

Gurney held the view that the main distinction of kind between his "alert" and his "deep" stage of hypnosis was to be found in the domain of memory, while memory also afforded the means for distinguishing the hypnotic state as a whole from the normal one. As a general rule (though with numerous exceptions), the events of ordinary life are remembered in the trance, while the trance events are forgotten on waking, but tend to recur to the memory on rehypnotization. But the most interesting part of his observations consisted in showing alternations of memory in the alert and deep stages of the trance itself—the ideas impressed in the one state being almost always forgotten in the other, and as invariably again remembered when the former state recurs. On experimenting further, he met with a stage in which there was a distinct third train of memory, independent of the others; and this, of course, suggests a further doubt as to there being any fixed number of stages in the trance.

Some experiments illustrating this were given in detail in a paper by Gurney under the title "Stages of Hypnotic Memory," in *Proceedings* S.P.R., vol. iv. pp. 515 *et seq.,* from which I quote, with abridgments, the following passages:

§ I made the trials with a considerable number of "subjects," in different parts of England, employing three different hypnotizers, to each of whom the results were as new and surprising as they were at first to myself; there seems reason to think, therefore, that the results are tolerably normal, and not due to any special idiosyncrasies of operator or "subject"; as they certainly were not due to any guidance, or any interference with the free play of the "subject's" mind, in the remarks addressed to him during the progress of the experiment. The mode of effecting the passage from one stage to another has usually consisted in gentle passes over the face, without contact. It is most impressive to find that a few noiseless movements of one person's fingers, at a short distance from another person's face, have completely obliterated that with which the latter's attention two or three seconds ago was entirely engrossed, and have brought back within his mental horizon that which no other means in the world—

no other physical operation, not the clearest verbal reminder, not the fear of death, nor the offer of £1000 reward—could have induced or enabled him to recall.

With the assistance of Mr. G. A. Smith (whom I will in future call S.), I have lately made a fresh series of experiments in hypnotic memory, in which some further points have been observed; and it may make the matter more intelligible to give the details of a few cases. The great point, of course, is to use the right means for ascertaining whether the thing told is or is not remembered, and to avoid reminding the subject of it.

As I have said, the rule is to obtain *two* states or stages. [Some instances of this are given in the paper.] If the attempt is made to carry the trance-condition beyond state B, the effect is either to bring the "subject" into an apparently deep sleep, in which he is incapable of answering, and probably of hearing; or to create such a desire for sleep, and aversion to being questioned, that he becomes more or less intractable. With one "subject" I have found that even the second stage, on one or two occasions, could not be obtained. But there are other cases where the course of the trance allows a distinct *third* stage of memory to manifest before unconsciousness sets in. The following instance will make this clear.

In state A, S——t was hypnotized; and the fact of his being in state A was ascertained by his remembering an incident previously told him when in that state—that a balloon had been seen passing over the King's Road—and forgetting two incidents previously told him when in state B—that an engine-boiler had burst at Brighton station, and that two large dogs had been having a fight in the Western Road. He was now told that a foreign flag had been seen floating over the Pavilion, and was then carried on into state B, when S. said, "People may well complain."

S——T.   "Yes."

S.   "Why?"

S——T.   "Why, the nuisance—those dogs fighting in the Western Road." (The idea proper to state B is revived.)

S.   "No, I meant about the flag."

S——T.   "What flag? There are plenty of flags about." (The idea proper to state A is forgotten.)

S.   "No, I meant that cart running away in Montpelier Road"—a new idea, which will belong henceforth to the B class.

S——T.   "What cart?" Then, scornfully, "Cart running away! It's the horse that runs away."

He was then informed more particularly that a horse with a cart had bolted in Montpelier Road; and the deepening passes were continued.

S.   "So they found it bottom upwards."

There was no answer; the "subject" had lapsed into sleep. He was called by name, and a few reverse passes were made, when he woke with an "Eh?"

S.   "They found it bottom upwards."

S——T.   "What? When?"

S.   "A boat, I mean." He was then told that a very high tide had washed away a boat on the beach; but that after a time it had drifted ashore. This idea was suggested in what proved to be a separate and third stage, C, when he was on the very verge of lapsing into unconsciousness; and he did lapse immediately afterwards. He was roused, and S. said, "That's the effect of not tying it securely." S——t's answers now showed that the rousing had carried him over stage C, and that he was once more in stage B. He said, "Tied? They never tie them."

S.   "No wonder it was washed away then."

S——T.   "Washed away! Did it go over the cliff?"

S.   "No; what do you mean?"

S——T.   "That horse and cart you were talking about."

Here, then, was the stage B idea, the boat of stage C being forgotten. It remained to ascertain that what I have called stage C was not identical with stage A—that there had been a real progression beyond stage B, and not a mere oscillation between the A and B states. Accordingly, some reverse passes were made, with the view of bringing the subject into the A state; and S. said, "I dare say it will get knocked about on the beach."

S——T.   "What knocked about?"

S.   "What I was telling you about."

S——T.   "Why, have they taken it on the beach now, then?"

S.   "It *was* on the beach."

S——T.   "Why, you said it was on the Pavilion."

S.   "What do you mean?"

S——T.   "That large flag."

Here, then, was the stage A idea, and the memory of the boat of stage C proved as unrevivable as it had been in stage B. S——t was now carried down without pause into the state of deep sleep—the most certain way of lighting on stage C being to go beyond it in this way, and then to revive the "subject" just enough to enable him to understand and answer. He was called by name several times, and a few reverse passes were made before he answered, "Eh? what?" S. replied in words which would apply equally to carts or boats; but, as I expected, they were understood as applying to *boats*—the stage C idea.

S.   "Is it customary to tie them?"

S——T. "Yes."

S. "I thought you said it wasn't." (He had said before that it was not customary to tie *carts*.)

S——T. "Oh yes; sometimes they tie them to capstans, sometimes to larger vessels."

He was now questioned about the cart, but had no remembrance of it; also about the dog fight (which, the reader will recall, was another stage B idea), with the same result. Some upward passes were now made, and S. said, "Did you say they tie them to a capstan?"

S——T. "No; they throw the reins loose over the horse's back."

S. "A lot of people saw it coming down."

S——T. "What, the horse and cart?"

Here is evidently the reappearance of stage B; and proceeding again on the upward or lightening course, we found the A idea, the flag on the Pavilion, duly remembered. This was on February 28th. On March 2nd the same process was briefly repeated, and it was found that the subject still remembered each of the topics already mentioned when its appropriate stage was reached, and at that stage alone. §

The later experiments of Mrs. Sidgwick on the same subject, in which eight or nine distinct trains of memory were found—each recurring when the corresponding stage of depth of the trance was reached—seem to show conclusively that the number may vary almost indefinitely. Gurney's experiments, quoted above, on stages of memory in the hypnotic trance were several times repeated by Mrs. Sidgwick and Miss Johnson in the course of their experiments on thought-transference with hypnotized subjects at Brighton, the hypnotizer being again Mr. G. A. Smith. Miss Johnson informs me that it was generally found possible to obtain three stages; but the memories did not always remain distinct. Thus one subject who kept the recollections of the three stages distinct one day, when re-hypnotized on the next day, succeeded with some effort in remembering the topics belonging to *all three* stages of the day before, and these recollections persisted through the three stages induced on this day, although the fresh topics suggested for each of these stages remained distinct. This probably indicates that there is a stratum of consciousness in which all the recollections are retained.

The most interesting experiments, however, occurred with another subject, T., who on one occasion exhibited *eight* different stages with distinct memories.

It must be understood that the test of distinctness of these memories does not consist in each statement made to the subject being forgotten as each deeper stage of hypnosis (produced by downward passes) was reached—which might be due merely to a general forgetfulness or inattention—but in the spontaneous recrudescence of each memory in its corresponding stage when the operation was reversed and a lighter and lighter stage continually produced by upward passes.

The following account of the occasion referred to is written by Miss Johnson, from her notes taken at the time, July 9th, 1891. The only other persons present were Mrs. Sidgwick, Mr. Smith, and T.

§ T. was hypnotized by Mr. Smith, and told that Mrs. Sidgwick was going to talk to him—Mr. Smith meanwhile, at the intervals between her statements, making passes over him—downwards or upwards, according to whether it was desired to make the hypnotic state more or less deep—but saying nothing.

Stage A.   Mrs. Sidgwick told T. that the Hotel Métropole had been burnt down that afternoon; all the people had escaped, but great damage had been done.

[After downward passes] *Stage B.*   T. told that the coach was upset coming into Brighton—the Comet—one or two people were rather hurt; the horses ran away, and turning round a corner too quickly upset the coach.

[After downward passes] *Stage C.*   Told that the Emperor of Germany had to go back to Germany tomorrow, on account of the death of one of his relations.

[After downward passes] *Stage D.*   T., in answer to a question whether he remembered anything, said he only remembered that Mr. Smith had said Mrs. Sidgwick was going to talk to him; he could not remember that she had said anything.

He was then told that there had been a railway accident on the Brighton line near Hayward's Heath—a bad accident—the train had run off the line. He remarked that it was probably a false report.

[After downward passes] *Stage E.*   T. was told that the lights went out at the theatre last night and everything was left in darkness, but it only lasted for a few moments.

[After downward passes] *Stage F.*   He was told that the key of the theatre door had been lost and no one could get in for a long time; the people were all kept waiting outside.

He seemed rather drowsy, expressed no interest in what he was told, and only spoke in answer to questions as briefly as possible. Mrs. Sidgwick asked him once or twice what she had been telling him; at last he said sleepily, "Key lost."

[After upward passes] *Return of Stage E.* In answer to the question what he had been told, he replied that the lights went out at the theatre.

[After downward passes] *Stage F.* In answer to the same question, replied that the key had been lost.

[After downward passes] *Stage G.* He was told that two goat carriages racing along the front had run into one another, and were smashed. He seemed still more drowsy, and could hardly be got by questions to repeat this story.

[After downward passes] *Stage H.* He was told that Mr. Smith had been playing a guitar and all the strings broke at once. He repeated this story after being asked what Mrs. Sidgwick had said, and even volunteered the remark that Mr. Smith could get fresh strings.

[After downward passes] *Stage K.* Mrs. Sidgwick asked several times, "Can you hear me?" T. at last said, "Yes." Mrs. Sidgwick asked, "Do you think Mr. Smith will ever get that put right?" No answer, though the question was repeated many times. At length she said, "Mr. Smith dropped his watch into the sea." No answer or remark could be elicited from T.

[After upward passes] *Stage H.* In answer to the question what Mr. Smith had better do, T. replied, "Strings—I don't know anything about strings."

[After upward passes] *Stage G.* In answer to a similar vague question, he showed that he remembered about the goat carriages.

[After upward passes] *Stage F.* In answer to the question whether it was not funny, he replied, "What? the people standing outside and getting wet? No, that wasn't amusing."

[After upward passes] *Stage E.* He remarked, "Ask Mr. Smith who put the lights out—several fellows who were there never told me—funny thing." At this point he began to talk spontaneously in a lively way. (Mrs. Sidgwick notes: "I independently noted that it was at this stage he became comparatively lively, and I did not notice any special increase of liveliness afterwards.")

[After upward passes] *Stage D.* He said, "They'll have to pay a lot of money. But it was better than a bridge breaking down, or being in a tunnel."

[After upward passes] *Stage C.* T. remarked, "I suppose the Queen will be put out, but the papers say it's inconvenient to her his coming to England. You don't know who died?"

[After upward passes] *Stage B.* He said, "It's a sharp turn round that corner, if you come down that hill. The horses got frightened at the corner, I suppose. Coaching must be very nice." Further spontaneous remarks of the same kind followed, and when Mrs. Sidgwick asked him what else they were talking about besides that coach, he only repeated the coach story in detail and said he knew of nothing else.

[After upward passes] *Stage A.*   He said, "You'd think I might have heard of it—a fire at a large place like that."

After more upward passes T. awoke or very nearly awoke, opening his eyes. Mrs. Sidgwick asked him what they were talking about; he said he had an idea it was "Something about the Métropole; I was dreaming; I dreamt it was on fire or something."

He was rehypnotized almost at once; Mr. Smith made a good many downward passes, then woke him suddenly and asked if he could remember dreaming about anything. After making an effort to remember, he said he had a confused idea of Mr. Smith sitting in a fire, "Mr. Smith sitting here—three of you sitting here, and something about a fire." All the experimenters thought that this referred to the last time he had been awake, not to what he had been told during the previous hypnosis.

Mrs. Sidgwick revised Miss Johnson's notes immediately after the sitting, and added the following note of her own:

"The above notes give a brief account of T.'s answers, etc. . . . the questions put by Mrs. Sidgwick being generally omitted; but on each occasion going up the scale, the subject was started by her after the passes with questions carefully selected so as not to hint what subject he was expected to speak about. Going down the scale, she first asked a question which he might have answered in connection with the subject of the previous stage, and asked him whether he remembered nothing, then told him the new story.

"In going up, he always remembered the subject appropriate to that stage at once." §

We have already seen that in cases of alternating personalities the number of personalities similarly varies. The student who now follows or repeats Gurney's experiments, with the increased knowledge of split personalities which recent years have brought, cannot fail to be struck with the analogies between Gurney's artificial light and deep states, with their separate chains of memory, and those morbid alternating personalities, with their complex cleavages with which we dealt in Chapter Two. The hypnotic stages are in fact secondary or alternating personalities of very shallow type, but for that very reason all the better adapted for teaching us from what kinds of subliminal disaggregation the more serious splits in personality take their rise.

Hypnotic sleep is at once stable and responsive; strong in its resistance to such stimuli as it chooses to ignore; ready in its accessibility to such appeals as it chooses to answer.

Prick or pinch the hypnotized subject, and although some stratum of his personality may be aware, in some fashion, of your act, the sleep will generally remain unbroken. But if you speak to him, or even speak before him, then, however profound his apparent lethargy, there is something in him which will hear.

All this is true even of earlier stages of trance. Deeper still lies the stage of highest interest—that sleep-waking in which the subliminal self is at last set free, is at last able not only to receive but to respond; when it begins to tell us the secrets of the sleeping phase of personality, beginning with directions as to the conduct of the trance or of the cure, and going on to who knows what insight into who knows what world afar?

Even now it may not be without surprise that the reader finds described under *inhibition of attention* a phenomenon so considerable and so apparently independent as *hypnotic suppression of pain.* Yet this induced analgesia has from the first been one of the main triumphs of hypnotism. Among others:

The most rudimentary form of restraint or inhibition lies in our effort to preserve the infant or young child from acquiring what we call "bad tricks." These morbid affections of motor centers, trifling in their inception, will sometimes grow until they are incurable by any régime or medicament—nay, till an action so insignificant as sucking the thumb may work the ruin of a life.

Among these morbid tricks *kleptomania* has an interest of its own, on account of the frequent doubt whether it is not put forward as a mere excuse for pilfering. It may thus happen that the cure is the best proof of the existence of the disease.

Agoraphobia, which makes a man dread to cross an open space; and its converse, *claustrophobia,* which makes him shrink from sitting in a room with closed doors; or the still more distressing *mysophobia,* which makes him constantly uneasy lest he should have become dirty or defiled— for all these disorders, one may broadly say, hypnotic suggestion is the best and often the only cure. With other conditions hypnotic suggestion often deals in a curious way. The suggestion is not generally felt as a strengthening of the central will. It resembles rather a molecular redisposition; it leaves the patient indifferent to the stimulus, or even disgusted with it. The man for whom alcohol has combined the extremes of delight and terror now lives in a world in which alcohol does not exist at all. Excessive smoking has also been successfully treated by suggestion, and even for the slave of morphia the same sudden freedom is sometimes achieved.

I come now to the division of hypnotic achievement with which I next propose to deal—the influence, namely, of suggestion upon man's *perceptive* faculties—its power to educate his external organs of sense. This wide subject is almost untouched as yet; and there is no direction in which one could be more confident of interesting results from further experiment.

Two points may be mentioned first: Improvement of vision; and increased attention, as stimulated by suggestion, upon the power of hearing.

And the stimulating influence of hypnotism on *imagination* is perhaps the most conspicuous phenomenon which the whole subject offers. Everyone knows that a hypnotized subject is easily hallucinated—that if he is told to see a non-existent dog, he sees a dog—that if he is told *not* to see Mr. A., he sees everything in the room but Mr. A.

Another characteristic of these suggested hallucinations tells in exactly the same direction. It is possible to suggest no mere isolated picture —a black cat on the table, or the like—but a whole complex series of responses to circumstances not at the time predictable. This point is well illustrated by what are called "negative hallucinations" or "systematized anæsthesiæ." Suppose, for instance, that I tell a hypnotized subject that when he awakes there will be no one in the room with him but myself. He awakes and remembers nothing of this order, but sees me alone in the room. Other persons present endeavor to attract his attention in various ways. Sometimes he will be quite unconscious of their noises and movements; sometimes he will perceive them, but will explain them away, as due to other causes, in the same irrational manner as one might do in a dream. Or he may perceive them, be unable to explain them, and feel considerable terror until the "negative hallucination" is dissolved by a fresh word of command. It is plain, in fact, throughout, that some element in him is at work all the time in obedience to the suggestion given, is keeping him by ever fresh modifications of his illusion from discovering its unreality.

Another indication of the subliminal power at work to produce these hallucinations is their remarkable *range*—a range as wide, perhaps, as that over which therapeutic effects are obtainable by suggestion. The post-hypnotic hallucination may affect not sight and hearing alone (to which spontaneous hallucinations are in most cases confined), but all kinds of vaso-motor responses and organic sensations—the hypnotic subject will often sweat and shiver at your bidding as you transplant him from the Equator to frosty Caucasus.

Well, then, given this strength and vigor of hallucination, one sees a possible extension of knowledge in more than one direction. To begin with, by suggesting to the subject that he is feeling or doing something which is beyond his normal range of faculties, we may perhaps enable him to perceive or to act as thus suggested.

Here, as elsewhere, it is desirable to push as far as possible our inquiry into phenomena which may still count as normal, so as to see if any bridge or passage between normal and supernormal be anywhere indicated; and here, as elsewhere, we have to regret the lamentable scarcity of purely psychological experiments over the whole hypnotic field. We are habitually forced to base our psychological inferences on therapeutic practice; and in directions where there has been no therapeutic effort there are gaps in our knowledge, which those hypnotists who have good subjects at their disposal should be invited to fill up.

What we need is to address to a sensitive subject a series of strong suggestions of the increase of his sensory range and power. We must needs begin by suggesting hallucinatory sensations: the subject should be told that he perceives some stimulus which is too feeble for ordinary perception. If you can make him *think* that he perceives it, he probably will after a time perceive it; the direction given to his attention heightening either peripheral or central sensory faculty. You may then be able to attack the question as to how far his specialized end-organs are really concerned in the perception. It may then be possible to deal in a more fruitful way with those alleged cases of *transposition of senses* which have so great a theoretical interest as being apparently intermediate between hyperæsthesia (unusually keen sensation) and clairvoyance (perception at a distance). If we once admit (as I, of course, admit) the reality of clairvoyance, it is just in some such way as this that we should expect to find it beginning.

I start from the thesis that the perceptive power within us precedes and is independent of the specialized sense-organs, which it has developed for earthly use.

I conceive further that under certain circumstances this primary clairvoyant faculty resumes direct operations, in spite of the fleshly barriers which are constructed so as to allow it to operate through certain channels alone.

In this attitude of mind, then, I approach the recorded cases of transposition of special sense. Perhaps the best evidence for this is to be found in some experiments made by Professor Fontan of Toulon, and described in his paper on *Hystéro-épilepsie Masculine: Suggestion, Inhibition, Transposition des Sens*, in the *Revue Philosophique*, August, 1887. A full account of this is given in *Proceedings* S.P.R., vol. v. pp. 263–268; but I have space here for a short extract only.

§ The subject, B., is a sailor, aged twenty-two, apparently robust, but suffering from hysteria, with attacks of catalepsy. When he came under Dr. Fontan's care his left side was wholly devoid of feeling, and the sense of smell was absent on that side; sight and hearing diminished; taste normal. A hysterogenous *zone* on the right side remained unaffected by any treatment. Hypnotic suggestion suspended the anæsthesia for a few hours at a time, but the magnet, and the magnet only, removed it permanently, and practically cured the patient.

[Transpositions of hearing, taste and smell are next described.]

Transposition of sight is, of course, the most bewildering of these supernormalities. It was suggested to the subject that he could only see with his fingers, and the psychical blindness was reinforced by placing a screen close to the subject's face, so that he could not see his own hands, nor the objects offered, nor the faces or gestures of the bystanders.

Printed letters were first tried; and the subject, who could scarcely read in his normal state, deciphered a few of these with difficulty. A number of skeins of colored wool, which he had never seen, were then placed before him, and he was told to choose the red ones. He felt the wools, rejected unhesitatingly the colors not asked for, and arranged the red in a series. He did this also with the green and with the blue wools. The wools were again mixed, and he was told to put the red ones on the right, the green on the left. But he was now exhausted, and recognized nothing.

The same experiments were repeated next day with fresh specimens of wool. And next the room was completely darkened, B.'s hand was placed in a box containing various patterns of wool, which he had never either seen or touched, and he was told to choose the blue ones. "He seized them," says Dr. Fontan, in a letter rather more detailed than the printed account, "with such rapidity, such force, tossing aside all those which he did not want, that we supposed that the experiment had failed. Shut up in a dark room, where we could not see each other, we did not know what was going on, and fearing some access of frenzy, I precipitated myself on the subject and hypnotized him strongly, by pressing the globes of his eyes. He had had time enough during this scene, which did not last five seconds, to choose the wools, and to hide them in his bosom. At no other time did he show such eagerness for the suggested color." He had, in fact, selected four blue skeins, which he clutched so closely that he had to be altogether inhibited before they could be taken from him.

The next experiment was perhaps the best of all. The wools were placed on a table *under a strong sheet of glass*. B. (psychically blinded and with the screen interposed) placed his hand on the glass, and was ordered to indicate the red wool. He resisted for a time, but "ended by consenting to search for the red wools, whose position he indicated by a tap on the glass, which left no room for doubt." He repeated this process several times with the green, the blue, and the yellow wools, and always with complete success.

Once more. Five photographs, of which one only was of a child, were placed on the table, and he was told to find the child's photograph. "He felt the faces, turned them with head upwards, felt over the child's figure carefully, and gave the photograph to me correctly." §

We are now going on to suggestions more directly affecting central faculty, in which *highest-level* centers begin to be involved. For I want to prepare the reader for an intermediate stage in which high faculties are used, in obedience to suggestion, for purely capricious ends. I speak of *calculations* subliminally performed in the carrying out of post-hypnotic suggestions.

Dr. Milne Bramwell's experiments (to mention these as a sample of the rest) were post-hypnotic suggestions involving arithmetical calculations; the entranced subject, for instance, being told to make a cross when 20,180 minutes had elapsed from the moment of the order. Their primary importance lay in showing that a subliminal or hypnotic memory persisted across the intervening gulf of time and prompted obedience to the order when at last it fell due. But incidentally, it became clear that the subject, whose arithmetical capacity in common life was small, worked out these sums subliminally a good deal better than she could work them out by her normal waking intelligence.

Of course, all that was needed for such simple calculations was close attention to easy rules; but this was just what the waking mind was unable to give, at least without the help of pencil and paper. If we lay this long and careful experiment, concerned though it was with very easy problems, side by side with the accounts already given of the solution of problems in somnambulic states, which states were forgotten on waking, it seems clear that there is yet much to be done in the education of subliminal memory and acumen as a help to supraliminal work.

Important in this connection is an account by Dr. Dufay of help given by him to an actress in the representation of her *rôles* by hypnotization.

Now we come to the effects of suggestion on the vasomotor system. Simple effects of this type form the commonest of "platform experiments."

The mesmerist holds ammonia under his subject's nose, and tells him it is rose-water. The subject smells it eagerly, and his eyes do not water. The suggestion that the stinging vapor is inert has inhibited the vasomotor reflexes which would ordinarily follow, and which no ordinary effort of will could restrain. *Vice versâ*, when the subject smells rose-water, described as ammonia, he sneezes and his eyes water. These results, which his own will could not produce, follow on the mesmerist's word. No one who sees these simple tests applied can doubt the genuineness of the influence at work.

This delicate responsiveness of the vasomotor system has given rise to some curious spontaneous phenomena, and has suggested some experiments, which are probably as yet in their infancy. The main point of interest is that at this point spontaneous self-suggestion, and subsequently suggestion from without, have made a kind of first attempt at the modification of the human organism in what may be called fancy directions. I speak of the phenomenon commonly known as "stigmatization," from the fact that its earliest spontaneous manifestations were suggested by imaginations brooding on the stigmata of Christ's passion—the marks of wounds in hands and feet and side. This phenomenon, which was long treated both by *savants* and by devotees as though it must be either fraudulent or miraculous, is now found (like a good many other phenomena previously deemed subject to that dilemma) to enter readily within the widening circuit of natural law. Stigmatization is, in fact, a form of vesication; and suggested vesication—with the quasi-burns and real blisters which obediently appear in any place and pattern that is ordered—is a high development of that same vasomotor plasticity of which the ammonia-rose-water experiment was an early example.

The best known and in some respects best observed modern case of stigmatization is that of Louise Lateau. The facts are now thoroughly established and generally accepted by physiologists, and, from the point of view of this book, they fall naturally enough among subliminal responses to self-suggestion. They have an interesting bearing, too, on mediæval traditions of stigmatization in St. Francis of Assisi and others.

§   Louise Lateau of Bois d'Haine, Hainault, Belgium ... had good health up to the age of seventeen, was accustomed to hard work, ... was noted for her common sense and power of self-control, and bore a good character with all her neighbors and acquaintances, showing no traces, either physical or moral, of any hysterical tendencies.

An illness of indefinite character, involving intense neuralgic pains, began in 1867 and lasted for months. In April, 1868 she was thought to be dying, and received the Sacrament. From that day she rapidly improved. Three days later the stigmata first appeared, and thirteen weeks later she began to exhibit the phenomena of ecstasy. Blood began issuing from certain locations on her skin every Friday—on the back and palm of each hand, on the dorsum and sole of each foot, on the forehead, and on the chest. The bleeding usually lasted twenty-four hours.

It was the religious authorities who requested Dr. Lefebvre, an eminent Louvain specialist in nervous diseases, to undertake the examination of the case. She was under his superintendence from August 30th, 1868, for twenty weeks, during which time he took more than a hundred medical friends to examine the phenomena. §

The chief authority for this case is Dr. Lefebvre's report, *Louise Lateau de Bois d'Haine: sa Vie, ses Extases, ses Stigmates* (Louvain, 1870). Dr. Warlomont examined her six years later, and found that the places of the stigmata had become continuously painful, and that there was an additional stigma on the right shoulder.

Three cases of the production of cruciform marks by hypnotism reported by Dr. M. H. Biggs, of Lima, appeared in the *Journal* S.P.R., vol. iii. p. 100, and I quote one of them

§ ... Another case was the first of this kind of experiment that I tried; it was in Santa Barbara, California. I was staying there in 1879 with a friend, Mr. G., a long-resident chemist in that town. His wife had a kind of half servant and half companion, a girl of about eighteen, who complained to me one day of a pain through her chest. Without her knowing what I intended to do, I tried magnetism; she fell into a deep magnetic sleep in a few minutes. With this subject I tried many interesting experiments, which I will pass over. One day I magnetized her as usual, and told her, "You will have a red cross appear on the upper part of your chest, only on every Friday. In the course of some time the words *Sancta* above the cross, and *Crucis* underneath it will appear also; at same time a little blood will come from the cross." In my vest pocket I had a cross of rock crystal. I opened the top button of her dress and placed this cross on the upper part of the manubrium, a point she could not see unless by aid of a looking-glass, saying to her, "*This* is the spot where the cross will appear." This was on a Tuesday. When Friday came I said, after breakfast, "Come, let me magnetize you a little; you have not had a dose for several days." She was always willing to be magnetized, as she always expressed herself as feeling very much rested and comfortable afterwards. In a few minutes she was in a deep sleep. I unbuttoned the top part of her dress, and there, to my complete and utter astonishment, was a pink cross, exactly over the place where I had put the one of crystal. It appeared every Friday, and was invisible on all other days. This was seen by Mr. and Mrs. G., and my old friend and colleague, Dr. B., who had become much interested in my experiments in magnetism, and often suggested the class of experiments he wished to see tried. . . .

[Part of the letter "S" once appeared but the full words *Sancta* and *Crucis* never did.] §

Even though we have not gone into the influence of suggestion on *character,* and many other important aspects of this multifaceted subject, still the case for hypnotism is now fairly complete; and this chapter might here draw to a close.

The reader, however, knows that my initial promise would not in reality be thus fulfilled. My own definition of sleep was of much wider scope. I believe that during sleep the subliminal self has other functions beyond the recuperation of the organism. Those other functions are concerned in some unknown way with the spiritual world; and the indication of their exercise is given by the sporadic occurrence, in the sleeping phase, of supernormal phenomena. Such phenomena, as we shall presently see, occur also at various points in hypnotic practice. To them we must now turn, if our account of the phenomena of induced somnambulism is to be complete.

Yet here, in order to give completeness to our intended review, we shall need a certain apparent extension of the scope of this chapter. We shall need to consider a group of cases which might have been introduced at various points in our scheme, but which are perhaps richest in their illustrations of the supernormal phenomena of hypnotism.

The evidence for *telepathy*—for psychical influence from a distance— has grown to goodly proportions, for a new form of experiment has been found possible from which the influence of suggestion can be entirely excluded. It has now, as I shall presently try to show, been actually proved that the hypnotic trance can be induced from a distance so great, and with precautions so complete, that telepathy or some similar supernormal influence is the only efficient cause which can be conceived.

I had the good fortune to take a part in one of the best of a series of experiments in this "telepathic hypnotism." These experiments are not easy to manage, since it is essential at once to prevent the subject from suspecting that the experiment is being tried, and also to provide for his safety in the event of its success. In Dr. Gibert's experiment, for instance, it was a responsible matter to bring this elderly woman in her dream-like state through the streets of Havre. It was needful to provide her with an unnoticed escort; and, in fact, several persons had to devote themselves for some hours to a single experiment.

The subject of these experiments in telepathic hypnotization was Professor Pierre Janet's well-known subject, Madame B. ("Léonie"), and the first experiments were carried out with her at Havre, by Professor Janet and Dr. Gibert, a leading physician there, and described in the *Bulletins de la Société de Psychologie Physiologique,* Tome I., p. 24, and in the *Revue Philosophique,* August, 1886. I summarize those relating to hypnotization at a distance.

§ *October* 3, 1885.—M. Gibert tries to put her to sleep from distance of half a mile; M. Janet finds her awake; puts her to sleep; she says, "I know very well that M. Gibert tried to put me to sleep, but when I felt him I looked for some water, and put my hands in cold water. I don't want people to put me to sleep in that way; it puts me out, and makes me look silly." She had, in fact, held her hands in water at the time when M. Gibert willed her to sleep.

October 9.—M. Gibert succeeds in a similar attempt; she says in trance, "Why does M. Gibert put me to sleep from his house? I had not time to put my hands in my basin." ... §

I give next extracts from my own notes of experiments, April 20th to 24th, 1886, taken at the time in conjunction with my brother, Dr. A. T. Myers, and forming the bulk of a paper presented to the Société de Psychologie Physiologique on May 24th (also published in *Proceedings* S.P.R., vol. iv. pp. 131–37).

Dr. A. T. Myers was present at the experiments throughout. Other observers were Dr. Gibert, Professor Paul Janet, Professor Pierre Janet, Dr. Jules Janet, Dr. Ochorowicz, and M. Marillier.

§ In order that the phenomenon of *sommeil à distance* may be satisfactory, we have to guard against three possible sources of error, namely, fraud, accidental coincidence, and suggestion by word or gesture.

The hypothesis of *fraud* on the part of operators or subject may here be set aside. The operators were Dr. Gibert and Professor Pierre Janet, and the detailed observations of Professor Pierre Janet, elsewhere published, sufficiently prove the genuineness of Madame B.'s somnambulic sleep.

The hypothesis of *accidental coincidence* would be tenable, though not probable, did the events of April 20th to 24th constitute the whole of the observed series. But the number of coincidences noticed by Dr. Gibert, Professor Janet, and others has been so large that the action of mere chance seems to be quite excluded. This, however, brings us to the third source of doubt, whether the sleep may not on *all* occasions have been induced by some *suggestion,* given perhaps unconsciously, by word or gesture. It was thus that I was at first inclined to explain the first two cases [not given], but the other cases here given seem to negative the supposition. . . .

On the morning of the 22nd, . . . we . . . selected by lot an hour (11 A.M.) at which M. Gibert should will, from his dispensary, which is close to his house, that Madame B. should go to sleep in the Pavillon. It was agreed that a rather longer time should be allowed for the process to take effect, as it had been observed that she sometimes struggled against the influence, and averted the effect for a time by putting her hands in cold water, etc. At 11:25 we entered the Pavillon quietly, and almost at once she descended from her room to the *salon,* profoundly asleep. Here, however, suggestion might again have been at work.

In the evening (22nd) we all dined at M. Gibert's, and in the evening M. Gibert made another attempt to put her to sleep at a distance from his house in the Rue Séry—she being at the Pavillon, Rue de la Ferme—and to bring her to his house by an effort of will. At 8:55 he retired to his study, and MM. Ochorowicz, Marillier, Janet, and A. T. Myers went to the Pavillon, and waited outside in the street, out of sight of the house. At 9:22 Dr. Myers observed Madame B. coming half-way out of the garden-gate, and again retreating. Those who saw her more closely observed that she was plainly in the somnambulic state, and was wandering about and muttering. At 9:25 she came out (with eyes persistently closed, so far as could be seen), walked quickly past MM. Janet and Marillier, without noticing them, and made for M. Gibert's house, though not by the usual or shortest route. She avoided lamp-posts, vehicles, etc., but crossed and recrossed the street repeatedly. No one went in front of her or spoke to her. After eight or ten minutes she grew much more uncertain in gait, and paused as though she would fall. Dr. Myers noted the moment in the Rue Faure; it was 9:35. At about 9:40 she grew bolder, and at 9:55 reached the street in front of M. Gibert's house. There she met him, but did not notice him, and walked into his house, where she rushed from room to room. M. Gibert had to take her hand before she recognized him. She then grew calm.

M. Gibert said that from 8:55 to 9:20 he thought intently about her, from 9:20 to 9:35 he thought more feebly; at 9:35 he gave the experiment up, and began to play billiards; but in a few minutes began to will her again. It appeared that his visit to the billiard-room had coincided with her hesitation and stumbling in the street. But this coincidence may of course have been accidental. . . . §

With regard to the cases next to be quoted, it must be observed that when the operator is within sight or hearing of the subject, either the production of hypnosis by mental suggestion alone, or its prevention by "silent willing" while ostensibly trying to produce it, is inconclusive as evidence of telepathy. The subject, having been previously hypnotized by the operator, must be assumed to be familiar—subliminally at least—with his particular habits of unconscious physical expression in connection with hypnotization, so that the slight unconscious indications of his intentions that would perhaps escape the notice of the ordinary bystanders might very likely be perceived by the subject.

The same objection cannot, of course, apply to the instances of hypnotization at a distance by the same experimenters.

The following account, contributed by Dr. E. Gley, of 37 Rue Claude Bernard, Paris, is a record of some observations of his friend, Dr. Dusart, published in the *Tribune Médicale,* in May, 1875.

§ The "subject" was a hysterical girl of fourteen, whom Dr. Dusart found very susceptible to hypnotism. He early remarked that his passes were ineffective if his attention was not strongly directed to the desired result; and this suggested to him to try the effect of purely mental suggestion. One day, before the usual hour for waking the patient had arrived, he gave her the mental command to awake. The effect was instantaneous: the patient woke, and again, in accordance with his will, began her hysterical screaming. He took a seat with his back to her, and conversed with other persons, without appearing to pay any attention to her; but on his silently giving her the mental suggestion to fall again into the trance, his will was again obeyed. More than one hundred experiments of the sort were made under various conditions, and with uniform success. On one occasion Dr. Dusart left without giving his usual order to the patient to sleep till a particular hour next morning. Remembering the omission, he gave the order mentally, when at a distance of 700 metres from the house. On arriving next morning at 7:30 he found the patient asleep, and asked her the reason. She replied that she was obeying his order. He said: "You are wrong; I left without giving you any order." "True," she said, "but five minutes afterwards I clearly heard you tell me to sleep till eight o'clock." Dr. Dusart then told the patient to sleep till she received the command to wake, and directed her parents to mark the exact hour of her waking. At 2 P.M. he gave the order mentally, at a distance of seven kilometres, and found that it had been punctually obeyed. This experiment was successfully repeated several times, at different hours.

After a time Dr. Dusart discontinued his visits, and the girl's father used to hypnotize her instead. Nearly a fortnight after this change it occurred to Dr. Dusart, when at a distance of ten kilometres, to try whether he still retained his power, and he willed that the patient should not allow herself to be entranced; then after half-an-hour, thinking that the effect might be bad for her, he removed the prohibition. Early next morning he was surprised to receive a letter from the father, stating that on the previous day he had only succeeded in hypnotizing his daughter after a prolonged and painful struggle; and that, when entranced, she had declared that her resistance had been due to Dr. Dusart's command, and that she had only succumbed when he permitted her. §

The next case is quoted from Dr. Dufay's paper already referred to (*Proceedings* S.P.R., vol. vi. p. 411). The author's caution in interpreting the phenomena adds to the value of his observations.

§ ... Madame C. was thirty-five years of age, of a nervous temperament, and slightly rheumatic. For some time she had been subject to periodical attacks of headache and sickness, which the usual remedies had failed to relieve. Under these circumstances, I did not hesitate to try the effect of magnetism on my first visit to her. At the end of five minutes the pain passed off and the sickness ceased, and on every subsequent occasion the same thing took place. If my arrival was delayed the troubles continued; but hardly had I pulled the bell, and before the door was opened, Madame C. fell into a calm sleep. It was quite a different thing if any one else rang the bell, for then the invalid complained bitterly of the noise that was splitting her head.

Later on she even felt my approach from the further end of the street: "Ah! what happiness!" she would say, "here is the doctor coming, I feel myself cured!" and Monsieur C. would open the window to make certain of it, and would see me in the distance. And his wife never made a mistake. Sometimes he would try to encourage her by telling her that he saw me coming, but she knew that this was not true, and the sickness continued.

In a case of this sort, how could I hesitate to make an attempt at influencing her from a distance? Moreover, I was driven to it by circumstances. At the height of an attack Monsieur C., who had already been twice to fetch me, discovered where I was to be found. Being with a patient whom I could not leave for several hours, I assured Monsieur C., without being at all certain of it myself, that his wife would be asleep and cured when he got home again. I had the satisfaction of verifying this three hours later, when I ordered a profound sleep to last till the following day, which repaired the fatigues of the morning. "Thus the possibility of magnetizing at a distance is not to be doubted," say my notes. But nowadays the objection of self-suggestion presents itself: I was expected; Monsieur C. had promised to bring me with him.

Am I going to find a more convincing example? Yes, certainly. It was, however, an act of simple curiosity without any therapeutic aim. Madame C. was in perfect health, but her name happening to be mentioned in my hearing, the idea struck me that I would mentally order her to sleep, without her wishing it this time, and also without her suspecting it. Then, an hour later I went to her house and asked the servant who opened the door whether an instrument, which I had mislaid out of my case, had been found in Madame C.'s room.

"Is not that the doctor's voice that I hear?" asked Monsieur C. from the top of the staircase; "beg him to come up. Just imagine," he says to me, "I was going to send for you. Nearly an hour ago my wife lost consciousness, and her mother and I have not been able to bring her to her senses. Her mother, who wished to take her into the country, is distracted. . . ."

I did not dare to confess myself guilty of this catastrophe, but was betrayed by Madam C., who gave me her hand, saying, "You did well to put me to sleep, Doctor, because I was going to allow myself to be taken away, and then I should not have been able to finish my embroidery."

To conclude, I was about to take a holiday of six weeks, and should thus be absent when one of the attacks was due. So it was settled between M. C. and myself that, as soon as the headache began, he should let me know by telegraph; that I should then do from afar off what succeeded so well near at hand; that after five or six hours I should endeavor to awaken the patient, and that M. C. should let me know by means of a second telegram whether the result had been satisfactory. He had no doubt about it; I was less certain. Madame C. did not know that I was going away.

The sound of moanings one morning announced to M. C. that the moment had come; without entering his wife's room he ran to the telegraph office, and I received his message at ten o'clock. He returned home again at that same hour, and found his wife asleep and not suffering any more. At four o'clock I willed that she should wake, and at eight o'clock in the evening I received a second telegram: "Satisfactory result, woke at four o'clock. Thanks."

And I was then in the neighborhood of Sully-sur-Loire, 28 leagues— 112 kilometres—from Blois. . . . §

And here at last we arrive at what is in reality the most interesting group of inquiries connected with the hypnotic trance.

We have just seen that the subliminal state of the hypnotized subject may be approached by ways subtler than mere verbal suggestion—by telepathic impacts and perhaps by some kindred supernormal type. We have now to trace the supernormal elements in the hypnotic *response.* Whether those elements are most readily excited by a directly subliminal appeal, or whether they depend mainly on the special powers innate in the hypnotized person, we can as yet but imperfectly guess. We can be pretty sure, at any rate, that they are not often evoked in answer to any rapid and perfunctory hypnotic suggestion; they do not spring up in miscellaneous hospital practice; they need an education and a development which is hardly bestowed on one hypnotized subject in a hundred. The first stage of this response lies in a subliminal relation established between the subject and his hypnotizer, and manifesting itself in what is called *rapport,* or in *community of sensation.* The earlier stages of *rapport*—conditions when the subject apparently hears or feels the hypnotizer only, and so forth—arise probably from mere self-suggestion or from the suggestions of the operator causing the conscious attention of the subject to be exclusively directed to him. Indications of the possible development of a real link between the two persons may rather be found in the cases where there is provable community of sensation—the hypnotized subject tasting or feeling what the hypnotizer (unknown to the subject) does actually at that moment taste or feel. Of this there was *much* evidence in the palmy days of Esdaile and Elliotson, when psychological experiment was pursued regardless of time or trouble; there is *some* evidence of our own recent collecting; and there will be, I venture to say, *far more* evidence so soon as the study of hypnotism devolves upon the psychologist without therefore being deserted by the physician. It must be observed, however, that in experiments of this kind with hypnotized persons, the hypnotist was generally—if not invariably—the only person who attempted to play the part of agent, so that the evidence of a special relation between him and his subject is inconclusive.

Experiments in "community of sensation" were made by the "Committee on Mesmerism" of the S.P.R. first in 1883. The first series (see *Proceedings* S.P.R., vol. i. pp. 224–27) were carried out with a boy named Wells, who was blindfolded and hypnotized by Mr. G. A. Smith. Out of twenty-four experiments in the transference of pains, the exact spot was correctly indicated by the subject twenty times.

On September 10th, 1883, Gurney made further experiments in the transference of pains and tastes with another subject, Conway. His account of them is as follows (see *Proceedings* S.P.R., vol. ii. p. 17).

§ Conway sat with his eyes closed, in a tolerably deep trance. Mr. Smith and I stood behind him, without contact, and Mr. Smith preserved absolute silence. I from time to time asked Conway whether he felt anything, but of course gave no guiding hint or indication of whether he was right or wrong.

I pinched Mr. Smith's right upper arm. Conway at once showed signs of pain, rubbed his right hand, then passed his left hand up to his right shoulder, and finally localized the exact spot.

I silently changed to Mr. Smith's *left* arm. In a very few seconds Conway's right hand flew to the corresponding place on his own left arm, and he rubbed it, uttering strong complaints.

I nipped the lobe of Mr. Smith's right ear. Conway first rubbed the right side of his neck close to his ear; he then complained of his right leg, and used threats. I then gave a severe nip to his *own* right ear, and he made no sign of any sort. He then rubbed close to the left ear, and finally localized the spot on that ear exactly corresponding to the place touched on Mr. Smith's right ear.

I now pinched the right side of Mr. Smith's right thigh. Conway, without receiving any hint that he was expected to feel anything, immediately began to rub the corresponding part of his *left* leg.

Mr. Smith now put a succession of substances into his mouth, according to my indications, still keeping behind Conway, and preserving total silence. I kept Conway's attention alive by asking him from time to time what the taste was like, but gave not the faintest guidance, except in the single case of cloves, when—to see if Conway would take a hint—I asked if it tasted like spice, and he said it did not.

Mustard.—"Something bitter." "It's rather warm."

Cloves.—"Some sort of fruit." "Mixed with spirits of wine." "Not like spice." "Tastes warm."

Bitter Aloes.—"Not nice." "Bitter and hot." "Sort of harshness." "Not sweet." (I had suggested that it was sweet.) "Not nice." "Frightful stuff." "Hurt your throat when you swallow it." "Bitterness and saltiness about it."

Sugar.—"It's getting better." "Sweetish taste." "Sweet." "Something approaching sugar."

Powdered Alum.—"Fills your mouth with water." "Precious hot." "Some stuff from a chemist's shop, that they put in medicine." "Leaves a brackish taste." "Makes your mouth water." "Something after the style of alum."

Cayenne Pepper.—Conway showed strong signs of distress. "Oh! you call it good, do you?" "Oh! give us something to rinse that down." "Draws your mouth all manner of shapes." "Bitter and acid, frightful." "You've got some Cayenne down my throat, I know." Renewed signs of pain and entreaties for water.

The subject was now waked. He immediately said, "What's this I've got in my mouth?" "Something precious hot." "Something much hotter than ginger." "Pepper and ginger." §

Further experiments of the same kind with the same subject, made by Gurney and Dr. A. T. Myers, are recorded in *Proceedings,* vol. ii. pp. 205–206.

The following case is quoted from Mrs. Sidgwick's paper "On the Evidence for Clairvoyance" in *Proceedings* S.P.R., vol. vii. pp. 30–99. It is one of a group of four cases given by Mrs. Sidgwick, which were observed by Mr. A. W. Dobbie, of Gawler Place, Adelaide, South Australia, with various hypnotic subjects of his own. Mr. Dobbie had at that time practiced hypnotism for ten or twelve years, chiefly with a view to alleviating suffering, and out of some five hundred subjects, had come across a few who seemed capable of clairvoyance. Mrs. Sidgwick made his acquaintance and talked over his cases with him during a visit of his to England in 1889. The account quoted here is a copy, Mr. Dobbie informed us, of the notes he "wrote down the moment the words were uttered."

§ Striking case of clairvoyance, which occurred May 28th, 1886, in the presence of the Hon. Dr. Campbell, M.L.C., Hon. David Murray, M.L.C., and Chief Secretary of South Australia, Mr. Lyall, and Mr. Fleming, solicitor:

The circumstances are briefly as follows, viz.: Dr. Campbell, being present at one of my usual clairvoyant evenings, handed me a gold sleeve-link, at the same time telling me that he had lost the fellow one to it, but had no idea as to what had become of it; he asked me to give the remaining one to one of my clairvoyants, and see if they could find the missing one. I should state that neither of the clairvoyants had ever seen either of the rooms they referred to, nor did they know the names of the children, or anything in connection with this case, so that it is either a case of genuine clairvoyance or else a most remarkable case of thought-reading.

I first handed the sleeve-link to the younger of the two sisters [Misses Eliza and Martha Dixon], who is not so lucid as her sister.

Miss Martha began by first accurately describing Dr. Campbell's features, then spoke of a little fair-haired boy who had a stud, or sleeve-link, in his hand, also of a lady calling him "Neil"; then said that this little boy had taken the link into a place like a nursery where there were some toys, especially a large toy elephant, and that he had dropped the link into this elephant through a hole which had been torn or knocked in the breast; also that he had taken it out again, and gave two or three other interesting particulars. We were reluctantly compelled to postpone further investigation until two or three evenings afterwards.

On the next occasion (in the interval, however, the missing sleeve-link had been found, but left untouched), I again placed the link in her hand, and the previous particulars were at once reproduced; but as she seemed to be getting on very slowly, it occurred to Dr. Campbell to suggest placing his hand on that of the clairvoyant, so I placed him *en rapport* and allowed him to do so, he simply touching the back of her hand with the points of his fingers. As she still seemed to have great difficulty (she is always much slower than her sister) in proceeding, it suddenly occurred to me that it would be an interesting experiment to place Miss Eliza Dixon *en rapport* with Miss Martha, so I simply joined their disengaged hands, and Miss Eliza immediately commenced as follows, viz.:

"I'm in a house, upstairs, I was in a bathroom, then I went into another room nearly opposite, there is a large mirror just inside the door on the left hand, there is a double-sized dressing-table with drawers down each side of it, the sleeve-link is in the corner of the drawer nearest the door. When they found it they left it there. I know why they left it there, it was because they wanted to see if we would find it. I can see a nice easy chair there, it is an old one, I would like it when I am put to sleep, because it is nice and low. The bed has curtains, they are a sort of brownish net and have a fringe of darker brown. The wall paper is of a light blue color. There is a cane lounge there and a pretty Japanese screen behind it, the screen folds up. There is a portrait of an old gentleman over the mantelpiece, he is dead, I knew him when he was alive, his name is the same as the gentleman who acts as Governor when the Governor is absent from the colony, I will tell you his name directly—it is the Rev. Mr. Way. It was a little boy who put the sleeve-link in that drawer, he is very fair, his hair is almost white, he is a pretty little boy, he has blue eyes, and about three years old. The link had been left on that table, the little boy was in the nursery, and he went into the bedroom after the gentleman had left. I can see who the gentleman is, it is Dr. Campbell. Doesn't that little boy look a young Turk, the link is quite a handful for his little hand, he is running about with it very pleased; but he doesn't seem to know what to do with it." . . .

"Now I can hear some one calling up the stairs, a lady is calling two names, Colin is one and Neil is the other, the other boy is about five years old and is darker than the other. The eldest, Colin, is going downstairs now, he is gone into what looks like a dining-room, the lady says, 'Where is Neil?' 'Upstairs, ma.' 'Go and tell him to come down at once.' The little fair-haired boy had put the link down; but when he heard his brother coming up he picked it up again. Colin says, 'Neil, you are to come down at once.' 'I won't,' says Neil. 'You're a goose,' replies Colin, and he turned and went down without Neil. What a young monkey! now he has gone into the nursery and put the link into a large toy elephant, he put it through a hole in front, which is broken. He has gone downstairs now, I suppose he thinks it is safe there.

"Now that gentleman has come into the room again and he wants that link; he is looking all about for it, he thinks it might be knocked down; the lady is there now too, and they are both looking for it. The lady says, 'Are you sure you put it there?' The gentleman says, 'Yes.'

"Now it seems like next day, the servant is turning the carpet up and looking all about for it; but can't find it.

"The gentleman is asking that young Turk if he has seen it, he knows that he is fond of pretty things. The little boy says 'No.' He seems to think it is fine fun to serve his father like that.

"Now it seems to be another day, and the little boy is in the nursery again, he has taken the link out of the elephant, now he has dropped it into that drawer, that is all I have to tell you about it, I told you the rest before."

[Dr. Campbell adds that:]

Every circumstance reported is absolutely correct. I know that neither of the clairvoyants has ever been inside of my door. My children are utterly unknown to them, either in appearance or by name. I may say also that they had no knowledge of my intention to place the link in their possession, or even of my presence at the séance, as they were both on each occasion in the mesmeric sleep when I arrived.

ALLAN CAMPBELL §

In Mrs. Sidgwick's paper "On the Evidence for Clairvoyance" in *Proceedings* S.P.R., vol. vii. pp. 30–99, an account is given of several striking cases of "travelling clairvoyance" on the part of a woman there called Jane, the wife of a Durham pitman (*op. cit.* pp. 53–62 and 82–94). She was hypnotized at intervals for many years from 1845 onwards, for the sake of her health, and used then to ask to "travel"—that is, to be guided by suggestion to places which she should clairvoyantly visit. The main evidence about her is contained in the contemporaneous notes of a Dr. F., which, however, do not appear to have been made before the truth of her statements was verified. I quote an extract from these notes.

§ I told a patient of my own, Mr. Eglinton, at present residing in the village of Tynemouth, that I intended to visit him [via the clairvoyant]. He stated that he would be present between 8 and 10 P.M. in a particular

room, so that there might be no difficulty in finding him. He was just recovering from a very severe illness, and was so weak that he could scarcely
walk. He was exceedingly thin from the effects of his complaint.

After the usual state had been obtained, I said, "We are standing beside
a railway station, now we pass along a road, and in front of us see a house
with a laburnum tree in front of it." She directly replied, "Is it the red
house with a brass knocker?" I said, "No, it has an iron knocker." I have
since looked, however, and find that the door has an old-fashioned brass
handle in the shape of a knocker. . . . [They moved along through the
house to the room where he thought Mr. Eglinton would be.]

After a little she described the door opening, and asked with a tone of
great surprise, "Is that a gentleman?" I replied, "Yes; is he thin or fat?"
"Very fat," she answered; "but has he a cork leg?" I told her that he had
no cork leg, and tried to puzzle her again about him. She, however, assured
me that he was very fat and had a great corporation. She also described him
as sitting by the table with papers beside him, and a glass of brandy and
water. "Is it not wine?" I asked. "No," she said, "it's brandy." "Is it not
whisky or rum?" "No, it is brandy," was the answer; "and now," she continued, "the lady is going to get her supper, but the fat gentleman does not
take any." I requested her to tell me the color of his hair, but she only
answered that the lady's hair was dark. I then inquired if he had any brains
in his head, but she seemed altogether puzzled about him, and said she
could not see any. I then asked her if she could see his name upon any of
the letters lying about. She replied, "Yes;" and upon my saying that the
name began with E, she spelt each letter of the name "Eglinton."

I was so convinced that I had at last detected her in a complete mistake
that I arose, and declined proceeding further in the matter, stating that, although her description of the house and the name of the person were correct, in everything connected with the gentleman she had guessed the opposite from the truth.

On the following morning Mr. E. asked me the result of the experiment, and after having related it to him, he gave me the following account: He had found himself unable to sit up to so late an hour, but wish-
ful fairly to test the powers of the clairvoyant, he had ordered his clothes
to be stuffed into the form of a figure, and to make the contrast more striking to his natural appearance, had an extra pillow pushed into the clothes
so as to form a "corporation." This figure had been placed near the table,
in a sitting position, and a glass of brandy and water and the newspapers
placed beside it. The name, he further added, was spelt correctly, though
up to that time I had been in the habit of writing it "Eglington," instead of
as spelled by the clairvoyant, "Eglinton." **§**

From "Facts in Clairvoyance," by Dr. Ashburner (*Zoist,* vol. vi. pp. 96–110). In the following case the information given by the clairvoyants related to facts which were apparently not known by normal means to any person.

Major Buckley, a well-known mesmerist, brought to Dr. Ashburner's house in London on February 12th, 1848, two young women, A. B. and E. L., whom he had brought down from Cheltenham that day. They had often been mesmerized by him, and Dr. Ashburner wished to investigate their alleged clairvoyant powers. On this first evening only the two subjects, Major Buckley, and Dr. Ashburner were present. The latter writes:

§ We assembled in my little library. I had provided myself with a dozen walnut-shells, bought at Grange's in Piccadilly, containing caraway comfits and, as I thought, a motto each, and two ounces of hazel-nut shells containing comfits and printed mottoes. These had been purchased by me about two hours before. [Major Buckley made a few slow passes and the girls said they were ready to begin.] A. B. having taken up one of the nut-shells provided by me, placed it upon the chimney-piece above her head. E. L. then did the same thing with one of the nut-shells allotted to her. I was fully aware of the objections of skeptics, that a possibility existed of changing these shells by sleight-of-hand. I watched the proceedings anxiously and accurately, to avoid the possibility of being deceived. The movements of these young women were slow and deliberate, not like the hocus-pocus quick jerk of the conjurer. A. B. first announced her readiness to read the motto in her nut-shell. She said that the words were—

> "The little sweetmeat here revealed,
> Lays, as good deeds should lay, concealed."

I wrote down to her dictation, then I cracked the shell, emptied out the comfits, and found among them a little strip of paper, several times folded, on which were printed the very words she had spoken. Remember, reader, she was not asleep; both the girls were wide awake, and joined in the conversation with Major Buckley and myself in the intervals of the phenomena which they were exhibiting.

Then E. L. read the motto in her hazel-nut shell. It ran thus—

> "An honest man may take a knave's advice,
> But idiots only will be cheated twice."

After I had written this down, and before I opened the shell by the aid of the nut-crackers, she said, "At the top, above the first line, is part of another motto; it runs thus—

'Who smiles to see me in despair.'

The word despair is cut close." When the nut-shell was opened and the motto unfolded, the description given by E. L. was found to be quite correct.

A. B. then took another shell, and in a very short time read these words, which I wrote down—

> "She's little in size,
> Has bright speaking eyes,
> And if you prove true,
> Will be happy with you."

The shell was broken open, and the words printed on the little slip of folded paper found among the sweetmeats within were word for word with those written down by me.

E. L. took her turn at reading. The words she read out were—

> "In every beholder a rival I view,
> I ne'er can be equalled in loving of you."

Having written down these words, the shell was opened, and it was found that E. L. had read the motto quite correctly.

The servant announced that Mr. Arnott wished to see me. He had come on professional business, and with no view of witnessing these phenomena. I asked Major Buckley's permission to introduce him. He came in and sat down. A. B. proposed that he should take up a nut-shell from the table, and she offered to read the motto while he held it in his hand. He seemed hardly to be aware of what wonder he was to witness. He took up a nut, held it in his closed hand, and A. B. read thus—

> "The pangs of absence, how severe,
> Have they ne'er waked thy bitter tear?"

Mr. Arnott took the nut-crackers, broke his nut-shell, and found that A. B. had read quite correctly. His laugh and look of surprise told enough of the conviction of his mind. The event had become a fact. How to account for it was another matter. He could not deny that he had witnessed the fact. §

A curious case of prevision of the details of an illness—exercised not in spontaneous somnambulism, but in hypnosis—was given in Dr. Alphonse Teste's *Manuel Pratique du Magnétisme Animal* (1841), and recently reprinted in the *Revue des Études Psychiques,* January, February, and March, 1901, p. 74, from which I summarize it.

§ The subject, Mme. M., was a patient of Dr. Teste's, who had often proved clairvoyant. On a certain Friday, being alone with her and her husband, Dr. Teste hypnotized her and tried to find out how far she could foretell the future. She proceeded to tell them what would happen, *but only in relation to herself.* She said that on the following Tuesday, between 3 and 3:30, something—she could not tell what or where—would frighten her; she would have a fall, which would cause a miscarriage; at 3:30 she would faint for eight minutes, and would be very ill for the rest of the day and night. On Wednesday there would be considerable hemorrhage; on Thursday she would be much better, and would get up, but at 5:30 P.M. the hemorrhage would come on again and be followed by delirium; she would then have a good night, but would lose her reason on Friday evening. This state would last for three days, after which she would recover. In answer to questions, she declared that no precautions could possibly avert the accident. On awaking she ignored, as usual, everything that had happened in her trance. Dr. Teste impressed on her anxious husband the necessity of keeping her in complete ignorance of the prediction, and himself took careful notes of all the details of it, which he showed the next day to a medical friend of his, Dr. Latour.

On the Tuesday he came to Mme. M.'s house, and found her lunching with her husband, apparently in the best of health and spirits. He said that he wished to spend the day with them. Soon afterwards he hypnotized her for a few minutes, when she repeated her prediction exactly, saying as before that she could not tell what would frighten her, nor where it would be. On waking she again knew nothing of the prediction.

Dr. Teste and her husband determined to take all possible precautions against the accident, and, as the hour approached, not to let her out of their sight for a moment. Nevertheless, a few minutes after 3:30 she went out of the room, accompanied by her husband, suddenly saw a rat— an animal to which she had an intense antipathy; the shock of seeing it caused her to fall, and the results of the accident followed exactly as she had predicted. §

This case—though a remarkable instance of self-suggestion—obviously affords no clear evidence of anything further, since Mme. M.'s prevision related simply to her own actions. She could not tell beforehand what would be the cause of her fright; the rat—if it was a real, and not a hallucinatory one—seems to have acted as a mere *point de repère*[1] for the suggestion to attach itself to. If there had been no rat, Mme. M.'s subliminal self would probably have conjured up some other cause of fright, real or imaginary, and the effects would have followed in due course.

Here, then, my review of hypnotism might not unfitly close; and I might venture to hope that I had welded many scattered and obscure phenomena into at least something more of apparent unity than previous writers have achieved.

And yet from my point of view—attaching to hypnotism the grave importance which has here been attached to it—one line of reflection seems still lacking before we can pass on with satisfaction to another topic. I am bound to say something further as to its prospect in the future. A systematic appeal to the deeper powers in man—conceived with the generality with which I have here conceived it—must be fitted on in some way to the whole serious life of man; it must present itself to him as a development of faiths and instincts which lie already deep in his heart. In other words, there must needs be some *scheme of self-suggestion* —some general theory which can give the individual a basis for his appeal, whether he regards that appeal as directed to an intelligence outside himself or to his own inherent faculties and informing soul. These helps to the power of generalization—to the feeling of confidence—we must consider now.

The schemes of self-suggestion which have actually been found effective have covered a range as ·wide as all the superstition and all the religion of men. Each form of supernatural belief in turn has been utilized as a means of securing that urgently-needed temporal blessing—relief from physical pain. We see the same tendency running through fetichistic, polytheistic, monotheistic forms of belief. Beginning with fetichistic peoples, we observe that *charms* of various kinds—inert objects, arbitrary gestures, meaningless words—have probably been actually the most general means which our race has employed for the cure of disease. What is, however, even more remarkable is the efficacy which charms still continue in some cases to possess, even when they are worn merely as an experiment in self-suggestion by a person who is perfectly well aware of their intrinsic futility. The experiments on this subject given below seem to show that the mere continual contact of some small unfamiliar object

[1] *Point de repère.*—Guiding mark. Used of some (generally inconspicuous) real object which a hallucinated subject sometimes sees along with his hallucination, and whose behavior under magnification, etc. suggests to him similar changes in the hallucinatory figure.

will often act as a reminder to the subliminal self, and keep some nervous disturbances in check. Until one reads these modern examples, one can hardly realize how veritably potent for good may have been the savage amulet, the savage incantation.

The following account of experiments in the efficacy of charms appeared in the *Journal* S.P.R., vol. vi. p. 152:

§ . . . The uncivilized Africans, among whom I have spent many years (sixteen), make large use of charms, worn on the person, in cases of illness. Missionaries and traders agree that they occasionally derive great benefit from this "superstition." . . . I was curious to know whether any evidence could be obtained pointing to a probable cause for their effect.

In order to do this I imitated the African, but did my best to exclude the factor of faith. I prepared a "charm," consisting of a few hieroglyphics written on paper. This was wrapped up and sewn into a piece of tape, and tied firmly on the bare arm of the subject of the experiment. It was to be worn night and day for a few days, no time limit being given. I gave the subjects to understand that I was only asking them to assist in an experiment; that the charm was only paper with writing on it; that they were not to expect any improvement, but simply to tell me if such happened. If any faith element remained it was against my wish, and must be a quantity resisting all methods of expulsion, even in people of education. Now for the results in detail: (1) Myself, age forty-six. I have, all my life, been subject to some nervous trick or twitching of a muscle; sometimes of the face, the head, the shoulder, etc. This took the form of a peculiar snort from time to time, and I was aware that it must be unpleasant. I therefore tried earnestly to suppress it, but without effect. I wore a charm, and it immediately disappeared. Some few days after I found myself at it again, and found that the charm had slipped from *where I could feel it* to the elbow. On replacing it the annoyance ceased. The same lapse occurred two or three times, but I always found the charm had slipped. After a few weeks I discontinued its use, and the bad habit has not recommenced.

Miss B. M., age, say twenty-five, complained of chronic cold in the head, remaining persistently for several months. I gave her a charm, and four days afterwards she told me the cold had quite gone. She said, half ashamed to confess her credulity, that she really thought the charm had cured her.

M. H., age, say forty-two, rheumatic; is reported to me to be much the same.

M. L., age, say forty, troubled with chronic fits of sneezing, is reported entirely free.

Recent case: M. D., age, say fifty, has chronic bronchitis and difficulty of breathing. I gave her *my* charm to wear three days ago, and she says she is very much better.

J. M., age, say fifty-five, has suffered for fifteen years from locomotor ataxy; has insupportable pains, for which reason he often drinks a pint of whisky per day, without any sign of intoxication (so he says). I gave him a charm, which he only wore when the pains became violent—not to prevent their attack. He says the thing is a snare and a delusion; it has done him no good.

P. H., aged twenty-one; has four times had rheumatic fever; heart affected; no constitution. He was recovering from last attack, and I gave him a charm, which he immediately lost. He continues to improve.

R. C. PHILLIPS §

For a number of instances of the cure of *warts* by charms, see *Journal* S.P.R., vol. viii. pp. 7–10, 40, 96, 226, and vol. ix. pp. 100, 121, 225.

The transition from fetichistic to polytheistic conceptions of cure is, of course, a gradual one. It may be said to begin when curative properties are ascribed to objects not arbitrarily, nor on account of the *look* of the objects themselves, but on account of their having been blessed or handled by some divine or semi-divine personage, or having formed part of his body or surroundings during some incarnation. Thus Lourdes water, bottled and exported, is still held to possess curative virtue on account of the Virgin's original blessing bestowed upon the Lourdes spring. But generally the influence of the divine or divinized being is more directly exercised, as in oracles, dreams, invisible touches, or actual appearances of the gods to the adoring patient. It will be seen as we proceed how amply the tradition of Lourdes has incorporated these ancient aids to faith.

Much further removed from primitive belief is the appeal made by Christian Scientists to the aid of Jesus Christ—either as directly answering prayer, or as enabling the worshippers to comprehend the infinite love on which the universe is based, and in face of which pain and sickness become a vain imagination or even a sheer nonentity.

Nor, again, is this attempt to *rise above* pain at all exclusively dependent upon the Christian revelation. "Mind-healing" is a generalized term which includes not only so-called Christian Science, but a number of other ways of so regarding the universe as to triumph, while still in the body, over bodily distress and infirmity. Oriental ideas of the unreality of matter (Maya), stoical ideas of the sage's command over external circumstances, mystical ideas of the painless ecstasy into which the purified spirit can enter at will—all these conceptions have the advantage of being independent of dogmatic systems, with the accompanying disadvantage of being difficult for ordinary minds to grasp. Mind-healing is a modern name for all this ancient and lofty protest against the tyranny of the flesh.

The points of view thus briefly hinted at do, no doubt, differ widely from one another. To the believer in mind-cure—the denier of physical evils—that anguished supplication of the Lourdes pilgrim for the removal of pains, which the sufferer holds as the most urgent of realities, would be in the highest degree distasteful. To both mind-curer and Lourdes pilgrim alike the charms and fetiches of the African savage would seem contemptible or shocking.

To the readers of this chapter, however, there will be nothing surprising in my own inclination to include almost all these efforts at health under the general category of schemes of self-suggestion. *Almost* all, I say; reserving thus for future notice the special case—a small element in the general total—of possible cure by definite spirit-agency. But with regard to the great bulk of these psychical cures, the differences involved are subjective rather than objective; are differences in the frames of mind of the sufferers rather than in any scientific evidence as to the nature of the healing agency.

It would not be difficult, I think, to show in detail the crudity even of those schemes of thought which have proved in practice the most helpful in the relief of pain. This crudity, indeed, is inevitable; we are in the very earliest days of self-suggestion; a few pioneers only are groping after ways in which the suggestions may be made to *take hold*—and the task is quite as difficult for the self-suggester as for the hypnotist. The present duty, therefore, of psychical criticism is not so much to expose the inconsistencies of each in turn, as to indicate the lines on which this difficult attempt may be pushed with the best chance of lasting success.

Especially must one insist on the underlying philosophical aspiration, not merely for the prolongation of life on earth, but for the abrogation and annihilation of evil, including physical pain. The strength of the mind-curer's position lies in the true thesis that evil is a less real, a less permanent thing than good. It is well that self-suggestion should be turned in this direction, through whatever strange perversions or exaggerations the ultimate goal be won.

The so-called "Miracles of Lourdes" present a somewhat different problem. They resemble rather a resuscitation of antique methods of self-suggestion than an attempt at breaking new ground. In describing these as a form of self-suggestion I should at once explain I am by no means denying (what I am, in fact, presently about to assert) that some inflow from the spiritual world may be an essential element in all these triumphs over the infirmities of the flesh. All that I deny is that there is any real evidence whatever for the agency of the Virgin Mary in these cures. The story is a picturesque one, and one may fairly credit the original seeress, Bernadette, with the possession of some kind of psychical faculty. Further than that the legend cannot, I think, be maintained. Judged by our habitual canons of evidence—which, as the reader knows, do, in fact, admit the veridical character of many apparitions—there is no reason to suppose that the figure which appeared to Bernadette was more than a purely subjective hallucination; still less reason to assume that that apparition was in any way connected with the subsequent cures. As to those cures themselves, moreover—in spite of many loud assertions, in spite of what I must call the pseudo-accuracy, the pseudo-candor, of some of the advocates of the miraculous at Lourdes—neither my brother[1] nor I could discover any well-attested incident which raised them into a different category from the marvels which hypnotic suggestion is effecting daily in the clinics of many physicians.

To the student of suggestion, indeed, to the psychologist, the story of Lourdes is a mine of attractive material. Yet from a point of view perhaps profounder still, I cannot but sympathize with those wiser Catholics who bitterly regret the whole series of incidents; who stand aloof from that organized traffic in human ignorance, from the money-changers in the temple—nay, even from that cowardly craving for earth-life prolonged at any cost which drives the leprous and the cancerous to implore a deferment of their entry into the promised heaven.

These words will sound, perhaps, needlessly severe. It is hard to keep the balance when one sees, as one surely does at Lourdes, forces—which, if rightly directed, may indefinitely bless and elevate mankind—distorted and abused in such fashion as must ultimately lead to some infidel reaction—some crushing desertion and downfall of ancient faith. It is *not* true, a thousand times it is *not* true, that a bottle of water from a spring near which a girl saw a hallucinatory figure will by miraculous virtue heal a Turk in Constantinople; but it *is* true that on some influx from the unseen world—an influence dimly adumbrated in that Virgin figure and that sanctified spring—depends the life and energy of this world of every day.

---

[1] "Mind-Cure, Faith-Cure, and the Miracles of Lourdes," by A. T. Myers, M.D., F.R.C.P., and F. W. H. Myers, *Proceedings* S.P.R., vol. ix. pp. 160–210.

To me, at least, it seems that no real explanation of hypnotic vitalization can, in fact, be given except upon the general theory supported in this work—the theory that a world of spiritual life exists, an environment profounder than those environments of matter which in a sense we know.

Within, beyond, the world of matter—as a still profounder, still more generalized aspect of the Cosmos—must lie the world of spiritual life. That the world of spiritual life does not depend upon the existence of the material world I hold as now proved by actual evidence. That it is in some way continuous with the world of matter I can well suppose. What does not originate in matter originates *there;* and beyond the material world there must be not one stage only, but countless stages in the infinity of things.

In my view each man is essentially a spirit, controlling an organism which is itself a complex of lower and smaller lives. The spirit's control is not uniform throughout the organism, nor in all phases of organic life. In waking life it controls mainly the centers of supraliminal thought and feeling, exercising little control over deeper centers, which have been educated into a routine sufficient for common needs. But in subliminal states—trance and the like—the supraliminal processes are inhibited, and the lower organic centers are retained more directly under the spirit's control. As you get into the profounder part of man's being, you get nearer to the source of his human vitality. You get thus into a region of essentially greater *responsiveness* to spiritual appeal than is offered by the superficial stratum which has been shaped and hardened by external needs into a definite adaptation to the earthly environment.

The ultimate lesson of hypnotic suggestion, especially in the somnambulic state, is, therefore, that we thus get, by empirical artifices, at these strata of greater plasticity—plasticity not to external but to internal forces—where the informing spirit controls the organism more immediately, and can act on it with greater freedom.

The highest development of sleep thus involves at once more penetrative bodily recuperation, and more independent spiritual activity. The spirit is more powerful either to draw spiritual energy into the organism, or to act in partial independence of the organism. The cases already cited of "travelling clairvoyance" have, in fact, generally occurred during sleep-waking states, originally induced for some healing purpose. I take this to mean that the spirit can in such states more easily either *modify* the body, or partially *quit* and return to the body. In other words, it can for the time either pay the body more attention, with benefit, or less attention, without injury. I use the word *attention* because, in the impossibility of conceiving how a spirit can affect or control an organism, the most fitting term seems to be that by which we designate our own attempts at concentrating the personality. I would say in crude terms that the soul keeps the body alive by attending to it, and can attend to central operations more directly than to superficial ones—to the activities of sleep more directly than to those of waking. Hence in deep states it can partially withdraw attention from the organism and bestow it elsewhere, while remaining capable of at once resuming its ordinary attitude towards that organism. Bodily death ensues when the soul's attention is wholly and irrevocably withdrawn from the organism, which has become from physical causes unfit to act as the exponent of an informing spirit. Life means the maintenance of this attention; achieved by the soul's absorption of energy from the spiritual environment. For if our individual spirits and organisms live by dint of this spiritual energy, underlying the chemical energy by which organic change is carried on, then we must presumably renew and replenish the spiritual energy as continuously as the chemical. To keep our chemical energy at work, we live in a warm environment, and from time to time take food. By analogy, in order to keep the spiritual energy at work, we should live in a spiritual environment, and possibly from time to time absorb some special influx of spiritual life.

Let men realize that their most comprehensive duty, in this or other worlds, is intensity of spiritual life; nay, that their own spirits are co-operative elements in the cosmic evolution, are part and parcel of the ultimate vitalizing Power.

Chapter Six

SENSORY AUTOMATISM

Each of the several lines of inquiry thus far has led us, through widely varying phenomena, in substantially the same direction. For the most part, dream introduces us only to incoherent thought, somnambulism only to irrational action. Yet from time to time we have found in dreams indications of a memory which surpasses waking memory; nay, which even implies that something within us has exercised in waking hours a perception more minute and comprehensive than our supraliminal consciousness ever knew. During various forms of sleep itself, moreover, something of unusual faculty seems to be exercised; mathematical or philological ingenuity may surpass its waking level; the senses may show a delicacy of which we had not judged them capable. And in the background of all this we catch glimpses of still higher faculty; of those supernormal powers of telepathy and clairvoyance on whose existence our belief in a unitary Self must ultimately be so largely based.

Then in hypnotic phenomena and in the analogous cases of spontaneous somnambulism we perceive elements of this supernormal faculty mingling with heightened faculty of familiar types. From every side we have indications of something complex and obscure in the structure of human personality; of something transcending sensory experience.

Considering together, under the heading of sensory and motor *automatism,* the whole range of that subliminal action of which we have as yet discussed fragments only, we shall gradually come to see that its distinctive faculty of telepathy or clairvoyance is in fact an introduction into a realm where the limitations of organic life can no longer be assumed to persist. Considering, again, the evidence which shows that that portion of the personality which exercises these powers during our earthly existence does actually continue to exercise them after our bodily decay, *we shall recognize a relation—obscure but indisputable—between the subliminal and the surviving self.*

I begin, then, with my definition of *automatism,* as the widest term under which to include the range of subliminal emergences into ordinary life. Different classes of those uprushes have already received special names. The turbulent uprush and downdraught of hysteria; the helpful uprushes of genius, the profound and recuperative changes which follow on hypnotic suggestion; these have been described under their separate headings. But the main mass of subliminal manifestations remains un-described. I have dealt little with veridical hallucinations, not at all with automatic writing nor with the utterances of spontaneous trance. The products of inner vision or inner audition I term *sensory automatisms*. The messages conveyed by movement of limbs or hand or tongue, initiated by an inner motor impulse beyond the conscious will—these are what I term *motor automatisms*. And I claim that when all these are surveyed together they will be seen to be endeavors of submerged tracts of our personality to present to ordinary waking thought fragments of a knowl-edge which no ordinary waking thought could attain.

First we come to a most important development of inward vision—namely, that vast range of phenomena which we call *hallucination*. *Dreams* actually *are* hallucinations of low intensity. *Imagination-images* may be carried to a hallucinatory pitch by good visualizers. And the *in-spirations of genius* may present themselves in hallucinatory vividness to the astonished artist.

In order to understand any one class of hallucinations, we ought to have all classes before us. At the lower limit of the series, the analysis of the physician should precede that of the psychologist. We already know to some extent, and may hope soon to know more accurately, what sen-sory disturbance corresponds to what nervous lesion. Yet these violent disturbances of inward perception—the snakes of the drunkard, the scarlet fire of the epileptic, the jeering voices of the paranoiac—these are perhaps of too gross a kind to afford more than a kind of neurological introduction to the subtler points which arise when hallucination is un-accompanied by any observable defect or malady.

Yet until quite recently—until Edmund Gurney took up the inquiry in 1882—this wide, important subject was treated, even in serious text-books, in a superficial and perfunctory way. Few statistics were collected; hardly anything was really known; rather there was a facile assumption that all hallucinations or sensory automatisms *must* somehow be due to physical malady, even when there was no evidence whatever for such a connection. I must refer my readers to Gurney's résumé in his chapter on "Hallucinations" in *Phantasms of the Living,* if they would realize the gradual confused fashion in which men's minds had been prepared for the wider view soon to be opened, largely by Gurney's own statistical and analytical work. The wide collection of first-hand experiences of sensory automatisms of every kind which he initiated, and which the S.P.R. "Census of Hallucinations" continued after his death, has for the first time made it possible to treat these phenomena with some surety of hand.

If purely subjective hallucinations of the senses affected insane or disordered brains alone—as was pretty generally the assumption, even in scientific circles, when this inquiry began—our task would have been much easier than it is. But the results of these inquiries show that a great number of sensory automatisms occur among sane and healthy persons, and that for many of these we can at present offer no explanation whatever. For some of them, however, we can offer at least an indication of a probable determining cause, whose mode of working remains wholly obscure.

In a few instances we can trace moral predisposing causes to expectation, grief, anxiety. These causes, however, turn out to be much less often effective than might have been expected from the popular readiness to invoke them. In two ways especially the weakness of this predisposing cause is impressed upon us. In the first place, the bulk of our percipients experience their hallucinations at ordinary unexciting moments; traversing their more anxious crises without any such phenomenon. In the second place, those of our percipients whose hallucination is in fact more or less coincident with some distressing external event, seldom seem to have been predisposed to the hallucination by a knowledge of the event. For the event was generally unknown to them when the corresponding hallucination occurred.

This last remark introduces us to the most interesting and important group of percepts—which are *veridical,* which are in some way generated by some event outside the percipient's mind, so that their correspondence with that event conveys some new fact. It is this group, of course, which gives high importance to the whole inquiry; which makes the study of inward vision no mere curiosity, but rather the opening of an inlet into forms of knowledge to which we can assign no bound.

The first and simplest step in the control of inner vision is one to which, as the reader of my chapter on hypnotism already knows, I attribute an importance much greater than is generally accorded to it. I refer to the hypnotizer's power not only of controlling but of *inducing* hallucinations in his subject.

Now, *crystal-vision,* like hypnotic trance, allows an occasional seer to develop this faculty of inward vision up to a point where it will sometimes convey to him information not attainable by ordinary means. On the whole it seems safest to attempt at present no further explanation of crystal-gazing than to say that it is an empirical method of externalizing pictures which are associated with changes in the sensorial tracts of the brain, due partly to internal stimuli, and partly to stimuli which may come from minds external to the scryer's own. Some interesting experiments on these and kindred questions will follow.

These experiments illustrate the gradual transition between the common forms of post-hypnotic hallucination, which, however surprising at first, are now undisputed, and the crystal-vision which I am anxious to present as no "occult practice" or superstitious fancy.

The following historical résumé is derived from Mr. Andrew Lang's *The Making of Religion* (Chapter V., "Crystal Visions, Savage and Civilized," p. 90), and Miss A. Goodrich-Freer's "Recent Experiments in Crystal Vision" (*Proceedings* S.P.R., vol. v. p. 486), in both of which numerous references to the history of the subject and the facts here adduced are given. The crystal was only one of many objects used in a similar way as a means of obtaining supernormal knowledge through induced hallucinations; *e.g.,* vessels containing liquid—usually water—water in springs, mirrors of polished steel, liquid poured into the palm of the hand, a drop of blood, or ink, and various objects having a reflecting surface, such as the beryl or other gems, the blade of a sword, a ball of polished stone, or the human finger-nail. Crystal-gazing in some such form has been practiced for at least 3000 years and is practically of world-wide distribution, having been found among the customs of Assyria, Persia, Egypt—ancient and modern—Greece, Rome, China, Japan and India, North American Indians, Africans of Fez, Zulus, Maoris. It was also practiced by the Incas, and is still by Australian savages and Polynesians, the Shamans of Siberia and Eastern Russia, and in Madagascar. Usually a more or less elaborate ritual formed part of the procedure, and in all ages and many places the Seer—variously called Speculator, Scryer, Viewer, or Reader—was usually a child "who had not known sin."

Among the Greeks, several different methods were used. (1) Hydromancy, practiced chiefly at the temple of Demeter in Patræ. Before the temple was a fountain, into which a mirror was let down by a small cord, so that its lower edge just touched the water. From the various figures and images seen in it, predictions were made as to the progress of diseases in the patients who came to consult the oracle. (2) Lecanomancy, divination by a bowl containing water, or oil and wine. (3) Catoptromancy, in which mirrors alone were used. (4) Gastromancy, in which glass vessels filled with water and surrounded by torches were used. A demon was invoked and a boy appointed to observe the appearance produced by the demon's action on the water. (5) Onychomancy, in which a boy's nails covered with oil and soot were turned to the sun, the reflection of whose rays produced images supposed to represent certain things. (6) Crystallomancy, where polished and enchanted crystals were used.

In India we find divination by mirrors and also a method in which the ashes of incense moistened with castor-oil are poured into the palm of the child seer. The Arabians also use a mirror in which they see visions after long fasting and prayers.

In Polynesia, Ellis relates that when any one has been robbed, the priest, after praying, has a hole dug in the floor of the house and filled with water. Then he gazes into the water, over which the god is supposed to place the spirit of the thief. The image of the thief is then supposed to be reflected in the water and perceived by the priest.

Among the Apaches also, one of the chief duties of the medicine-men was to find out the whereabouts of lost or stolen property, and for this purpose crystal-gazing was employed.

Other Red Indians make their patients gaze into the water, in which they see the pictures of what food or medicine will do them good.

The art, which was attributed in early times to divine power, came to be regarded in the Middle Ages by the Christian Church as the work of evil spirits, and the *Specularii*—as they were then called—were looked upon as heretics and treated accordingly. They continued, however, to flourish, and the art lingered on till the sixteenth century, when it received a new impetus and reached its highest development in the hands of the famous Dr. John Dee (1527–1608), whose "Shew-stone" is now to be seen in the British Museum. His seer—a man named Kelly—professed not only to see various spirits in the crystal, but also to hear them speak, and long conversations were carried on with them. Other sounds were also said to be heard in or near the stone, and occasionally apparitions were seen in its neighborhood. Sometimes writing was seen in it instead of figures. The stone was generally set in a frame of gold on a table, and its use was prefaced with long prayers.

The practice was carried on both in England and on the Continent of Europe through the seventeenth and eighteenth centuries, and has, in fact, never become extinct.

The following cases are extracted from Miss A. Goodrich-Freer's paper on "Recent Experiments in Crystal Vision" (*Proceedings* S.P.R., vol. v., 1889, pp. 505–519).

§ To quote from my note-book. . . . I had carelessly destroyed a letter without preserving the address of my correspondent. I knew the county, and searching in a map recognized the name of the town, one unfamiliar to me, but which I was sure I should know when I saw it. But I had no clue to the name of house or street, till at last it struck me to test the value of the crystal as a means of recalling forgotten knowledge. A very short inspection supplied me with "H. House" (the entire word—one I know in no other connection—was supplied) in grey letters on a white ground, and having nothing better to suggest from any other source, I risked posting my letter to the address so strangely supplied. A day or two brought me an answer, headed H. House in grey letters on a white ground. §

The next is a possibly telepathic case:

§ On Monday evening, February 11, I took up the crystal, with the deliberate intention of seeing in it a figure, which happened to occupy my thoughts at the moment, but I found the field pre-occupied by a small bunch of daffodils—a prim little posy, not larger than might be formed by two or three fine heads. This presented itself in various positions, in spite of my hurry to be rid of it, for I rashly concluded my vision to be a consequence of my having the day before seen, on a friend's dinner-table, the first daffodils of the season. The resemblance was not complete, for those I had seen were loosely arranged and intermixed with ferns and ivy, whereas my crystal-vision had no foliage, and was a compact little bunch. It was not till Thursday, 14th, that I received, as a wholly unexpected "Valentine," a painting, on a blue satin ground, of a bunch of daffodils, corresponding exactly with my crystal picture, and learnt that the artist had spent some hours on Monday, previous to my vision, in making studies of the flowers in various positions. §

Sir Joseph Barnby, the well-known musician, relates (in *Proceedings* S.P.R., vol. viii. pp. 499–515) an instance where a young protégée of Lord and Lady Radnor's, Miss A., looked in her crystal ball during his visit at Longford Castle.

§ She described a bedroom in which a lady was drying her hands on a towel. The lady was tall, dark, slightly foreign in appearance and with rather "an air" about her. Sir Joseph says, "This described with such astonishing accuracy my wife, and the room she was then occupying at a hotel in Eastbourne, that I was impelled to ask for particulars as to dress, etc." Miss A. stated that the dress was of serge, with a good deal of braid on the bodice and a strip of braid down one side of the skirt. "This threw me off the scent, as before I had started for Longford my wife had expressed regret that she had not a serge dress with her. My astonishment was great, therefore, on returning to Eastbourne to find my wife wearing a serge dress exactly answering to the description given above." She had had it made after he left.

Miss A. had never seen Sir Joseph's wife, but one night about sixteen months later they all attended the same minstrel show. His wife was across the room when he chanced to meet Lady Radnor and Miss A. She said,

"You will remember my seeing a lady in the bedroom while looking in my crystal; *that* is the lady I saw." It was his wife to whom she referred. **§**

Quite apart from the *veridicality* of some of these cases of crystal vision —the intrinsic evidence which they contain of knowledge outside the experimenter's ordinary knowledge—they occur to a greater or less extent with so many persons of sanity and probity that we can not doubt their existence.

In turning, as we must now turn, to the *spontaneous* cases of sensory automatism, we must needs single out first some fundamental phenomenon, illustrating some principle from which the rarer or more complex phenomena may be in part at least derived. Nor will there be difficulty in such a choice. Theory and actual experience point here in the same direction. If this inward vision, this inward audition, on whose importance I have been insisting, are to have any such importance—if they are to have any validity at all—if their contents are to represent anything more than dream or meditation—they must receive knowledge from other minds or from distant objects—knowledge which is *not* received by the external organs of sense. Telepathy, in short, must be the prerequisite of all these supernormal phenomena.

Actual experience, as we shall presently see, confirms this view of the place of telepathy. For when we pass from the induced to the spontaneous phenomena we shall find that these illustrate before all else this transmission of thought and emotion directly from mind to mind.

We are obliged, for the sake of clearness of evidence, to start from telepathic communications intentionally planned to be so trivial, so devoid of associations or emotions, that it shall be impossible to refer them to any common memory or sympathy; to anything save a direct transmission of idea, or impulse, or sensation, or image, from one to another mind.

The history of the first sporadic attempts at this form of experiment in the early days of mesmerism, of the various steps by which recent workers have developed and systematized the investigation, and of the varied, yet concordant, results already obtained, must, I think, be regarded as one of the most important chapters in psychology.

The first experimental study of thought-transference was connected with the discovery that the somnambulistic state could be artificially induced, and the greater number of observations made during this early stage were carried out in this country during the second quarter of the nineteenth century. Thought-transference in these cases took the form of *community of sensation* between operator and subject, depending, as was supposed, on a specific *rapport* between them. The phenomenon was not studied by itself, but regarded as belonging essentially to mesmerism; consequently it shared in the discredit into which the latter fell.

The first impetus to the more recent scientific study of telepathy was given by Professor W. F. Barrett, F.R.S., who brought forward some results of his own with a hypnotized girl, in a paper read before the British Association in 1876. In the course of the correspondence arising out of his paper, Professor Barrett learnt of other instances, which he carefully investigated, in which telepathy had been observed in the normal waking state. Later, in the years 1881–2, a long series of experiments in which Professor Sidgwick, Professor Balfour Stewart, Edmund Gurney, myself, and others joined with Professor Barrett, seemed to establish the possibility of a new mode of communication from mind to mind. And these early results have been confirmed by further experiments continued down to the present time by observers both in this country and abroad.

The experiments cited here have been selected because particular care had been given to rule out fraud (either conscious or unconscious), and because of the intelligence of the experimenters, the scientific standing of some of them, and the general spirit in which their work was done. Full records were published in the *Proceedings* S.P.R., vols. i., ii., and iii.

In this series of experiments there were two percipients, and a considerable group of agents, each of whom, when alone with one or other of the percipients, was successful in transferring his impression.

We owe these remarkable experiments to the sagacity and energy of Mr. Malcolm Guthrie, J.P., of Liverpool. At the beginning of 1883, Mr. Guthrie happened to read an article on thought-transference in a magazine, and though completely skeptical, he determined to make some trials on his own account. He was then at the head of an establishment which gave employment to many hundreds of persons; and he was informed by a relative who occupied a position of responsibility in this establishment that she had witnessed remarkable results in some casual trials made by a group of his employees after business hours. He at once took the matter into his own hands, and went steadily, but cautiously, to work. He restricted the practice of the novel accomplishment to weekly meetings; and he arranged with his friend, Mr. James Birchall, the hon. secretary of the Liverpool Literary and Philosophical Society, that the latter should make a full and complete record of every experiment made. Mr. Guthrie thus describes the proceedings:

§ I have had the advantage of studying a series of experiments *ab ovo*. I have witnessed the genuine surprise which the operators and the subjects have alike exhibited at their increasing successes, and at the results of our excursions into novel lines of experiment. The affair has not been the discovery of the possession of special powers, first made and then worked up by the parties themselves for gain or glory. The experimenters in this case were disposed to pass the matter over altogether as one of no moment, and only put themselves at my disposal in regard to experiments in order to oblige me. The experiments have all been devised and conducted by myself and Mr. Birchall, without any previous intimation of their nature, and could not possibly have been foreseen. In fact they have been to the young ladies a succession of surprises. No set of experiments of a similar nature has ever been more completely known from its origin, or more completely under the control of the scientific observer.

In the earlier experiments, the ideas transferred were of colors, geometrical figures, cards, and visible objects of all sorts, which the percipient was to name. We tried also the perception of *motion,* and found that the movements of objects exhibited could be discerned. The idea was suggested by an experiment tried with a card, which in order that all present should see, I moved about, and was informed by the percipient that it was a card, but she could not tell which one because it seemed to be moving about. On a subsequent occasion, in order to test this perception of motion, I bought a toy monkey, which worked up and down on a stick by means of a string drawing the arms and legs together. The answer was: "I see red and yellow, and it is darker at one end than the other. It is like a flag moving about—it is moving. . . . Now it is opening and shutting like a pair of scissors." §

The reproduction of diagrams was introduced in October, 1883, and in that and the following month about 150 trials were made. The whole series has been carefully mounted and preserved by Mr. Guthrie. No one could look through them without perceiving that the hypothesis of chance or guesswork is out of the question; that in most instances some idea, and in many a complete idea, of the original must, by whatever means, have been present in the mind of the person who made the reproduction.

The conditions which follow were uniformly observed in all cases. The originals were for the most part drawn in another room from that in which the percipient was placed. The few executed in the same room were drawn while the percipient was blindfolded, at a distance from her, and in such a way that the process would have been wholly invisible to her or any one else, even had an attempt been made to observe it. During the process of transference, the agent looked steadily and in perfect silence at the original drawing, which was placed upon an intervening wooden stand; the percipient sitting opposite to him, and behind the stand, blindfolded and quite still. The agent ceased looking at the drawing, and the blindfolding was removed, only when the percipient professed herself ready to make the reproduction, which happened usually in times varying from half a minute to two or three minutes. Her position rendered it absolutely impossible that she should obtain a glimpse of the original.

I give on the following pages a few not unduly favorable specimens. The agents concerned were Mr. Guthrie; Mr. Steel, the President of the Liverpool Literary and Philosophical Society; Mr. Birchall, mentioned above; Mr. Hughes, B.A., of St. John's College, Cambridge; and myself. The names of the percipients were Miss Relph and Miss Edwards.

We must clearly realize that in telepathic experiment we encounter just the same difficulty which makes our results in hypnotism so unpredictable and irregular. We do not know how to get our suggestions to *take hold* of the subliminal self. They are liable to fail for two main reasons. Either they somehow never *reach* the subliminal centers which we wish to affect, or they find those centers preoccupied with some self-suggestion hostile to our behest. This source of uncertainty can only be removed by a far greater number of experiments than have yet been made. Yet there is one provisional interpretation of telepathic experiment which must be noticed because, if true, it may conceivably connect our groping work with more advanced departments of science. I refer to the suggestion that telepathy is propagated by "brain waves." These waves are conceived as passing from one brain to another, and arousing in the *second* brain an excitation or image similar to those from which they start in the *first.*

The above points have been fair matter of argument almost since our research began. But as our evidence has developed, our conception of telepathy has needed to be more and more generalized in other and new directions, less compatible with the vibration theory. Three such directions may be briefly specified here—namely, the relation of telepathy to clairvoyance, to time, and to disembodied spirits.

The hypothesis which I suggested in *Phantasms of the Living* itself, in my "Note on a possible mode of psychical interaction," seems to me to have been rendered increasingly plausible by evidence of many kinds since received; evidence of which the larger part falls outside the limits of this present work. I still believe—and more confidently than in 1886—that a "psychical invasion" does take place; that some movement bearing some relation to space as we know it is actually accomplished; and some presence is transferred, and may or may not be discerned by the invaded person; some perception of the distant scene in itself is acquired, and may or may not be remembered by the invader.

No. 1. Original Drawing.   No. 1. Reproduction.

Mr. Guthrie and Miss Edwards.

No. 2. Original Drawing.   No. 2. Reproduction.

Mr. Guthrie and Miss Edwards.

No. 3. ORIGINAL DRAWING.

No. 3. REPRODUCTION.

Mr. Guthrie and Miss Edwards.

No. 4. ORIGINAL DRAWING.

No. 4. REPRODUCTION.

Mr. Guthrie and Miss Edwards.

No. 5. Original Drawing.   No. 5. Reproduction.

Mr. Guthrie and Miss Edwards.

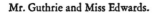

No. 6. Original Drawing.

Mr. Guthrie and Miss Edwards.

No. 6. Reproduction.

Miss Edwards almost directly said, "Are you thinking of the bottom of the sea, with shells and fishes?" and then, "Is it a snail or a fish?"—then drew as above.

No. 7. Original Drawing.   No. 7. Reproduction.

Mr. Gurney and Miss Relph.

No. 8. Original Drawing.

Mr. Birchall and Miss Relph.

No. 8. Reproduction.

Miss Relph said she seemed to see a lot of rings, as if they were moving, and she could not get them steadily before her eyes.

No. 9. Original Drawing.   No. 9. Reproduction.

Mr. Birchall and Miss Relph.

No. 10. Original Drawing.

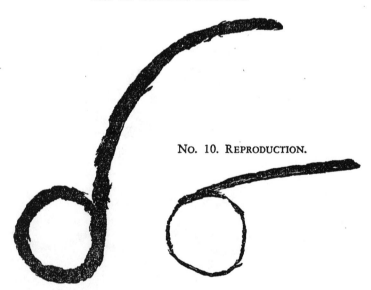

No. 10. Reproduction.

Mr. Birchall and Miss Edwards.

But the words which I am here beginning to use carry with them associations from which not the scientific reader alone may well shrink in disgust. I am falling into the language of a "palæolithic psychology"—into the habits of thought of the savage who believes that you can travel in dreams and infest your enemy as a haunting spirit. Fully realizing the offense which such expressions must give—the apparent levity of a return to conceptions so enormously out of date—I see no better line of excuse than simply to retrace to my reader the way in which the gradual accretion of evidence has obliged me, for the mere sake of covering all the phenomena, to use phrases and assumptions which go far beyond those which Edmund Gurney and I employed in our first papers on this inquiry in 1883.

The facts of the case, then, are briefly as follows. When in 1882 our small group began the collection of evidence bearing upon "veridical hallucinations"—or apparitions which coincided with other events in such a way as to suggest a casual connection—we found that the subject had hardly as yet been seriously attacked. Cases, indeed, of various kinds had been vaguely recorded; but scarcely any of these reached the evidential level on which we wished our narratives to stand. Our own collection was miserably scanty as compared with the magnitude of the harvest waiting to be reaped; but at the same time it was copious enough to indicate those types of coincidental apparition which were at once commonest and most capable of evidential treatment. These were apparitions of living persons, coinciding with some crisis which those persons were undergoing at a distance; and especially the apparitions of persons who might indeed be regarded as still living, but who were undergoing the crisis of death. These cases, I say, were the first to attain to a number and a weight which carried conviction to our own minds, and in various papers in the S.P.R. *Proceedings,* and then in *Phantasms of the Living,* they were set forth in evidential form, and were connected with experimental telepathy, being themselves regarded as spontaneous examples, upon a more impressive scale, of these transferences of impression from one to another mind.

But at the same time there were scattered among these cases from the first certain types which were with difficulty reducible under the conception of telepathy pure and simple—even if such a conception could be distinctly formed. Sometimes the apparition was seen by more than one percipient at once—a result which we could hardly have expected if all that had passed were the transference of an impression from the agent's mind to another mind, which then bodied forth that impression in externalized shape according to laws of its own structure. There were instances, too, where the percipient seemed to be the agent also—in so far that it was he who had an impression of having somehow visited and noted a distant scene, whose occupant was not necessarily conscious of any immediate relation with him. Or sometimes this "telepathic clairvoyance" developed into "reciprocity," and each of the two persons concerned was conscious of the other—the *scene* of their encounter being the same in the vision of each, or at least the experience being in some way common to both. These and cognate difficulties were present to my mind from the first; and in the "Note on a suggested mode of psychical interaction," I indicated briefly the extension of the telepathic theory to which they seemed to me to point.

Meantime cases of certain other definite types continued to come steadily to hand, although in lesser numbers than the cases of apparition at death. To mention two important types only—there were apparitions of the so-called *dead* and there were cases of *precognition.* With regard to each of these classes, it seemed reasonable to defer belief until time should have shown whether the influx of first-hand cases was likely to be permanent; whether independent witnesses continued to testify to incidents which could be better explained on these hypotheses than on any other. Before Edmund Gurney's death in 1888 our cases of apparitions and other manifestations of the dead had reached a degree of weight and consistency which, as his last paper showed, was beginning to convince him of their veridical character; and since that date these have been much further increased and especially have drawn from Mrs. Piper's and other trance-phenomena an unexpected enlargement and corroboration. The evidence for communication from the departed is now in my personal estimate quite as strong as that for telepathic communication between the living; and it is moreover evidence which inevitably alters and widens our conception of telepathy between living men.

The evidence for precognition, again, was from the first scantier, and has advanced at a slower rate. But at whatever point one or another inquirer may happen at present to stand, I urge that this is the reasonable course for conviction to follow. First analyze the miscellaneous stream of evidence into definite types; then observe the frequency with which these types recur, and let your sense of their importance gradually grow, if the evidence grows also.

"What definite reason do I know why this should *not* be true?"—this is the question which needs to be pushed home again and again if one is to realize—and not in the ordinary paths of scientific speculation alone—how profound our ignorance of the Universe really is.

My own ignorance, at any rate, I recognize to be such that my notions of the probable or improbable in the Universe are not of weight enough to lead me to set aside any facts which seem to me well attested, and which are not shown by experts actually to conflict with any better-established facts or generalizations. Wide though the range of established science may be, it represents, as its most far-sighted prophets are the first to admit, a narrow glance only into the unknown and infinite realm of law.

The evidence, then, leading me thus unresisting along, has led me to this main difference from our early treatment of veridical phantasms. Instead of starting from a root-conception of a telepathic impulse merely passing from mind to mind, I now start from a root-conception of the dissociability of the self, of the possibility that different fractions of the personality can act so far independently of each other that the one is not conscious of the other's action.

Naturally the two conceptions coincide over much of the ground. Where experimental thought-transference is concerned—even where the commoner types of coincidental phantasms are concerned—the second formula seems a needless and unprovable variation on the first. But as soon as we get among the difficult types—reciprocal cases, clairvoyant cases, collective cases, above all, manifestations of the dead—we find that the conception of a telepathic impulse as a message dispatched and then left alone, as it were, to effect its purpose needs more and more of straining, of manipulation, to fit it to the evidence. On the other hand, it is just in those difficult regions that the analogies of other splits of personality recur, and that phantasmal or automatic behavior recalls to us the behavior of segments of personality detached from primary personality, but operating through the organism which is common to both.

The innovation which we are here called upon to make is to suppose that segments of the personality can operate in apparent separation from the organism. Such a supposition, of course, could not have been started without proof of telepathy, and could with difficulty be sustained without proof of survival of death. But, given telepathy, we have *some* psychical agency connected with man operating apart from his organism. Given survival, we have an element of his personality operating when his organism is destroyed. There is therefore no very great additional burden in supposing that an element of his personality may operate apart from his organism, while that organism still exists.

If we have once got a man's *thought* operating apart from his body— if my fixation of attention on the two of diamonds does somehow so modify another man's brain a few yards off that he seems to see the two of diamonds floating before him—there is no obvious halting-place on *his* side till we come to "possession" by a departed spirit, and there is no obvious halting-place on *my* side till we come to "travelling clairvoyance," with a corresponding visibility of my own phantasm to other persons in the scenes which I spiritually visit.

Dissociation of personality, combined with activity in the spiritual environment; such will be the formula which will most easily cover those actually observed facts of veridical apparition on which we must now enter at considerable length.

It must be remembered, in the first place, that all these veridical or coincidental cases stand out together as a single group from a background of hallucinations which involve no coincidence, which have no claim to veridicality. Meantime we have to rely on the evidence afforded by external coincidence—on the mere fact, to put such a coincidence in its simplest form, that I see a phantom of my friend Smith at the moment when Smith is unexpectedly dying at a distance. A coincidence of this general type, if it occurs, need not be difficult to substantiate, and we have in fact substantiated it with more or less completeness in several hundred cases. The conclusion will obviously be that there is a causal connection between the death and the apparition. To overcome this presumption it would be necessary either to impugn the accuracy of the informant's testimony, or to show that chance alone might have brought about the observed coincidences.

There are, notwithstanding, several sources of error which may affect the testimony of honest and educated persons to events that are both unusual and of a sort unrecognized by contemporary science.

First, as to errors of *observation* these can only relate to real objects, seen and misinterpreted, e.g. a real figure seen out of doors and at some distance may be wrongly recognized, and the person supposed to have been seen may happen to have died on that day.

In most cases, however, the experience is clearly hallucinatory, and the next class of errors—those of *inference*—are therefore unimportant. The only question is—not, how did the witness interpret his impression, but, what did he seem to himself at the time to perceive?

Errors of *narration* and of *memory* may be more serious. As to the former, there is the tendency to exaggerate to make the account graphic and picturesque; but this would vitiate oral rather than written accounts, and—as might be expected from general experience—affects especially second-hand accounts.

Errors of *memory* are much more difficult for a thoroughly honest person to avoid, since very few are aware of the untrustworthiness of their own memory. This ignorance aids unconscious tendencies to bring events into harmony with one's own beliefs and opinions—whether religious or scientific—and with each other; to exaggerate the clearness and precision of recollections, and to simplify them, either by bringing any group of events into a connected whole or merely by dropping some of the details.

The total effect may be an exaggeration of the marvelous elements in a story, or occasionally the reverse; *e.g.* a waking hallucination may be remembered as a dream.

For a thorough discussion of the arguments for and against chance-coincidence, the reader should consult the "Report on the Census of Hallucinations," *Proceedings* S.P.R., vol. x., where every source of error as yet discovered has been pretty fully considered.

And yet the conclusion to which the Committee which assembled this "Report" unanimously came is expressed in the closing words: "Between deaths and apparitions of the dying person a connection exists which is not due to chance alone."

We have a right, I think, to say that only by another census of hallucinations, equally careful, more extensive, and yielding absolutely different results, could this conclusion be overthrown.

In forming this conclusion, apparitions at death are of course selected, because, death being an unique event in man's earthly existence, the coincidences between death and apparitions afford a favorable case for statistical treatment. But the coincidences between apparitions and crises other than death, although not susceptible of the same arithmetical precision of estimate, are, as will be seen, quite equally convincing. To this great mass of spontaneous cases we must now turn.

I must begin with cases where the action of the excursive fragment of the personality is of the weakest kind—the least capable of affecting other observers, or of being recalled into the agent's own waking memory.

Such cases, naturally enough, will be hard to bring up to evidential level. It must depend on mere chance whether these weak and aimless psychical excursions are observed at all; or are observed in such a way as to lead us to attribute them to anything more than the subjective fancy of the observers.

How can a casual vision—say, of a lady sitting in her drawing-room, of a man returning home at six o'clock—be distinguished from memory-images on the one hand and from what I may term "expectation-images" on the other? The picture of the lady may be a slightly modified and externalized reminiscence; the picture of the man walking up to the door may be a mere projection of what the observer was hoping to see.

I have assumed that these phantoms coincided with no marked event. The lady may have been thinking of going to her drawing-room; the man may have been in the act of walking home; but these are trivial circumstances which might be repeated any day.

Yet, however trivial, almost any set of human circumstances are sufficiently complex to leave room for coincidence. If the sitter in the drawing-room is wearing a distinctive article of dress, never seen by the percipient until it is seen in the hallucination; if the phantasmal homeward traveller is carrying a parcel of unusual shape, which the real man does afterwards unexpectedly bring home with him—there may be reason to think that there is a causal connection between the apparent agent's condition at the moment, and the apparition.

I will quote one of these "arrival-cases," so to term them, where the peculiarity of dress was such as to make the coincidence between vision and reality well worth attention. The case is interesting also as one of our earliest examples of a psychical incident carefully recorded at the time; so that after the lapse of nearly forty years it was possible to correct the percipient's surviving recollection by his contemporary written statement.

It is taken from *Phantasms of the Living*, vol. ii. p. 94, having been contributed by Major Bigge, of 2 Morpeth Terrace, S.W., who took the account out of a sealed envelope, in Gurney's presence, for the first time since it was written on the day of the occurrence. It reads:

§ An account of a circumstance which occurred to me when quartered at Templemore, Co. Tipperary, on 20th February, 1847.

This afternoon about 3 o'clock I was walking from my quarters towards the mess-room, when I distinctly saw Lt. Col. Reed walking from the buildings occupied by the officers toward the mess-room door; and I saw him go into the passage. He was dressed in a brown shooting-jacket, with grey summer regulation tweed trousers, and had a fishing-rod and a landing-net in his hand. Although at the time I saw him he was about 15 or 20 yards from me, and although anxious to speak to him at the moment, I did not do so, but followed him into the passage and turned into the ante-room on the left-hand side, where I expected to find him. On opening the door, to my great surprise, he was not there. The only person in the room was Quartermaster Nolan, who said he had not seen the colonel.

[Major Bigge then looked all over the building, but to his surprise the colonel was not to be found.]

I walked into the barrack-yard and joined Lt. Caulfield who was walking there; and I told the story to him, particularly describing the dress in which I had seen the colonel. We walked up and down the barrack-yard talking about it for about ten minutes, when to my great surprise I saw the colonel walk into the barracks through the gate which is in the opposite direction. He was in precisely the same dress in which I had seen him, and had a fishing-rod and landing-net in his hand. He was accompanied by Ensign Willington. Lt. Caulfield and I immediately walked to them, and we were joined by Lt. Col. Goldie and Captain Hartford, and I asked Col. Reed if he had not gone into the mess-room about ten minutes before. He replied he certainly had not, for he had been out fishing for more than two hours at some ponds about a mile from the barracks, and he had not been near the mess-room at all since the morning.

At the time I saw Col. Reed going into the mess-room, I was not aware that he had gone out fishing—a very unusual thing to do at this time of the year. . . . That I *did* see him I shall continue to believe until the last day of my existence.

WILLIAM MATTHEW BIGGE
Major, 70th Regiment §

In these *arrival* cases, there is, I say, a certain likelihood that the man's mind may be fixed on his return home, so that his phantasm is seen in what might seem both to himself and to others the most probable place.

But there are other cases were a man's phantasm is seen in a place where there is no special reason for his appearing, although these places seem always to lie within the beat and circuit of his habitual thought.

In such cases there are still possible circumstances which may give reason to think that the apparition is causally connected with the apparent agent. The phantasm of a given person may be seen *repeatedly* by different percipients, or it may be seen *collectively* by several persons at a time; or it may combine both these evidential characteristics, and may be seen several times and by several persons together.

Now considering the rarity of phantasmal appearances, considering that not one person in (say) five thousand is ever phantasmally seen at all; the mere fact that a given person's phantasm is seen even *twice*, by different percipients (for we cannot count a second appearance to the *same* percipient as of equal value), is in itself a remarkable fact; while if this happens *three or four times* we can hardly ascribe such a sequence of rare occurrences to chance alone.

I cite here the case of Mrs. Lucy Hawkins (née Eden, daughter of the late Primus of Scotland) from *Phantasms of the Living,* vol. ii. p. 78, considerably condensed from testimonies of Mrs. Hawkins herself, her cousins Miss Dickins and Mrs. Malcolm, and her son Edward Hawkins.

§ In the autumn of 1845 in Cherington, the residence of Mr. William Dickins, a large party of young people were playing hide-and-seek. Miss Dickins came around the corner of a building and saw her cousin, Lucy

Eden, standing under some trees about twenty yards ahead of her. Her sister, who at the moment appeared on the other side, also saw her and shouted to her. Their cousin Lucy, whose face they both saw distinctly, ran through a door into the fold-yard (or cow-yard) and disappeared, although scarcely a second elapsed before the sisters followed her through the door. When found a short time later, Lucy assured them she had not been anywhere near that spot at the time they saw her, and others supported her statement. This is attested to by both sisters, whose recollections after nearly forty years coincided closely.

Mrs. Hawkins states that at another time when she was about twenty, one of her little sisters reported to have seen her on the stairs, when she was actually seven miles off; but, Mrs. Hawkins says, "She might so easily have been mistaken that I have never put any faith in that appearance."

At another time an apparition of Mrs. Hawkins was said to have been seen in her own home by the nursery-maid, but this was not corroborated by the eye witness, who had since died.

On another occasion, in 1877, Mrs. Hawkins' son Edward saw her in the moonlight in his room at night, with her arms out ahead of her as if she were sleep walking. Edward Hawkins writes:

"I then sat up in bed, listening, but hearing nothing; and, on peering through the darkness saw that the door to get to which she would have had to pass in front of the light, was still shut. I then jumped out of bed, struck a light, and instead of finding my mother at the far end of the room, as I expected, found the room empty.

"I might add that I had, at that time, quite forgotten that my mother had ever appeared to anyone before, her last appearance having been about the year 1847, three years before I was born." §

Taken from *Phantasms of the Living,* vol. ii. p. 91. This account comes from Captain A. S. Beaumont, of 1 Crescent Road, South Norwood Park:

§ In September, 1873, when my father was living at 57 Inverness Terrace, I was sitting one evening, about 8:30 P.M., in the large dining-room. At the table, facing me, with their backs to the door, were seated my mother, sister, and a friend, Mrs. W. Suddenly I seemed to see my wife bustling in through the door of the back dining-room, which was in view from my position. She was in a *mauve* dress. I got up to meet her, though much astonished, as I believed her to be at Tenby. As I rose, my mother said, "Who is that?" not (I think) seeing any one herself, but seeing that

I did. I exclaimed, "Why, it's Carry," and advanced to meet her. As I advanced the figure disappeared. On inquiry, I found that my wife was spending that evening at a friend's house, in a mauve dress, which I had most certainly never seen. I had never seen her dressed in that color. My wife recollected that at that time she was talking with some friends about me, much regretting my absence, as there was going to be dancing, and I had promised to play for them. I had been unexpectedly detained in London.

ALEX. S. BEAUMONT §

And we now come to other cases, where the percipience has been collective, although it has not been repeated. Here is a case where two persons at one moment—a moment of no stress or excitement whatever—see the phantasm of a third; that third person being perhaps occupied with some supraliminal or subliminal thought of the scene in the midst of which she is phantasmally discerned. Both the percipients supposed at the moment, naturally enough, that it was their actual sister whom they saw: and one can hardly fancy that a mere act of tranquil recognition of the figure by one percipient would communicate to the other percipient a telepathic shock such as would make *her* see the same figure as well.

The account is taken from the "Report on the Census of Hallucinations" (*Proceedings* S.P.R., vol. x. p. 306).

§ Miss K. E. writes: Upon the afternoon in August, 1889 during which this curious incident happened, I wandered about my uncle's garden for a while, and half thought of going into the church, but changed my mind and did not. I went into the library, and being interested in genealogy, studied my uncle's family pedigree until teatime, when I remarked to my sisters that I had not been to the church all afternoon, and they told me that they had seen me there. I felt no unusual sensations during the afternoon, and am much mystified by the incident.

Her sister Miss C. J. E. writes: I was playing the harmonium in the church . . . when I saw my eldest sister walk up the aisle toward the chancel with a roll of papers under her arm. When I looked up again she had disappeared. I was eighteen years old. A younger sister was the only other person in the church with me at the time . . . My eldest sister looked just as usual and wore her hat and jacket, . . . she walked rather briskly, looking straight before her.

The other percipient, Miss H. E., writes: My sisters and I were spending the day with our uncle; as he is the rector his garden leads into the churchyard. In the course of the afternoon C. and I went into the church;

she began to play the harmonium and I stood on a stone coffin beside her
with my hand on her shoulder. . . . C. casually looked up; I did the
same, and saw K. walking to us up the church with—and this rather surprised me—a long bundle of papers in her hand . . . It was certainly
K. herself; I could see her face quite well. §

That special idiosyncrasy on the part of the agent which tends to make
his phantasm easily visible has never yet, so far as I know, received a
name, although for convenience' sake it certainly needs one. I propose
to use the Greek word ψυχορραγῶ, which means strictly "to let the soul
break loose," and from which I form the words *psychorrhagy* and *psychorrhagic,* on obvious analogies. When I say that Mrs. Beaumont or Mrs.
Hawkins, agents in cases cited, were born with the *psychorrhagic diathesis,*
I express what I believe to be an important fact, physiological as well as
psychological, in terms which seem pedantic, but which are the only ones
which mean exactly what the facts oblige me to say. That which "breaks
loose" on my hypothesis is not (as in the Greek use of the word) the
whole principle of life in the organism; rather it is some psychical element probably of very varying character, and definable mainly by its
power of producing a phantasm, perceptible by one or more persons, in
some portion or other of space. I hold that this phantasmogenetic effect
may be produced either on the mind, and consequently on the brain of
another person—in which case he may discern the phantasm somewhere
in his vicinity, according to his own mental habit or prepossession—or
else directly on a portion of space "out in the open" in which case several
persons may simultaneously discern the phantasm in that actual spot.

Let us apply the view to one of our most bizarre and puzzling cases
—that of Canon Bourne. From the *Journal* S.P.R., vol. vi. p. 129. The
case is recorded by the Misses H. M. and L. Bourne.

Additional evidence of the hallucinatory character of the figure seen
is afforded by the details having been more clearly discernible than those
of a real figure at the same distance would have been.

Miss L. Bourne writes:

§ On February 5th, 1887, my father, sister, and I went out hunting.
About the middle of the day my sister and I decided to return home with
the coachman, while my father went on. Somebody came and spoke to
us, and delayed us for a few moments. As we were turning to go home,
we distinctly saw my father, waving his hat to us and signing us to follow
him. He was on the side of a small hill, and there was a dip between
him and us. My sister, the coachman, and myself all recognized my

father, and also the horse. The horse looked so dirty and shaken that the coachman remarked he thought there had been a nasty accident. As my father waved his hat I clearly saw the Lincoln and Bennett mark inside, though from the distance we were apart it ought to have been utterly impossible for me to have seen it. At the time I mentioned seeing the mark in the hat, though the strangeness of seeing it did not strike me till afterwards.

Fearing an accident, we hurried down the hill. From the nature of the ground we had to lose sight of my father, but it took us very few seconds to reach the place where we had seen him. When we got there, there was no sign of him anywhere, nor could we see any one in sight at all. We rode about for some time looking for him, but could not see or hear anything of him. We all reached home within a quarter of an hour of each other. My father then told us he had never been in the field, in which we thought we saw him, the whole of that day. He had never waved to us, and had met with no accident.

My father was riding the only white horse that was out that day.

LOUISE BOURNE
H. M. BOURNE §

And now let us pass on from these psychorrhagic cases, which hardly concern anybody beyond the phantom-begetter himself—and do not even add anything to his own knowledge—to cases where there is some sort of communication from one mind to another, or some knowledge gained by the excursive spirit.

It is impossible to arrange these groups in one continuous logical series. But, roughly speaking, the degree in which the psychical collision is *recollected* on either side may in some degree indicate its *intensity,* and may serve as a guide to our provisional arrangement.

And following this scheme I shall begin with a group of cases which seem to promise but little information—cases, namely, where A, the agent, in some way impresses or invades P, the percipient—but nevertheless neither A nor P retains in supraliminal memory any knowledge of what has occurred.

But how can we outside inquirers know anything of telepathic incidents which the principals themselves fail altogether to remember?

In ordinary life we may sometimes learn from bystanders incidents which we cannot learn from the principals themselves. Can there be bystanders who look on at a psychical invasion?

The question is of much theoretical import. On my view that there

is a real transference of something from the agent, involving an alteration of some kind in a particular part of space, there might theoretically
be some bystander who might discern that alteration in space more clearly
than the person for whose benefit, so to say, the alteration was made. If,
on the other hand, what has happened is merely a transference of some
impulse "from mind to mind" then one can hardly understand how any
mind except the mind aimed at could perceive the telepathic impression.
Yet, in *collective* cases, persons in whom the agent feels no interest, nay,
of whose presence along with the intended percipient he is not aware,
do in fact receive the impression in just the same way as that intended
percipient himself.

From *Phantasms of the Living,* vol. i. p. 214. We received the first
account of this case—the percipient's evidence—through the kindness
of Mrs. Martin, of Ham Court, Upton-on-Severn, Worcester.

§ Helen Alexander (maid to Lady Waldegrave) was lying here very
ill with typhoid fever, and was attended by me. I was standing at the
table by her bedside, pouring out her medicine, at about 4 o'clock in the
morning of the 4th October, 1880. I heard the call-bell ring and was attracted by the door of the room opening, and by seeing a person entering
the room whom I instantly felt to be the mother of the sick woman. She
had a brass candlestick in her hand, a red shawl over her shoulders, and a
flannel petticoat on which had a hole in the front. I looked at her as
much as to say, "I am glad you have come," but the woman looked at
me sternly, as much as to say, "Why wasn't I sent for before?" I gave
the medicine to Helen Alexander, and then turned round to speak to
the vision, but no one was there. She had gone. She was a short, dark
person, and very stout. At about 6 o'clock that morning Helen Alexander
died. Two days after her parents and a sister came to Antony, and arrived
between 1 and 2 o'clock in the morning; I and another maid let them in,
and it gave me a great turn when I saw the living likeness of the vision
I had seen two nights before. I told the sister about the vision, and she
said that the description of the dress exactly answered to her mother's, and
that they had brass candlesticks at home exactly like the one described.
There was not the slightest resemblance between the mother and daughter.

FRANCES REDDELL §

This at first sight might be taken for a mere delusion of an excitable
or over-tired servant, modified and exaggerated by the subsequent sight
of the real mother. If such a case is to have evidential force, we must
ascertain beyond doubt that the description of the experience was given

in detail before any knowledge of the reality can have affected the percipient's memory or imagination. This necessary corroboration has been
kindly supplied by Mrs. F. A. Pole-Carew, of Antony, Torpoint, Devon-
port: "Reddell told me and my daughter of the apparition, about an hour
after Helen's death."

Now what I imagine to have happened here is this. The mother,
anxious about her daughter, paid her a psychical visit during the sleep of
both. In so doing she actually modified a certain portion of space, not
materially nor optically, but in such a manner that persons perceptive in
a certain fashion would discern in that part of space an image approximately corresponding to the conception of her own aspect latent in the
invading mother's mind. A person thus susceptible happened to be in
the room, and thus, as a bystander, witnessed a psychical invasion whose
memory the invader apparently did not retain, while the invaded person
—the due percipient—may or may not have perceived it in a dream, but
died and left no sign of having done so.

I will give one more instance of this *deflected* perception, where a dying (or dead) man, apparently wishing to appear to his sister, fails to
attract her attention, but is observed by a nurse, who has never seen him
in the flesh.

From *Phantasms of the Living,* vol. ii. p. 61. This case came from Mrs.
Clerke, of Clifton Lodge, Farquhar Road, Upper Norwood, S. E.

§ In the month of August, 1864, about 3 or 4 o'clock in the afternoon, I
was sitting reading in the verandah of our house in Barbadoes. My [col-
ored] nurse was driving my little girl, about eighteen months or so old,
in her perambulator in the garden. I got up after some time to go into
the house, not having noticed anything at all—when this woman said to
me, "Missis, who was that gentleman that was talking to you just now?"
"There was no one talking to me," I said. "Oh, yes, dere was, missis—a
very pale gentleman, very tall, and he talked to you, and you was very
rude, for you never answered him." I repeated there was no one, and got
rather cross with the woman, and she begged me to write down the day,
for she knew she had seen some one. I did, and in a few days I heard of
the death of my brother in Tobago. Now, the curious part is this, that *I*
did not see him, but she—a stranger to him—did; and she said that he
seemed very anxious for me to notice him.

MAY CLERKE §

I give now a strange case, which comes to us on good authority, where
we must suppose one man's subliminal impulse to have created a picture

of himself, his wife, a carriage and a horse, persistent enough to have been
watched for some seconds at least by three observers in one place, and
by a fourth and independent observer at another point in the moving
picture's career.

From *Phantasms of the Living,* vol. ii. p. 97. The narrator is the late
Rev. W. Mountford, of Boston, U.S.A., a minister and author of repute.

§ One day, some fifteen years ago, I was visiting some friends who resided in Norfolk. About four o'clock in the afternoon I stood at the window, and looking up the road I said, "Here is your brother coming." My
host advanced to the window and said, "Oh yes, here he is; and see,
Robert has got Dobbin out at last." Dobbin was a horse which, on account of some accident, had not been used for some weeks. The lady also
looked out of the window, and said to me, "And I am so glad, too, that
my sister is with him. They will be delighted to find you here." I recognized distinctly the vehicle in which they rode as being an open one, also
the lady and the gentleman, and both their dress and their attitudes. Our
friends passed at a gentle pace along the front of the window, and then
turning with the road round the corner of the house, they could not longer
be seen. After a minute my host went to the door and exclaimed, "Why,
what can be the matter? They have gone on without calling; a thing they
never did in their lives before. What can be the matter?"

Five minutes afterwards, while we were seated by the fireside, the
parlor door opened, and there entered a lady of about twenty-five years
of age; she was in robust health and in full possession of all her senses,
and she was possessed, besides, of a strong common-sense. She was pale
and much excited, and the moment she opened the door she exclaimed,
"Oh, aunt, I have had such a fright! Father and mother have passed me
on the road without speaking. I looked up at them as they passed by, but
they looked straight on and never stopped nor said a word. A quarter of
an hour before, when I started to walk here, they were sitting by the fire;
and now, what can be the matter? They never turned nor spoke, and yet I
am certain that they must have seen me."

Ten minutes after the arrival of this lady, I, looking through the window up the road, said, "But see, here they are, coming down the road
again." My host said, "No, that is impossible, because there is no path
by which they could get on to this road, so as to be coming down it again.
But sure enough, here they are, and with the same horse! How in the
world have they got here?" We all stood at the window, and saw pass
before us precisely the same appearance which we had seen before—lady
and gentleman, and horse and carriage. My host ran to the door and ex-

claimed, "How did you get here? How did you get on to the road to be coming down here again now?" "I get on the road? What do you mean? I have just come straight from home." "And did you not come down the road, and pass the house, less than a quarter of an hour ago?" "No," said the lady and gentleman both. "This is the first time that we have come down the road to-day." "Certainly," we all said, "you passed these windows less than a quarter of an hour ago. And, besides, here is Mary, who was on the road and saw you." "Nonsense!" was the answer. "We are straight from home, as you may be very sure." "Then you mean to say that really you did not pass by here ten or fifteen minutes ago?" "Certainly; for at that time, probably, we were just coming out of the yard and starting to come here." §

In the cases which I have lately been recounting there has been a psychical excursion, with its possibilities of clairvoyance; but the excursive element has not brought home any assignable knowledge to the supraliminal personality. I go on now to cases where such knowledge *has* thus been garnered.

From *Phantasms of the Living,* vol. i. p. 196. In the following the percipient, Mr. J. G. Keulemans, acquires information of what is happening at a distance through a mere mental impression, completely unexternalized, but yet conveying both the abstract idea of an event and the concrete picture of a scene.

§ My wife went to reside at the seaside on September 30th last, taking with her our youngest child, a little boy thirteen months old.

On Wednesday, October 3rd, I felt a strong impression that the little fellow . . . had fallen *out of the bed,* upon chairs, and then rolled down upon the floor. This was about 11 A.M., and I at once wrote to my wife, asking her to let me know how the little fellow was getting on. I thought it rather bold to tell my wife that the baby had, to my conviction, really met with an accident, without being able to produce any confirmatory evidence. Also I considered that she would take it as an insinuation of carelessness on her part; therefore I purposely wrote it as a *post scriptum:* "Mind little Gaston does not fall out of bed. Put chairs in front of it. You know accidents soon happen. The fact is, I am almost certain he has met with such a mishap this very morning."

Mr. Keulemans learned later that the baby had tumbled out of the bed upon the chairs placed at the side, and then found his way upon the floor, without being hurt. This occurred about 11 A.M. the same day he wrote the letter. §

From *Phantasms of the Living*, vol. ii. p. 37. The stage of visualization in the next case is particularly interesting. The narrator is Mrs. Taunton, of Brook Vale, Witton, Birmingham.

§ On Thursday evening, 14th November, 1867, I was sitting in the Birmingham Town Hall with my husband at a concert, when there came over me the icy chill which usually accompanies these occurrences. Almost immediately, I saw with perfect distinctness, between myself and the orchestra, my uncle, Mr. W., lying in bed with an appealing look on his face, like one dying. I had not heard anything of him for several months, and had no reason to think he was ill. The appearance was not transparent or filmy, but perfectly solid-looking; *and yet I could somehow see the orchestra, not through, but behind it.* I did not try turning my eyes to see whether the figure moved with them, but looked at it with a fascinated expression that made my husband ask if I was ill. I asked him not to speak to me for a minute or two; the vision gradually disappeared, and I told my husband, after the concert was over, what I had seen. A letter came shortly after telling of my uncle's death. He died at exactly the time when I saw the vision.

E. F. TAUNTON

[The signature of Mrs. Taunton's husband is also appended.]
RICH. H. TAUNTON §

The phantasm here was perfectly external, and is described as "perfectly solid-looking"; yet it certainly did not hold to the real objects around the same relation as a figure of flesh and blood would have held; it was in a peculiar way transparent. This feature is noticeable, as it is one which occasionally occurs also in hallucinations of the purely subjective class. It may thus be taken as one of the numerous minor indications of the hallucinatory character of telepathic phantasms.

From Mrs. Sidgwick's paper "On the Evidence for Clairvoyance," in *Proceedings* S.P.R., vol. vii. pp. 32–35. Mr. A. B. Wood writes to Mr. F. A. Nims, an Associate of the American Branch of the Society for Psychical Research, as follows:

§ MUSKEGON, April 29th, 1890.

In compliance with your suggestion, supplemented by the request of Mr. Richard Hodgson, I sought an interview with Mrs. Agnes Paquet, and obtained the following information regarding her strange experience on the day of her brother's death. . . .

A. B. WOOD

Statement of Accident.

On October 24th, 1889, Edmund Dunn, brother of Mrs. Agnes Paquet, was serving as fireman on the tug *Wolf,* a small steamer engaged in towing vessels in Chicago Harbor. At about 3 o'clock A.M., the tug fastened to a vessel, inside the piers, to tow her up the river. While adjusting the tow-line Mr. Dunn fell or was thrown overboard by the tow-line, and drowned. The body, though sought for, was not found until about three weeks after the accident, when it came to the surface near the place where Mr. Dunn disappeared.

Mrs. Paquet's Statement.

I arose about the usual hour on the morning of the accident, probably about six o'clock, feeling gloomy and depressed, which feeling I could not shake off. After breakfast I decided to steep and drink some tea, hoping it would relieve me of the gloomy feelings aforementioned. I went into the pantry, took down the tea canister, and as I turned around my brother Edmund—or his exact image—stood before me and only a few feet away. The apparition stood with back toward me, or, rather, partially so, and was in the act of falling forward—away from me— seemingly impelled by two ropes or a loop of rope drawing against his legs. The vision lasted but a moment, disappearing over a low railing or bulwark, but was very distinct. I dropped the tea, clasped my hands to my face, and exclaimed, "My God! Ed is drowned."

At about half-past ten A.M. my husband received a telegram from Chicago, announcing the drowning of my brother.

AGNES PAQUET §

A precognitive case given in my article on "The Subliminal Self; the Relation of Supernormal Phenomena to Time" (*Proceedings* S.P.R., vol. xi. pp. 334–593) is here quoted. The narrative comes from Dr. A. S. Wiltse of Skiddy, Kansas, personally known to Dr. Hodgson and myself as a careful and conscientious witness, who writes:

§ This incident occurred in Morgan County, Tennessee, I think in the spring of 1878. Mrs. Wiltse and myself had spent the day with her mother and step-father, Mr. and Mrs. Todd. We retired early, and Mrs. Wiltse almost immediately fell asleep.

Mr. Todd and myself being wakeful, lay and talked. There was but one room, in which there was an open fireplace containing fire mostly buried up with ashes, a large pine knot having been laid on top and so nearly buried in ashes as to give about a one candle power of light.

While we were talking, I saw a picture slide on to the wall at my feet, at such a height as to rest easily in the line of my vision. I called to Mr. and Mrs. Todd to cease talking, and told them what I saw. The picture was some feet in size each way, and remained before me long enough for me to describe it in detail to them. It was a landscape of a familiar local scene. The picture disappeared, then appeared again with the addition of a log house in the scene.

Both Todd and his wife said I had described the "Cass Davis House," which was about a mile distant, across the river. At this another picture slid on to the wall, the very counterpart of the second one, except that a good portion of the landscape was left out, but the house was there, the door of which was closed, and as I announced its appearance, I heard the muffled report of a gun on the inside of the house, and immediately afterwards the door flew open and a man rushed out seemingly in a great fright.

At this point Todd said, "See here, Doc., are you seeing these things, or just playing off a drive on us?" I assured him that I actually saw, or seemed to see the things I described, although they did not seem possessed of solidity, but were more as if one should breathe over a looking-glass, then stand at some distance from it and observe his image; it would look shadowy and dim.

In the meantime the door of the house in the picture had been left open so that I could see into the house, where I saw a man staggering toward the door with blood running from his mouth. He reached the door, where he supported himself by leaning against the door-facing, and steadied himself off the doorstep on to the ground. In so doing he left the print of his hand in blood upon the door-facing.

At this point the picture again disappeared and was immediately replaced by another much the same as the other, but in it the dead body of the man was lying on the ground some few feet from the door, while from the field advanced several people, with hoes and mattocks in their hands, who gathered round the body in apparent excitement and consternation, when the picture vanished and I saw nothing more.

I asked Todd if he was sure of the house; he assured me that it bore the exact description I had given. I asked if there was any rumor, or ever had been to his knowledge, of a tragedy having occurred there. "Not that he had ever heard of." I believe I said that "something of the kind has occurred there or else will. If it is past we may never know it; if it is to come, we may see."

When the corn which Todd had planted that day was ready for hoeing, I was with him again in the field a portion of a day, and together we left the field and started to go to Wartburg, the county seat about two miles distant. On the way we met *Cass Davis,* a quadroon, who asked us if we had heard of Henderson Whittaker killing himself. We had not, and he told us that during the (forenoon, I think) Whittaker went into the house, where Mr. Haun was sitting alone, and asked Haun to loan him his rifle to go hunting. Haun pointed to the corner where the rifle stood, saying, "I don't know whether it is loaded or not." Whittaker put his mouth over the muzzle to blow into the gun, pushing back the hammer with his foot. The foot slipped off and the gun was discharged into his mouth. Haun ran out into the field for help. The hands came up and I think found the young man dead in the yard. I have also been told that the hand print of blood was left upon the door-facing, but these lesser points can be learned best from parties who lived in the neighborhood at the time. The main points are absolutely certain. The tragedy occurred in the house I had described, and was of substantially the nature I had described from the picture-writing on the wall. §

Questions about this case were answered by Mr. William Todd. Others who testified were Maniphee Haun, James Bales, and W. T. Howard.

The following is condensed from accounts given by Mrs. Elgee of 18 Woburn Road, Bedford, and Mrs. Ramsay of Clevelands, Bassett, Southampton.

§ In the month of November, 1864 Mrs. Elgee, on her way to join her husband, Major Elgee of the 23rd Royal Welsh Fusiliers in India, was detained overnight in Cairo. With her was a young lady under her charge who was going to India to rejoin her parents. They were obliged to spend the night in a somewhat unfrequented hotel and were especially concerned as to their safety. Thus they locked the door of their room, and then put a chair against it with a travelling bag so arranged on the chair that it would fall off if the door was pushed. As it was warm they left open the only window in the room, for it led onto a small balcony, which was isolated and was three stories above the ground. [Mrs. Elgee continues:]

I suddenly woke from a sound sleep with the impression that somebody had called me, and, sitting up in bed, to my unbounded astonishment, by the clear light of early dawn coming in through the large window before mentioned, I beheld the figure of an old and very valued friend whom I knew to be in England. He appeared as if most eager to speak to me, and I addressed him with, "Good gracious! how did you come here?" So clear was the figure, that I noted every detail of his dress, even to three onyx shirt-studs which he always wore. He seemed to come a step nearer to me, when he suddenly pointed across the room, and on my looking round, I saw Miss D. sitting up in her bed, gazing at the figure with every expression of terror. On looking back, my friend seemed to shake his head, and retreated step by step, slowly, till he seemed to sink through that portion of the door where the settee stood.

[In the morning Mrs. Elgee determined not to say anything until Miss D. spoke about it.]

Presently, on Miss D. waking up, she looked about the room, and, noticing the chair and bag, made some remark as to their not having been much use. I said, "What do you mean?" and then she said, "Why, that man who was in the room this morning must have got in somehow." She then proceeded to describe to me exactly what I myself had seen. . . .

Of course, I was under the impression my friend was dead. Such, however, was not the case; and I met him some four years later, when, without telling him anything of my experience in Cairo, I asked him, in a joking way, could he remember what he was doing on a certain night in November, 1864. "Well," he said, "you require me to have a good memory"; but after a little reflection he replied, "Why, this was the time I was so harassed with trying to decide for or against the appointment which was offered me, and I so much wished you could have been with me to talk the matter over. I sat over the fire quite late, trying to think what you would have advised me to do." A little cross-questioning and comparing of dates brought out the curious fact that, allowing for the difference of time between England and Cairo, his meditations over the fire and my experience were simultaneous. Having told him the circumstances above narrated, I asked him had he been aware of any peculiar or unusual sensation. He said none, only that he had wanted to see me very much.

E. H. ELGEE

[Mrs. Ramsay (who is referred to above as "Miss D.") reports their conversation the next morning after the incident as follows:]

I believe I then told her it was not strange that I should look odd, for I "had seen a ghost." She started violently, and asked me to tell her what I saw. I described it as best I could, and she said *she had seen "it" too*, and that she knew it to be the form and face of a valued friend. She was much disturbed about it—as indeed, so was I, for I had never indulged in "hallucinations" and was not given to seeing visions. §

This case was interesting both evidentially and from its intrinsic character. The narrative, printed in *Phantasms of the Living* on the authority of one only of the witnesses concerned (Mrs. Elgee), led to the discovery of the *second* witness (Mrs. Ramsay)—whom we had no other means of finding—and has been amply corroborated by her independent account.

From the *Journal* S.P.R., vol. v. p. 147 is the following account of a very curious experience of Mr. James Dickinson, a photographer, of 43 Grainger St., Newcastle-on-Tyne.

On Saturday, the 3rd of January, 1891, Mr. Dickinson arrived at his place of business a few minutes before 8 A.M. A gentleman called to inquire if his photographs were finished. He was told no and to call again later in the day. Mr. Dickinson continues:

§ He said, "I have been traveling all night, and cannot call again." With that he turned abruptly, and went out. Anxious to retain his good will, I shouted after him, "Can I post what may be done?" but I got no answer. I turned once more to the book, looked at the number, and on a slip of paper wrote, "No. 7976, *Thompson, post.*" (This I wrote with pen and ink, and have the paper yet.) At nine o'clock, when Miss S. (clerk and reception-room attendant) came, I handed the slip of paper to her and asked her to have it attended to, telling her that the man had called for them, and seemed much disappointed that he had not received them before. Miss S., with considerable surprise, exclaimed: "Why, an old man called about these photographs yesterday (Friday), and I told him they could not be ready this week owing to the bad weather, and that we were nearly three weeks behind with our work." . . . I asked to be shown the negative, and about half-an-hour later Miss S. called me, saying, "This is Thompson's negative." I took it in my hands and looked at it carefully, remarking, "Yes, that is it; that is the chap who called this morning."

Mr. Dickinson relates that when he went to print Mr. Thompson's picture the negative inadvertently was dropped and broken. He wrote to Mr. Thompson "asking him to kindly give another sitting, and offering to recoup him for his trouble and loss of time."

On Friday, January 9th, Miss S. called Mr. Dickinson to come down from the printing-room upstairs, as the gentleman had called about the negative. I asked "What negative?" "Well," she replied, "the one we broke, Mr. Thompson's." I answered, "I am very busy, and cannot come down, but you know the terms I offered him; send him up to be taken at once." "But he is *dead!*" said Miss S. "Dead!" I exclaimed, and hastened to my office. Here I saw an elderly gentleman, who seemed in trouble. "Surely," said I, "you don't mean to say that this man is dead?" "It is only too true," he replied. "It must have been very sudden," I said sympathetically, "because I saw him only last Saturday." The old gentleman shook his head sadly, and said, "You are mistaken, for he died last Saturday."

"Nay," I returned, "I am not mistaken, for I recognized the negative by him." However, the father persisted in saying I was mistaken, and that it was he who called on the Friday and not his son. . . . "That is quite right," said Miss S., "but Mr. D. also saw a gentleman on Saturday morning, and when I showed Mr. D. the negative he said, 'Yes, that's the man who called.' I told Mr. D. *then* of your having called on the Friday." Still Mr. Thompson seemed to think that we were wrong . . . He told me that his son died on Saturday, January 3rd, at about 2:30 P.M.; he also stated that at the time I saw him (the sitter) he was unconscious, and remained so up to the time of his death. I have not had any explanation of this mysterious visit up to present date, February 26th, 1891.

It is curious to me that I have no recollection of hearing the man come upstairs, or of him going down. In appearance he was pale and careworn, and looked as though he had been very ill. This thought occurred to me when he said he had been traveling all night.

JAMES DICKINSON

[Miss S. signs the following statement:]

I am the Miss S. referred to in the foregoing narrative. I have read Mr. Dickinson's statement carefully, and I can testify that everything in it referring to me has been correctly stated.

ETHEL MAUD SIMMON

[This was also corroborated by the independent testimony of Mr. Thompson Sr.] §

The following case is taken from Mrs. Sidgwick's paper, "On the Evidence for Clairvoyance," in *Proceedings* S.P.R., vol. vii. p. 41.

§ Mr. S. R. Wilmot, a manufacturer of Bridgeport, Connecticut, sailed on October 3rd, 1863 from Liverpool for New York, on the steamer *City of Limerick,* of the Inman line, Captain Jones commanding. The night following a severe nine-day storm he had the first refreshing sleep since leaving port. "Toward morning I dreamed that I saw my wife, whom I had left in the United States, come to the door of my state room, clad in her night dress," he reports. "At the door she seemed to discover that I was not the only occupant of the room, hesitated a little, then advanced to my side, stooped down and kissed me, and after gently caressing me for a few moments, quietly withdrew.

"Upon waking I was surprised to see my fellow-passenger, whose berth was above mine, but not directly over it—owing to the fact that our room was at the stern of the vessel—leaning upon his elbow, and looking fixedly at me. 'You're a pretty fellow,' said he at length, 'to have a lady come and visit you in this way.' I pressed him for an explanation, which he at first declined to give, but at length related what he had seen while wide awake, lying in his berth. It exactly corresponded with my dream."

This gentleman was William J. Tait, a sedate 50 year old man who was not in the habit of practical joking. From the testimony of Mr. Wilmot's sister, Miss Eliza E. Wilmot, who was also on board ship, he was impressed by what he had seen. She says: "In regard to my brother's strange experience on our homeward voyage in the *Limerick,* I remember Mr. Tait's asking me one morning (when assisting me to the breakfast table, for the cyclone was raging fearfully) if I had been in last night to see my brother; and my astonishment at the question, as he shared the same stateroom. At my, '*No, why?*' he said he saw *some* woman, in white, who went up to my brother." Miss Wilmot said her brother then told her of his dream.

Mr. Wilmot continues: "The day after landing I went by rail to Watertown, Conn., where my children and my wife had been for some time, visiting her parents. Almost her first question when we were alone together was, 'Did you receive a visit from me a week ago Tuesday?' 'A visit from you?' said I, 'we were more than a thousand miles at sea.' 'I know it,' she replied, 'but it seemed to me that I visited you.' 'It would be impossible,' said I. 'Tell me what makes you think so.' "

His wife then told him that on account of the severity of the weather she had been extremely anxious about him. On the night in question she had lain awake for a long time thinking of him, and about four o'clock in the morning it seemed to her that she went out to seek him. Crossing the wide and stormy sea, she came at length to a low, black steamship, whose side she went up, and then descending into the cabin, passed through it to the stern until she came to his stateroom.

"Tell me," she said, "do they ever have staterooms like the one I saw, where the upper berth extends further back than the under one? A man was in the upper berth, looking right at me, and for a moment I was afraid to go in, but soon I went up to the side of your berth, bent down and kissed you, and embraced you, and then went away."

The description given by Mrs. Wilmot of the steamship was correct in all particulars, though she had never seen it. Mrs. Wilmot states that she thinks she told her mother the next morning about her dream; and I know that I had a very vivid sense all the day of having visited my husband; the impression was so strong that I felt unusually happy and refreshed, to my surprise." §

And here comes in a small but important group—the group of what I may call death-compacts prematurely fulfilled. We shall see in the next chapter that the exchange of a solemn promise between two friends to appear to one another, if possible, after death is far from being a useless piece of sentiment. Such posthumous appearances, it is true, may be in most cases impossible, but nevertheless there is real ground to believe that the previous tension of the will in that direction makes it more likely that the longed-for meeting shall be accomplished. If so, this is a kind of *experiment,* and an experiment which all can make.

We have two or three cases where this compact has been made, and where an apparition has followed—but before and not after the agent's death—at the moment, that is to say, of some dangerous accident, when the sufferer was perhaps all but drowned, or was stunned, or otherwise insensible.

From *Phantasms of the Living,* vol. i. p. 527. The next account was from a lady known to Mr. Gurney, whose only reason for withholding her name and address was her fear that a near relation might object to their publication.

§ Years ago, a friend and myself made the time-worn arrangement that whichever died first would endeavor to return to visit the other. Some years after, I asked this man's sister to remember me to him and say, did he remember his promise, and having received for answer "Perfectly, and I hope I shall appear to her and not she to me," the whole matter passed out of my mind. My friend was in New Zealand, his sister I don't know where. One night I awoke with a feeling some one was in the room. I must tell you that I always have a bright light burning on a table, not far from my bed. I looked about, and presently saw something behind the little table; felt myself grow perfectly cold; was not in the least frightened, rubbed my eyes to be sure I was quite awake, and looked at it steadfastly. Gradually a man's head and shoulders were perfectly formed, but in a sort of misty material, if I may use such a word. The head and features were distinct, but the whole appearance was not substantial and plain; in fact it was like a cloud, formed as a man's head and shoulders. At first I gazed and thought, who is it, some one must be here, but who? Then the formation of the head and forehead (which are most marked in my friend) made me exclaim to myself "Captain W——." The appearance faded away.

I got up and put the date down; and waited until news from New Zealand was possible. In due time we heard. . . . He had fallen off the coach, and was insensible for some time, and then, as he had said, his head was not clear for a while. I have never had the slightest doubt but that, while insensible, his spirit came here. The appearance to me was coincident with the time of his insensibility. I have never had but this one experience of an apparition.

E. W. R.

[In a subsequent letter, Miss R. adds:]

. . . I mentioned it to several people—quite three or four. One was extremely amused because my friend had not died; which she always used to assure me was—she was sure—a cause of sincere regret to me. §

In conversation, Miss R. especially, and unasked, confirmed the fact that the feeling of a presence in the room preceded the vision. She described the formation of the figure as like a cloud taking a definite shape. She further said that the hair of the head which appeared was distinctly *grey,* and that this was the chief reason why she did not sooner recognize the face. Her friend had *black* hair when she last saw him, and she had never thought of him otherwise; but she found out afterwards that he had become grey, and was so at the time of his accident. She also stated that she had ascertained beyond a doubt that her vision fell during the period of her friend's insensibility.

From *Phantasms of the Living,* vol. ii. p. 227. The next account is from Commander T. W. Aylesbury (late of the Indian Navy), of Sutton, Surrey.

§ The writer, when thirteen years of age, was capsized in a boat, when landing on the island of Bali east of Java, very early one morning and was nearly drowned. On coming to the surface, after being repeatedly submerged, the boy called his mother. This amused the boat's crew, who spoke of it afterwards, and jeered him a good deal about it. Months after, on arrival in England, the boy went to his home, and while telling his mother of his narrow escape, he said, "While I was under water, I saw you all sitting in this room; you were working something white. I saw you all —mother, Emily, Eliza, and Ellen." [His mother replied that they had heard him call at the time.] Commander Aylesbury adds:

I saw their features (my mother's and sisters'), the room and the furniture, particularly the old-fashioned Venetian blinds. My eldest sister was seated next to my mother. §

The following is an extract from a letter written to Commander Aylesbury by one of his sisters, and forwarded to us, in 1883:

§ I distinctly remember the incident you mention in your letter (the voice calling "Mother"); it made such an impression on my mind, I shall never forget it. We were sitting quietly at work one evening; it was about nine o'clock. I think it must have been late in the summer as we had left the street door open. We first heard a faint cry "Mother"; we all looked up, and said to one another, "Did you hear that? Some one cried out 'Mother.'" We had scarcely finished speaking, when the voice again called, "Mother," twice in quick succession, the last cry a frightened, agonizing cry. Mother was sadly upset about it. I remember she paced the room, and feared that something had happened to you. She wrote down the date the next day, and when you came home and told us how near you had been drowned, and the time of day, father said it would be about the time nine o'clock would be with us. I know the date and the time corresponded. §

The difference of time at the two places is a little more than seven hours; consequently nine in the evening in England would correspond with "very early in the morning" of the next day at the scene of the accident. But the incident happened too long ago for memory to be trusted as to the exactitude of the coincidence.

Lastly, the lessons of these spontaneous apparitions have been confirmed and widened by actual experiment. It is plain that just as we are not confined to noting small spontaneous telepathic transferences when they occur, but can also endeavor to reproduce them by experiment, so also we can endeavor to reproduce experimentally these more advanced telepathic phenomena of the invasion of the presence of the percipient by the agent. It is to be hoped, indeed, that such experiment may become one of the most important features of our inquiry.

From *Phantasms of the Living,* vol. i. pp. 104–109. The following case was especially remarkable in that there were two percipients. The narrative was copied by Gurney from a manuscript book of Mr. S. H. B.'s, to which he transferred it from an almanac diary, since lost.

§ On a certain Sunday evening in November, 1881, having been reading of the great power which the human will is capable of exercising, I determined with the whole force of my being, that I would be present in spirit in the front bedroom on the second floor of a house situated at 22 Hogarth Road, Kensington, in which room slept two ladies of my acquaintance, viz., Miss L. S. V. and Miss E. C. V., aged respectively 25 and 11 years. I was living at this time at 23 Kildare Gardens, a distance of about three miles from Hogarth Road, and I had not mentioned in any way my intention of trying this experiment to either of the above ladies, for the simple reason that it was only on retiring to rest upon this Sunday night that I made up my mind to do so. The time at which I determined I would be there was 1 o'clock in the morning, and I also had a strong intention of making my presence perceptible.

On the following Thursday I went to see the ladies in question, and in the course of conversation (without any allusion to the subject on my part) the elder one told me that on the previous Sunday night she had been much terrified by perceiving me standing by her bedside, and that she screamed when the apparition advanced towards her, and awoke her little sister, who saw me also.

I asked her if she was awake at the time, and she replied most decidedly in the affirmative, and upon my inquiring the time of the occurrence, she replied, about 1 o'clock in the morning.

This lady, at my request, wrote down a statement of the event and signed it.

This was the first occasion upon which I tried an experiment of this kind, and its complete success startled me very much.

Besides exercising my power of volition very strongly, I put forth an effort which I cannot find words to describe. I was conscious of a mysterious influence of some sort permeating in my body, and had a distinct impression that I was exercising some force with which I had been hitherto unacquainted, but which I can now at certain times set in motion at will.

S. H. B. §

Gurney requested Mr. B. to send him a note on the night that he intended to make his next experiment of the kind, and received the following note by the first post on Monday, March 24th, 1884.

§ *March 22nd,* 1884

DEAR MR. GURNEY—I am going to try the experiment tonight of making my presence perceptible at 44 Norland Square, at 12 P.M. I will let you know the result in a few days.—Yours very sincerely,   S. H. B. §

This is the statement of the results:

§ On Saturday night, March 22nd, 1884, at about midnight, I had a distinct impression that Mr. S. H. B. was present in my room, and I distinctly saw him whilst I was quite widely awake. He came towards me, and stroked my hair. I *voluntarily* gave him this information, when he called to see me on Wednesday, April 2nd, telling him the time and the circumstances of the apparition, without any suggestion on his part. The appearance in my room was most vivid, and quite unmistakable.

L. S. VERITY

[Miss A. S. Verity corroborates as follows:]

I remember my sister telling me that she had seen S. H. B., and that he had touched her hair, *before* he came to see us on April 2nd.

A. S. V. §

The experiment in the following case succeeded on the first trial. The agent was Miss Edith Maughan (now Mrs. G. Rayleigh Vicars), and the account is taken from the *Proceedings* S.P.R., vol. x. p. 273. Miss Maughan writes:

§ One night in September, 1888 I was lying awake in bed reading. . . I had recently been studying with interest various cases of astral projection in *Phantasms of the Living,* and I distinctly remember making up my mind that night to try whether I could manage to accomplish a projection of myself by force of will-concentration.

The room next to mine was occupied by a friend of mine [Miss Ethel Thompson], who was an old acquaintance, and not at all of an excitable turn of mind. I perfectly recall lying back on my pillow with a resolute but half-doubtful and amused determination to make Miss Thompson see me. The candle was burning on a chair at the side of my bed, and I heard only the ticking clock as I "willed" with all my might to appear to her. After a few minutes I felt dizzy and only half-conscious.

I don't know how long this state may have lasted, but I do remember emerging into a conscious state and thinking I had better leave off, as the strain had exhausted me.

I gave up, and changed into an easy position, thinking I had failed and needlessly fatigued myself for an impossible fancy. I blew out my candle; at the instant I was startled by hearing an indistinct sound from the next room.

It was Miss Thompson's voice raised slightly, but I could not distinguish more than the actual sound, which was repeated, and then there was silence. Soon after my clock struck two (A.M.), and I fell asleep.

Next morning I noticed that Miss Thompson looked rather tired at breakfast, but I asked no questions. Presently she said, "Had I gone into her room to frighten her during the night?" I said I had not left my room. She declared that I seemed to her to come in and bend over her and disappeared immediately thereafter. From what she said I concluded it must have been between 1 and 2 A.M. Her own account is in the possession of the Psychical Society. All I have to add is that I was in my ordinary state of health, and not at all excited, but merely bent on trying an experiment. §

From the *Journal* S.P.R., vol. vii. p. 99. This case is specially interesting in being *reciprocal*, as well as *experimental*. It must be observed, however, that the attempt to produce an apparition of himself seems to have been only a secondary object on the part of the agent; his main desire being to discover himself something of the percipient's condition. The following is the account of the agent, Mr. B. F. Sinclair:

§ On the 5th of July, 1887, I left my home in Lakewood to go to New York to spend a few days. My wife was not feeling well when I left, and after I had started I looked back and saw her standing in the door looking disconsolate and sad at my leaving. The picture haunted me all day, and at night, before I went to bed, I thought I would try to find out if possible her condition. I had undressed, and was sitting on the edge of the bed, when I covered my face with my hands and willed myself in Lakewood at home to see if I could see her. After a little, I seemed to be standing in her room before the bed, and saw her lying there looking much better. I felt satisfied she was better, and so spent the week more comfortably regarding her condition. On Saturday I went home. When she saw me, she remarked, "I don't know whether I am glad to see you or not, for I thought something had happened to you. I saw you standing in front of the bed the night (about 8:30 or before 9) you left, as plain as could be, and I have been worrying myself about you ever since. I sent to the office and to the depôt daily to get some message from you." After explaining my effort to find out her condition, everything became plain to her. She had seen me when I was trying to see her and find out her condition. I thought at the time I was going to see her and make her see me.

B. F. SINCLAIR §

Two important points are the *amount of effort* made by the experimenter, and the degree of his *consciousness of success*. In these self-projections we have before us, I do not say the most useful, but the most extraordinary achievement of the human will. What can lie further outside any known capacity than the power to cause a semblance of oneself to appear at a distance? What can be a more *central* action—more manifestly the outcome of whatsoever is deepest and most unitary in man's whole being? Here, indeed, begins the justification of the conception that we should now see the subliminal self no longer as a mere chain of eddies or backwaters, in some way secluded from the main stream of man's being, but rather as itself the central and potent current, the most truly identifiable with the man himself. Other achievements have their manifest limit; where is the limit here? The spirit has shown itself in part dissociated from the organism; to what point may its dissociation go? It has shown some independence, some intelligence, some permanence. To what degree of intelligence, independence, permanence, may it conceivably attain? Of all vital phenomena, I say, this is the most significant; this self-projection is the one definite act which it seems as though a man might perform equally well before and after bodily death.

Chapter Seven

PHANTASMS OF THE DEAD

The course of our argument has gradually conducted us to a point of capital importance. A profound and central question, approached in irregular fashion from time to time in previous chapters, must now be directly faced. From the actions and perceptions of spirits still in the flesh, and concerned with one another, we must pass on to inquire into the actions of spirits no longer in the flesh, and into the forms of perception with which men still in the flesh respond to that unfamiliar and mysterious agency.

There need be no real break here in my previous line of argument. The subliminal self, which we have already traced through various phases of growing sensitivity, growing independence of organic bonds, will now be studied as sensitive to yet remoter influences—as maintaining an independent existence even when the organism is destroyed. Our subject will divide itself conveniently under three main heads. *First,* it will be well to discuss briefly the nature of the evidence to man's survival of death which may theoretically be obtainable. *Secondly,* and this must form the bulk of the present chapter, we need a classified exposition of the main evidence to survival thus far obtained; so far as sensory automatism—audition or apparition—is concerned. Motor automatism—automatic writing and trance-utterance—must be left for later discussion. *Thirdly,* there will be need of some consideration of the meaning of this evidence as a whole, and of its implications alike for the scientific and for the ethical future of mankind. Much more, indeed, of discussion (as well as of evidence) than I can furnish will be needed before this great conception can be realized or argued from with the scientific thoroughness due to its position among fundamental cosmical laws. Considering how familiar the notion—the vague shadowy notion—of "immortality" has always been, it is strange indeed that so little should have been done in these modern days to grasp or to criticize it.

Beginning, then, with the inquiry as to what kind of evidence ought to be demanded for human survival, we are met first by the bluff statement which is still often uttered even by intelligent men, that *no* evidence would convince them of such a fact; "neither would they be persuaded though one rose from the dead."

Extravagant as such a profession sounds, it has a meaning which we shall do well to note. These resolute antagonists mean that no new evidence can carry conviction to them unless it be *continuous* with old evidence; and that they cannot conceive that evidence to a world of spirit can possibly be continuous with evidence based upon our experience of a world of matter. I agree with this demand for continuity; and I agree also that the claims usually advanced for a spiritual world have not only made no attempt at continuity with known fact, but have even ostentatiously thrown such continuity to the winds. The popular mind has expressly desired something startling, something outside Law and above Nature.

I can hardly too often repeat that my object in these pages is of a quite opposite character. Believing that all cognizable Mind is as continuous as all cognizable Matter, my ideal would be to attempt for the realm of mind what the spectroscope and the law of gravitation have effected for the realm of matter, and to carry that known cosmic uniformity of substance and interaction upwards among the essences and operations of an unknown spiritual world.

In popular parlance, we are looking out for *ghosts*. What connotation, then, are we to give to the word "ghost"—a word which has embodied so many unfounded theories and causeless fears? It would be more satisfactory, in the present state of our knowledge, simply to collect facts without offering speculative comment. But it seems safer to begin by briefly pointing out the manifest errors of the traditional view; since that tradition, if left unnoticed, would remain lodged in the background even of many minds which have never really accepted it.

In the first place, we have no warrant for the assumption that the phantom seen, even though it be somehow *caused* by a deceased person, *is* that deceased person, in any ordinary sense of the word. Instead of appealing to the crude analogy of the living friend who, when he has walked into the room, *is* in the room, we shall find for the ghost a much closer parallel in those hallucinatory figures or phantasms which living persons can sometimes project at a distance. When Mr. S. H. B., for instance, caused by an effort of will an apparition of himself to a waking percipient out of sight, he was himself awake and conscious in the place where, not his phantom, but his body, stood. Whatever, then, that phantom *was*—however generated or conditioned—we cannot say that it was *himself*. And equally unjustifiable must be the common parlance which speaks of the ghost as though it were the deceased person himself—a *revenant* coming back amongst living men.

And in the second place, just as we must cease to say that the phantom *is* the deceased, so also must we cease to ascribe to the phantom the motives by which we imagine that the deceased might be swayed. We must therefore excluded from our definition of a ghost any words which assume its intention to communicate with the living. It may bear such a relation to the deceased that it can reflect or represent his presumed wish to communicate, or it may not. If, for instance, its relation to his *post-mortem* life be like the relation of my dreams to my earthly life, it may represent little that is truly his, save such vague memories and instincts as give a dim individuality to each man's trivial dreams.

So let us describe a "ghost" as *a manifestation of persistent personal energy,* or as an indication that some kind of force is being exercised after death which is in some way connected with a person previously known on earth. In this definition we have eliminated, as will be seen, a great mass of popular assumptions. Yet we must introduce a further proviso, lest our definition still seem to imply an assumption which we have no right to make. It is theoretically possible that this force or influence, which after a man's death creates a phantasmal impression of him, may indicate no continuing action on his part, but may be some residue of the force or energy which he generated while yet alive.

Strange as this notion may seem, it is strongly suggested by many of the cases of *haunting* which are referred to later in this chapter. We shall presently find that there is strong evidence for the recurrence of the same hallucinatory figures in the same localities, but weak evidence to indicate any purpose in most of these figures, or any connection with bygone individuals, or with such tragedies as are popularly supposed to start a ghost on its career. In some of these cases of frequent, meaningless recurrence of a figure in a given spot, we are driven to wonder whether it can be some deceased person's past frequentation of that spot, rather than any fresh action of his after death, which has generated what I have termed the veridical after-image—veridical in the sense that it communicates information, previously unknown to the percipient, as to a former inhabitant of the haunted locality.

Such are some of the questions which our evidence suggests. And I may point out that the very fact that such bizarre problems should present themselves at every turn does in a certain sense tend to show that these apparitions are not purely subjective things—do not originate merely in the percipient's imagination. For they are not like what any man would have imagined. What man's mind does tend to fancy on such topics may be seen in the endless crop of fictitious ghost stories, which furnish, indeed, a curious proof of the persistence of preconceived notions. For they go on being framed according to canons of their own, and deal with a set of imaginary phenomena quite different from those which actually occur. The actual phenomena, I may add, could scarcely be made romantic. One true "ghost story" is apt to be very like another, and most of them to be fragmentary and apparently meaningless. Their meaning, that is to say, lies in their conformity, not to the instinct of mankind which fabricates and enjoys fictitious tales, but to some unknown law, not based on human sentiment or convenience at all.

And thus, absurdly enough, we sometimes hear men ridicule the phenomena which actually do happen, simply because those phenomena do not suit their preconceived notions of what ghostly phenomena ought to be—not perceiving that this very divergence, this very unexpectedness, is in itself no slight indication of an origin *outside* the minds which obviously were so far from anticipating anything of the kind.

A communication (if such a thing exists) from a departed person to a person still on earth is, at any rate, a communication from a mind in one state of existence to a mind in a very different state of existence. And it is, moreover, a communication from one mind to another which passes through some channel other than the ordinary channels of sense, since on one side of the gulf no material sense-organs exist. Whatever else, indeed, a "ghost" may be, it is probably one of the most complex phenomena in nature. It is a function of two unknown variables—the incarnate spirit's sensitivity and the discarnate spirit's capacity of self-manifestation. Our attempt, therefore, to study such intercourse may begin at either end of the communication—with the percipient or with the agent. We shall have to ask, How does the incarnate mind receive the message? and we shall have to ask also, How does the discarnate mind originate and convey it?

We have in this chapter to record and analyze such sensory experiences of living men as seem referable to the action of some human individuality persisting after death. We have also obtained some preliminary notion as to the kind of phenomena for which we can hope, especially as to what their probable limitations must be, considering how great a gulf between psychical states any communication must overpass.

Let us now press the actual evidential question somewhat closer. Let us consider, for it is by no means evident at first sight, what conditions a visual or auditory phantasm is bound to fulfill before it can be regarded as indicating the influence of a discarnate mind. The discussion may be best introduced by quoting the words in which Edmund Gurney opened it in 1888:

§ There remain three, and I think only three, conditions which might establish a presumption that an apparition or other immediate manifestation of a dead person is something more than a mere subjective hallucination of the percipient's senses. Either (1) more persons than one might be independently affected by the phenomenon; or (2) the phantasm might convey information, afterwards discovered to be true, of something which the percipient had never known; or (3) the appearance might be that of a person whom the percipient himself had never seen, and of whose aspect he was ignorant, and yet his description of it might be sufficiently definite for identification. But though one or more of these conditions would have to be fully satisfied before we could be convinced that any particular apparition of the dead had some cause external to the percipient's own mind, there is one more general characteristic of the class which is sufficiently suggestive of such a cause to be worth considering. I mean the disproportionate number of cases which occur *shortly after* the death of the person represented. Such a time-relation, if frequently enough encountered, might enable us to argue for the objective origin of the phenomenon in a manner analogous to that which leads us to conclude that many phantasms of the living have an objective (a telepathic) origin. For, according to the doctrines of probabilities, a hallucination representing a known person would not *by chance* present a definite time-relation to a special cognate event—viz., the death of that person—in more than a certain percentage of the whole number of similar hallucinations that occur; and if that percentage is decidedly exceeded, there is reason to surmise that some other cause than chance—in other words, some objective origin for the phantasm—is present. §

I shall begin with a sample of a small group of cases, which I admit to be anomalous and non-evidential—for we cannot prove that they were more than subjective experiences—yet which certainly should not be lost, filling as they do, in all their grotesqueness, a niche in our series otherwise as yet vacant. If man's spirit is separated at death from his organism, there must needs be cases where that separation, although apparently, is not really complete. There must be subjective sensations corresponding to the objective external facts of apparent death and subsequent resuscitation. Nor need it surprise those who may have followed my general argument, if those subjective sensations should prove to be dreamlike and fantastic. Here, as so often in our inquiries, the very oddity and unexpectedness of the details—the absence of that solemnity which one would think the dying man's own mind would have infused into the occasion—may point to the existence of some reality beneath the grotesque symbolism of the transitional dream.

It is possible that we might learn much were we to question dying persons, on their awakening from some comatose condition, as to their memory of any dream or vision during that state. If there has in fact been any such experience it should be at once recorded, as it will probably fade rapidly from the patient's supraliminal memory, even if he does not die directly afterwards.

Just such an instance, with ultimate recovery of the patient, Dr. Wiltse, was printed in the *St. Louis Medical and Surgical Journal*, November, 1889, and in the *Mid-Continental Review*, February, 1890. Dr. Wiltse has since obtained for us the sworn depositions of the witness of importance. The experience is long, and for the most part of a thoroughly dreamlike type; but in any view it is extremely unusual, nor can it be fairly understood from extracts alone. I quote, therefore, the essential part of the case in full (from *Proceedings* S.P.R., vol. viii. p. 180):

§ [After describing his gradual sinking in the summer of 1889 under an unusual disease—typhoid fever with subnormal temperature and pulse—Dr. Wiltse (of Skiddy, Kansas) continues as follows:] I asked if I was perfectly in possession of my mind, so that what I might say should be worthy of being relied upon. Being answered in the decided affirmative, I bade adieu to family and friends, giving such advice and consolation to each and all as I deemed best, conversed upon the proofs *pro* and *con* of immortality, and called upon each and all to take testimony for themselves by watching the action of my mind, in the bodily state in which they saw me, and finally, as my pupils fell open, and vision began to fail, and my voice to weaken, feeling a sense of drowsiness come over me, with a strong effort, I straightened my stiffened legs, got my arms over the breast, and clasped the fast stiffening fingers, and soon sank into utter unconsciousness.

I passed about four hours in all without pulse or perceptible heartbeat, as I am informed by Dr. S. H. Raynes, who was the only physician present. During a portion of this time several of the bystanders thought I was dead, and such a report being carried outside, the village church bell was tolled. Dr. Raynes informs me, however, that by bringing his eyes close to my face, he could perceive an occasional short gasp, so very light as to be barely perceptible, and that he was upon the point, several times, of saying, "He is dead," when a gasp would occur in time to check him.

He thrust a needle deep into the flesh at different points from the feet to the hips, but got no response. Although I was pulseless about four hours, this state of apparent death lasted only about half-an-hour.

I lost, I believe, all power of thought or knowledge of existence in absolute unconsciousness. I came again into a state of conscious existence and discovered that I was still in the body, but the body and I had no longer any interests in common. I looked in astonishment and joy for the first time upon myself—the me, the real Ego, while the not me closed it upon all sides like a sepulchre of clay.

With all the interest of a physician, I beheld the wonders of my bodily anatomy, intimately interwoven with which, even tissue for tissue, was I, the living soul of that dead body. I learned that the epidermis was the outside boundary of the ultimate tissues, so to speak, of the soul. I realized my condition and reasoned calmly thus. I have died, as men term death, and yet I am as much a man as ever. I am about to get out of the body. I watched the interesting process of the separation of soul and body. By some power, apparently not my own, the Ego was rocked to and fro, laterally, as a cradle is rocked, by which process its connection with the tissues of the body was broken up. After a little time the lateral motion ceased, and along the soles of the feet beginning at the toes, passing rapidly to the heels, I felt and heard, as it seemed, the snapping of innumerable small cords. When this was accomplished I began slowly to retreat from the feet, toward the head, as a rubber cord shortens. I remember reaching the hips and saying to myself, "Now, there is no life below the hips." I can recall no memory of passing through the abdomen and chest, but recollect distinctly when my whole self was collected into the head, when I reflected thus: I am all in the head now, and I shall soon be free. I passed around the brain as if I were hollow, compressing it and its membranes, slightly, on all sides, toward the center and peeped out between the sutures of the skull, emerging like the flattened edges of a bag of membranes. I recollect distinctly how I appeared to myself something like a jelly-fish as regards color and form. As I emerged, I saw two ladies sitting at my head. I measured the distances between the head of my cot and the knees of the lady opposite the head and concluded there was room for me to stand, but felt considerable embarrassment as I reflected that I was about to emerge naked before her, but comforted myself with the thought that in all probability she could not see me with her bodily eyes, as I was a spirit. As I emerged from the head I floated up and down and laterally like a soap-bubble attached to the bowl of a pipe until I at last broke loose from the body and fell lightly to the floor, where I slowly rose and expanded into the full stature of a man. I seemed to be translucent, of a bluish cast and perfectly naked. With a painful sense of embarrassment I fled toward the partially opened door to escape the eyes of the two ladies whom I was facing as well as others who I knew were about me, but upon reaching the door I found myself clothed, and satisfied upon that point I turned and faced the company. As I turned, my left elbow came in contact with the arm of one of two gentlemen who were standing in the door. To my surprise, his arm passed through mine without apparent resistance, the severed parts closing again without pain, as air reunites. I looked quickly up at his face to see if he had noticed the contact, but he gave me no sign, only stood and gazed toward the couch I had just left. I directed my gaze in the direction of his, and saw my own dead body. It was lying just as I had taken so much pains to place it, partially upon the right side, the feet close together and the hands clasped across the breast. I was surprised at the paleness of the face. I had not looked in a glass for some days and had imagined that I was not as pale as most very sick people are. I congratulated myself upon the decency with which I had composed the body and thought my friends would have little trouble on that score.

I saw a number of persons sitting and standing about the body, and particularly noticed two women apparently kneeling by my left side, and I knew that they were weeping. I have since learned that they were my wife and my sister, but I had no conception of individuality. Wife, sister or friend were as one to me. I did not remember any conditions of relationship. I could distinguish sex, but nothing further.

I now attempted to gain the attention of the people with the object of comforting them as well as assuring them of their own immortality. I bowed to them playfully and saluted with my right hand. I passed about among them also, but found that they gave me no heed. Then the situation struck me as humorous and I laughed outright.

They certainly must have heard that, I thought, but it seemed otherwise, for not one lifted their eyes from my body. It did not once occur to me to speak and I concluded the matter by saying to myself: "They see only with the eyes of the body. They cannot see spirits. They are watching what they think is I, but they are mistaken. That is not I. This is I and I am as much alive as ever."

I turned and passed out at the open door, inclining my head and watching where I set my feet as I stepped down on to the porch.

I crossed the porch, descended the steps, walked down the path and into the street. There I stopped and looked about me. I never saw that street more distinctly than I saw it then. I took note of the redness of the soil and of the washes the rain had made. I took a rather pathetic look about me, like one who is about to leave his home for a long time. Then I discovered that I had become larger than I was in earth life and congratulated myself thereupon. I was somewhat smaller in the body than I just liked to be, but in the next life, I thought, I am to be as I desired.

... "How well I feel," I thought. "Only a few minutes ago I was horribly sick and distressed. Then came that change, called death, which I have so much dreaded. It is past now, and here am I still a man, alive and thinking, yes, thinking as clearly as ever, and how well I feel; I shall never be sick again. I have no more to die." And in sheer exuberance of spirits I danced a figure, then turned about and looked back in at the open door, where I could see the head of my body in a line with me. I discovered then a small cord, like a spider's web, running from my shoulders back to my body and attaching to it at the base of the neck in front.

[He started walking down the street.] I had walked but a few steps when I again lost my consciousness, and when I again awoke found myself in the air, where I was upheld by a pair of hands, which I could feel pressing lightly against my sides. The owner of the hands, if they had one, was behind me, and shoving me through the air at a swift but a pleasant rate of speed. By the time I fairly realized the situation I was pitched away and floated easily down a few feet, alighting gently upon the beginning of a narrow, but well-built roadway, inclined upward at an angle of something less than 45 degrees.

I looked up and could see sky and clouds above me at the usual height. I looked down and saw the tops of green trees and thought: It is as far down to the tree tops as it is high to the clouds. [He walked up the roadway for what he judged to be about 20 minutes.]

Suddenly I saw at some distance ahead of me three prodigious rocks blocking the road, at which sight I stopped, wondering why so fair a road should be thus blockaded, and while I considered what I was to do, a great and dark cloud, which I compared to a cubic acre in size, stood over my head. Quickly it became filled with living, moving bolts of fire, which darted hither and thither through the cloud. They were not extinguished by contact with the cloud. I could see them as one sees fish in deep water.

I was aware of a presence, which I could not see, but which I knew was entering into the cloud from the southern side. The presence did not seem, to my mind, as a form, because it filled the cloud like some vast intelligence.... Then from the right side and from the left of the cloud a tongue of black vapor shot forth and rested lightly upon either side of my head, and as they touched me thoughts not my own entered into my brain.

These, I said, are his thoughts and not mine; they might be in Greek or Hebrew for all power I have over them. But how kindly am I addressed in my mother tongue that so I may understand all his will.

Yet, although the language was English, it was so eminently above my power to reproduce that my rendition of it is far short of the original.... The following is as near as I can render it:

"This is the road to the eternal world. Yonder rocks are the boundary between the two worlds and the two lives. Once you pass them, you can no more return into the body. If your work is complete on earth, you may pass beyond the rocks. If, however, upon consideration you conclude that . . . it is not done, you can return into the body."

The thoughts ceased and the cloud passed away, moving slowly toward the mountain in the east. I turned and watched it for some time, when suddenly, and without having felt myself moved, I stood close to and in front of the three rocks. I was seized with a strong curiosity then to look into the next world.

There were four entrances, one very dark, at the left between the wall of black rock and the left hand one of the three rocks, a low archway between the left hand and the middle rock, and a similar one between that and the right hand rock, and a very narrow pathway running around the right hand rock at the edge of the roadway.

I was tempted to cross the boundary line. I hesitated and reasoned thus: "I have died once and if I go back, soon or late, I must die again. If I stay some one else will do my work, and so the end will be as well and as surely accomplished, and shall I die again? I will not, but now that I am so near I will cross the line and stay." So determining I moved cautiously along the rocks.

I reached the exact center. Here, like Cæsar at the Rubicon, I halted and parleyed with conscience. It seemed like taking a good deal of responsibility, but I determined to do it, and advanced the left foot across the line. As I did so, a small, densely black cloud appeared in front of me and advanced toward my face. I knew that I was to be stopped. I felt the power to move or to think leaving me. My hands fell powerless at my side, my head dropped forward, the cloud touched my face and I knew no more.

Without previous thought and without apparent effort on my part, my eyes opened. I looked at my hands and then at the little white cot upon which I was lying, and realizing that I was in the body, in astonishment and disappointment, I exclaimed: "What in the world has happened to me? Must I die again?"

I was extremely weak, but strong enough to relate the above experience despite all injunctions to be quiet. . . . I made a rapid and good recovery [and this paper is written] just eight weeks from "the day I died," as some of my neighbors speak of it.

There are plenty of witnesses to the truth of the above statements, in so far as my physical condition was concerned. Also to the fact that just as I described the conditions about my body and in the room, so they actually were. I must, therefore, have seen things by some means. §

Here, at any rate, whatever view we take as to the source or the content of Dr. Wiltse's vision, the fact remains that the patient, while in a comatose state, almost pulseless, and at a temperature much below the normal, did, nevertheless, undergo a remarkably vivid series of mental impressions. It is plain, therefore, that we may err in other cases by assuming prematurely that all power of perception or inference has ceased.

We have very few cases where actual apparitions give evidence of any *continuity* in the knowledge possessed by a spirit of friends on earth. Such evidence is, naturally enough, more often furnished by automatic script or utterance. But there is one case where a spirit is recorded as appearing repeatedly—in guardian angel fashion—and especially as foreseeing and sympathizing with the survivor's future marriage.

The account of this case is taken from the "Report on the Census of Hallucinations" in the *Proceedings* S.P.R., vol. x. pp. 387–91.

§ From St. Petersburg, Russia comes a letter dated April 29, 1891 from Eugene Mamtchitch telling about a girl whom he had known for several years before she died at the age of 15. Her name was Palladia and she was the daughter of a wealthy Russian landlord.

He says that in 1875, two years after her death, while in Kieff at a séance he heard taps and thought it was a joke. But at home he was able to communicate via alphabet with Palladia. She said: "Replace the angel, it is falling." He visited her grave, found it buried under snow, with the marble statue of an angel with cross quite askew. Later she appeared to him and after that she appeared frequently. On rare occasions she gave a warning or announcement.

Once in 1879 he spoke to her. He suddenly saw her looking at him with joy and serenity. He asked, "What do you feel?" "Peace," she answered. "I understand," he replied.

The young lady whom he later married saw her one day while visiting in his home. She was told, "Don't be afraid of me, I am good and affectionate."

Mr. Mamtchitch's setter dog ran in fright once when she appeared, and his little son also saw her. The little boy's face was peaceful and happy. §

Less uncommon are the cases where an apparition, occurring singly and not repeated, indicates a continued knowledge of the affairs of earth. That knowledge runs mainly, as we shall presently see, in two directions. There is often knowledge of some circumstance connected with the deceased person's own death, as the appearance of his body after dissolution, or the place of its temporary deposit or final burial. And there is often knowledge of the impending or actual death of some friend of the deceased person's. On the view here taken of the gradual passage from the one environment into the other, both these kinds of knowledge seem probable enough. I think it likely that some part of the consciousness after death may for some time be dreamily occupied with the physical scene. And similarly, when some surviving friend is gradually verging towards the same dissolution, the fact may be readily perceptible in the spiritual world. When the friend has actually died, the knowledge which his predecessor may have of his transition is knowledge appertaining to events of the next world as much as of this.

But apart from this information, acquired perhaps on the borderland between two states, apparitions do sometimes imply a perception of more definitely terrene events, such as the moral crises (as marriage, grave quarrels, or impending crimes) of friends left behind on earth. Here is a case of impressive warning, in which the phantom was seen by two persons, one of whom had already had a less evidential experience.

From *Proceedings* S.P.R., vol. vi. p. 25. Mrs. P. relates first an experience in her youth just after her father's death:

§ I was just about to slip quietly down into bed, when on the opposite side of it (that on which the nurse was sleeping) the room became suddenly full of beautiful light, in the midst of which stood my father absolutely transfigured, clothed with brightness. He slowly moved towards the bed, raising his hands, as I thought, to clasp me in his arms; and I ejaculated: "Father!" He replied, "Blessed for ever, my child! For ever blessed!" I moved to climb over nurse and kiss him, reaching out my arms to him; but with a look of mingled sadness and love he appeared to float back with the light towards the wall and was gone! I offer no explanation, and can only say most simply and truthfully that it all happened just as I have related.

[Now comes the case which has evidential importance. Mrs. P. writes:]

In the year 1867 I was married. Our life was exceedingly bright and happy until towards the end of 1869, when my husband's health appeared to be failing, and he grew dejected and moody.

On Christmas Eve of that year we arranged to go to bed early, consequently at 9 o'clock we went upstairs, having as usual carefully bolted the doors. About 9:30 we were ready to extinguish the lamp. Suddenly I saw a gentleman standing at the foot of the bed, dressed as a naval officer, with a cap on his head having a projecting peak. The face was in shadow *to me,* and the more so that the visitor was leaning upon his arms which rested on the foot-rail of the bedstead. I was too astonished to be afraid, but simply wondered who it could be; and, instantly touching my husband's shoulder (whose face was turned from me), I said, "Willie, who is this?" My husband turned, and for a second or two lay looking in intense astonishment at the intruder; then lifting himself a little, he shouted "What on earth are you doing here, sir?" Meanwhile the form, slowly drawing himself into an upright position, now said in a commanding, yet reproachful voice, "Willie! Willie!"

I looked at my husband and saw that his face was white and agitated. As I turned towards him he sprang out of bed as though to attack the man, but stood by the bedside as if afraid, or in great perplexity, while the figure calmly and slowly moved towards the wall. As it passed the lamp, a deep shadow fell upon the room as of a material person shutting out the light from us by his intervening body, and he disappeared, as it were, into the wall.

[Sitting upon the bedside, her husband put his arms about her and said, "Do you know what we have seen?" She replied, "Yes, it was a spirit." She told him she feared it might be her brother Arthur, who was in the navy and at that time on a voyage to India. Her husband exclaimed, "Oh! no, it was my father!" His father, who had been a naval officer in his youth, had been dead fourteen years. Mrs. P. had never seen her husband's father.]

She continues:

As the weeks passed on my husband became very ill, and then gradually disclosed to me that he had been in great financial difficulties; and that, at the time his father was thus sent to us, he was inclining to take the advice of a man who would certainly—had my husband yielded to him (as he had intended before hearing the warning voice)—have led him to ruin, perhaps worse. §

I add another case of similar type, the message in which, while felt by the percipient to be convincing and satisfactory, was held too private to be communicated in detail. It is plain that just in the cases where the message is most intimately veracious, the greatest difficulty is likely to be felt as to making it known to strangers.

From *Proceedings* S.P.R., vol. viii. p. 236. I owe the narrative to the kindness of Mr. Morell Theobald, who printed it first in *Light* for March 5th, 1892. The percipient confirms this early narrative, as does his father.

§ On the evening of Wednesday, October 24th, 1860, having retired to bed about nine o'clock, I had slept, I conclude, about two hours, making it then about eleven o'clock P.M. I was awoke from my sleep by a hand touching my forehead, and the well-known voice of Mrs. B. pronouncing my name, E. I started up, and sat in bed, rubbed my eyes, and then saw Mrs. B. From the head to the waist the figure was distinct, clear, and well-defined: but from the waist downwards it was all misty and the lower part transparent. She appeared to be dressed in black silk. Her countenance was grave and rather sad, but not unhappy.

The words she first uttered were: "I have left dear John"; what followed related entirely to myself, and she was permitted by a most kind Providence to speak words of mercy, promise, and comfort, and assurance that what I most wished would come to pass. She came to me in an hour of bitter mental agony, and was sent as a messenger of mercy.

I would have spoken more to her, but the form faded, and in answer to an earnest appeal, a voice came to me which, though apparently hundreds of miles away, was distinct and clear, saying, "Only believe," and she was gone.

Throughout the interview I felt no fear, but an inward, heavenly peace. It was new moon, but the room was as light as day! §

Mr. C. has forwarded to us a printed extract from the *South Australian Register* of October 25th, 1860, which includes a notice of the death of Mrs. B. on October 24th, at Bank Street, Adelaide.

Further reminded of his contemporary account, the percipient writes, May 1st, 1892: "I appear to have spoken, but have no distinct recollection of doing so. What she did say was entirely personal." It related to the removal of a painful misunderstanding with a friend. "So far as I know she had never seen, or even heard of, the friend alluded to."

The supposed conversation in this case may have been more dream-like than the percipient imagined. It may have taken place, so to say, in his own mind, without definite auditory externalization.

From the *Journal* S.P.R., vol. v. p. 10. The four incidents which follow were written out for me in 1888 by a lady whom I will term Mrs. V., who has had other experiences somewhat similar, which, for private reasons, she does not wish to give. I am well acquainted with Mrs. V., and with her husband, who has held an important position in India.

§ I. In 1874 I was in India, at a hill station. On the 7th June, between one and three o'clock in the morning, I woke with the sensation that half my life had been taken from me (I can only describe the feeling in this vague way). I sat up and pressed my side in wonder at what was happening. I then saw most beautiful lights at the end of the room; these lights gave place to a cloud, and after a few moments the face of a dear sister, then living (as I believed), appeared in the cloud, which remained a little while and then gradually faded away. I became much alarmed and at once felt I should hear bad news of my sister, who was living in London and had been very ill, though the last accounts we had received had been better. I told my husband what had happened, and when a telegram was brought by a friend at eight o'clock that morning I knew what its contents must be. The telegram contained the news of my sister's death during the previous night.

II. In 1885 I was present in church at the confirmation of my sister's youngest boy. I was in the left-hand gallery of the church, the boy in the body of the church, on the right side. As I was kneeling, I looked towards the opposite gallery, which was of dark wood. There I saw the half figure of my sister; the head and arms outstretched high above the boy, as if blessing him. For the moment I thought it was impossible, and closed my eyes for a few seconds. Opening them again I saw the same beautiful form, which almost immediately vanished.

III. In India, in the winter of 1881, the husband of an acquaintance was lying dangerously ill at a hotel about five miles from us. Knowing this, I went frequently to inquire after him. One particular evening I remained with his wife some time, as the doctor thought his condition most critical. When I returned home, about ten o'clock that night, I ordered beef essences and jellies to be made to send early the next morning.

The night was perfectly calm and sultry, not a leaf stirring. About twelve o'clock the venetians in my bedroom suddenly began to shake and knockings were heard, which seemed to proceed from a box under my writing-table. The knocking and shaking of the venetians went on for half-an-hour or more, off and on.

During this time I heard a name whispered, A—— B——, of which the Christian name was unknown to me, the surname being the maiden name of the sick man's wife. I felt so certain that I was wanted at the hotel that I wished to start at once, but I was advised not to do so at that hour of the night. Early the next morning a messenger arrived with a note begging me to go at once to the hotel, as my friend's husband had died at one o'clock. When I reached the hotel, she told me how she had wished to send for me during the night whilst his death was impending. I went at once to stay with her till after the funeral, and found that the Christian name I had heard whispered was the name of her brother who had died seven years previously.

IV. In 1884 we were staying in a villa in the south of France. One night, soon after we arrived, I went from my room upstairs to fetch something in the drawing-room (which was on the ground floor), and saw a slight figure going down the stairs before me in a white garb with a blue sash and long golden hair. She glided on into a room near the hall door. This startled and impressed me so much that I afterwards went to the house-agent and asked if any one had lately died in that house with long golden hair. He replied that an American lady, young and slight, with golden hair, had died there a few months before—in the very room into which I had seen the figure gliding. §

From these instances of knowledge shown by the departed of events which seem wholly terrene, I pass to knowledge of events which seem in some sense more nearly concerned with the spirit-world. In the cases to which I shall now allude the degree of foresight seems not greater than that of ordinary spectators, except in the case to be first given, where, though the family did not foresee the death, a physician might, for aught we know, have been able to anticipate it. However explained, the case is one of the best-attested, and in itself one of the most remarkable, that we possess.

The account, which I quote from *Proceedings* S.P.R., vol. vi. p. 17, was sent in 1887 to the American Society for Psychical Research by Mr. F. G., of Boston. Professor Royce and Dr. Hodgson vouch for the high character and good position of the informants; and the percipient's father and brother are first-hand witnesses as regards the most important point—the effect produced by a certain symbolic item in the phantom's aspect. Mr. G. writes:

§ SIR,—Replying to the recently published request of your Society for actual occurrences of psychical phenomena, I respectfully submit the following remarkable occurrence to the consideration of your distinguished Society, with the assurance that the event made a more powerful impression on my mind than the combined incidents of my whole life. I have never mentioned it outside of my family and a few intimate friends, knowing well that few would believe it, or else ascribe it to some disordered state of my mind at the time; but I well know I never was in better health or possessed a clearer head and mind than at the time it occurred.

In 1867 my only sister, a young lady of eighteen years, died suddenly of cholera in St. Louis, Mo. My attachment for her was very strong, and the blow a severe one to me. A year or so after her death the writer became a commercial traveler, and it was in 1876, while on one of my Western trips, that the event occurred.

I had "drummed" the city of St. Joseph, Mo., and had gone to my room at the Pacific House to send in my orders, which were unusually large ones, so that I was in a very happy frame of mind indeed. My thoughts, of course, were about these orders, knowing how pleased my house would be at my success. I had not been thinking of my late sister, or in any manner reflecting on the past. The hour was high noon, and the sun was shining cheerfully into my room. While busily smoking a cigar and writing out my orders, I suddenly became conscious that some one was sitting on my left, with one arm resting on the table. Quick as a flash I turned and distinctly saw the form of my dead sister, and for a brief second or so looked her squarely in the face; and so sure was I that it was she, that I sprang forward in delight, calling her by name, and, as I did so, the apparition instantly vanished. Naturally I was startled and dumbfounded, almost doubting my senses; but the cigar in my mouth, and pen in hand, with the ink still moist on my letter, I satisfied myself I had not been dreaming and was wide awake. I was near enough to touch her, had it been a physical possibility, and noted her features, expression, and details of dress, etc. She appeared as if alive. Her eyes looked kindly and perfectly natural into mine. Her skin was so life-like that I could see the glow or moisture on its surface, and, on the whole, there was no change in her appearance, otherwise than when alive.

Now comes the most remarkable *confirmation* of my statement, which cannot be doubted by those who know what I state actually occurred. This visitation, or whatever you may call it, so impressed me that I took the next train home, and in the presence of my parents and others I related what had occurred. My father, a man of rare good sense and very practical, was inclined to ridicule me, as he saw how earnestly I believed what I stated; but he, too, was amazed when later on I told them of a bright red line or *scratch* on the right-hand side of my sister's face, which I distinctly had seen. When I mentioned this my mother rose trembling to her feet and nearly fainted away, and as soon as she sufficiently recovered her self-possession, with tears streaming down her face, she exclaimed that I had indeed seen my sister, as no living mortal but herself was aware of that scratch, which she had accidentally made while doing some little act of kindness after my sister's death. She said she well remembered how pained she was to think she should have, unintentionally, marred the features of her dead daughter, and that unknown to all, how she had carefully obliterated all traces of the slight scratch with the aid of powder, etc., and that she had never mentioned it to a human being from that day to this. In proof, neither my father nor any of our family had detected it, and positively were unaware of the incident, yet *I saw the scratch as bright as if just made.* So strangely impressed was my mother, that even after she had retired to rest she got up and dressed, came to me and told me *she knew* at least that I had seen my sister. A few weeks later my mother died, happy in her belief she would rejoin her favorite daughter in a better world. §

I have ranked this case as a perception by the spirit of her mother's approaching death. That coincidence is too marked to be explained away: the son is brought home in time to see his mother once more by perhaps the only means which would have succeeded; and the mother herself is sustained by the knowledge that her daughter loves and awaits her.

From *Proceedings* S.P.R., vol. vi. p. 20. The following account was received from Miss Pearson, 15 Fitzroy Square, London, W.C.

§ The house, 19 St. James Place, Green Park, had been taken on a very long lease by my grandfather, a solicitor, in large county practice, having his offices in Essex Street, Strand. There my father was born and his two sisters, Ann and Harriet. Aunt Ann died in 1858, leaving all she possessed to Aunt Harriet, who remained in the house. They had been devotedly attached to each other. In November, 1864 I was summoned to Brighton. My Aunt Harriet was then very ill there. . . .

About 1 or 2 A.M. on the morning of December 23rd, both Mrs. Coppinger [Miss Pearson's cousin] and myself started up in bed; we were neither of us sleeping, as we were watching every sound from the next room.

We saw some one pass the door, short, wrapped up in an old shawl, a wig with three curls each side and an old black cap. Mrs. Coppinger called out, "Emma, get up, it is old Aunt Ann." I said, "So it is, then Aunt Harriet will die today." We jumped up, and Mrs. John Pearson [the wife of a nephew] came rushing out of the room and said, "That was old Aunt Ann. Where is she gone to?" . . .

No explanation has ever been given of this appearance, except that it was old Aunt Ann come to call her sister, and she died at 6 P.M. that day.

EMMA M. PEARSON §

I place next by themselves a small group of cases which have the interest of uniting the group just recounted, where the spirit anticipates the friend's departure, with the group next to be considered, where the spirit welcomes the friend already departed from earth. It is not very uncommon for dying persons to say, or to indicate when beyond speech, that they see spirit friends apparently near them. But, of course, such vision becomes evidential only when the dying person is unaware that the friend whose spirit he sees has actually departed, or is just about to depart, from earth. Such a conjuncture must plainly be rare; it is even rather surprising that these "Peak in Darien" cases, as they have been termed, should be found at all. We give herewith two cases of fair attestation.

From *Proceedings* S.P.R., vol. iii. p. 92. The writer is Colonel ——, a well-known Irish gentleman who must remain anonymous.

§ Some sixteen years since Mrs. —— said to me, "We have some people staying here all next week. Do you know any person I could get to sing with the girls?" I suggested that my gunmaker, Mr. X., had a daughter with a fine voice, who was training as a public singer, and that I would write to X. and ask if he would allow her to come down and spend a week with us. On my wife's approval I wrote, and Miss X. came down for a week, and then left. As far as I know, Mrs. —— never saw her again. Shortly after I called on X., thanked him for allowing his daughter to come to us, and said we were all much pleased with her. X. replied: "I fear you have spoilt her, for she says she never passed so happy a week in her life." Miss X. did not come out as a singer, but shortly after married Mr. Z., and none of us ever saw her again.

Six or seven years passed and Mrs. ——, who had been long ill, was dying, in fact she did die the following day. I was sitting at the foot of her bed talking over some business matters that she was anxious to arrange, being perfectly composed and in thorough possession of her senses. She changed the subject, and said, "Do you hear those voices singing?" I replied that I did not; and she said, "I have heard them several times today, and I am sure they are the angels welcoming me to Heaven; but," she added, "it is strange, there is one voice amongst them I am sure I know, and cannot remember whose voice it is." Suddenly she stopped and said, pointing straight over my head, "Why, there she is in the corner of the room; it is Julia X.; she is coming on; she is leaning over you; she has her hands up; she is praying; do look; she is going." I turned but could see nothing. Mrs. —— then said, "She is gone." All these things I imagined to be the phantasies of a dying person.

Two days afterwards, taking up the *Times* newspaper, I saw recorded the death of Julia Z., wife of Mr. Z. I was so astounded that in a day or so after the funeral I asked Mr. X. if Mrs. Z., his daughter, was dead. He said, "Yes, poor thing, she died of puerperal fever. On the day she died she began singing in the morning, and sang and sang until she died."

[Colonel —— adds later:]

Mrs. Z. died on February 2nd at six or thereabout in the morning, 1874. Mrs. —— died, February 13th, 1874, at about four in the evening. I saw notice of Mrs. Z.'s death on February 14th. Mrs. —— never was subject to hallucinations of any sort. §

In the next case (quoted from *Proceedings* S.P.R., vol. xiv. p. 288) a dying mother had an apparently telepathic vision of an absent son who happened to be dying at the same time. The account comes from Miss Flo Hicks, daughter of Colonel C. F. Hicks.

§ I was in my late mother's bedroom between the hours of five and six in the evening, on the 3rd of October, 1887, when she asked me to open the door, as some one was outside and wanted to come in. I said, "Oh, mother, the door is open, and there is no one outside," and then I opened the door wider. Then I shut the door. She then said, "Poor Eddie, he looks very ill; he has had a fall." I said to her, "Oh, mother, how you go on; he is all right the last time we heard." She said, "Oh, he is looking very ill." The next morning she died. I heard from letters received that my poor brother Eddie [had fallen from his horse and] died in Australia on the same day and about the same time.

F. HICKS §

From this last group, then, there is scarcely a noticeable transition to the group where departed spirits manifest their knowledge that some friend who survived them has now passed on into their world. That such recognition and welcome does in fact take place, later evidence, drawn especially from trance-utterances, will give good ground to believe. Only rarely, however, will such welcome—taking place as it does in the spiritual world—be reflected by apparitions in *this*.

I quote one of the most complete cases of this type, which was brought to us by the Census of Hallucinations (*Proceedings* S.P.R., vol. x. pp. 380–82). From Miss L. Dodson:

§ On June 5th, 1887, a Sunday evening, between eleven and twelve at night, being awake, my name was called three times. I answered twice, thinking it was my uncle, "Come in, Uncle George, I am awake," but the third time I recognized the voice as that of my mother, who had been dead sixteen years. I said, "Mamma!" She then came round a screen near my bedside with two children in her arms, and placed them in my arms and put the bedclothes over them and said, "Lucy, promise me to take care of them, for their mother is just dead." I said, "Yes, mamma." She repeated, "*Promise* me to take care of them." I replied, "Yes, I promise you"; and I added, "Oh, mamma, stay and speak to me, I am so wretched." She replied, "Not yet, my child," then she seemed to go round the screen again, and I remained, feeling the children to be still in my arms, and fell asleep. When I awoke there was nothing. Tuesday morning, June 7th, I received the news of my sister-in-law's death. She had given birth to a [second child] three weeks before, which I did not know till after her death. I had not known she was ill.

LUCY DODSON §

From *Proceedings* S.P.R., vol. x. p. 214. The account is written by Mrs. J. P. Smith:

§ In June, 1879, I was a teacher in Macclesfield. A friend, Mrs. ——, was near her confinement. She told me she was afraid she would die. I went into the county of Durham for a holiday. While there I was roused from sleep by Mrs. —— as I supposed. She was shaking me, and saying, "I have passed away, but the baby will live." Then the figure left the room by the door. I got out of bed and went to my sister and related the incident. We agreed to make a note of it. Next day I received a letter from a friend in Macclesfield saying that Mrs. —— was dead but the baby was alive.

I was in the best of health and about twenty-nine years of age.

No other persons were present. §

Mrs. Smith, who is the mistress of the Infants' School at Amble, informs us that this is the only experience of the kind she has ever had, and that to the best of her recollection the apparition was seen about an hour or two after the death.

The following case is taken from *Phantasms of the Living*, vol. 1. p. 449. Mr. Clarke, a tradesman in Hull, writes:

§ Widow Palliser was a woman who had seen better days, and worked for my firm, Clarke & Son, Clothiers, Queen Street, Hull. She had an only son, Matthew. I assisted her in getting him to sea. One morning she came to me with tears rolling down her cheeks, and said, "Mat's dead; I saw him drowned! Poor Mat, the last words he said were, 'Oh! my dear mother.' He threw up his hands and sank to rise no more." I asked how she knew. She said, "I saw him going on board his ship, and the plank that he walked upon slipped on one side, and he fell overboard between the quay and the ship and was drowned. My own mother, who had been dead many years, came to the foot of my bed and said, 'Poor Mat's gone; he's drowned.' " I then said, "Why, Mat's in New York." "Yes," she said, "he was drowned last night at New York; I saw him." Mrs. P.'s object in coming to me was to ask if I would write to the agent in New York to ascertain the facts. I said I would, and wrote stating that a poor widow had an only son on board such a ship, and she had a vision that an accident (I said nothing about drowning) had happened to her son, and I would take it as a great favor if he would ascertain and tell me all particulars. In about three to five weeks (she came day by day to ask if we had received a reply, always saying that she knew what the answer would be), at length, the letter arrived. We sent for Mrs. P., and before the letter was opened by my son, I said to her, "What will be its contents?" She at once and decidedly said that Mat was drowned on the very night that she saw him, that in going on board the ship the plank slipped and he fell overboard between the quay and the ship. Mrs. P. was then wearing mourning for Mat.

When the letter was opened it revealed the identical information—that Mat had fallen off a plank and drowned between the quay and the ship at the time she stated.

My son and half-a-dozen young men can verify this if needed.

Mrs. P. died soon after.

M. W. Clarke §

I now come to a considerable group of cases where the departed spirit shows a definite knowledge of some fact connected with his own earth-life, his death, or subsequent events connected with that death. The knowledge of subsequent events, as of the spread of the news of his death, or as to the place of his burial, is, of course, a greater achievement than a mere recollection of facts known to him in life, and ought strictly, on the plan of this series, to be first illustrated. But it will be seen that all these stages of knowledge cohere together; and their connection can better be shown if I begin at the lower stage—of mere earth-memory. Now here again, as so often already, we shall have to wait for automatic script and the like to illustrate the full extent of the deceased person's possible memory. Readers of the utterances, for instance, of "George Pelham" (see Chapter Nine), will know how full and accurate may be these recollections from beyond the grave. Mere apparitions, such as those with which we are now dealing, can rarely give more than one brief message, probably felt by the deceased to be of urgent importance.

I will quote at length a well-attested case where the information communicated in a vision proved to be definite, accurate, and important to the survivors. From *Proceedings* S.P.R., vol. viii. pp. 200–205. The first report of the case appeared in *The Herald* (Dubuque, Iowa), February 11th, 1891, as follows:

§ It will be remembered that on February 2nd, Michael Conley, a farmer living near Ionia, Chickasaw County, was found dead in an outhouse at the Jefferson house. He was carried to Coroner Hoffmann's morgue, where, after the inquest, his body was prepared for shipment to his late home. The old clothes which he wore were covered with filth from the place where he was found, and they were thrown outside the morgue on the ground.

His son came from Ionia, and took the corpse home. When he reached there, and one of the daughters was told that her father was dead, she fell into a swoon, in which she remained for several hours. When at last she was brought from the swoon, she said, "Where are father's old clothes? He has just appeared to me dressed in a white shirt, black clothes, and felt slippers, and told me that after leaving home he sewed a large roll of bills inside his grey shirt with a piece of my red dress, and the money is still there." In a short time she fell into another swoon, and when out of it demanded that somebody go to Dubuque and get the clothes. She was deathly sick.

The entire family considered it only a hallucination, but the physician advised them to get the clothes, as it might set her mind at rest. The son telephoned Coroner Hoffmann, asking if the clothes were still in his possession. He looked and found them in the backyard, although he had supposed they were thrown in the vault, as he had intended. He answered that he still had them, and on being told that the son would come to get them, they were wrapped in a bundle.

The young man arrived last Monday afternoon, and told Coroner Hoffmann what his sister had said. Mr. Hoffmann admitted that the lady had described the identical burial garb in which her father was clad, even to the slippers, although she never saw him after death, and none of the family had seen more than his face through the coffin lid. Curiosity being fully aroused, they took the grey shirt from the bundle, and within the bosom found a large roll of bills sewed with a piece of red cloth. The young man said his sister had a red dress exactly like it. The stitches were large and irregular, and looked to be those of a man. The son wrapped up the garments and took them home with him yesterday morning, filled with wonder at the supernatural revelation made to his sister. §

If we may accept the details of this narrative, which seems to have been carefully and promptly investigated, we find that the phantasm communicates two sets of facts: one of them known only to strangers (the dress in which he was buried), and one of them known only to himself (the existence of the inside pocket and the money therein). In discussing from what mind these images originate it is, of course, important to note whether any living minds, known or unknown to the percipient, were aware of the facts thus conveyed.

There are few cases where the communication between the percipient and the deceased seems to have been more direct than here. The hard, prosaic reality of the details of the message need not, of course, surprise us. On the contrary, the father's sudden death in the midst of earthly business would at once retain his attention on money matters and facilitate his impressing them on the daughter's mind. One wishes that more could be learned of the daughter's condition when receiving the message. It seems to have resembled trance rather than dream.

Dr. Binns, an author of some scientific repute in his day, gives the following narrative in his *Anatomy of Sleep,* p. 462, adding that "perhaps there is not a better authenticated case on record." It consists of a letter written October 21st, 1842, by the Rev. Charles M'Kay, a Catholic priest, to the Countess of Shrewsbury. I abbreviate it here:

§ In July, 1838, I left Edinburgh to take charge of the Perthshire missions. On my arrival in Perth I was called upon by a Presbyterian woman, Anne Simpson, who for more than a week had been in the utmost anxiety to see a priest. This woman stated that a woman lately dead named Maloy, slightly known to Anne Simpson, had appeared to her during the night for several nights urging her to go to the priest, who would pay a sum of money, three and tenpence, which the deceased owed to a person not specified.

I made inquiry, and found that a woman of that name had died, who had acted as washerwoman and followed the regiment. Following up the inquiry I found a grocer with whom she had dealt, and on asking him if a female named Maloy owed him anything, he turned up his books, and told me she did owe him three and tenpence. I paid the sum. Subsequently the Presbyterian woman came to me, saying that she was no more troubled. §

From *Phantasms of the Living,* vol. i. p. 556. The account was received in 1882, from Captain G. F. Russell Colt, of Gartsherrie, Coatbridge, N. B.

§ I had a very dear brother (my eldest brother), Oliver, lieutenant in the 7th Royal Fusiliers. He was about nineteen years old, and had at that time been some months before Sebastopol. I corresponded frequently with him; and once when he wrote in low spirits, not being well, I said in answer that he was to cheer up, but that if anything did happen to him, he must let me know by appearing to me in my room. This letter (I learned subsequently) he received as he was starting to receive the Sacrament from a clergyman who has since related the fact to me. Having done this, he went to the entrenchments and never returned, as in a few hours afterwards the storming of the Redan commenced. He, on the captain of his company falling, took his place, and led his men bravely on. He had just led them within the walls, though already wounded in several places, when a bullet struck him on the right temple and he fell amongst heaps of others, where he was found in a sort of kneeling posture (being propped up by other dead bodies) thirty-six hours afterwards. His death took place, or rather he fell, though he may not have died immediately, on the 8th September, 1855.

That night I awoke suddenly, and saw facing the window of my room, by my bedside, surrounded by a light sort of phosphorescent mist, as it were, my brother kneeling. I tried to speak but could not. . . . I decided that it must be fancy, and the moonlight playing on a towel, or something out of place. But on looking up, there he was again, looking lovingly, imploringly, and sadly at me. I turned, and still saw poor Oliver. I shut my eyes, walked through it, and reached the door of the room. As I turned the handle, before leaving the room, I looked once more back. The apparition turned round his head slowly and again looked anxiously and lovingly at me, and I saw then for the first time a wound on the right temple with a red stream from it. His face was of a waxy pale tint, but transparent-looking, and so was the reddish mark. But it is almost impossible to describe his appearance. I only know I shall never forget it. I left the room and went into a friend's room, and lay on the sofa the rest of the night. I told him why. I told others in the house, but when I told my father, he ordered me not to repeat such nonsense, and especially not to let my mother know. [It was about a fortnight later that the death was confirmed.] §

When a compact to appear, if possible, after death is made, it should be understood that the appearance need not be to the special partner in the compact, but to any one whom the agent can succeed in impressing. It is likely enough that many such attempts, which have failed on account of the surviving friend's lack of appropriate sensitivity, might have succeeded if the agent had tried to influence some one already known to be capable of receiving these impressions.

The following case (quoted from *Phantasms of the Living,* vol. ii. p. 216, foot-note) was received from the Rev. Arthur Bellamy, of Publow Vicarage, Bristol:

§ When a girl at school my wife made an agreement with a fellow pupil, Miss W., that the one of them who died first should, if Divinely permitted, appear after her decease to the survivor. In 1874 my wife, who had not seen or heard anything of her former school-friend for some years, casually heard of her death. The news reminded her of her former agreement, and then, becoming nervous, she told me of it. I knew of my wife's compact, but I had never seen a photograph of her friend, or heard any description of her. [Mr. Bellamy told Gurney, in conversation, that his mind had not been in the least dwelling on the compact.]

A night or two afterwards as I was sleeping with my wife, a fire brightly burning in the room and a candle alight, I suddenly awoke, and saw a lady sitting by the side of the bed where my wife was sleeping soundly. At once I sat up in the bed, and gazed so intently that even now I can recall her form and features. Had I the pencil and the brush of a Millais, I could transfer to canvas an exact likeness of the ghostly visitant. I remember that I was much struck, as I looked intently at her, with the careful arrangement of her coiffure, every single hair being most carefully brushed down. How long I sat and gazed I cannot say, but directly the apparition ceased to be, I got out of bed to see if any of my wife's garments had by any means optically deluded me. I found nothing in the line of vision but a bare wall. Hallucination on my part I rejected as out of the question, and I doubted not that I had really seen an apparition. Returning to bed, I lay till my wife some hours after awoke and then I gave her an account of her friend's appearance. I described her color, form, all of which exactly tallied with my wife's recollection of Miss W. Finally I asked, "But was there any special point to strike one in her appearance?" "Yes," my wife promptly replied; "we girls used to tease her at school for devoting so much time to the arrangement of her hair." This was the very thing which I have said so much struck me. Such are the simple facts.

I will only add that till 1874 I had never seen an apparition, and that I have not seen one since.

ARTHUR BELLAMY §

I conclude this group by quoting another compact case where the apparition coincides with a funeral. From the "Report on the Census of Hallucinations," *Proceedings* S.P.R., vol. x. p. 371. Mrs. B. writes as follows:

§ At Fiesole, on March 11th, 1869, I was giving my little children their dinner at half-past one o'clock. It was a fine hot day. As I was in the act of serving macaroni and milk from a high tureen, I raised my head. Just then the wall opposite me seemed to open, and I saw my mother lying dead on her bed in her house. Some flowers were at her side and on her breast; she looked calm, but unmistakably dead, and the coffin was there.

It was so real that I could scarcely believe that the wall was really brick and mortar, and not a transparent window—in fact, it was a wall dividing the hotel in which we were living from the Carabinieri.

I was so distressed at the vision that I wrote to my mother to give her my address, and entreat her to let me know how she was. By return of post came the statement that she had died on March 5th, and was buried on the 11th.

When I was married my mother made me promise as I was leaving home to be sure to let her know in any way God permitted if I died, and she would try to find some way of communicating to me the fact of her death, supposing that circumstances prevented the usual methods of writing or telegraphing. I considered the vision a fulfillment of this promise, for my mind was engrossed with my own grief and pain—the loss of baby, and my neuralgia, and the anxieties of starting a new life. §

I have now traced certain *post-mortem* manifestations which reveal a recollection of events known at death, and also a persistence of purpose in carrying out intentions formed before death. In this next group I shall trace the knowledge of the departed a little further, and shall discuss some cases where they appear cognizant of the aspect of their bodies after death, or of the scenes in which those bodies are temporarily deposited or finally laid. Such knowledge may appear trivial—unworthy the attention of spirits transported into a higher world. But it is in accordance with the view of a gradual transference of interests and perceptions—a period of intermediate confusion. Such may follow especially upon a death of a sudden or violent kind, or perhaps upon a death which interrupts very strong affections.

In certain cases of violent death there seems to have been an intention on the deceased person's part to show the condition in which his body is left. Such was Mrs. Storie's dream, or rather series of visions. Such, too, was Mrs. Menneer's dream, where the additional evidence obtained brings out a special meaning in the severed *head,* beyond the mere fact of decapitation. Such was an equally striking dream, which I have left for quotation in this place, because it forms a link between this group—where *post-mortem* knowledge of the body's aspect is in question—and the next following group, which will deal with the still stranger phenomenon of *post-mortem* knowledge of dissemination of the news of death. The case is taken from *Proceedings* S.P.R., vol. iii. (1885) p. 95.

Mr. D. did not wish his name to be published, but Gurney saw him, and talked over the subject with him. Mr. D. narrates as follows:

§ I am the owner of a very old mechanical business in Glasgow, with for twenty years past a branch in London, where I have resided for that period, and in both of which places my professional reputation is of the highest order.

Some thirty-five years ago I took into my employment a tender, delicate-looking boy, Robert Mackenzie, who was in dire straits, being literally homeless and starving. He worked for me for a number of years and always evidenced an intensity of gratitude.

In 1862 I settled in London, and have never been in Glasgow since. Robert Mackenzie, and my workmen generally, gradually lost their individuality in my recollection. About ten to twelve years ago my employees had their annual soirée and ball. This was always held, year after year, on a Friday evening. Mackenzie, ever shy and distant, refused to mingle in the festivities, and begged of my foreman to be permitted to serve at the buffet. This, however, I only learned after what I am now about to relate. On the Tuesday morning following, immediately before 8 A.M., in my house on Campden Hill, I had the following manifestation—I cannot call it a dream; but let me use the common phraseology. I dreamt, but with no vagueness as in common dreams, no blurring of outline or rapid passages from one thing disconnectedly to another, that I was seated at a desk, engaged in a business conversation with an unknown gentleman, who stood at my right hand. Towards me, in front, advanced Robert Mackenzie, and feeling annoyed, I addressed him with some asperity, asking him if he did not see that I was engaged. He retired a short distance with exceeding reluctance, turned again to approach me, as if most desirous for an immediate colloquy, when I spoke to him still more sharply as to his want of manners. On this, the person with whom I was conversing took his leave, and Mackenzie once more came forward. "What is all this, Robert?" I asked somewhat angrily. "Did you not see I was engaged?" "Yes, sir," he replied; "but I must speak with you at once." "What about?" I said; "what is it that can be so important?" "I wish to tell you, sir," he answered, "that I am accused of doing a thing I did not do, and that I want *you* to know it, and to tell you so, and that you are to forgive me for what I am blamed for, because I am innocent." Then, "I did not do the thing they say I did." I then naturally asked, "But how can I forgive you if you do not tell me what you are accused of?" I can never forget the emphatic manner of his answer in the Scottish dialect, "Ye'll sune ken" (you'll soon know). This question was repeated at least twice

—I am certain the answer was repeated thrice, in the most fervid tone. On that I awoke, and was in that state of surprise and bewilderment which such a remarkable dream might induce, and was wondering what it all meant, when my wife burst into my bedroom, much excited, and holding an open letter in her hand, exclaimed, "Oh, James, here's a terrible end to the workmen's ball—Robert Mackenzie has committed suicide!" With now a full conviction of the meaning of the vision, I at once quietly and firmly said, "No, he has not committed suicide." "How can you possibly know that?" "Because he has just been here to tell me."

By the following post my manager informed me that he was wrong in writing me of suicide. That on Saturday night, Mackenzie, on going home, had lifted a small black bottle containing *aqua fortis* (which he used for staining the wood of birdcages, made for amusement), believing this to be whisky, and pouring out a wine-glassful, had drunk it off at a gulp, dying on the Sunday in great agony. . . .

D. §

Two singular cases in this group remain, where the departed spirit, long after death, seems pre-occupied with the spot where his bones are laid. The first of these cases approaches farce. From the *Journal* S.P.R., vol. vi. p. 230. The following account was sent to Mr. Podmore by Miss F. Atkinson, of Willesden Lane, N.W.

§ On Saturday, July 1st, 1893, I was in L—— for the purpose of looking over the old churches with a friend with whom I was staying. Among others we went to St. M——'s. My friend had been telling me of a very dear old friend of the family who was buried in that church, and who had left a sum of money to have a window put in to his memory, and had even had the window prepared for the glass to be put in, but that the person who had inherited his fortune neglected his wish.

After we had looked over the church, we came to the window which ought to have been filled in. I remember that the neglect of his wish quite made me angry, and I said, looking at the window, "If I was Dr. —— I should come back and throw stones at it."

Just then I saw an old gentleman behind us, but thinking he was looking over the church took no notice. But my friend got very white and said, "Come away, there *is* Dr. ——!" Not being a believer in apparitions, I simply for the moment thought she was crazy, though I knew they were a ghost-seeing family. But, when I moved, still looking at him, and the figure before my very eyes vanished, I had to give in. For the few moments he was visible I saw him distinctly; he was short and broad, and wore an old-fashioned tie, and a waistcoat cut low and showing a great deal of shirt-front. One hand was resting on a pew, and one down at his side holding his very tall hat. But the thing that struck me most was the sun shining on his white hair, and making it look like silver; even now I can see him distinctly in my mind's eye. It certainly surprised me to see what was apparently "too solid flesh" disappear before my very eyes, and when we got outside my friend told me that his was the figure which came to different members of their family so often, and, indeed, had been the cause of their leaving one house. One of her sisters had been so affected by it, that she will never sleep alone, or go upstairs alone. When we got home I easily recognized the doctor by his photograph.

F. ATKINSON §

The next case is remarkable for the frequent repetition of the percipient's experience. It is one of those that suggest, as we have said, a kind of local imprint left by past events, and perceptible at times to persons endowed with some special form of sensitiveness. I quote from *Proceedings* S.P.R., vol. v. p. 418, the account, given by Mr. D. M. Tyre, 157 St. Andrew's Road, Pollokshields, Glasgow.

§ He relates that his people had taken a lease on a house which was built far up on a hill overlooking one of the most beautiful lochs in Dumbartonshire, just on the boundary of the Highlands. He and his two sisters were sent there early in May to have the house put in order and attend to the garden. They had a lot of work to do, and as the home was nearly a mile from any neighbors, they were left to their own resources.

One day his elder sister J. and he were away to the village for supplies. When they returned, about 6 P.M., they found his other sister L. in a rather excited state, saying that an old woman had taken up her quarters in the kitchen and was lying in the bed. But when L. pointed to the old woman, saying, "There she is," neither of the other two could see her.

He says:

"I looked in the bed and so did my elder sister, but the clothes were flat and unruffled, and when we said that there was nothing there she was quite surprised, and pointing with her finger, said, 'Look, why there's the old wife with her clothes on and lying with her head towards the window'; but we could not see anything. Then for the first time it seemed to dawn upon her that she was seeing something that was not natural to us all, and she became very much afraid, and we took her to the other room and tried to soothe her, for she was trembling all over. The very idea of any one being in the bed was ridiculous, so we attributed it to imagination, and life at the house went on as usual for about two days, when one afternoon, as we were sitting in the kitchen round the fire, it being a cold, wet day outside, L. startled us by exclaiming, 'There is the old woman again, and lying the same way.' L. did not seem to be so much afraid this time, so we asked her to describe the figure; and with her eyes fixed on the bed, she went on to tell us how that the old wife was not lying under the blankets, but on top, with her clothes and boots on, and her legs drawn up as though she were cold; her face was turned to the wall, and she had on what is known in the Highlands as a 'sow-backed mutch,' that is, a white cap which only old women wear; it has a frill round the front and sticks out at the back. She also wore a drab-colored petticoat, and a checked shawl round her shoulders, drawn tight. Such was the description given; she could not see her face, but her right hand was hugging her left arm, and she saw that the hand was yellow and thin, and wrinkled like the hands of old people who have done a lot of hard work in their day."

[This apparition appeared to L. so often that they got used to it, and used to talk about it among themselves as "L's. old woman." When their family came down from the city they began to get acquainted with their neighbors.]

"On one occasion my elder sister brought up the subject before a Mrs. M'P., our nearest neighbor, and when she described the figure to her, Mrs. M'P. well-nigh swooned away, and said that it really was the case; the description was the same as the first wife of the man who lived in the house before us, and that he cruelly ill-used his wife, to the extent that the last beating she never recovered from. He realized her condition and was afraid, and went down to Mrs. M'P., saying that his wife was very ill. When Mrs. M'P. went up to the house she found Kate with her clothes on, lying with her face to the wall for the purpose of concealing its very badly bruised condition. . . . "

D. M. Tyre §

I hold it probable that those communications, of which telepathy from one spirit to another forms the most easily traceable variety, are in reality infinitely varied and complex, and show themselves from time to time in forms which must for long remain quite beyond our comprehension.

The next class of cases in this series well illustrates this unexpectedness. It has only been as the result of a gradual accumulation of concordant cases that I have come to believe there is some reality in the bizarre supposition that the departed spirit is sometimes specially aware of the time at which news of his death is about to reach some given friend.

A hint is given by certain cases where the percipient states that a cloud of unreasonable depression fell upon him about the time of his friend's death at a distance, and continued until the actual news arrived; when, instead of becoming intensified, it lifted suddenly. In one or two such cases there was an actual presence or apparition, which seemed to hang about until the news arrived, and then disappeared. Or, on the other hand, there is sometimes a happy vision of the departed preluding the news, as though to prepare the percipient's mind for the shock. The suggested inference is that in such cases the spirit's attention is more or less continuously directed to the survivor until the news reaches him. This does not, of course, explain how the spirit learns as to the arrival of the news; yet it makes that piece of knowledge seem a less isolated thing.

In a case published in *Proceedings* S.P.R., vol. iii. p. 90, Mr. Wambey heard a phantasmal voice as though in colloquy with his own thought. He was planning a congratulatory letter to a friend, when the words, "What! write to a dead man? write to a *dead* man?" sounded clearly in his ears. He later learned that the friend had been dead for some days.

I add here a case where a message seemed to be given by the decedent's voice in a dream. From *Proceedings* S.P.R., vol. v. p. 455.

§ Mr. George King of Westbourne Park, W., tells of bidding his brother goodbye as he left by ship for Brazil in 1874. His brother had once before survived a shipwreck. Mr. King was not worrying about his brother before this dream. He writes that one night he went home and retired shortly after midnight. He does not think he had been dreaming, but suddenly he found himself in the midst of a brilliant assembly, such as he had recently left at King's College. He stood in evening dress on the steps at the entrance to a great and crowded hall and he had a delicious feeling of pleasure and peace.

He writes:

"Suddenly my brother appeared and advanced towards me. He was in evening dress, like all the rest, and was the very image of buoyant health. I was much surprised to see him, and, going forward to meet him, I said: 'Hallo! D., how are you here?' He shook me warmly by the hand, and replied: 'Did you not know I have been wrecked again?' At these words a deadly faintness came over me. I seemed to sink to the ground. After momentary unconsciousness I awoke, and found myself in my bed. I was in a cold perspiration, and had paroxysms of trembling, which would not be controlled. I argued with myself on the absurdity of getting into a panic over a dream, but all to no purpose, and for long I could not sleep. Towards morning I again slumbered, and the fear passed off from me."

As it turned out, his brother's ship had foundered in a terrific gale in the Bay of Biscay and his brother was drowned at just about the time of his dream. §

I give below a grotesque incident where the indication is of *impatience* on the part of the deceased person, who perceives the news of his death being delayed in reaching his wife.

From *Proceedings* S.P.R., vol. viii. p. 218. The following account was written out by me on December 22nd, 1888, from notes taken during an interview with Mrs. Davies the same day; and was afterwards revised and signed by Mrs. Davies.

§ The account states that a neighbor of Mrs. Davies named Mrs. J. Walker, whose husband was in India, had moved away without leaving a forwarding address. But Mrs. Davies' brother occasionally saw Mrs. Walker's brother. One day when she was visiting the new neighbor who had moved into the house where Mrs. Walker formerly lived, Mrs. Davies was given a letter which had come from India for Mrs. Walker. She continues:

"I promised to give it to my brother, and took it home. It was a dirty-looking letter, addressed in an uneducated handwriting, and of ordinary bulk. I placed it on the chimney-piece in our sitting-room, and sat down alone. I expected my brother home in an hour or two. The letter, of course, in no way interested me. In a minute or two I heard a ticking on the chimney-piece, and it struck me that an old-fashioned watch which my mother always had standing in her bedroom must have been brought downstairs. I went to the chimney-piece, but there was no watch or clock there or elsewhere in the room. The ticking, which was loud and sharp, seemed to proceed from the letter itself. Greatly surprised, I removed the letter and put it on a sideboard, and then in one or two other places; but the ticking continued, proceeding undoubtedly from where the letter was each time. After an hour or so of this I could bear the thing no longer, and went out and sat in the hall to await my brother. When he came in I simply took him into the sitting-room and asked him if he heard anything. He said at once, 'I hear a watch or clock ticking.' There was no watch or clock, as I have said, in the room. He went to where the letter was and exclaimed, 'Why, the letter is ticking.' We then listened to it together, moved it about, and satisfied ourselves that the ticking proceeded from the letter, which, however, plainly contained nothing but a sheet of paper. The impression which the ticking made was that of an urgent call for attention. My brother took the letter to Mrs. J. W. either that night (it was very late) or next morning. On opening it, she found that her husband had suddenly died of sunstroke, and the letter was written by some servant or companion to inform her of his death. The ticking no doubt made my brother and myself hand on the letter more promptly than we might otherwise have done.

"The incident of the letter made a deep impression on me."

ANNA DAVIES §

From the "Report on the Census of Hallucinations," *Proceedings* S.P.R., vol. x. p. 373, is an interesting example (the only one in the Census) of a *primâ facie* veridical hallucination coinciding with the arrival of a letter bearing on the subject. Another remarkable feature in the case is the persistent repetition of the percept. The account was written by Miss E. L. M. in 1889.

§ On the morning of January 14th, 1876, I was in the B. schoolroom, a small village near to A. in Hants, when I saw what appeared to me to be a favorite cousin. She was close beside me, and appeared in good health, as I had every reason to suppose her to be. I should here explain that I held in my hand a letter which had just been brought to me, *and which I had not yet opened,* telling me that my cousin was seriously ill with scarlet fever. The fact was that at the time she was actually dead, her death having occurred after the posting of the letter. I was waiting for children to assemble in school, and was in good health and in no grief or anxiety. I knew immediately that it was my cousin whom I saw, and believed her to be at the time at her own home. I could not understand what she meant by saying "Good-bye," which I cannot say I heard, but *saw* by the movement of her lips.

The village children and my sister were present. The former I have no reason to think saw anything, and my sister only laughed at me. I continued to see her all day, and when indoors my sister would persist in strumming on the piano, although I remonstrated with her, "How can you keep on with that noise when Jessie is dead?" I received a letter the next morning informing me that she was dead, after which I saw her only at intervals that day and part of the next, when the appearances ceased. §

On the strength of all these cases, and of some less striking, I repeat my suggestion that in our ignorance as to the degree of knowledge of earthly affairs possessed by the departed, and of the causes which permit or stimulate their apparition, this possibility of their following the diffusion of news of their own death may be well worth our continued attention.

Having thus discussed cases where the apparition shows varying degrees of knowledge or memory, I pass on to the somewhat commoner type, where the apparition lacks the power or the impulse to communicate any message much more definite than that all-important one—of his own continued life and love.

In the following, which I quote from *Proceedings* S.P.R., vol. v. p. 409, the apparition was seen several weeks after the death. The account came from Mrs. Clark, 8 South View, Forest Hall, Newcastle-on-Tyne.

§ I send you a short account, describing what I experienced at the time of the apparition of my friend, who was a young gentleman much attached to myself, and who would willingly (had I loved him well enough) have made me his wife. I became engaged to be married, and did not see my friend (Mr. Akhurst) for some months, until within a week of my marriage (June, 1878), when in the presence of my husband he wished me every happiness, and regretted he had not been able to win me.

I had been married about two years and had never seen Mr. Akhurst, when one day my husband told me Mr. Akhurst was in Newcastle and was coming to supper and was going to stay the night. When my husband and he were talking, he said my husband had been the more fortunate of the two, but he added if anything happened to my husband he could leave his money to whom he liked and his widow to him, and he would be quite content. I mention this to show he was still interested in me.

Three months passed and baby was born. When she was about a week old, very early one morning I was feeding her, when I felt a cold waft of air through the room and a feeling as though some one touched my shoulder; my hair seemed to bristle all over my head and I shuddered. Raising my eyes to the door (which faced me), I saw Akhurst standing in his shirt and trousers looking at me, when he seemed to pass through the door. In the morning I mentioned it to my husband. I did not hear of Mr. Akhurst's death for some weeks after, when I found it corresponded with that of the apparition.

He was found lying on the bed with his shirt and trousers on, just as he had thrown himself down after taking an overdose of a sleeping draught.

EMILY CLARK §

The next case I quote is from *Phantasms of the Living,* vol. i. p. 444.
In December, 1880 Mr. J. G. Keulemans was living, he tells us, with his
family in Paris. The outbreak of an epidemic of small-pox caused him to
remove three of his children, including a favorite little boy, Isidore, to
London, whence he received, in the course of the ensuing month, several
letters giving an excellent account of their health.

§ On the 24th of January, 1881, at half-past seven in the morning, I was
suddenly awoke by hearing his voice, as I fancied, very near me. I saw a
bright, opaque, white mass before my eyes, and in the center of this light
I saw the face of my little Isidore, his eyes bright, his mouth smiling.
The apparition, accompanied by the sound of his voice, was too short
and too sudden to be called a dream: it was too clear, too decided, to be
called an effect of imagination. So distinctly did I hear his voice that I
looked round the room to see whether he was actually there. The sound I
heard was that of extreme delight, such as only a happy child can utter. I
thought it was the moment he woke up in London, happy and thinking
of me. I said to myself, "Thank God, little Isidore is happy as always." §

Mr. Keulemans describes the ensuing day as one of peculiar brightness and cheerfulness. He took a long walk with a friend, with whom he
dined; and was afterwards playing a game of billiards, when he again
saw the apparition of his child. This made him seriously uneasy, and in
spite of having received within three days the assurance of the child's
perfect health, he expressed to his wife a conviction that he was dead.
Next day a letter arrived saying that the child was ill; but the father
was convinced that this was only an attempt to break the news; and, in
fact, the child had died, after a few hours' illness, at the exact time of the
first apparition.

One specially impressive characteristic of apparitions (as has been
already remarked) is their occasional *collectivity*—the fact that more
percipients than one sometimes see or hear the phantasmal figure or voice
simultaneously. When one is considering the gradual decline in definiteness and apparent purpose from one group of apparitions to another, it
is natural to ask whether this characteristic—in my view so important—
accompanies especially the higher, more intelligent manifestations.

I cannot find that this is so. On the contrary, it is, I think, in cases of
mere *haunting* that we oftenest find that the figure is seen by several persons at once, or else by several persons successively. I know not how to
explain this apparent tendency. Could we admit the underlying assumptions, it would suit the view that the "haunting" spirits are "earthbound,"
and thus somehow nearer to matter than spirits more exalted. Yet instances

of collectivity are scattered through all classes of apparitions; and the irregular appearance of a characteristic which seems to us so fundamental affords another lesson how great may be the variety of inward mechanism in cases which to us might seem constructed on much the same type.

The next account is taken from *Phantasms of the Living,* vol. ii. p. 213. It is given by Mr. Charles A. W. Lett, of the Military and Royal Naval Club, Albemarle Street, W.

§ On the 5th April, 1873 my wife's father, Captain Towns, died at his residence, Cranbrook, Rose Bay, near Sydney, N. S. Wales. About six weeks after his death my wife had occasion, one evening about nine o'clock, to go to one of the bedrooms in the house. She was accompanied by a young lady, Miss Berthon, and as they entered the room—the gas was burning all the time—they were amazed to see, reflected as it were on the polished surface of the wardrobe, the image of Captain Towns. It was barely half figure, the head, shoulders, and part of the arms only showing—in fact, it was like an ordinary medallion portrait, but life-size. The face appeared wan and pale, as it did before his death, and he wore a kind of grey flannel jacket, in which he had been accustomed to sleep. Surprised and half alarmed at what they saw, their first idea was that a portrait had been hung in the room, and that what they saw was its reflection; but there was no picture of the kind.

Whilst they were looking and wondering, my wife's sister, Miss Towns, came into the room, and before either of the others had time to speak she exclaimed, "Good gracious! Do you see papa?" One of the housemaids happened to be passing downstairs at the moment, and she was called in, and asked if she saw anything, and her reply was, "Oh, miss! the master." Graham—Captain Towns' old body servant—was then sent for, and he also immediately exclaimed, "Oh, Lord save us! Mrs. Lett, it's the Captain!" The butler was called, and then Mrs. Crane, my wife's nurse, and they both said what they saw. Finally, Mrs. Towns was sent for, and, seeing the apparition, she advanced towards it with her arm extended as if to touch it, and as she passed her hand over the panel of the wardrobe the figure gradually faded away, and never again appeared, though the room was regularly occupied for a long time after.

These are the simple facts of the case, and they admit of no doubt; no kind of intimation was given to any of the witnesses; the same question was put to each one as they came into the room, and the reply was given without hesitation by each.

C. A. W. LETT §

From the *Proceedings* of the American Society for Psychical Research, vol. i. p. 446. This is a case of two apparently synchronous "visions of consolation" representing the same deceased person. The percipients were the mother and husband of a lady who had been dead five months. She died in December, 1879, and the incidents occurred about the end of April, 1880. Mrs. Crans, the mother, was then residing in New York, and her son-in-law, Mr. C. A. Kernochan, in Central City, Dakota. Mrs. Crans writes to Dr. Hodgson as follows:

§ . . . After lying down to rest, I remember feeling a drifting sensation, of seeming almost as if I was going out of the body. My eyes were closed; soon I realized that I was, or seemed to be, going fast somewhere. All seemed dark to me; suddenly I realized that I was in a room; then I saw Charley lying in a bed asleep; then I took a look at the furniture of the room, and distinctly saw every article—even to a chair at the head of the bed, which had one of the pieces broken in the back. . . . In a moment the door opened and my spirit-daughter Allie came into the room and stepped up to the bed and stooped down and kissed Charley. He seemed to at once realize her presence, and tried to hold her, but she passed right out of the room about like a feather blown by the wind. . . . I told [several people] my experience, and the following Sunday I wrote, as was always my custom, to my son-in-law, Charley, telling him of all my experience, describing the room as I saw it furnished.

It took a letter six days to go from here to Dakota, and the same length of time, of course, to come from there here; and at the end of six days judge of my surprise to receive a letter from Charley telling me thus: "Oh, my darling mamma Crans! My God! I dreamed I saw Allie last Friday night!" He then described just as I saw her; how she came into the room and he cried and tried to hold her, but she vanished. Then at the end of six days, when my letter reached him, and he read of my similar experience, he at once wrote me that all I had seen was correct, even to every article of furniture in the room, also as his dream had appeared to him. . . .

Mrs. N. J. Crans §

In the case which I shall next quote, the evidence, though coming from a young boy, is clear and good, and the incident itself is thoroughly characteristic.

We owe this case (which I quote from *Proceedings* S.P.R., vol. viii. p. 173) to the kindness of Lady Gore Booth, from whom I first heard the account by word of mouth. Her son (then a schoolboy aged 10) was the percipient, and her youngest daughter, then aged 15, also gives a first-hand account of the incident as follows:

§ On the 10th of April, 1889, at about half-past nine o'clock A.M., my youngest brother and I were going down a short flight of stairs leading to the kitchen, to fetch food for my chickens, as usual. We were about half-way down, my brother a few steps in advance of me, when he suddenly said—"Why, there's John Blaney, I didn't know he was in the house!" John Blaney was a boy who lived not far from us, and he had been employed in the house as hall-boy not long before. I said that I was sure it was not he (for I knew he had left some months previously on account of ill-health), and looked down into the passage, but saw no one. The passage was a long one, with a rather sharp turn in it, so we ran quickly down the last few steps, and looked round the corner, but nobody was there, and the only door he could have gone through was shut. As we went upstairs my brother said, "How pale and ill John looked, and why did he stare so?" I asked what he was doing. My brother answered that he had his sleeves turned up, and was wearing a large green apron, such as the footmen always wear at their work. An hour or two afterwards I asked my maid how long John Blaney had been back in the house. She seemed much surprised, and said, "Didn't you hear, miss, that he died this morning?" On inquiry we found he had died about two hours before my brother saw him. My mother did not wish that my brother should be told this, but he heard of it somehow, and at once declared that he must have seen his ghost.

MABEL OLIVE GORE BOOTH

[The actual percipient's independent account is as follows:]

March, 1891.

We were going downstairs to get food for Mabel's fowl, when I saw John Blaney walking round the corner. I said to Mabel, "That's John Blaney!" but she could not see him. When we came up afterwards we found he was dead. He seemed to me to look rather ill. He looked yellow; his eyes looked hollow, and he had a green apron on.

MORDAUNT GORE BOOTH §

I add a somewhat similar case. The figure of the grandmother looking at the clock resembles the figure of the pantry-boy seen in the offices, but was seen by both persons in a position to see it, instead of by one only.

From *Proceedings* S.P.R., vol. v. p. 437. The account is given by Mrs. Judd.

§ My grandmother was a tall, stately, and handsome woman, even at an advanced age. Her latter years were spent with my mother (her daughter), and in her eighty-fourth year she died. She had suffered long; she had attained a great age; therefore, though we missed her, our grief was not of that poignant and excessive kind which produces hallucination.

My sister and myself had always slept in a room adjoining hers, and—for want of space in her apartment—there stood by our bedside a large old-fashioned clock, which had been presented to our grandmother on her wedding-day. More precious than gold was this old clock to her heart; "by it," she often said, "have I hundreds of times watched the slow hours pass in my early married days when my husband had to leave me; by it have I timed the children's return from school"; and she begged us, her grandchildren, to leave our bedroom door unlocked at night that she might consult the old clock when she rose each morning. We have often opened our sleepy eyes at four on a summer morning and smiled to see the stately figure already there. For up to the last illness she retained the habits of her youth, and rose at what we deemed fearfully primitive hours.

About three weeks after her death I awoke one morning in October, and saw distinctly the well-known tall figure, the calm old face, the large dark eyes uplifted as usual to the face of the old clock. I closed my eyes for some seconds, and then slowly reopened them. She stood there still. A second time I closed my eyes, a second time opened them. She was gone.

I was looked upon by my family in those days, and particularly by the sister who shared my room, as romantic. Therefore I carefully kept to myself the vision of the morning and pondered over it alone.

At night, however, when we were once more preparing for rest, my sister—my eminently practical and unromantic sister—spoke to me. "I cannot go to bed without telling you something, only don't laugh, for I am really frightened; I saw grandmamma this morning!" I was amazed. I inquired of her the hour, what the vision was like, where it stood, what it was doing, etc., and I found that in every respect her experience was similiar to mine. She had preserved silence all day for fear of ridicule.

CAROLINE JUDD

Some years ago, a few months after the death of my grandmother, I awoke in the dim light just before dawn, to see an appearance exactly like her standing in the old accustomed place from whence, when alive, she was wont to consult an old clock, her own property, at very early hours. I said nothing to any one till we retired again for the night, when I found to my surprise, my sister, who slept with me, had seen the same appearance at the same time.   MARY DEAR   (Mrs. Judd's sister) §

I will conclude this group with three cases closely similar, all well attested.

From *Phantasms of the Living*, vol. ii. p. 619. This, if telepathically originated, is an interesting instance of the appearance of a phantasm to certain percipients on local, not personal, grounds. It comes from Miss Edith Farquharson, with the following independent account from her sister Mrs. Marianne Murray:

§ Our home was in Perthshire; but in the winter of 1868 my father took a house for four months in Edinburgh, in order to give us a change. The house belonged to General Stewart, who had a delicate daughter, and he let it, to take the daughter to Torquay for the winter. We did not know the Stewarts, so our imagination could not have assisted in any way to account for the curious apparition that was seen. I myself did not *see* it, but I was in the room with my sister and little cousin, who both did. . . . Well, the apparition took place on Good Friday night at about twelve o'clock. This little cousin, who was only about six years old, had come into town from the country, and as our house was very full she had a shake-down beside our bed on my side. I was the first to be awakened by hearing her calling out in a frightened way. So I said, "What is the matter, Addie?" "Oh," she said, "Cousin Marianne, I am so frightened. A figure has been leaning over me, and whenever I put out my hands to push it off it leant back on your bed!" At this I was alarmed and awoke my sister, who lifted her head from her pillow and looked up, when she saw a figure gliding across the foot of our bed wrapped in a shawl, with a hat and veil on. She whispered to me in French, "*Il y a quelqu'un*," thinking it was a thief, whereat we both jumped out of bed together and went to the next room to get our brother, Captain Farquharson. . . . While he was coming to our help, we kept our eyes fixed on our door in case any one should have escaped, but we saw nothing, and after our all searching every corner of the bedroom we came to the conclusion that no one had been there, for everything was intact. We then questioned little Addie as to what she had seen, and what the figure was like. She described it as that of a lady with a shawl, a hat, and a veil over her face, and said that as I spoke she had gone across the foot of the bed in the same direction that my sister had seen her go. . . .

Then the next morning we were relating our adventures, when a ring came to the door, and the servant said a gentleman wanted to speak to my father. . . . He came to say he had received a telegram that morning that Miss Stewart had died in Torquay during the night, and they wanted to bring her body to Edinburgh. We heard afterwards from friends of the Stewarts that the bedroom we had had been hers.

We have none of us ever had any hallucinations either before or after this strange affair.

MARIANNE MURRAY §

From *Proceedings* S.P.R., vol. vi. p. 57. The following incident occurred to a gentleman personally known to me. The initials here given are not the true ones. On October 12th, 1888, Mr. J. gave me orally the following account of his experience in the X. Library, in 1884, which I took down from memory next day, and which he revised and corrected:

§ In 1880 I succeeded a Mr. Q. as librarian of the X. Library. I had never seen Mr. Q., nor any photograph or likeness of him, when the following incidents occurred. . . . I was . . . alone in the library one evening late in March, 1884. . . . I gathered up some books in one hand, took the lamp in the other, and prepared to leave the librarian's room, which communicated by a passage with the main room of the library. As my lamp illuminated this passage, I saw apparently at the further end of it a man's face. I instantly thought a thief had got into the library. This was by no means impossible, and the probability of it had occurred to me before. I turned back into my room, put down the books, and took a revolver from the safe, and, holding the lamp cautiously behind me, I made my way along the passage —which had a corner, behind which I thought my thief might be lying in wait—into the main room. Here I saw no one, but the room was large and encumbered with bookcases. I called out loudly to the intruder to show himself several times, more with the hope of attracting a passing policeman than of drawing the intruder. Then I saw a face looking round one of the bookcases. I say looking *round*, but it had an odd appearance as if the *body* were *in* the bookcase, as the face came so closely to the edge and I could see no body. The face was pallid and hairless, and the orbits of the eyes were very deep. I advanced towards it, and as I did so I saw an old man with high shoulders seem to *rotate* out of the end of the bookcase, and with his back towards me and with a shuffling gait walk rather quickly from the bookcase to the door of a small lavatory, which opened from the library and had no other access. I heard no noise. I followed the man at once into the lavatory; and to my extreme surprise found no one there. . . . I confess I began to experience for the first time what novelists describe as an "eerie" feeling. . . .

Next morning I mentioned what I had seen to a local clergyman, who on hearing my description, said, "Why, that's old Q.!" Soon after I saw a photograph (from a drawing) of Q., and the resemblance was certainly striking. Q. had lost all his hair, eyebrows and all, from (I believe) a gunpowder accident. His walk was a peculiar, rapid, high-shouldered shuffle. Later inquiry proved he had died at about the time of year at which I saw the figure. §

As often happens when (as I do here) one knows the percipient and his *milieu*, even the very plot of ground on which he dodged about to watch the phantom, one feels a reality in the incident which the most satisfactory depositions from a distance will not always bring. The case is quoted from *Phantasms of the Living*, vol. i. p. 212.

The first account of it was sent to us by the Rev. C. T. Forster, Vicar of Hinxton, Saffron Walden, as follows:

§ My late parishioner, Mrs. de Fréville, was a somewhat eccentric lady, who was specially morbid on the subject of tombs, etc.

About two days after her death, which took place in London, May 8th, in the afternoon, I heard that she had been seen that very night by Alfred Bard [a gardner who had once been in her employ]. I sent for him, and he gave me a very clear and circumstantial account of what he had seen.

He is a man of great observation, being a self-taught naturalist, and I am quite satisfied that he desires to speak the truth without any exaggeration.

I must add that I am absolutely certain that the news of Mrs. de Fréville's death did not reach Hinxton till the next morning, May 9th.

C. T. FORSTER

[Mrs. Bard states that:]

When Mr. Bard came home, he said, "I have seen Mrs. de Fréville tonight, leaning with her elbow on the palisade, looking at me. I turned again to look at her and she was gone. She had cloak and bonnet on." He got home as usual between nine and ten. It was on the 8th of May, 1885.

SARAH BARD §

The *Times* obituary confirms the date of the death.

The incident suggests that Bard had come upon Mrs. de Fréville's spirit, so to say, unawares. One cannot imagine that she specially wished him to see her, and to see her engaged in what seems so needless and undignified a retracing of currents of earthly thought. Rather this seems a rudimentary *haunting*—an incipient lapse into those aimless, perhaps unconscious, reappearances in familiar spots which may persist (as it would seem) for many years after death.

A somewhat similar case is that of Colonel Crealock in *Proceedings*

S.P.R., vol. v. p. 432) where a soldier who had been dead some hours was seen by his superior officer in camp at night rolling up and taking away his bed.

It is, indeed, mainly by dwelling on these intermediate cases, between a message-bringing apparition and a purposeless haunt, that we have most hope of understanding the typical haunt which, while it has been in a sense the most popular of all our phenomena, is yet to the careful inquirer one of the least satisfactory. One main evidential difficulty generally lies in identifying the haunting figure, in finding anything to connect the history of the house with the vague and often various sights and sounds which perplex or terrify its flesh and blood inhabitants. We must, at any rate, rid ourselves of the notion that some great crime or catastrophe is always to be sought as the groundwork of a haunt of this kind. To that negative conclusion the cases now to be described, and the cases which have just been described, do concordantly point us. Mrs. de Fréville was concerned in no tragedy; she was merely an elderly lady with a fancy for sepulchres.

From *Proceedings* S.P.R., vol. iii. p. 110. The narrative is written by General Sir Arthur Becher, of St. Faith's Mede, Winchester.

§ General Becher, who held a very high appointment on the Staff in India, went, accompanied by his son and A.D.C., to the Hill Station of Kussowlie, about March, 1867, to examine a house he had secured for his family to reside in during the approaching hot season. They both slept in the house that night. During the night the General awoke suddenly and saw the figure of a native woman standing near his bed, and close to an open door which led into a bathroom. He called out, "Who are you?" and jumped out of bed, when the figure retreated into the bathroom, and in following it the General found the outer door locked and the figure had disappeared.

He went to bed again, and in the morning he wrote in pencil on a doorpost, "Saw a ghost," but he did not mention the circumstance to his wife.

A few days after, the General and his family took possession of the house for the season, and Lady Becher used the room the General had slept in for her dressing room. About 7 P.M. on the first evening of their arrival, Lady Becher was dressing for dinner, and on going to a wardrobe (near the bathroom door) to take out a dress, she saw, standing in the bathroom a native woman, and, for the moment thinking it was her own ayah, asked her "what she wanted," as Lady Becher never allowed a servant in her room while dressing. The figure then disappeared by the same door as on the former occasion, which, as before, was found locked! Lady Becher was not much alarmed, but felt that something unusual had occurred, and at dinner mentioned the event to the General and his son, when the General repeated what had occurred to him on the former occasion. That same night their youngest son, a boy about eight years of age [whom they were sure had no knowledge of the ghost], was sleeping in the same room as his father and mother, his bed facing an open door leading into the dressing room and bathroom, before mentiond. In the middle of the night the boy started up in his bed in a frightened attitude and called out, "What do you want, ayah? what do you want?" in Hindustani, evidently seeing a female figure in the dressing room near his bed. His mother quieted him and he fell asleep, and the figure was not seen by *us* on that occasion, nor was it ever again seen, though we lived for months in the house. But it confirmed our feeling that the same woman *had appeared to us all three,* and on inquiry from other occupants we learned that it was a frequent apparition on the first night or so of the house being occupied.

A native Hill, or Cashmere woman, very fair and handsome, had been murdered some years before in a hut a few yards below the house, and immediately under the door leading into the bath and dressing room, through which, on all three occasions, the figure had entered and disappeared. My son sleeping in another side of the house never saw it.

I could give the names of some other subsequent occupants who have told us much the same story. §

From *Proceedings* S.P.R., vol. viii. p. 178. The following narrative was sent to us with the true names, but with a request to conceal them, and some local details, on account of the painful nature of the incident described. Our informant, whom I will call Mrs. M., writes under date December 15th, 1891.

§ Before relating my experience of having seen a ghost, I should like my readers thoroughly to understand that I had not the slightest idea that the house in which my husband and I were living was haunted, or that the family residing there for many years before us had had any family troubles. One night on retiring to my bedroom about 11 o'clock, I thought I heard a peculiar moaning sound, and some one sobbing as if in great distress of mind. I listened very attentively, and still it continued; so I raised the gas in my bedroom, and then went to the window and drew the blind aside. There on the grass was a very beautiful young girl in a kneeling posture before a soldier, in a general's uniform, sobbing, and clasping her hands together, entreating for pardon; but, alas! he only waved her away from him. So much did I feel for the girl, that without a moment's hesitation I ran down the staircase to the door opening upon the lawn, and begged her to come in and tell me her sorrow. The figures then disappeared [gradually dissolved]! Not in the least nervous did I feel then; went again to my bedroom, took a sheet of writing-paper and wrote down what I had seen. [Mrs. M. has found and sent us this paper. The following words are written in pencil on a half sheet of notepaper: "March 13th, 1886. Have just seen visions on lawn: a soldier in general's uniform, a young lady kneeling to him. 11:40 P.M."]

It appears the story is only too true. The youngest daughter of this very old, proud family had had an illegitimate child; and her parents and relatives would not recognize her again, and she died broken-hearted. The soldier, a distinguished officer, was a near relative (also a connection of my husband's); and it was in vain she tried to gain his forgiveness.

So vivid was my remembrance of the features of the soldier that some months after the occurrence, when I happened to be calling with my husband at a house where there was a portrait of him, I stepped before it and said: "Why, look! There is the General!" And sure enough it *was*. §

Mrs. M. then mentions that a respectable local tradesman, hearing of the incident, remarked: "That is not an uncommon thing to see *her* about the place, poor soul! She was a badly used girl."

This case may remind us of what I have termed a *veridical after-image* of past events or emotions with no active counterpart in the present. We are, indeed, always uncertain as to the degree of the deceased person's active participation in post-mortem phantasms, as to the relation of such manifestations to the central current of his continuing individuality. But it is in dealing with these persistent pictures of a bygone earth-scene that this perplexity reaches its climax.

In each of the two next cases the interval after death was considerable, and the percipient was an absolute stranger to the deceased. This condition must, of course, usually involve the disadvantage that the identification of the appearance with a particular person can be based only on the percipient's subsequent description of what he had seen. But in the case which I shall quote first, this sort of identification was reinforced by the percipient's recognition of a photograph of the deceased. The account, taken from *Proceedings* S.P.R., vol. v. p. 416, comes from Mr. John E. Husbands, of Melbourne House, Town Hall Square, Grimsby.

§ DEAR SIR,—The facts are simply these. I was sleeping in a hotel in Madeira in January, 1885. It was a bright moonlight night. The windows were open and the blinds up. I felt some one was in my room. On opening my eyes, I saw a young fellow about twenty-five, dressed in flannels, standing at the side of my bed and pointing with the first finger of his right hand to the place I was lying. I lay for some seconds to convince myself of some one being really there. I then sat up and looked at him. I saw his features so plainly that I recognized them in a photograph which was shown me some days after. I asked him what he wanted; he did not speak, but his eyes and hand seemed to tell me I was in his place. As he did not answer, I struck out at him with my fist as I sat up, but did not reach him, and as I was going to spring out of bed he slowly vanished through the door, which was shut, keeping his eyes upon me all the time.

Upon inquiry I found that the young fellow who appeared to me died in that room I was occupying. . . .

JOHN E. HUSBANDS §

The following is from Miss Falkner, of Church Terrace, Wisbech, who was resident at the hotel when the above incident happened.

§ The figure that Mr. Husbands saw while in Madeira was that of a young fellow who died unexpectedly months previously, in the room which Mr. Husbands was occupying. Mr. H. had never heard of him or his death. He told me the story the morning after he had seen the figure, and I recognized the young fellow from the description. It impressed me very much, but I did not mention it to him or any one. I loitered about until I heard Mr. Husbands tell the same tale to my brother; we left Mr. H. and said simultaneously, "He has seen Mr. D."

No more was said on the subject for days; then I abruptly showed the photograph. Mr. Husbands said at once, "That is the young fellow who appeared to me the other night, but he was dressed differently"—describing a dress he often wore—"cricket suit (or tennis) fastened at the neck with sailor knot." I must say that Mr. Husbands is a most practical man, and the very last one would expect "a spirit" to visit.

K. FALKNER §

From *Proceedings* S.P.R., vol. v. p. 466. It is possible here that a real person may have been mistaken for an apparition, but the details, as reported, tell strongly against this view. The account is given by Mrs. Clerke, 68 Redcliffe Square, S.W.

§ In the autumn of 1872, I stayed at Sorrento with my two daughters, and established myself for some months at the Hotel Columella, which stands on the high road, within half a mile of the town.

On the evening in question we left the dining-room before the tea was finished, anxious, after the heat of the day, to enjoy the freshness and beauty of the terrace. After a few moments, I returned to my bedroom to fetch a candlestick and a shawl.

I got [them] and was preparing to return . . . when, on turning towards the half-open door, I saw it filled by the figure of an old woman. She stood motionless, silent, immovable, framed by the doorway, with an expression of despairing sadness, such as I had never seen before. I don't know why I was frightened, but some idea of its being an imbecile or mad woman flashed through my mind, and in an unreasoning panic I fled through the bedrooms to the terrace. My daughter, on hearing of my fright, returned to the rooms, but all was in its wonted stillness; nothing was to be seen.

The next morning I spoke to the women of the house of the old woman who had come to my room, as I thought she might be in some way connected with the establishment, and they were dismayed at my account of her, and assured me that there was no one answering the description in the house. I perceived there was much consternation caused by my narration, but paid little attention to it at the time.

A fortnight afterwards we had a visit from the parish priest, a friend of our landlord, and the spiritual adviser of the family. At a loss for conversation, I told him of my visitor. The padre listened to me with the greatest gravity, and said, after a pause: "Madam, you have accurately described the old mistress of this house, who died six months before you came in the room over yours. The people of the hotel have been already with me about it; it has caused them much anxiety lest you should leave, as they recognized in your description the old padrona, as she was called."

This explained to me various presents of fruit and special attentions I had received. Nothing more came of it, and I saw the apparition no more. In our walks we looked for even some semblance of the dress in which the woman appeared, but never saw it. Short as my glance towards her was, I could have painted her likeness had I been an artist. She was pale, of the thick pallor of age, cold grey eyes, straight nose, thick bands of yellowish grey hair crossing her forehead. She wore a lace cap with the border closely quilted all round, a white handkerchief crossed over her chest, and a long white apron. Her face was expressionless, but fixed and sad. I could not think she had any knowledge of where she was, or who stood before her, and certainly, for breaking through the barrier of the unseen, it was a most objectless visit.

I ought to mention that I had no knowledge of there having been such a person in existence until her likeness stood at my bedroom door.

KATE M. CLERKE §

Unless the actual evidence be disallowed in a wholesale manner, we shall be forced, I think, to admit the continued action of the departed as a main element in these apparitions. I do not say as the *only* element. I myself hold, as already implied, that the thought and emotion of living persons does largely intervene, as aiding or conditioning the independent action of the departed. I even believe that it is possible that, say, an intense fixation of my own mind on a departed spirit may aid that spirit to manifest at a special moment—and not even to me, but to a percipient more sensitive than myself. In the boundless ocean of mind innumerable currents and tides shift with the shifting emotion of each soul.

But now we are confronted by another possible element in these vaguer classes of apparitions, harder to evaluate even than the possible action of incarnate minds. I mean the possible *results* of past mental action, which, for ought we know, may persist in some perceptible manner, without fresh reinforcement, just as the results of past bodily action persist. And since we are coming now to cases into which the element of meaningless sound will enter largely, it seems right to begin their discussion with a small group in which there is evidence for the definite agency of some dying or deceased person in connection with inarticulate sounds, or I should rather say of the *connection* of some deceased person with the sounds; since the best explanation may perhaps be that they are *sounds of welcome*—before or after actual death—corresponding to those *apparitions of welcome* of which we have already had specimens.

The following is taken from *Phantasms of the Living*, vol. ii. p. 639. A gentleman named H. E. L. who is a master at Eton College wrote to us telling about the beautiful music heard by people in the house just about ten minutes after his mother died. He did not hear it himself. He enclosed two memorandums written by witnesses. In one Miss E. I., an accomplished musician, writes:

§ I will copy the memorandum which I made in my diary just after the death of my dear friend and connection, Mrs. L.

"*July 28th,* 1881.

"Just after dear Mrs. L.'s death between two and three A.M., I heard a most sweet and singular strain of singing outside the windows; it died away after passing the house. All in the room heard it, and the medical attendant, who was still with us, went to the window as I did, and looked out, but there was nobody. It was a bright and beautiful night. It was as if several voices were singing in perfect unison a most sweet melody, which died away in the distance. Two persons had gone from the room to fetch something, and were coming upstairs at the *back* of the house, and heard the singing and stopped, saying, 'What is that singing?' They could not *naturally* have heard any sound outside the windows in the front of the house from where they were. I cannot think that any explanation can be given to this—as I think—supernatural singing; but it would be very interesting to me to know what is said by those who have made such matters a subject of study."

E. I. §

The fact that Mr. L. did not share the experience is strong evidence that the sounds were not objectively caused by persons singing outside the house; and this is further confirmed by the slight difference which there appears to have been between the impressions received.

It is not contrary to our analogies that the person most deeply concerned in the death should in this case fail to hear them. But the point on which I would here lay stress is that phantasmal sounds—even non-articulate sounds—may be as clear a manifestation of personality as phantasmal figures. Among non-articulate noises music is, of course, the most pleasing; but sounds, for instance, which imitate the work of a carpenter's shop, may be equally human and intelligent. In some of the cases of this class we see apparent attempts of various kinds to simulate sounds such as men and women produce. To claim this humanity, to indicate this intelligence, seems the only motive of sounds of this kind.

The next case taken from the *Journal* S.P.R., vol. vi. p. 27 is another instance of a kind of auditory hallucination, the hearing of music, that seems to occur much more rarely than the hearing of voices. Some similar cases —also associated with deaths—were published in *Phantasms of the Living.* (See vol. ii. pp. 221 and 223.) The fact that the sounds were heard collectively suggests at first sight that they may have been real— an explanation which it is always more difficult to exclude in auditory than in visual cases. But the whole circumstances, when closely examined, make this explanation an extremely unlikely one.

The following account was given by Miss Horne, daughter of the percipient, in a letter to which Mrs. Horne's signature was afterwards added, so that the account, though written in the third person, is really a first-hand one.

§ It is nearly thirty years ago now, but it is as vividly impressed on her memory, as if it had happened yesterday.

She was sitting in the dining-room (in a self-contained house), which was behind the drawing-room, with Jamie, my eldest brother, on her knee, who was then a baby scarcely two years old. The nurse had gone out for the afternoon, and there was no one in the house except the maid downstairs. The doors of the dining-room and drawing-room both happened to be open at the time. All at once she heard the most divine music, very sad and sweet, which lasted for about two minutes, then gradually died away. My brother jumped from mamma's knee, exclaiming "Papa! papa," and ran through to the drawing-room. Mamma felt as if she could not move and rang the bell for the servant, whom she told to go and see who was in the drawing-room. When she went into the room, she found my brother standing beside the piano and saying "No papa!" Why the child should have exclaimed these words was that papa was very musical, and used often to go straight to the piano when he came home. Such was the impression on mamma that she noted the time to a *minute,* and six weeks after she received a letter saying her sister had died at the Cape, and the time corresponded exactly to the *minute* that she had heard the music. I may tell you that my aunt was a very fine musician.

[Miss] Emily M. Horne
[Mrs.] Eliza Horne §

I think that the curious question as to the influence of certain *houses* in generating apparitions may be included under the broader heading of Retrocognition. Manifestations which occur in haunted houses depend, let us say, on something which has taken place a long time ago. In what way do they depend on that past event? Are they a sequel, or only a residue? Is there fresh operation going on, or only fresh perception of something already accomplished? Or can we in such a case draw any real distinction between a continued action and a continued perception of a past action?

The following case is in some respects one of the most remarkable and best authenticated instances of "haunting" on record, although, as will be seen, the evidence for the identity of the apparition is inconclusive. The case was fully described in a paper entitled "Record of a Haunted House," by Miss R. C. Morton, in *Proceedings* S.P.R., vol. viii. pp. 311–332. Besides the account of the principal percipient, Miss R. C. Morton, the paper contains independent first-hand statements from six other witnesses—a friend, Miss Campbell, a sister and brother of Miss Morton's who lived in the house, and a married sister who visited there, and two former servants; also plans of the whole house. For the full details I must refer the reader to the original paper; I have space here only for abbreviated extracts from Miss Morton's account.

An account of the case first came into my hands in December, 1884, and this with Miss Morton's letters to her friend, Miss Campbell, are the earliest written records. On May 1st, 1886, I called upon Captain Morton at the "haunted house," and afterwards visited him at intervals, and took notes of what he told me. I also saw Miss Morton and Miss E. Morton, and the two former servants whose accounts are given in Miss Morton's paper. The phenomena as seen or heard by all the witnesses were very uniform in character, even in the numerous instances where there had been no previous communication between the percipients. Miss Morton is a lady of scientific training, and was at the time her account was written (in April, 1892) preparing to be a physician. The name "Morton" is substituted for the real family name. With that exception the names and initials are the true ones.

After describing the house and garden, Miss Morton proceeds:

§ It was built about the year 1860; the first occupant was Mr. S., an Anglo-Indian, who lived in it for about sixteen years. During this time, in the month of August, year uncertain, he lost his wife, to whom he was passionately attached, and to drown his grief took to drinking. About two years later, Mr. S. married again. His second wife, a Miss I. H., was in hopes of curing him of his intemperate habits, but instead she also took to drinking, and their married life was embittered by constant quarrels, frequently resulting in violent scenes. The chief subjects of dispute were the management of the children (two girls, and either one or two boys, all quite young) of the first Mrs. S., and the possession of her jewelry, to preserve which for her children, Mr. S. had some of the boards in the small front sitting-room taken up by a local carpenter and the jewels inserted in the receptacle so formed. Finally, a few months before Mr. S.'s death, on July 14th, 1876, his wife separated from him and went to live in Clifton. She was not present at the time of his death, nor, as far as is known, was she ever at the house afterwards. She died on September 23rd, 1878.

[In April, 1882, Captain Morton leased the house and moved in with his family. The following June Miss Morton first saw the apparition. She writes:]

I had gone up to my room, but was not yet in bed, when I heard some one at the door, and went to it, thinking it might be my mother. On opening the door, I saw no one; but on going a few steps along the passage, I saw the figure of a tall lady, dressed in black, standing at the head of the stairs. After a few moments she descended the stairs, and I followed for a short distance, feeling curious what it could be. I had only a small piece of candle, and it suddenly burnt itself out; and being unable to see more, I went back to my room.

The figure was that of a tall lady, dressed in black of a soft woollen material, judging from the slight sound in moving. The face was hidden in a handkerchief held in the right hand. This is all I noticed then; but on further occasions, when I was able to observe her more closely, I saw the upper part of the left side of the forehead, and a little of the hair above. Her left hand was nearly hidden by her sleeve and a fold of her dress. As she held it down a portion of a widow's cuff was visible on both wrists, so that the whole impression was that of a lady in widow's weeds. There was no cap on the head but a general effect of blackness suggests a bonnet, with long veil or a hood.

During the next two years—from 1882 to 1884—I saw the figure about half-a-dozen times; at first at long intervals, and afterwards at shorter, but I only mentioned these appearances to one friend, who did not speak of them to any one. During this period, as far as we know, there were only three appearances to any one else. . . .

On July 21st, 1884 I went into the drawing-room, where my father and sisters were sitting, about nine in the evening, and sat down on a couch close to the bow window. A few minutes after, as I sat reading, I saw the figure come in at the open door, cross the room and take up a position close behind the couch where I was. I was astonished that no one else in the room saw her, as she was so very distinct to me. My youngest brother, who had before seen her, was not in the room. She stood behind the couch for about half-an-hour, and then as usual walked to the door. I went after her, on the excuse of getting a book, and saw her pass along the hall, until she came to the garden door, where she disappeared. I spoke to her as she passed the foot of the stairs, but she did not answer, although as before she stopped and seemed as though *about* to speak. On July 31st, some time after I had gone up to bed, my second sister E., who had remained downstairs talking in another sister's room, came to me saying that some one had passed her on the stairs. I tried then to persuade her that it was one of the servants, but next morning found it could not have been so, as none of them had been out of their rooms at that hour, and E.'s more detailed description tallied with what I had already seen. §

The apparition was seen frequently by various members of the household during the rest of 1884 and the year 1885, and occasionally during 1886. It gradually became less distinct when it appeared and after 1889 it was never seen again.

During this time Miss Morton spoke to the lady whenever she saw her, but never received a reply, tried to touch her and tried to get her picture, but with no results. She fastened string across the stairway, but the ghost walked right through it.

Altogether during this period over a dozen people saw the apparition, and her footsteps were heard by at least twenty people, many of whom had not previously heard of her existence. She has been connected with the second Mrs. S.

In the *Journal* S.P.R., vol. vi. p. 146, November, 1893, an account was given by Miss M. W. Scott, of Lessudden House, St. Boswell's, Roxburghshire, of an apparition seen several times by herself, and occasionally by others, on a country road near her home. Her first experience was in May, 1892, when, walking down a short incline on her way home, she saw a tall man dressed in black a few yards in front of her. He turned a corner of the road, being still in view of her, and there suddenly disappeared. On following him round the corner, Miss Scott found a sister of hers, also on her way home, who had just seen a tall man dressed in black, whom she took for a clergyman, coming to meet her on the road. She looked away for a moment, and on looking towards him again could see no one anywhere near. Miss Scott on overtaking her found her looking up and down the road and into the fields in much bewilderment. It appeared that they had not seen the man at exactly the same moment nor in exactly the same place, but from their description of the surroundings it seems impossible that it could have been a real person, who had contrived to get away unnoticed.

On August 17th, 1900, Miss Scott wrote to say that she had recently seen the apparition twice, the most recent occasion having been "only last night." She describes it as follows:

§ *July 24th,* 1900.—I am writing to let you know the dates that I have again seen the apparition. . . . On the evening of July 24th I was standing speaking to a friend, exactly upon the part known as the property of that "mysterious he." I had forgotten the very existence of our supernatural neighbor, and while we conversed upon indifferent subjects, I inadvertently glanced carelessly down the expanse beyond, when I perceived the tall black figure walking on in advance with his back towards us. How he came to be there I had not the faintest idea, not having remarked his advent. I made no comment to my companion, but, wishing her a hasty adieu, hurried away as quickly as possible to try and make up upon him, but he instantly vanished—there was no one to be seen either high or low. It was just eight o'clock in the evening, as I heard the hour chime in the village almost at the same time. He was dressed in the same way,

namely, all in black, and was only proceeding about twenty yards away
. . . .

M. W. Scott §

Here, then, is a natural place of pause in our inquiry. We have worked as far as we can on the data which we have had under our view. The *sensory automatisms* with which we have dealt in this and the preceding chapter have proved to us, in my view, the connection of definite apparitions with individual men, both during bodily life and after bodily death. They have, in short, proved by logical reasoning the existence and the persistence of a spirit in man.

But great as this achievement is, it opens out more problems than it solves; it leaves us even more eager than at first for a fuller insight into this new dim-lit world. We feel that, important though the facts of phantasmal appearances may be, we want to get deeper, to reach some psychological discussion not dependent on time-coincidences nor on the details of some evanescent observation. We instinctively seek, in short, just that knowledge which will now be in some measure afforded to us through the study of that wide range of phenomena which I have classed together as *motor automatisms.*

The suddenness, the brevity of an apparition may be actually an evidential aid if we are simply establishing, say, a death coincidence. But when we have proceeded to a somewhat further stage—when we are looking for information from the inside as to the nature of spiritual operations—then, as I have said, the power of question and answer, of prolonged scrutiny, becomes all-important. We certainly cannot claim any more universal trustworthiness for motor than for sensory automatisms. The proportion of misleading to veridical written messages is probably even greater than the proportion of merely subjective to veridical apparitions. But while the apparition is gone in a moment, the written or spoken matter may renew itself for years, allowing us to test both its authenticity and its truthfulness—two different matters—with every touchstone which our leisure can devise.

It must be, then, on the study of motor automatisms that our general view of the spiritual world now opening to us must mainly be based. Those longer colloquies of automatic speech and script will introduce us to points of philosophy which fleeting apparitions cannot teach.

But one point already stands out from the evidence—in this long string of narratives, complex and bizarre though their details may be, we yet observe that the character of the appearance varies in a definite manner with their distinctness and individuality. Haunting phantoms, incoherent and unintelligent, may seem restless and unhappy. But as they rise into definiteness, intelligence, individuality, the phantoms rise also into love and joy. I cannot recall one single case of a proved posthumous combination of intelligence with wickedness. All that world-old conception of Evil Spirits, of malevolent Powers, which has been the basis of so much of actual devil-worship and of so much more of vague supernatural fear—all this insensibly melts from the mind as we study the evidence before us. In that faintly opening world of spirit I can find nothing worse than living men; I seem to discern not an intensification but a disintegration of selfishness, malevolence, pride. And is not this a natural result of any cosmic moral evolution?

I have thus indicated one point of primary importance on which the undesignedly coincident testimony of hundreds of first-hand narratives supports a conclusion, not yet popularly accepted, but in harmony with the evolutionary conceptions which rule our modern thought. Nor does this point stand alone. I can find, indeed, no guarantee of absolute and idle bliss; no triumph in any exclusive salvation. But the student of these narratives will, I think, discover throughout them uncontradicted indications of the persistence of Love, the growth of Joy, the willing submission to Law.

Could a proof of our survival be obtained, it would carry us deeper into the true nature of the universe than we should be carried by an even perfect knowledge of the material scheme of things. It would carry us deeper both by achievement and by promise. The discovery that there was a life in man independent of blood and brain would be a cardinal, a dominating fact in all science and in all philosophy. And the prospect thus opened to human knowledge, in this or in other worlds, would be limitless indeed.

I do not venture to suppose that the evidence set forth in these volumes, even when considered in connection with other evidence now accessible in our *Proceedings,* will at once convince the bulk of my readers that the momentous, the epoch-making discovery has been already made. Nay, I cannot even desire that my own belief should at once impose itself upon the world. Let men's minds move in their wonted manner: great convictions are sounder and firmer when they are of gradual growth. But I do think that to the candid student it should by this time become manifest that the world-old problem can now in reality be hopefully attacked; that there is actual and imminent possibility that the all-important truth should at last become indisputably known; and, therefore, that it befits all "men of goodwill" to help toward this knowing with what zeal they may.

Neither the religious nor the scientific reader can longer afford to ignore the *facts* presented here, to pass them by. They must be met, they must be understood, unless Science and Religion alike are to sink into mere obscurantism. And the one and only way to understand them is to learn more of them; to collect more evidence, to try more experiments, to bring to bear on this study a far more potent effort of the human mind than the small group who have thus far been at work can possibly furnish. Judged by this standard, the needed help has still to come. Never was there a harvest so plenteous with laborers so few.

Chapter Eight

MOTOR AUTOMATISM

Our main theme, I repeat once more, is the analysis of human personality, undertaken with the object of showing that in its depths there lie indications of life and faculty not limited to a planetary existence, or to this material world.

What we have already recounted seems, indeed, impossible to explain except by supposing that there is a spiritual world in which the individualities of our departed friends still actually subsist.

The reader, however, who has followed me thus far must be well aware that a large class of phenomena, of high importance, is still awaiting discussion. *Motor* automatisms—though less familiar to the general public than the phantasms which I have classed as *sensory* automatisms—are in fact even commoner, and even more significant.

Motor automatisms, as I define them, are phenomena of very wide range. We have encountered them already many times in this book. We met them in the first place in a highly developed form in connection with multiplex personality in Chapter Two. Numerous instances were there given of motor effects, initiated by secondary selves without the knowledge of the primary selves, or sometimes in spite of their actual resistance. All motor action of a secondary self is an automatism in this sense, in relation to the primary self.

But in what way then, it will be asked, do you distinguish the supernormal from the merely abnormal? Why assume that in these aberrant states there is anything besides hysteria, besides epilepsy, besides insanity?

The answer to this question has virtually been given in previous chapters. The reader is already accustomed to the point of view which regards all psychical as well as all physiological activities as necessarily either developmental or degenerative, tending to evolution or to dissolution.

Analogy, therefore, both physiological and psychical, warns us not to conclude that any given psychosis is merely degenerative until we have examined its results closely enough to satisfy ourselves whether they tend to bring about any enlargement of human powers, to open any new inlet to the reception of objective truth. If such there prove to be, then, with whatever morbid activities the psychosis may have been intertwined, it contains indications of an evolutionary impulse as well, something which we may represent as an effort towards self-development, self-adaptation, self-renewal.

Thus, for instance, Telepathy is surely a step in *evolution*.

These remarks, I hope, may have sufficiently cleared the ground to admit of our starting afresh on the consideration of such motor automatisms as are at any rate not morbid in their effect on the organism, and which I now have to show to be *evolutive* in character.

I may say at once that some of the automatic movements with which we shall have to deal—certain utterances and writings given in a state of "possession"—must rank, in my view, among the most important phenomena yet observed by man.

Since the subliminal self, like the telegraphist, begins its effort with full knowledge, indeed, of the alphabet, but with only weak and rude command over our muscular adjustments, it is likely that its easiest mode of communication will be through a repetition of simple movements, so arranged as to correspond to letters of the alphabet.

And here, I think, we have attained to a conception of the mysterious and much-derided phenomenon of "table-tilting" which enables us to correlate it with known phenomena, and to start at least from an intelligible basis, and on a definite line of inquiry.

A few words are needed to explain "table-turning," "spirit-rapping," and the like.

If one or more persons of a special type, at present definable only by the question-begging and barbarous term "mediumistic," remain quietly for some time with hands in contact with some easily movable object, and desiring its movement, that object will sometimes begin to move. If, further, they desire it to indicate letters of the alphabet by its movements—as by tilting once for *a*, twice for *b*, etc., it will often do so, and answers unexpected by any one present will be obtained.

Thus far, whatever our interpretation, we are in the region of easily reproducible facts, which many of my readers may confirm for themselves if they please.

But beyond the simple movements it is alleged by many persons that further physical phenomena occur; namely, that the table moves in a direction, or with a violence, which no unconscious pressure can explain; and also that percussive sounds or "raps" occur, which no unconscious action, or indeed no agency known to us, could produce. These raps communicate messages like the tilts, and it is to them that the name of "spirit-rapping" is properly given. But spiritualists generally draw little distinction between these four phenomena—mere table-turning, responsive table-tilting, movements of inexplicable vehemence, and responsive raps —attributing all alike to the agency of departed spirits of men and women, or at any rate to disembodied intelligences of some kind or other.

I am not at present discussing the physical phenomena of spiritualism, and I shall therefore leave on one side all the alleged movements and noises of this kind for which unconscious pressure will not account. I do not prejudge the question as to their real occurrence; but assuming that such disturbances of the physical order do occur, there is at least no need to refer them to disembodied spirits. If a table moves when no one is touching it, this is not obviously more likely to have been effected by my deceased grandfather than by myself. We cannot tell how *I* could move it; but then we cannot tell how *he* could move it either.

Faraday's explanation of table-turning as the result of the summation of many unconscious movements—obviously true as it is for some of the simplest cases of table-movement—does not touch the far more difficult question of the origination of intelligent messages, conveyed by distinct and repeated movements of some object. The ordinary explanation—I am speaking, of course, of cases where fraud is not in question—is that the sitter unconsciously sets going and stops the movements so as to shape the word in accordance with his expectation. Now that he unconsciously sets going and stops the movements is part of my own present contention, but that the word is thereby shaped in accordance with his expectation is often far indeed from being the case. Several of the examples to follow in this chapter illustrate the bizarre capriciousness of these replies—their want of relation to anything anticipated or desired by the persons in contact with the table. Similar instances might be indefinitely multiplied; but any one who is really willing to take the trouble can satisfy himself on this point by experiment with a sufficiently varied list of trustworthy friends. To those indeed who are familiar with automatic *written* messages, this question as to the unexpectedness of the *tilted* messages will present itself in a new light. If the written messages originate in a source beyond the automatist's supraliminal self, so too may the tilted messages; even though we admit that the tilts are caused by his hand's pressure of the table just as directly as the script by his hand's manipulation of the pen.

One piece of evidence which I cite in order to show that *written* messages are not always the mere echo of expectation, is a case where *anagrams* were automatically written, which their writer was not at once able to decipher. Following this hint, I have occasionally succeeded in getting anagrams tilted out for myself by movements of a small table which I alone touched. I should add that although I have never succeeded in *writing* automatically, I have nevertheless, after some hundreds of trials, continued over many years, attained the power of eliciting by unconscious pressure tilted responses which do not emanate from my own conscious self. That they do, however, emanate from *some* stratum of my being—from that fragmentary and incoherent workshop where dreams are strung together—seems to me, as already indicated, the most probable hypothesis.

The anagrams—or rather jumbles of letters forming a short word—which I have myself obtained, have been of the simplest kind. But occasionally I have not at once recognized the word thus given, but have been aware of a distinct interval before the word which my own unconscious muscular action had thus confusedly "tilted out" was grasped by my conscious intelligence. This is a kind of experiment which might with advantage be oftener repeated; for the extreme incoherence and silliness of the responses thus obtained does not prevent the process itself from being in a high degree instructive.

We cannot always answer the primary questions, Is the subliminal impulse sensory or motor? is it originated in the automatist's own mind, or in some mind external to him?

A small group of cases may naturally be mentioned here. From two different points of view they stand for the most part at the entrance of our subject. I speak of motor inhibitions, prompted at first by subliminal memory. First are two cases (Mrs. Hadselle's) where the motor effect produced was the important part of the experience, but which show in intimate connection general *malaise,* motor impulse, and auditory hallucination.

From the *Proceedings* S.P.R., vol. ix. p. 33. In this case the conscious desire of the agent seems to have been the pre-determining cause of the percipient's impression.

The percipient, Mrs. Hadselle, writes to Dr. Hodgson as follows:

§ 28 BRADFORD STREET, PITTSFIELD, MASS., *May* 28*th,* 1888.
Less than two years ago a curious thing happened to me. I had been in Wash. Co., N.Y., giving half a dozen readings, and was on my way to Williamstown. . . . With ticket purchased, I was serenely seated in the car, box, bundle, and bag beside me, the conductor's "All aboard" was at that instant in my ears, when I sprang to my feet with the force of an inward command, "Change your ticket and go to Elizabeth (N.J.). *Change your ticket and go to Elizabeth. Change your——*" Here a gentleman in the opposite seat—an utter stranger—rose and said: "Madam, have you forgotten something, can I help you?" I said: "Do you think the train will wait for me to change my ticket?" For there appeared to be no alternative. As I spoke I moved towards the platform; he followed, and seeing that the office was but a few steps distant said: "Go, I'll see that you are not left." I

did go, and in a moment more was on my way to Elizabeth, *though I had not before even thought of such a thing.* Next morning, on reaching my friend's house, she threw her arms about me and sobbed out: "Oh, I have wanted you so." Then she led me to a room where an only and beloved sister lay in life's last battle. In an hour it was ended.

My poor grief-stricken friend declared then—declares now—that my sudden change of purpose was a direct answer to her repeated though unspoken demand for my presence. And who shall say it was not?

C. A. C. HADSELLE

[The gentleman who helped Mrs. Hadselle to change her ticket, the Rev. James Wilson, then of Greenwich, N.Y., writes in answer to Dr. Hodgson's inquiries:]

I recollect the circumstance of "assisting a lady" at Greenwich ticket office, who exchanged her ticket at the last moment, because of a change of purpose; and it was in November, 1886. She sent me a few lines afterwards, detailing certain facts touching a sick friend at the point of her destination—not clearly recalled at this moment.

J. T. WILSON §

From the *Proceedings* S.P.R., vol. ix. p. 35. Mrs. Hadselle sent at the same time as the above another narrative, of which she said:

§ I send you with this a bit of experience which I had years ago.

[The account is taken from the *Berkshire County Eagle,* May 10th, 1888, Pittsfield, Mass., and is there headed "The Unspoken Warning—A Mother's Experience."]

One bitter cold day in winter a merry party of us, nestled down under furry robes, went to meet an appointment with a friend living a few miles distant, with whom we were to spend the afternoon and in the evening attend a concert to be held near by. The sleighing was delightful, the air keen and inspiriting, the host and hostess genial as the crackling fires in the grates, and the invited guests, of whom there were many besides ourselves, in that peculiar visiting trim which only old-time friends, long parted, can enjoy. . . . Just before tea, [however] I was seized with a sudden and unaccountable desire to go home, accompanied by a dread or fear of something, I knew not what, which made the return appear, not a matter of choice, but a thing imperative. I tried to reason it away, to revive anticipations of the concert; I thought of the disappointment it would be to those who came with me to give it up, and running over in my mind the condition in which things were left at home, could find no ground for alarm.

For many years a part of the house had been rented to a trusty family. In their care had been left Eddie, a boy of ten years, the only one of the family remaining at home, who knew that when he returned from school he was expected to bring in wood and kindlings for the morning fire and otherwise pass the time as he pleased, only that he must not go into the street to play, or on to the pond to skate. He had been left many times in this way, and had never given occasion for the slightest uneasiness; still, as this nameless fear grew upon me, it took the form of a conviction that danger of some sort threatened this beloved child.

I was rising to go and ask Mr. A. to take me home, when some one said, "You are very pale; are you ill?" "No," I answered, and dropping back in the chair, told them how strangely I had been exercised for the last few minutes; adding, "I really must go home." There was a perfect chorus of voices against it, and for a little time I was silenced, though not convinced. ... But at tea my trembling hand almost refused to carry food to my lips, and I found it utterly impossible to swallow a mouthful. A death-like chill crept over me, and I knew that every eye was on me as I left the room. Mr. A. rose, saying in a changed voice and without ceremony, "Make haste; bring the horse round, we must go right away. I never saw her in such a state before; there is something in it." He followed me to the parlor, but before he could speak I was pleading as for dear life that not a moment be lost in starting for home....

We returned in the cutter—urging the horse to his best. Only once was the silence broken in that three-mile journey, and that was when the house was in full view. I said, "Thank God, the house is not on fire." "That was my own thought," said Mr. A., but there was no slackening of speed.

On nearing home a cheerful light was glimmering from Mrs. E.'s window; before the vehicle had fairly stopped we were clear of it, and opening the door, said in the same breath, "Where's Eddie?" "Eddie? why, he was here a little while ago," answered Mrs. E., pleasantly striving to dissipate the alarm she saw written on our countenances....

Mr. A. crossed the hall to our own room and turned the knob. The door was locked. What could that mean? Eddie was either on the inside or had taken the key away with him. Mr. A. ran round to a window with a broken spring which could be opened from the outside. It went up with a clang, but a dense volume of smoke drove him back. After an instant another attempt was made, and this time, on a lounge directly under the window, he stumbled on the insensible form of little Eddie, smothered in smoke. Limp and apparently lifeless, he was borne into the fresh cold air, and after some rough handling was restored to consciousness.

Eddie said that on returning from school he made a good fire, and as the wood was snowy thought he would put it in the oven to dry; something he had never done before; and it seemed so nice and warm he thought he would lie down awhile. . . . Every one said that with a delay of five or even three minutes we should have been too late.

MRS. C. A. C. HADSELLE §

Inhibitions—sudden arrests or incapacities of action—form a simple, almost rudimentary, type of motor automatisms. And an inhibition—a sudden check on action of this kind—will be a natural way in which a strong but obscure impression will work itself out. Such an impression, for instance, is that of *alarm*, suggested by some vague sound or odor which is only subliminally perceived. And thus in this series of motor automatisms, just as in our series of dreams, or in our series of sensory automatisms, we shall find ourselves beginning with cases where the subliminal self merely shows some slight extension of memory or of sensory perception.

From a paper by Mrs. Verrall, entitled "Some Experiments on the Supernormal Acquisition of Knowledge," in the *Proceedings* S.P.R., vol. xi. p. 191.

§ In these cases a piece of information not consciously possessed at the moment is conveyed to the conscious intelligence by means of an apparent mechanical difficulty, which on examination turns out not to exist. The information thus obtained is usually negative; that is, this apparent mechanical difficulty prevents my doing something unnecessary or undesirable, which I should know to be such if I thought about it, but which from thoughtlessness I am on the point of doing. An illustration will make my meaning clearer.

Constantly, when using my typewriter, it has happened to me to find a difficulty in pressing a key, so great a difficulty as to oblige me to look to see what is wrong. I then see that what is wrong is that my finger was on the wrong key, but there is, in fact, no difficulty whatever in depressing the key if I determine to do so. The effect of this apparent mechanical difficulty is to draw my attention in time to the mistake I am on the point of making.

. . .

[Again,] I wrote, in the afternoon, five letters, and then stretched out my left hand to the stationery case to take the necessary envelopes. I wanted five, and as I can usually take a small number without error expected to take five. But I did not get enough; I found that I only had three, and tried to take a couple more. But one of these two slipped through my fingers, and I only held one. I was quite vexed at my maladroitness, gave up a further attempt for the present and proceeded to fold my letters, put them into envelopes, and address them. When I came to the fifth letter, I remembered that I had an envelope ready addressed for this letter, and it was actually lying on my table while I was trying to take the five envelopes. I may have seen it, but if I did, it was unconsciously; it was only when I found that I could not get five envelopes that I discovered that I did not require more than four. §

Parallel to this trivial case of inability to grasp an unneeded envelope is a case of sudden check from throwing into the fire a bundle of banknotes mistaken for useless papers.

From the *Proceedings* S.P.R., vol. vii. p. 344. The following is a case in which, as I conceive, the subliminal self has observed what the supraliminal has failed to notice.

§ From Mrs. E. K. ELLIOTT, wife of the Rev. E. K. Elliott

About twenty years ago I received some letters by post, one of which contained £15 in bank notes. After reading the letters I went into the kitchen with them in my hands. I was alone at the time, no one being near me, except the cook, and she was in the scullery. Having done with the letters, I made a motion to throw them into the fire, when I distinctly felt my hand arrested in the act. It was as though another hand were gently laid upon my own, pressing it back. Much surprised, I looked at my hand, and then saw that it contained not the letters I had intended to destroy, but the bank notes, and that the letters were in the other hand. I was so surprised that I called out, "Who is here?" I called the cook and told her, and also told my husband on the first opportunity. I never had any similar experience before or since.

E. K. ELLIOTT §

Similarly there are cases where some sudden muscular impulse or inhibition has probably depended on a subliminal perception or interpretation of a sound which had not reached the supraliminal attention. For instance, two friends walking together along a street in a storm just evade by sudden movements a falling mass of masonry. Each thinks that he has received some *monition* of the fall; each asserting that he heard no noise whatever to warn him. Here is an instance where subliminal perception may have been slightly quicker and more delicate than supraliminal; and may have warned them just in time.

In the next case (quoted from *Proceedings* S.P.R., vol. xi. p. 416) there may have been some subliminal hyperæsthesia of hearing which dimly warned Mr. Wyman of the approach of the extra train.

Mr. Wm. H. Wyman writes to the Editor of the *Arena* as follows:

§ DUNKIRK, N.Y., *June 26th,* 1891.

Some years ago my brother was employed and had charge as conductor and engineer of a working train on the Lake Shore and Michigan Southern Railway, running between Buffalo and Erie. On one occasion I was with him. As we approached near Westfield Station, running about 12 miles per hour, and when within about one mile of a long curve in the line, my brother all of a sudden shut off the steam, and quickly stepping over to the fireman's side of the engine, he looked out of the cab window, and then to the rear of his train to see if there was anything the matter with either. Not discovering anything wrong he put on steam, but almost immediately again shut it off and gave the signal for breaks and stopped. After inspecting the engine and train and finding nothing wrong, he seemed very much excited, and for a short time he acted as if he did not know where he was or what to do. I asked what was the matter. He replied that he did not know, when, after looking at his watch and orders, he said that he felt that there was some trouble on the line of the road. I suggested that he had better run his train to the station and find out. He then ordered his flagman with his flag to go ahead around the curve, which was just ahead of us, and he would follow with the train. The flagman started and had just time to flag an extra express train, with the General Superintendent and others on board, coming full forty miles per hour. The Superintendent inquired what he was doing there, and if he did not receive orders to keep out of the way of the extra. My brother told him that he had not received orders and did not know of any extra train coming; that we had both examined the train reports before leaving the station. The train then backed to the station, where it was found that no orders had been given. The train dispatcher was at once discharged from the road, and from that time to this both my brother and myself are unable to account for his stopping the train as he did. I consider it quite a mystery, and cannot give or find any intelligent reason for it. Can you suggest any?

The above is true and correct in every particular. §

Here, again, is an averted railway accident, where smell may possibly have played some part. From *Proceedings* S.P.R., vol. xi. p. 419.

§ Train No. 2 of the B. and O. R. R., due in Chicago at 6:20 A.M., Sunday, in the month of August, 1883 (have forgotten exact date), was on time, running at about thirty-five miles an hour. On approaching Salt Creek Trestle Work, about forty miles east of Chicago, the engineer, Mr.

C. W. Moses, felt that something that he could not define compelled him to stop before attempting to cross over. He applied the air and came to a full stop at the approach. I occupied front seat in smoker, it being the second car from engine. The time was about 4:30 A.M. I immediately went forward and joined the engineer where we found thirty feet of the woodwork burned, the rails being held to place by charred stringers. We went across, by climbing down and up the bank on the other side, and woke up the watchman who was employed to look after the bridge, who, on seeing us and the condition of things in general, took to his heels and is running still, as far as I know. I would say that in more than a score of years engaged in railroad work, that was the most narrow escape I ever experienced; for undoubtedly, with a fall of thirty feet and the length of over a hundred, we would not only have been disabled, but burned.

Now you especially ask as to what impelled Mr. Moses in his action. He only stated to me at the time that something especially pressing on him told him he should stop, and he acted on the impulse. There had been fires all along the side of track at other points, but he paid no attention to them.

I. J. STEWART, Conductor C. J. and M. R. R.
[Formerly of the B. and O. R. R.] §

See also a case given in *Proceedings* S.P.R., vol. viii. p. 345, where a lady hurrying up to the door of a lift, is stopped by seeing the figure of a man standing in front of it, and then finds that the door is open, leaving the well exposed, so that she would probably have fallen down it, if she had not been checked by the apparition.

And now I give a case of sudden motor inhibition where no warning can well have been received from hyperæsthetic sensation. We have come, it seems, to spirit guardianship.

(From *Proceedings* S.P.R., vol. xi. p. 459.)

§ Four years ago, I made arrangements with my nephew, John W. Parsons, to go to my office after supper to investigate a case. We walked along together, both fully determined to go up into the office, but just as I stepped upon the door sill of the drug store, in which my office was situated, some invisible influence stopped me instantly. I was much surprised, felt like I was almost dazed, the influence was so strong, almost like a blow, I felt like I could not make another step. I said to my nephew, "John, I do not feel like going into the office now; you go and read Flint and Aitken on the subject." He went, lighted the lamp, took off his hat, and just as he was reaching for a book the report of a large pistol was heard. The ball entered the window near where he was standing, passed near to and over his head, struck the wall and fell to the floor. Had I been standing where he was, I would have been killed, as I am much taller than he. The pistol was fired by a man who had an old grudge against me, and had secreted himself in a vacant house near by to assassinate me.

I am fully satisfied that the invisible and unknown intelligence did the best that could have been done, under the circumstances, to save us from harm.

D. J. PARSONS, M.D., Sweet Springs, Mo. §

In the next group of cases which I shall cite, we reach a class of massive motor impulses which are almost entirely free from any sensory admixture. The first account is taken from the *Journal* S.P.R., vol. viii. p. 125. Mr. Garrison writes:

§ MR. RICHARD HODGSON,—DEAR SIR,—Answering your letter of July 15th in regard to my experience connected with the death of my mother, I will make the following statement. My mother, Nancy J. Garrison, died on Friday night, October 4th, 1888, at her home three miles northeast of Ozark, Christian County, Missouri.

[He states that he was living at Fordland, 18 miles away. He was at a church meeting with his wife and child when he suddenly felt a desire to see his mother. He continues:]

And then the impulse to go to her became so strong that I gave the baby to a neighbor-woman and left the church without telling my wife. She was in another part of the house.

The train going west which would have taken me to Rogersville. seven miles of the distance to my mother's place, was due at 10:30 P.M., but before I got home and changed my clothes and returned to the depot, the cars had left the station. I still felt that I must see my mother, and started down the railroad track alone, and walked to Rogersville. Here I left the railroad and walked down the wagon way leading from Marshfield to Ozark, Mo. It was about three o'clock A.M. when I reached my mother's house. I knocked at the door two or three times and got no response. Then I kicked the door, but still made no one hear me. At last I opened the door with my knife and walked in and lighted a lamp. Then my sister, Mrs. Billie Gilley, the only person who had been living with my mother, awoke, and I asked her where mother was. She replied that she was in bed, and I said, "She is dead," for by that time I felt that she could not be alive. She had never failed to wake before when I had entered the room at night.

I went to my mother's bed and put my hand on her forehead. It was cold. She had been dead about three hours, the neighbors thought, from the condition of her body. She had gone to bed about ten o'clock at night, feeling better than usual. She and my sister had talked awhile after going to bed. They were aiming to come to Ozark the next morning, and intended to get up early.

The above facts cover my experience as fully as I can tell the story. I have no explanation for the matter. It is as much a mystery to me now as ever. I could not believe such a strange affair if told by any one else, and yet I could swear to every fact stated.

THOMAS B. GARRISON §

In another case, Mr. Skirving (see below) was irresistibly compelled to leave his work and go home—*why,* he knew not—at the moment when his wife was in fact calling for him in the distress of a serious accident. See also a case given in *Phantasms of the Living,* vol. ii. p. 377, where a bricklayer has a sudden impulse to run home, and arrives just in time to save the life of his little boy, who had set himself on fire. From *Phantasms of the Living,* vol. i. p. 285.

§ [Mr. Alexander Skirving writes that he always took his lunch to work as it was too far to go home. But on a certain day he suddenly had an intense desire to go home. It was ten in the morning and he hated to leave but:]

I got fidgety and uneasy, and felt as if I must go, even at the risk of being ridiculed by my wife, as I could give no reason why I should leave my work and lose 6d. an hour for nonsense. However, I could not stay, and I set off for home under an impulse which I could not resist.

When I reached my own door and knocked, the door was opened by my wife's sister, a married woman, who lived a few streets off. She looked surprised, and said, "Why, Skirving, how did you know?" "Know what?" I said. "Why, about Mary Ann." I said, "I don't know anything about Mary Ann" (my wife). "Then what brought you home at present?" I said, "I can hardly tell you. I seemed to want to come home. But what is wrong?" I asked. She told me that my wife had been run over by a cab and been most seriously injured about an hour ago, and she had called for me ever since, but was now in fits, and had several in succession. I went upstairs, and though very ill she recognized me, and stretched forth her arms and took me round the neck and pulled my head down into her bosom. The fits passed away directly, and my presence seemed to tranquilize her, so that she got into sleep, and did well. Her sister told me that she had uttered the most piteous cries for me to come to her, although there was not the least likelihood of my coming. This short narrative has only one merit; it is strictly true.

ALEXANDER SKIRVING §

Some of my readers may have seen so-called "spirit-drawings," designs, sometimes in color, whose author asserts that he drew them without any plan, or even knowledge of what his hand was going to do. This assertion may be quite true, and the person making it may be perfectly sane. For, of course, the mere fact that a man writes messages or draws pictures which he does not consciously originate will not, when taken alone, prove anything beyond this fact itself as to the writer's condition. He may be perfectly sane, in normal health, and with nothing unusual observable about him.

The following is a typical case of automatic drawing, recorded at a time when the subject of automatism was almost unknown, not only to the educated layman but also to psychologists and physiologists. I quote the account from *Spirit Drawings: a Personal Narrative,* by W. M. Wilkinson. Second edition (1864), pp. 9–11.

§ In August, 1856, a heavy and sudden affliction came upon us, in the removal of a dear boy—our second son [aged eleven]—into the spiritual world.

One morning his brother, then about twelve years old, had a piece of paper before him, and a pencil in his hand, with which he was about to draw some child's picture; when gradually he found his hand filling with some feeling before unknown to him, and then it began to move involuntarily upon the paper, and to form letters, words, and sentences. The feeling he described as of a pleasing kind, entirely new to him, and as if some power was within him apart from his own mind, and making use of his hand. The handwriting was different to his own, and the subject-matter of the writing was unknown to him till he read it with curiosity as it was being written. [This occurred frequently after that.]

Sometimes, when he wished to write, his hand moved in drawing small flowers, such as exist not here; and sometimes, when he expected to draw a flower, the hand moved into writing. The movement was, in general, most rapid, and unlike his own mode of writing or drawing; and he had no idea of what was being produced, until it was in process of being done. Often, in the middle of writing a sentence, a flower or diagram would be drawn, and then suddenly the hand would go off in writing again. §

A few weeks later the boy's mother, who had never learnt to draw, found that she possessed the same faculty, and by devoting about an hour a day to the practice, produced a large series of drawings of flowers, geometrical forms, and various objects which her family regarded as symbolical. They often obtained also automatic writing purporting to come from the dead child and to explain the meaning of the drawings. The latter developed into architectural sketches and landscapes, and Mrs. Wilkinson gradually began to paint, as well as draw, automatically. Mr. Wilkinson also developed the faculty of automatic writing and drawing.

The subject of automatic writing is a creation of the last few decades, and is at present in so rapidly developing a condition that it is not easy to know at what stage of proof or explanation it is here best to begin. In calling the subject novel I do not indeed mean to deny that this and similar practices are traceable in many lands and in remote antiquity. But among civilized men, in Europe and America, the phenomenon came first into notice as an element in so-called "modern spiritualism," about the middle of the nineteenth century. It then remained for another generation a kind of plaything or drawing-room amusement—planchette being called upon for answers to such questions as "What young lady am I thinking of?" "What horse is going to win the Derby?"

It was in the United States that these sporadic messages were first developed and systematized. Through the unlettered mind of Andrew Jackson Davis a kind of system of philosophy was given. Through Judge Edmonds many messages of serious import were given, although they contain little evidence to the agency of an external intelligence. *The Healing of the Nations* was another work of the same general type. But the automatic writings of W. Stainton Moses—about 1870–80—were perhaps the first continuous series of messages given in England which lifted the subject into a higher plane.

These writings marked a new departure of most serious moment. Mr. Moses—a man whose statements could not be lightly set aside—claimed for them that they were the direct utterances of departed persons, some of them lately dead, some dead long ago. Such a claim seemed at first too prodigious for belief; and—as will be seen later—it is in fact still under discussion. But Mr. Moses' writings—however to be explained—strongly impressed Edmund Gurney and myself, and added to our desire to work at the subject in as many ways as we could.

It was plain that these writings—which *might* be of almost immeasurable importance—could not be judged aright without a wide analysis of similar scripts, without an experimental inquiry into what the human mind, in states of somnambulism or the like, could furnish of written messages, apart from the main stream of consciousness. By his experiments on writing obtained in different stages of hypnotic trance, Gurney acted as the pioneer of a long series of researches which, independently set on foot by Professor Pierre Janet in France, have become of high psychological, and even medical, importance. What is here of prime interest is the indubitable fact that fresh personalities can be artificially and temporarily created, which will write down matter quite alien from the first personality's character, and even matter which the first personality never knew. That matter may consist merely of reminiscences of previous periods when the second personality has been in control. But, nevertheless, if these writings are shown to the primary personality, he will absolutely repudiate their authorship—alleging not only that he has no recollection of writing them, but also that they contain allusions to facts which he never knew. Some of these messages, indeed, although their source is so perfectly well defined—although we know the very moment when the secondary personality which wrote them was called into existence—do certainly look more alien from the automatist in his normal state than many of the messages which claim to come from spirits of lofty type. It is noticeable, moreover, that these manufactured personalities sometimes cling obstinately to their fictitious names, and refuse to admit that they are in reality only aspects or portions of the automatist himself. This must be remembered when the persistent *claim* to some spiritual identity—say Napoleon—is urged as an argument for attributing a series of messages to that special source. There is much else which may be learnt from these self-suggested automatisms; and the discussions in my earlier chapters refer to several points which should be familiar to all who would seriously analyze the more advanced, more difficult, motor phenomena.

And here it must be strongly asserted that, however important it may be to work to the full that preliminary inquiry, it is still more important to collect the richest possible harvest of those more advanced cases. To such collection Mr. Moses' writings acted as a powerful stimulant; and ever since my first sight of his MSS. I have made it a principal object to get hold of automatic script from trustworthy sources.

During those twenty-seven years I have personally observed at least fifty cases where there was every reason to suppose that the writing was genuinely *automatic;* albeit in most of the cases it was uninteresting and non-evidential.

This number is, at any rate, sufficient to enable me to generalize as to the effects of this practice on healthy persons rather less inadequately than writers who generalize from hearsay, or observation of hospital patients.

In two cases I think that the habit of automatic writing (carried on in spite of my warning, by persons over whom I had no influence), may have done some little harm, owing to the obstinate belief of the writers that the obvious trash which they wrote was necessarily true and authoritative. In the remaining cases no apparent harm was done; nor, so far as I know, was there any ill-health or disturbance in connection with the practice. Several of the writers were persons both physically and mentally above the average level.

My own conclusion is that when the writing is presumptuous or nonsensical, or evades test questions, it should be stopped; since in that case it is presumably the mere externalization of a kind of dream-state of the automatist's; but that when the writing is coherent and straightforward, and especially when some facts unknown to the writer are given as tests of good faith, the practice of automatic writing is harmless, and may lead at any moment to important truth. The persons, in short, who should avoid this experiment are the self-centered and conceited. It is dangerous only to those who are secretly ready—and many are secretly ready—to regard themselves as superior to the rest of mankind.

What has now been said may suffice as regards the varieties of mechanism—the different forms of motor automatism—which the messages employ. I shall pass on to consider the *contents* of the messages, and shall endeavor to classify them according to their apparent sources.

A. In the first place, the message may come from the percipient's own mind; its contents being supplied from the resources of his ordinary memory, or of his more extensive subliminal memory; while the *dramatization* of the message—its assumption of some other mind as its source—will resemble the dramatizations of dream or of hypnotic trance.

Of course the absence of facts unknown to the writer is not in itself a proof that the message does not come from some other mind. We cannot be sure that other minds, if they can communicate, will always be at the pains to fill their messages with evidential facts. But, equally of course, a message devoid of such facts must not, on the strength of its mere assertions, be claimed as the product of any but the writer's own mind.

B. Next above the motor messages whose content the automatist's own mental resources might supply, we may place the messages whose content seems to be derived telepathically from the mind of some other person still living on earth; that person being either conscious or unconscious of transmitting the suggestion.

C. Next comes the possibility that the message may emanate from some unembodied intelligence of unknown type—other, at any rate, than the intelligence of the alleged agent. Under this heading come the views which ascribe the messages on the one hand to "elementaries," or even devils, and on the other hand to "guides" or "guardians" of superhuman goodness and wisdom.

D. Finally we have the possibility that the message may be derived, in a more or less direct manner, from the mind of the departed friend from whom the communication does actually claim to come.

My main effort has naturally been thus far directed to the proof that there are messages which do *not* fall into the lowest class, *A*—in which class most psychologists would still place them all. And I myself—while reserving a certain small portion of the messages for my other classes—do not only admit but assert that the great majority of such communications represent the subliminal workings of the automatist's mind alone. It does not, however, follow that such messages have for us no interest or novelty.

As Professor William James says in *Psychology,* vol. i. p. 394: "One curious thing about trance utterances is their generic similarity in different individuals. . . . It seems exactly as if one author composed more than half of the trance messages, no matter by whom they are uttered. Whether all subconscious selves are peculiarly susceptible to a certain stratum of the *Zeitgeist*[1] and get their inspiration from it, I know not."

Is this indeed the drift of the *Zeitgeist*—as Professor James suggests—steady beneath the tossings and tumblings of individual man? Or is it something independent of age or season? Is there some pattern in the very fabric of our nature which begins to show whenever we scratch the glaze off the stuff?

I need not here multiply instances of the simpler and commoner forms of this type, and I will merely quote in illustration two short cases recounted by Mr. H. Arthur Smith (author of *The Principles of Equity,* and a member of the Council of the Society for Psychical Research) who has had the patience to analyze many communications through "Planchette."

From *Proceedings* S.P.R., vol ii. p. 233. Mr. Smith and his nephew placed their hands on the Planchette, and a purely fantastic name was given as that of the communicating agency.

§ Q. "Where did you live?"   A. "Wem." This name was quite unknown to any of us. I am sure it was to myself, and as sure of the word of the others as of that of any one I know.

Q. "Is it decided who is to be Archbishop of Canterbury?"   A. "Yes."

[1] The spirit of the age; trend of thought and feeling in a period.

Q. "Who?" A. "Durham." As none of us remembered his name, we asked.

"What is his name?" A. "Lightfoot." Of course, how far the main statement is correct, I don't know. The curiosity at the time rested in the fact that the name was given which none of us could recall, but was found to be right. §

Now, this is just one of the cases which a less wary observer might have brought forward as evidence of spirit agency. An identity, it would be said, manifested itself, and gave an address which none present had ever heard. But I venture to say that there cannot be any real proof that an educated person has never heard of Wem. A permanent recorded fact, like the name of a town which is to be found (for instance) in Bradshaw's Guide, may at any moment have been presented to Mr. Smith's eye, and have found a lodgment in his subliminal memory.

Similarly in the answers "Durham" and "Lightfoot" we are reminded of cases where in a dream we ask a question with vivid curiosity, and are astonished at the reply; which nevertheless proceeds from *ourselves* as undoubtedly as does the inquiry. The prediction in this case was wrong.

In the next case, although it is possible that the lady's mental action may have contributed, as Mr. Smith supposes, to the very result which she so little desired, the word written may have emanated from the subliminal self of the *writer* alone.

§ Present—H. A. Smith (A), R. A. H. Bickford-Smith (B), another gentleman (C), and two ladies (D and E). . . .

Our method of procedure at the time was as follows: C, sitting at one end of the room, wrote down a name of an author, showing it to no one in the room; B had his hands on the Planchette, no one else being in contact with him or it. C fixed his attention on the written name, and our design was to see whether that name would be written through the medium of the Planchette. The ladies were meanwhile sewing in silence, and taking no part in the experiments. It happened that one of the ladies had at the time, owing to some painful family circumstances, the name of a gentleman (not present) painfully impressed on her mind. The name was not a common one, and though all present knew something of the circumstances, they had not been mentioned during the evening, and no one had mentioned the name in question, which we will call "Bolton." C then wrote "Dickens" on his paper, and was "willing" B with all his might to write this, when, to the surprise of every one, Planchette rapidly wrote "Bolton." This was not only surprising to us, but painful; and no comments were made at the time, the subject being changed as rapidly as possible. It would appear from this that the effect of C's volitional concentration was overmatched by the intensity of the lady's thought, though not directed to the same object.

H. ARTHUR SMITH §

I quote next a more complex case ("Clelia") furnished by a gentleman whom I call Mr. A. It is a very good instance of the capricious half-nonsense which has often been referred to the agency of spirits. The indisputable evidence for complex subliminal mentation which this case seems to me to furnish lies in the fact that here Mr. A.'s pen wrote not only unintelligible abbreviations, but absolute anagrams of sentences; anagrams, indeed, of the crudest kind, consisting of mere transpositions of letters, but still *puzzles* which the writer had to set himself to decipher *ab extra.* The chances against drawing a group of letters *at random* which will form several definite words and leave no letters over are, of course, very great.

From the *Proceedings* S.P.R., vol. ii. pp. 226–31. Mr. A. describes his experience with automatic writing by pen as follows:

§ CLELIA, OR UNCONSCIOUS CEREBRATION

The experiment was made Easter, 1883, on one day, and, after an interval of a week, continued on three consecutive days; four days in all. On the first day I became seriously interested; on the second puzzled; on the third I seemed to be entering upon entirely novel experiences, half awful and half romantic; upon the fourth the sublime ended very painfully in the ridiculous.

FIRST DAY

. . .

Q. 2. *What* is it that *now moves* my pen? A. 2. Religion. Q. 3. What moves my pen to write *that* answer? A. 3. Conscience. Q. 4. What is religion? A. 4. Worship.

Q. 5. Worship of what? A. 5. wbwbwbwbwbwb——. Q. 6. What is the meaning of wb? A. 6. Win, buy. Q. 7. What? A. 7. Know-(ledge).

. . .

SECOND DAY

Q. 1. What is man? (*i.e.* What is the nature of his being?) A. 1. Flise.

My pen was at first very violently agitated, which had not been the case upon the first day. It was quite a minute before it wrote as above. Upon the analogy of *wb*, I proceeded.

Q. 2. What does F stand for? A. 2. Fesi. Q. 3. 1? A. 3. le. Q. 4. i? A. 4. ivy. Q. 5. s? A. 5. sir. Q. 6. e? A. 6. eye. Fesi le ivy sir eye.

Q. 7. Is this an anagram? A. 7. Yes. Q. 8. How many words in the answer? A. 8. Four.

I tried for a few minutes to solve it without success. Not caring to spend much time in trying to solve what might have no solution, I gave it up.

THIRD DAY

Q. 1. (rep.) What is man? A. 1. Tefi Hasl Esble Lies.
This answer was written right off.

Q. 2. Is this an anagram? A. 2. Yes. Q. 3. How many words in the answer? A. 3. V (*i.e.,* five). Q. 4. What is the first word? A. 4. See. Q. 5. What is the second word? A. 5. Eeeeee——. Q. 6. See? Must I interpret it myself? A. 6. Try.

Presently I got out, "Life is the less able." Next I tried the anagram given upon the previous day, and at last obtained, "Every life is yes." But my pen signified that it preferred the following order of words, "Every life yes is." . . .

I do not know whether any other interpretations can be given to the letters. But these fulfill the requirements as to the number of words; and the action of the pen, assisting in the process of interpretation, pointing to the letters, accepting these and rejecting those combinations, left no doubt in my mind that I had hit the meaning.

It was not without something of awe that I put:

Q. 7. Who art thou? A. 7. *Clelia! !* Q. 8. Thou art a woman? A. 8. Yes. Q. 9. Hast thou ever lived upon the earth? A. 9. No. Q. 10. Wilt thou? A. 10. Yes. Q. 11. When? A. 11. Six years. Q. 12. Wherefore dost thou speak with me? A. 12. E if Clelia e l.

It was with increasing excitement that I perceived as an interpretation, "I Clelia feel." But upon my asking whether this was right, "Clelia" wrote again thus: E if Clelia e l. 20.

Q. 13. Is 20 your age? A. 13. ∞. (She was eternal.) Q. 14. Then 20 what? A. 14. Words. . . .

FOURTH DAY

I began my questioning in the same exalted mood, but, to my surprise, did not get the same answer.

Q. 1. Wherefore dost thou speak with me?   A. 1. [Wavy line. Repetition and emphasis: Wherefore dost *thou* speak with *me?*]

However, I thought this "a solemn and piercing rejoinder," and proceeded to consider my motives, and purify them from all earthly and unspiritual alloy. Then—

Q. 2. Wherefore dost thou answer me?   A. 2. [Wavy line. Wherefore dost *thou* answer *me?*]   Q. 3. Do I answer myself?   A. 3. Yes. Q. 4. Is Clelia here?   A. 4. No.   Q. 5. Who is it, then, now here? A. 5. Nobody.   Q. 6. Does Clelia exist?   A. 6. No.   Q. 7. With whom did I speak yesterday?   A. 7. No one. . . .

My pen now became altogether wild, sometimes affirming and sometimes denying the existence of Clelia. . . . Almost the last anagram I received was: Wvfs yoitet—testify, vow. . . .

Note: I have never known any one named Clelia. I have not been in the habit of writing anagrams, though I have done so in boyhood. §

The cases of automatic writing thus far given have shown us an independent activity of the subliminal self holding colloquies with the supraliminal; but they have shown us nothing more. Yet we shall find, if we go on accumulating instances of the same general type, that traces of clairvoyance and telepathy begin insensibly to show themselves; not at first with a distinctness or a persistence sufficient for actual proof, but just in the same gradual way in which indications of supernormal faculty stole in amid the disintegration of split personalities; or in which indications of some clairvoyant outlook stole in amid the incoherence of dream. Many of these faint indications, valueless, as I have said, for purely evidential purposes, are nevertheless of much theoretical interest, as showing how near is the subliminal self to that region of supernormal knowledge which for the supraliminal is so definitely closed.

Mr. Schiller's case, given below, is a good example of these obscure transitions between normal and supernormal, and introduces us to several phenomena which we shall afterwards find recurring again and again.

From the *Proceedings* S.P.R., vol. iv. pp. 216–24. This is a case typical at least in its main features, and specially suitable for record on account of the care with which the phenomena were noted down as they occurred. The case was sent to us by Mr. F. C. S. Schiller, now Fellow of Corpus Christi College, Oxford, and I have myself been present at one of the experiments where Mr. F. C. S. Schiller and his brother, Mr. F. N. Schiller, of St. John's College, Cambridge, obtained some of the old French writing. Some experiments in telepathy and clairvoyance were also tried, but with no great success, and the description of these is omitted here.

§ The experiments in question were conducted during a great part of the Long Vacation, with my brother, whom I will call F., and my sister L., as "mediums," writing conjointly at first, but afterwards separately. Of course, there could thus be no doubt as to the good faith of the "mediums," even if the course of the experiments had not afforded convincing proof that the phenomena were independent of their conscious mind. There appeared at different times no less than nine "spirits." Although the evidence was not conclusive in establishing the identity of the various "spirit" personages, there could be no doubt of their complete independence of the mediums' conscious will. Both F. and L. were at first entirely ignorant of what planchette was writing, and F. remained so to the end, nor did the occupations of his conscious self appear in the least to affect the progress of the writing. I have seen planchette write in the same slow and deliberate way both while he was telling an amusing anecdote in an animated way and while he was absorbed in an interesting novel; and frequently whole series of questions would be asked and answered without his knowing what had been written or thinking that anything else than unmeaning scrawls had been produced.

In L.'s case it is true that after some time she came to know what letters were being formed and was able to interpret the movements of her hand. This, of course, made it difficult to avoid, at times, a certain half-conscious influence on the writing, and makes it necessary to allow for the personal equation. But it is clear that this influence must tend to harmonize the answers of planchette with the opinions and will of the medium, and as a matter of fact I observed frequent cases, especially with L., of a conflict between her will and opinions and those of planchette. . . .

The spirit of a "careless rhymer," after writing verses in English, French, and German, professed its ability to do so in the classical languages. [He produced some Greek, but F. then remembered that he had read the *Iliad* a long time ago, and the "spirit's" Greek was a quotation from this. Then occurred an] entirely unknown language, namely Hindustani. A "spirit" gave his name as "Lokenadrath," and wrote in an extraordinary Oriental style, rather resembling some of Marion Crawford's rhapsodies. On introducing the words "Allah il Allah," he was asked whether he was a Mohammedan. "Hindi apkahai." I have since been informed[1] that ["apkahai" means] "I am yours," "At your service," and that "Lokenadrath" should be "Lokendranath," and means "lord of princes"; and one or two other fragments of Hindustani were similarly

[1] On the authority of (1) an Anglo-Indian lady; (2) a Balliol Brahmin of Bambay. [The whole phrase means "A Hindu is at your service." The Oriental rhapsodies were found to be mainly centoes of *Mr. Isaacs*, worked together so as to make sense.]

inaccurate.[1] Now, as F. left India as a baby of eight months, and has never since, to the best of my belief, heard any Hindustani spoken, this is surely a most curious case of unconscious memory, if such it was. . . .

An interesting experiment was tried of writing with two planchettes, F. having one hand on each. I suggested this in order to elucidate the connection between left-handed writing and "mirror-writing," and fully expected that the two hands would write the same communications. To my astonishment, however, the communications, though written simultaneously, were different and proceeded from different "spirits." I regard this as conclusive proof that the phenomena have nothing to do with the medium's consciousness, for, as every one can easily experience for himself, it is quite impossible, at least without long practice, to write two *different* words at the same time.

Whenever F. wrote with two planchettes, the left hand wrote mirror-writing, which was often very hard to decipher.

To sum up then I will only say that the matter of the various communications (*i.e.* excluding the card and alphabet experiments, etc.) does not seem to me to afford absolute proof that the knowledge displayed could not possibly have been latent in the writer's mind, while at the same time this is extremely *improbable* in a large number of cases. Moreover, both the matter and the manner of the communications display powers beyond any at present recognized as normal.

F. C. S. SCHILLER §

The next case which I shall quote combines various motor automatisms in a very unusual way. I give it at length partly on account of its strangeness and partly in deference to the high scientific authority on which I received it. The account is taken from an article by Dr. A. T. Myers and myself in *Proceedings* S.P.R., vol. ix. p. 182.

The writer of the following narrative is a physician occupying an important scientific post on the Continent of Europe. He is known to us by correspondence and through a common friend—himself a *savant* of European reputation—who has talked the case over with Dr. X. and his wife, and has read the statement which we now translate and abbreviate. We are bound to conceal Dr. X.'s identity, and even his country; nor is this unreasonable, since the *bizarrerie* of the incidents to be recorded would be felt as greatly out of place in his actual scientific surroundings. The Dr. Z. who here appears in the somewhat dubious character of a

---

[1] I have now found out (December, 1886) that Lokenadrath's description of his nationality is not as totally unintelligible as I had hitherto thought it. He called himself a "Jude poerano," and I have been told that "poerano" is Romany for *gipsy*.

mesmerizing spirit, was also, as it happens, a *savant* of European repute, and a personal friend of Dr. X.'s.

§ Mme. X. is a lady healthy in body and mind, well-balanced, of sound judgment, strong common sense, and a calm and firm character. She is the very opposite of what would be termed a nervous or hysterical subject. . . .

In September, 1890, while we were staying in the country, Mme. X. sprained her right foot. It became inflamed and painful; and the left foot also became painful. For all that winter Mme. X. was obliged to lie up, the foot being kept from all movement by plaster or silicate dressings. . . There was inflammation of the tissues of several of the joints of the right foot, and we were seriously alarmed.

At this point certain friends talked to Mme. X. about the alleged facts of spiritism, of which until that date she had had a very vague notion. They praised the beneficent intervention of spirits in disease; but had much difficulty in inducing her to admit the mere possibility of facts of this nature. I can affirm, therefore, that it was only with great difficulty that these friends succeeded in vanquishing Mme. X.'s skepticism—which was moreover supported by my own objections to spiritism—and at last persuaded her to submit herself to the action of the invisibles. The spirit-guide of a group of which one of our friends was a member advised the intervention of the (spirit)-doctor Z. A day was arranged when Dr. Z. was to visit Mme. X., and she was informed of the date. Owing to other preoccupations we completely forgot this *rendezvous*. On the day named —it was in April, 1891—Dr. Z. announced himself by raps in the table. Only then did we recollect the *rendezvous* agreed upon. I asked Dr. Z. his opinion on the nature of the injury to Mme. X.'s foot. By tilts of the table, through Mme. X.'s mediumship, he gave the word "tuberculosis." He meant that there was tuberculosis of the joints, and of this there had been some indications. Had Mme. X. been predisposed to tubercle I doubt not that this would have supervened. Personally, I much feared this complication, and Dr. Z.'s answer (as I at once thought) might well be the mere reflection of my fears. . . We now know that there was in fact no tuberculosis. In any case, Dr. Z. ordered a merely soothing remedy, sulphur ointment. Some days later, at our request, Dr. Z. reappeared and promised to undertake the cure of Mme. X.'s feet.

I come now to the phenomena, mainly subjective, which Mme. X.'s case began to present. On August 17th, 1891, the patient felt for the first time a unique sensation, accompanied by formication and sense of weight in the lower limbs, especially in the feet. This sensation gradually spread over the rest of the body, and when it reached the arms, the hands and forearms began to rotate. These phenomena recurred after dinner every evening, as soon as the patient was quiet in her arm-chair. . .

[Later] the phenomena changed in character, and gained in interest. The patient had begun to be able to walk without much difficulty; but all forced and voluntary movement of the foot was still painful, although when the movement was initiated by the occult agency no pain whatever was felt. One evening, after the usual séance, the patient felt her head move against her will. An intelligent intercourse was thus set up between the patient and the unseen agent or agents. The head nodded once for "Yes," twice for "No," three times for a strong affirmation. These movements were sometimes sudden and violent enough to cause something like pain. Words and phrases could, of course, be spelt out in this way. This form of correspondence has never wholly ceased; although the intensity of the phenomenon has now much diminished. The occult agent now impresses one or other of Mme. X.'s hands with movements which trace in the air the form of letters of the alphabet—a plan which works well and quickly.

Mme. X. is also a writing medium; and this power first showed itself in a strange way. . . . She was writing a letter one day, with no thought of these unseen agencies, when suddenly she felt her hand checked. Warned by a special sensation, she still held the pen. Her hand placed itself on a sheet of paper and began rapidly to write alarming predictions. The writings retained this tone only for a few hours; and soon the communications became trivial in character, and, save in some exceptional instances, have since remained so.

Another phenomenon followed shortly afterwards. One day Mme. X. felt herself lifted with force from her arm-chair and compelled to stand upright. Her feet and her whole body then executed a systematic calisthenic exercise, in which all the movements were regulated and made rhythmic with finished art. This was renewed on following days, and towards the end of each performance—sometimes of an hour's or two hours' duration—the movements acquired extreme energy. Mme. X. has never had the smallest notion of chamber-gymnastics, Swedish or otherwise, and these movements would have been very painful and fatiguing had she attempted them of her own will. Yet at the end of each performance she was neither fatigued nor out of breath.

Mme. X. was accustomed to bandage her own foot every morning. One day she was astonished to feel her hands seized and guided by an occult force. From that day onwards the bandaging was done according to all the rules of the art, and with a perfection which would have done credit to the most skillful surgeon of either hemisphere. Although very adroit with her hands, Mme. X. had never had occasion to practice nursing or to study minor surgery, yet the bandages thus *automatically* applied were irreproachable, and were admired by every one. When Mme. X. wished to renew the bandages, she placed the strips all rolled up upon a table within reach of her hand, and her hand then automatically took the bandage which best suited the occult operation.

Mme. X. is accustomed to arrange her own hair. One morning she said laughingly, "I wish that a Court hairdresser would do my hair for me; my arms are tired." At once she felt her hands acting automatically, and with no fatigue for her arms, which seemed to be held up; and the result was a complicated *coiffure,* which in no way resembled her usual simple mode of arrangement....

At the Paris Exhibition of 1889 Mme. X. once saw the "Javanese dance," consisting of rhythmic motions of the body with contortions of the arms. The occult agents caused her to repeat this dance several times with perfect execution.

Disliking these phenomena, Mme. X. has tried very hard to free herself from this control, and has to a great extent succeeded, by the use of cold water, by strongly resisting all communications, and by "passes of disengagement" executed by a hypnotizer. This has reduced the phenomena almost entirely to automatic writing, which vague or fantastic when dealing with ordinary topics, is precise and intelligent on medical questions.

Thus far the phenomena recorded have been purely subjective; in those which follow there is something objective also. When one has the honor to be treated by a physician of Dr. Z.'s celebrity (!) ordinary kindness bids one sometimes think of benefiting one's neighbor. One of the officials of my department had suffered for many years from pleurodynia, which occasionally laid him up altogether, and also from frequent attacks of sick headache. Dr. Z. was consulted and prescribed an internal treatment which, to my great surprise, consisted mainly of "dosimetric granules"; which this great official surgeon had not in his lifetime employed. He also caused Mme. X. to perform "passes of disengagement" for ten or fifteen minutes at a time. It was noticeable that while these passes were made with extreme violence, Mme. X.'s hands were arrested at the distance of a millimetre at most from the patient's face, without ever touching him in the least. Mme. X. could never of herself have given to her movements such a degree of precision. For two years now the patient has felt no more of his pleurodynia, and his *migraine* is, if not altogether cured, at least greatly reduced.

Under other circumstances I have myself consulted Dr. Z. as to patients under my professional care. On each occasion he has given a precise diagnosis and has indicated a treatment, consisting mainly of dosimetric granules, sometimes associated with other treatment. These facts have been repeated many times, and I owe great gratitude to Dr. Z. for the advice which he has given me. His prescriptions were always rational; and when I showed fears as to certain doses which appeared to me too large, he took pains to reassure me, but stuck to his prescriptions. I have never had to repent having followed the advice of my eminent colleague in the other world; and I am bound to state distinctly that every time that a medical question has been submitted to him the replies and advice of Dr. Z. have been of an astonishing clearness and precision. §

In reply to inquiries Dr. X. adds the following remarks:

§ It is not impossible that Mme. X. should have at some time heard myself or others pronounce the names of the medicaments prescribed. But when she gave me an exact diagnosis, and formulated in detail a rational treatment, I am sure that this did not come from her own mind. She has never studied any branch of medicine—neither the therapeutic art itself, nor the minor art of composing formulæ. Nor could I have been acting suggestively, since my own ideas were often quite different from those which the occult agent dictated; unless, indeed, my unconscious self acted upon Mme. X.'s consciousness, which seems to me a somewhat too elaborate view.

The dosimetric granules are a convenient mode of administering alkaloids, glycosides, and other toxic principles, and I have often been alarmed at the doses which Dr. Z. prescribed. I confess that I was astonished to find that an occult agent who thus claimed to be a bygone Professor should have selected a form of medication on which the Faculty look with no approving eye.

As to Mme. X.'s foot, I have a *firm conviction* that it was healed by the rhythmical movements imposed, and by the "magnetization" of the occult agent.

You ask me whether I consider these agents as belonging to the human type. Provisionally, Yes; unless we admit that there exists, superposed upon our world, another world of beings distinct from humanity, but knowing it and studying it as we study the other regions of nature, and assuming for the sake of amusement or for some other motive the *rôle* of our departed friends. §

Dr. X. concludes with warnings against the dangers of such influence or possession; dangers which he thinks that Mme. X. avoided by her calmness of temperament and resolute maintenance of self-control.

Dr. X. sent us two of the prescriptions written by Mme. X.'s hand. We compared them with British Pharmacopœal prescriptions, by the aid of Burggraeve's *Guide de Médecine Dosimétrique* (Paris, 1872). Both prescriptions are in fair accord with English practice; the doses of arsenic in the one case, of strychnia in the other, being rather stronger than usually given. Each prescription contains several ingredients, in what seems reasonable proportion.

The main curiosity of such cases as these lies in their very persistence and complexity; it would be a waste of space to quote any of the longer ones in such a way as to do them justice. And, fortunately, there is no need for me to give any of my own cases; since a specially good one has been specially well observed and reported in a book with which many of my readers are probably already acquainted—Professor Flournoy's *Des Indes à la planète Mars: Etude sur un cas de Somnambulisme avec Glossolalie* (Paris and Geneva, 1900).

Professor Flournoy's book indicates in a remarkable way how things have moved in the psychology of the last twenty years. The book—a model of fairness throughout—is indeed, for the most part, critically *destructive* in its treatment of the quasi-supernormal phenomena with which it deals. But what a mass of conceptions a competent psychologist now takes for granted in this realm, which the official science of twenty years ago would scarcely stomach our hinting at!

One important point may be noticed at once as decisively corroborating a contention of my own made long ago, and at a time when it probably seemed fantastic to many readers. Arguing for the potential *continuity* of subliminal mentation (as against those who urged that there were only occasional flashes of submerged thought, like scattered dreams), I said that it would soon be found needful to press this notion of a continuous subliminal self to the utmost, if we were not prepared to admit a continuous spiritual guidance or possession. Now, in fact, with Professor Flournoy's subject the whole discussion turns on this very point. There is unquestionably a continuous and complex series of thoughts and feelings going on beneath the threshold of consciousness of Mlle "Hélène Smith" (a pseudonym). Is this submerged mentation due in any degree or in any manner to the operation of spirits other than Mlle Smith's own? That is the broad question.

Mlle Smith, I should at once say, is not, and never has been, a paid medium. At the date of M. Flournoy's book, she occupied a leading post on the staff of a large store at Geneva, and gave séances to her friends simply because she enjoyed the exercise of her mediumistic faculties, and was herself interested in their explanation.

Her organism is regarded, both by herself and by others, as a quite healthy one. Mlle Smith, says Professor Flournoy, declares distinctly that she is perfectly sound in body and mind and indignantly repudiates the idea that there is any hurtful anomaly or the slightest danger in mediumship as she practices it.

"I am so far from being abnormal," she writes, "that I have never been so clear-sighted, so lucid, so capable of judging rapidly on all points, as since I have been developed as a medium." No one appears to dispute this estimate, which the facts of Mlle Smith's progress in her line of business distinctly confirm.

"It is in fact incontestable" (continues Professor Flournoy, p. 41), "that Hélène has a head extremely well organized; and that from a business point of view she manages admirably the very important and complicated department of which she is at the head in this large shop where she is employed; so that to accuse her of being morbid simply because she is a medium is . . . inadmissible so long as the very nature of mediumship remains a thing so obscure and open to discussion as is still the case. . . .

"It is clear that there exist amid the ranks of the learned faculty certain spirits narrow and limited, strong in their own specialties, but ready to cast their anathemas at whatever does not fit in with their preconceived ideas, and to treat as morbid, pathological, insane, everything which differs from the normal type of human nature, such as they have conceived it on the model of their own small personalities. . . .

"But in the first place the essential criterion in judging of a human being's value is not the question whether he is in good or bad health, like or unlike other people, but whether he fulfills adequately his special task— how he acquits himself of the functions incumbent on him, and what may be expected or hoped from him. I am not aware that Miss Smith's psychical faculties have ever interfered with her accomplishment of any of her duties; rather they have helped her therein; for her normal and conscious activity has often found an unexpected assistance—which non-mediums lack!—in her subliminal inspirations and her automatisms, which effect a useful end.

"In the second place, it is far from being demonstrated that mediumship is a pathological phenomenon. It is abnormal, no doubt, in the sense of being *rare, exceptional;* but rarity is not morbidity. The few years during which these phenomena have been seriously and scientifically studied have not been enough to allow us to pronounce on their true nature. It is interesting to note that in the countries where these studies have been pushed the furthest, in England and America, the dominant view among the *savants* who have gone deepest into the matter is not at all unfavorable to mediumship; and that, far from regarding it as a special case of hysteria, they see in it a faculty superior, advantageous, healthy."

There is in her phenomena every kind of automatic irruption of subliminal into supraliminal life. As Professor Flournoy says (p. 45): "Phenomena of hypermnesia, divinations, mysterious findings of lost objects, happy inspirations, exact presentiments, just intuitions, teleological (purposive or helpful) automatisms, in short, of every kind; she possesses in a high degree this small change of genius—which constitutes a more than sufficient compensation for the inconvenience resulting from those distractions and moments of absence of mind which accompany her visions; and which, moreover, generally pass unobserved."

At séances—where the deeper change has no inconveniences—Hélène undergoes a sort of self-hypnotization which produces various lethargic and somnambulistic states. And when she is alone and safe from interruption she has spontaneous visions, during which there may be some approach to ecstasy. At the séances the main actor is Hélène's guide Leopold who speaks and writes through her, and is, in fact, either her leading spirit-control or (much more probably) her most developed form of secondary personality. It should be added that, although somewhat pompous, Leopold always appears both sensible and dignified. "Leopold," says Professor Flournoy (p. 134) "certainly manifests a very honorable and amiable side of Mlle Smith's character, and in taking him as her 'guide' she has followed inspirations which are doubtless among the highest in her nature."

I must indeed confess myself unable to explain why it is that beneath the frequent incoherence, frequent commonplaceness, frequent pomposity of messages purporting to come from the spirit world there should almost always be a substratum of better sense, of truer catholicity, than is usually to be heard except from the leading minds of the generation. It is possible that these utterances may bear in reality some obscure relation to truths profounder than we have as yet normally acquired. Yet these as often involve tenets which are unsupported by evidence, and are probably to be referred to mere self-suggestion.

Prominent among such tenets is one which forms a large part of Mlle Smith's communications; namely, the doctrine of *reincarnation,* or of successive lives spent by each soul upon this planet.

The simple fact that such was probably the opinion both of Plato and of Virgil shows that there is nothing here which is alien to the best reason or to the highest instincts of men. Nor, indeed, is it easy to realize any theory of the *direct creation* of spirits at such different stages of advancement as those which enter upon the earth in the guise of mortal man. There *must,* one feels, be some kind of continuity—some form of spiritual Past. Yet for reincarnation there is at present no valid evidence; and it must be my duty to show how its assertion in any given instance—Mlle Smith's included—constitutes in itself a strong argument in favor of self-suggestion rather than extraneous inspiration as the source of the messages in which it appears.

On the general scheme here followed, each incarnation, if the last has been used aright, ought to represent some advance in the scale of being. If one earth-life has been misused, the next earth-life ought to afford opportunity for expiation—or for further practice in the special virtue which has been imperfectly acquired. Thus Mlle Smith's present life in a humble position may be thought to atone for her overmuch pride in her last incarnation—as Marie Antoinette.

But the mention of Marie Antoinette suggests the risk which this theory fosters—of assuming that one is the issue of a distinguished line of spiritual progenitors; insomuch that, with whatever temporary sets-back, one is sure in the end to find oneself in a leading position.

Pythagoras, indeed, was content with the secondary hero Euphorbus as his bygone self. But in our days Dr. Anna Kingsford and Mr. Edward Maitland must needs have been the Virgin Mary and St. John the Divine. And Victor Hugo, who was naturally well to the front in these self-multiplications, took possession of most of the leading personages of antiquity whom he could manage to string together in chronological sequence. It is obvious that any number of re-born souls can play at this game; but where no one adduces any evidence it seems hardly worth while to go on.

Meantime the question as to reincarnation has actually been put to a very few spirits who have given some real evidence of their identity. So far as I know, no one of these has claimed to know anything personally of such an incident; although all have united in saying that their knowledge was too limited to allow them to generalize on the matter.

Hélène's controls and previous incarnations—to return to our subject —do perhaps suffer from the general fault of aiming too high. She has to her credit a control from the planet Mars; one pre-incarnation as an Indian Princess; and a second (as I have said) as Marie Antoinette.

In each case there are certain impressive features in the impersonation; but in each case also careful analysis negatives the idea that we can be dealing with a personality really revived from a former epoch, or from a distant planet, and leaves us inclined to explain everything by that subliminal inventiveness of which we already know so much.

The *Martian* control was naturally the most striking at first sight. Its reality was supported by a Martian language, written in a Martian alphabet, spoken with fluency, and sufficiently interpreted into French to show that such part of it, at any rate, as could be committed to writing was actually a grammatical and coherent form of speech; but it was a language corresponding in every particular with simple French idioms, and including such words as *quisa* for *quel*, *quisé* for *quelle*, *vétèche* for *voir*, *vèche* for *vu* —the fantastic locutions of the nursery. Having transmogrified *monsieur* into *métiche*, Hélène further transmutes *les messieurs* into *cée métiché*— in naïve imitation of ordinary French usage. And this tongue is supposed to have sprung up independently of all the influences which have shaped terrene grammar in general or the French idiom in particular! And even after Professor Flournoy's analysis of this absurdity I see newspapers speaking of this Martian language as an impressive phenomenon! They seem willing to believe that the evolution of another planet, if it has culminated in conscious life at all, can have culminated in a conscious life into which we could all of us enter affably, with a suitable Ollendorff's phrase-book under our arms; "*eni cée métiché oné qudé*"—"ici les hommes (messieurs) sont bons"—"here the men are good"—and the rest of it.

To the student of automatisms, of course, all this irresistibly suggests the automatist's own subliminal handiwork. It is a case of "glossolaly," or "speaking with tongues." We have no modern case where such utterance has proved to be other than gibberish. I have had various automatic hieroglyphics shown to me, with the suggestion that they may be cursive Japanese, or perhaps an old dialect of Northern China; but I confess that I have grown tired of showing these fragments to the irresponsive expert, who suggests that they may also be vague reminiscences of the scrolls in an Oriental tea-tray.

It seems indeed to be a most difficult thing to get telepathically into any brain even fragments of a language which it has not learned. A few simple Italian, and even Hawaiian, words occur in Mrs. Piper's utterances, coming apparently from departed spirits, but these, with some Kaffir and Chinese words given through Miss Browne, form, I think, almost the only instances which I know. And, speaking generally, whatever is elaborate, finished, pretentious, is likely to be of subliminal facture; while only things scrappy, perplexed, and tentative have floated to us veritably from afar.

Analysis of the so-called Martian language proves it to be no exception to this rule. It is, in fact, a childish, though elaborate, imitation of French whose true parallel lies in those languages of the nursery which little brothers and sisters sometimes invent—as a tongue not understanded of their elders.

Further, it has sometimes been alleged that discarnate spirits may be concerned in the composition of such romances, on the hypothesis that if they do act upon human minds, they probably so act sometimes to amuse *themselves,* as well as to please or inform *us.* I know of no evidence, indeed, of their having any power to *injure* us, but it is thought by some that there is a good deal of evidence of tricky, playful interference, and that a kind of literary impulse to write or act out *romances,* through the intermediacy of some human being, may be one form of this mystifying intervention. There is, however, no need to postulate the existence of tricky spirits when the phenomena can be adequately accounted for by the known tendencies of the subliminal self, as exemplified in such cases as the "Clelia" and Newnham writings, and Sally Beauchamp.

I pass on from these reincarnational romances to certain minor, but interesting phenomena. These are small acts of helpfulness—*beneficent* actions, as we might term them, in contrast with the *injurious,* or combined groups of *hurtful* actions, with which hysteria has made us familiar. We have already printed several incidents of this type in our *Proceedings* and *Journal.* (See, for instance, the trivial but instructive case of Mrs. Verrall and the envelopes.)

"One day," says Professor Flournoy (p. 55), "Miss Smith, when desiring to lift down a large and heavy object which lay on a high shelf, was prevented from doing so because her raised arm remained for some seconds as though petrified in the air and incapable of movement. She took this as a warning, and gave up the attempt. At a subsequent séance Leopold stated that it was he who had thus fixed Hélène's arm to prevent her from grasping this object, which was much too heavy for her, and would have caused her some accident.

"Another time, a shopman, who had been looking in vain for a certain pattern, asked Hélène if by chance she knew what had become of it. Hélène answered mechanically and without reflection—'Yes, it has been sent to Mr. J.' (a client of the house). At the same time she saw before her the number 18 in large black figures a few feet from the ground, and added instinctively, 'It was sent eighteen days ago.' This was in the highest degree improbable, but was found to be absolutely correct."

The next question is as to whether supernormal faculty of any kind is manifested in Hélène's phenomena. There does appear to be some telepathy and of telepathy Professor Flournoy speaks as follows:

"One may almost say that, if telepathy did not exist, it would be necessary to invent it. I mean by this that a direct action between living beings, independently of the organs of sense, is a thing so in accord with all that we know of nature that it would be difficult not to assume its existence *a priori*, even were no sign of it perceptible. ..."

And now as to the question of possible telepathy from the dead in Hélène's case. The instance with most in its favor is described by Professor Flournoy as follows (p. 406):

§ In a sitting at my house (February 12th, 1899) Mlle Smith has a vision of a village on a height covered with vines; she sees a small old man coming down thence by a stony road. He looks like a "demi-monsieur"— buckled shoes, large soft hat, shirt-collar unstarched, with points rising to his cheeks, etc. A peasant in a blouse whom he meets bows to him as to a personage of importance; they talk a *patois* which Hélène cannot follow. She has an impression that she knows the village; but she cannot identify it. Soon the landscape disappears, and the old man, now clothed in white and seen in a luminous space [implying that he is in the next world] seems to come nearer. ... Then she ... takes a pen, and holding it between thumb and forefinger writes slowly in an unknown handwriting, *Chaumontet syndic.* Then returns the vision of the village; we wish to know its name and she ends by perceiving a guide-post on which she spells out *Chessenaz* —a name unknown to us. Finally having, at my desire, asked the old man the date when he was syndic, she hears him answer, 1839. Nothing more can be learnt; the vision disappears and gives place to a possession by Leopold, who in his big Italian voice talks at length about various matters. I question him on the incident of the unknown village and syndic; his answers, interrupted by long digressions, are to this effect: "I am looking—I turn my thoughts along that great mountain with a tunnel in it whose name I do not know [Leopold who returns from the eighteenth century, is naturally not well up in modern geographical names; but this is the hill of Forte de l'Ecluse]; I see the name of Chessenaz—a village on a height—a road leading up to it. Look in that village; you will find the name [Chaumontet]: try to verify the signature; you will get a proof that the signature is really that of this man."

I ask him whether he sees all this in Hélène's memories—"*No*";—or whether she has ever been at Chessenaz: "Ask her; she will know; I have not followed her in all her excursions."

Hélène, when awake, could give no information. But next day I found on the map a little village of Chessenaz in the department of Haute-Savoie, at twenty-six kilometres from Geneva. ...

[A fortnight later Helen sees the vision of the other day reappear—the village, the little old man; but accompanied by a *curé,* who seems intimate with him, and whom he calls "my dear friend Bournier." Leopold promises that this *curé* will write his name for Helen.]

At the next sitting in my house, March 19th, I remind Leopold of this promise. . . . The *curé* at last takes her hand as the syndic had done and writes very slowly the words *Burnier salut. . . .*

I wrote to the Mairie at Chessenaz, and the Mayor, M. Saunier, was good enough to answer me at once. "During the years 1838 and 1839," he said, "the syndic of Chessenaz was Jean Chaumontet, whose signature I find in various documents of that date. We had also for *curé* M. André Burnier, from November, 1824 to February, 1841, during which period all the *actes des naissances,* bear his signature. But I have found in our archives a document with both signatures, which I send you."

[Reproductions are given (p. 409) of the actual signatures, and of the signatures given by Mlle Smith. The handwritings were markedly similar.] §

This case of Professor Flournoy's, then—this classical case, as it may already be fairly termed—may serve here as our culminant example of the free scope and dominant activity of the unassisted subliminal self. The telepathic element in this case, if it exists, is relatively small; what we are watching in Mlle Hélène Smith resembles a kind of exaggeration of the submerged constructive faculty without the innate originality of mind which made even the dreams of R. L. Stevenson a source of pleasure to thousands of readers.

In reference to the main purpose of this work, such cases as these, however curious, can be only introductory to automatisms of deeper moment. In our attempt to trace an evolutive series of phenomena indicating ever higher human faculty, the smallest telepathic incident, the most trivial proof, if proof it be, of communication received without sensory intermediation from either an incarnate or a discarnate mind, outweighs in importance the most complex ramifications and burgeonings of the automatist's own submerged intelligence.

I pass on, then, to evidence which points, through motor automatisms, to supernormal faculty; and I shall begin by citing certain experiments (due to Professor Richet and to Mr. G. M. Smith) in the simplest of all forms of motor automatism, viz., table-tilting, with results which only telepathy can explain.

Some early experiments in thought-transference through table-tilting were published by Professor Richet in the *Revue Philosophique* for December, 1884. A critical discussion of these by Gurney appeared in the

Proceedings S.P.R. vol. ii. pp. 239–64, and a briefer report in *Phantasms of the Living,* vol. i. pp. 72–81. I quote from the latter a description of the method used:

§ The place of a planchette was taken by a table, and M. Richet prefaces his account by a succinct statement of the orthodox view as to "table-turning." Rejecting altogether the three theories which attribute the phenomena to wholesale fraud, to spirits, and to an unknown force, he regards the gyrations and oscillations of séance-tables as due wholly to the unconscious muscular contractions of the sitters. It thus occurred to him to employ a table as an indicator of the movements that might be produced by "mental suggestion." The plan of the experiments was as follows. Three persons (C, D, and E), took their seats in a semi-circle, at a little table on which their hands rested. One of these three was always a "medium"—a term used by M. Richet to denote a person liable to exhibit intelligent movements in which consciousness and will apparently take no part. Attached to the table was a simple electrical apparatus, the effect of which was to ring a bell whenever the current was broken by the tilting of the table. Behind the backs of the sitters at the table was another table, on which was a large alphabet, completely screened from the view of C, D, and E, even had they turned round and endeavored to see it. In front of this alphabet sat A, whose duty was to follow the letters slowly and steadily with a pen, returning at once to the beginning as soon as he arrived at the end. At A's side sat B, with a note-book; his duty was to write down the letter at which A's pen happened to be pointing whenever the bell rang. This happened whenever one of the sitters at the table made the simple movement necessary to tilt it. Under these conditions, A and B are apparently mere automata. C, D, and E are little more, being unconscious of tilting the table, which appears to them to tilt itself; but even if they tilted it consciously, and with a conscious desire to dictate words, they have no means of ascertaining at what letter A's pen is pointing at any particular moment; and they might tilt for ever without producing more than an endless series of incoherent letters. Things being arranged thus, a sixth operator, F, stationed himself apart both from the tilting table and from the alphabet, and concentrated his thought on some word of his own choosing, which he had not communicated to the others. The three sitters at the first table engaged in conversation, sang, or told stories; but at intervals the table tilted, the bell rang, and B wrote down the letter which A's pen was opposite to at that moment. Now, to the astonishment of all concerned, these letters, when arranged in a series, turned out to produce a more or less close approximation to the word of which F was thinking. §

The general result—of which full details are given in the original articles referred to—was that the amount of coincidence between the letters of the words chosen by F and those tilted out by the table was considerably greater than would most probably have been produced by chance.

In the next case there is an apparent element of *prophecy;* and I quote it in order to show how fallacious this appearance is, and how easily an ordinary mental anticipation of the future, if it in any way becomes *externalized,* may look like a revelation. Miss Summerbell is well known to me as a careful observer. From *Proceedings* S.P.R., vol. iii. p. 2.

§ I have used Planchette a great deal, but the result has generally been nonsense; but I remembered two occasions when it correctly interpreted the thought of some one in the room, whose hands were *not* upon it. About a year ago, we were amusing ourselves by asking it what Christmas presents we should have. My hands were upon Planchette, and I *believe* Miss Lay's, but in any case it is quite certain that neither of the persons who were touching it could possibly know the answer to the question I asked. I said, "What will Miss T. have at Christmas?" Miss T. was in the room, but not near the table. Planchette immediately wrote down a rather large sum of money. I asked, "Who is to give it?" It wrote "B. and one other." Some weeks afterwards I met Miss T., who asked me if I remembered what Planchette had written. I remembered it perfectly. She said, "I have received more than that sum, but I knew about it at the time, though not the exact sum, and I believe that must have been thought-reading, for I am certain that nobody in the room knew of it but myself." The money was given by a relative whose surname begins with B., and another person.

On another occasion, we asked a friend to dictate a question, the answer to which we did not know. She said, "Who is coming to breakfast tomorrow?" Miss Lay and I placed our hands upon Planchette and asked the question. It wrote "Lucas." Our friend said that was the name of the gentleman who was coming to breakfast. Neither Miss Lay nor I had ever heard of him before. Our friend said, "Ask his Christian name." We asked; it wrote "William." "Is that right?" we asked our friend. "I don't know," she answered; "I never heard his Christian name." Then somebody else, who was *not* touching Planchette, remembered that there was a song by him somewhere among the music. We looked, and at length found the song by "William Lucas"—of whom we had never heard before, nor have we heard of him since.

L. D. SUMMERBELL §

The prophecy of the Christmas gift was doubtless a mere reflection of

Miss T.'s anticipation—transferred telepathically to the writer's sub-liminal self, and as regards the Christian name "William," we may assume that (as in the case of the word *Wem* in a previous narrative) the name printed on the song, although no one consciously remembered it, had been vaguely noticed by Mr. Lucas' friend at some previous time, and now re-appeared from the stores of unconscious memory.

In another case, Mr. Allbright, of Mariemont, Birmingham, a chemical manufacturer asked a young lady, of whose complete ignorance of the facts of his business he felt quite sure, for the name of a waste product oc-curring on a large scale in his manufactory. He *meant* the answer to be "gypsum," but "chloride of calcium" was written, and this was also true; although, had he thought of this substance, he would have thought of it by its trade name of "muriate of lime." Again, he asked what was his firm's port of importation. He meant the answer to be "Gloucester," but "Wales" was written; and this again was true at the time, as he was just then import-ing through Cardiff. These answers startled him so disagreeably that he re-fused to make further experiments. But I cite the case here for the express purpose of pointing out that no insuperable difficulty is presented by the fact that the answers, while substantially known to the inquirer, were not those on which his supraliminal mind was fixed.

In my next case an answer is given which is in fact true, although the questioner believed it at the time to be false. The account, which I quote from *Proceedings* S.P.R., vol. iii. p. 5, came from Mr. W. Riddell of Dun-ster, Somerset.

§ The way I became acquainted with "Planchette" was as follows: A friend of my wife's (Miss B.) is staying with us, and one day she was talk-ing about "Planchette," and saying that she had one at her home, in Lon-don, and had seen some remarkable answers given by it when a certain young lady had her hands on it. Both my wife and I laughed at the idea, saying nothing would make us believe in it. Miss B., to prove herself right, sent for her "Planchette." In the course of a day or two it arrived, and hav-ing put it together Miss B. and I tried it, but without any result beyond a few lines up and down the paper. Then my wife put her hands on it with Miss B., and in a very short time it began to move, and on being asked answered questions very freely, some rightly and some quite wrongly. Amongst those answered rightly were the following. (I may here observe that not only did my wife and myself not believe in it, but we were antago-nistic to it in feeling.) Our first question was asked by myself, my wife and Miss B. having their hands on it. I said, "How many shillings has Miss B. in her purse?" Ans.—"Four"; right. I then asked how many coins I had in

mine. Ans.—"Five"; right. I thought I had many more. I then took a playing card from a pack in a box, looked at it, put it face down on a table, and
asked for its color. Ans.—"Red"; right. Number—"Seven"; right. Name
—"Hearts"; right. This, I must confess, seemed to me very wonderful, as
neither my wife nor Miss B. could possibly have known anything about
the card. I then took a visiting card from the bottom of the basket, and
having looked at it, placed it face downwards on the table, and asked
"Planchette" for the name on it. This it seemed quite unable to give, but
after a long time it wrote "clergyman," which was a wonderful answer, as
the card was that of a Rev. —— who was here two winters ago, helping
our rector. After this we did not get anything more satisfactory. §

Now, here, as no complete list of the answers has been preserved, we
cannot feel sure that the answer "five," as to the number of coins in Mr.
Riddell's pocket, may not have been right by mere accident. But my point
is that, even excluding the idea of mere chance coincidence, there is still
nothing in the answer which obliges us to go beyond Mr. Riddell's own
mind. His subliminal self may well have been aware of the number of
coins in his pocket, although his supraliminal self was not.

All our evidence has tended to show that the telepathic power itself is a
variable thing; that it shows itself in flashes, for the most part spontaneously, and seldom persists through a series of deliberate experiments. And
if an automatist possessing power of this uncertain kind has exercised it at
irregular moments and with no scientific aim—and has kept, moreover, no
steady record of success and failure—then it becomes difficult to say that
even some brilliant coincidences afford cogent proof of telepathic action.
The case which is next cited presents these drawbacks; but it presents also
positive points of interest and corroborations of memory quite sufficient, I
think, to justify me in laying it before my readers as an example of telepathy acting—not just in the way in which we should like it to act, but in
the way in which it apparently does act; and with that strange intercur-
rence, moreover, which we so often find of something like clairvoyance
and premonition mingling with the reflection of thoughts which pass
through minds in *rapport* with the automatist's. But I quote the case as one
where telepathy from the living seems to play at least a considerable part
in supplying the contents of the messages.

From *Proceedings* S.P.R., vol. ix. pp. 44–48. The following account,
dated Thornes House, Wakefield, January 30th, 1893, is signed by Lady
Mabel Howard; her husband, Mr. Henry Howard, of Greystoke Castle,
Westmoreland, attesting the facts which lie within his cognizance.

§ A Mr. Harry Huth, who was staying at our hotel, was leaving the next day for Paris, and had arranged to dine the day after with a friend, a young doctor attached to the Embassy in Paris, from whom he had just received an invitation. He asked me to predict something about his journey. My hand wrote words to this effect: "You will have an accident on your journy; and you will not see your friend, and you cannot see him." He derided this, as the arrangement with the friend had just been made. As he went to Chur next day by sleigh his sleigh was overturned, and his journey was thus delayed for a day. When he got to Paris he found that his friend was dead.

Some time after my marriage (1885) there was a burglary at Netherby Hall, in Cumberland, a few valuable jewels being stolen. The robbers were caught three or four days later, but the jewels were not found. Next Sunday, I was asked by some friends to write where the jewels were. I wrote, "In the river, under the bridge at Tebay." Every one laughed at this; but the jewels were found there.

On the same night I wrote that my sister would be engaged to be married in September, 1887. At the end of September, 1887 she became engaged to a gentleman of whom there had been no idea at the time. [It is, of course, conceivable that the prediction, known to this lady, may have influenced the date of the event.]

At nearly the same date some connections of mine who had let a house, the lease of which was expiring, were expecting to hear whether any damage had been done, but did not speak of any particular possibility. I wrote that nothing was injured except a particular table in a particular spot. Next day they heard that this particular table, and this alone, had been injured.

The following statement, dated Downes, Crediton, Devonshire, April 8th, 1893, is signed by Sir Redvers Buller, K.C.B., and by Miss Dorothy Howard (daughter of Lady Audrey Buller):

"Lady Mabel Howard was stopping with us this week. She was writing with her pencil just after arriving. Some one asked: 'Where is Don?' The pencil immediately answered, 'He is dead.' Lady Mabel then asked who Don was and was told that he was a dog. No one in the room knew that he was dead; but on inquiry the next day, it was found that it was so. One of the party then asked how many fish would be caught in the river the next day. The pencil at once wrote *three,* which was the number obtained the next day.

"A little girl in the house, who attends a school in London, asked who was her greatest friend at this school. The pencil answered *Mary,* which was again a fact absolutely unknown to Lady Mabel."

DOROTHY E. HOWARD
REDVERS BULLER §

The following is another case which I quote from the *Proceedings* S.P.R., vol. xi. p. 395. Lady Vane writes:

§ HUTTON-IN-THE-FOREST, *April 8th,* 1894.

About a month ago I lost a book, a manuscript one, relating to this house. I thought I had left it in my writing-table in my sitting-room, and intended to add a note about some alterations just completed—but next day the book had vanished. I looked through every drawer and cupboard in my room and then asked Sir Henry to do the same, which he did twice. I also made the head housemaid turn everything out of them and helped her to do so—so that four thorough searches were made; but in vain. We also looked in the gallery and library (the only other rooms to which the book had been taken) and could not find it. On March 28th I asked Lady Mabel Howard to write about it. She wrote, "It is in the locked cupboard in the bookcase—hidden behind the books."

I said, "Then it *must* be in the library, because the bookcases are locked," and Lady Mabel wrote, "Not in the library." I said, "Then it must be in the ante-room in the cupboard," and asked if *I* should find it. Lady Mabel wrote, "No, send Sir Henry." I asked, "Will he find it?" and she wrote, "Of course."

Still thinking it could only be the ante-room or the library—on account of the locked cupboard and bookcase, I asked, "Which end of the room?"

Lady Mabel wrote, "The tapestry end." I asked, "Is it on the window side of the room or on the other?" and she wrote, "The other." A friend staying in the house looked in the bookcases in the library at the tapestry end, and in the cupboard in the ante-room (I had met with an accident and could not go myself) and could not find the book, so we gave it up.

On April 5th Sir Henry was in my sitting-room and suddenly said, "I have an idea! Lady Mabel meant *this* room. There is the bookcase and the locked cupboard in it—and the wall outside the door is covered with tapestry." I said, "You *have* looked in that cupboard twice, and so have I and the housemaid, and the book is not there—but look again if you like." Sir Henry unlocked the door of the cupboard and took out all the books (a half-a-dozen) and put them on the floor. The last he put back into the cupboard was a scrap-book for newspaper cuttings, and as it was rather dark at 6:30 P.M. he could not see the name on the back and therefore opened it to see what it was, and the lost manuscript book fell out.

Having searched this very small cupboard four times previously, either of us would have been ready to swear that this book was not in it.

MARGARET VANE
HENRY VANE §

Are we to describe this as a knowledge of past, of present, or of future? Or may we say that perception of this kind is not strictly conditioned by time, but includes some retrogressive knowledge as to how things reached their present condition, and also some pregressive inference as to their coming development? The element of forecast in the present case—the indication that it would be Sir Henry Vane who would find the book—is in itself very slight; but it cannot be ignored when we compare other messages of Lady Mabel Howard's. See, for instance, the messages to Mr. Huth, where the element of precognition was strongly marked. In this present case, the whereabouts of the book can hardly have been supraliminally known to any human being; since the workman or servant whose hands may have slipped it into the larger book was probably unaware of what it was, or even of his own unthinking action itself. If, however, it were Sir Henry or Lady Vane who unthinkingly placed the small book in the larger one—and this does not seem quite impossible—Lady Mabel's knowledge might have been drawn telepathically from their subliminal memory.

From the *Journal* S.P.R., vol. ix. pp. 15–16. The following incident seems to have been carefully watched and recorded, and was published, with names of guarantors, immediately after the event. It is extracted from a pamphlet, entitled *Spiritualisme: Faits Curieux,* par Paul Auguez (Dentu, Paris, 1858):

§ On December 10th, 1857, we addressed the following letter to M. Morin, vice-president of the Société du Mesmérisme, asking him to keep the letter *sealed* until the complete fulfillment of the sad event of which we related the prediction. The said prediction was as clearly expressed as it was wonderful in the extraordinary method of production. We retained a copy of this letter word for word. The original, stamped with the postmark, has been returned to us, after the verification of its date and contents, under the following circumstances:

"SIR,—About a year ago, after a fruitless experiment in hydromancy,[1] a young lady, who was with us making these experiments, suddenly saw a very strange scene reflected on the polished surface of a glass into which she had been looking a few minutes before. . . .

"She saw, she said, a room containing two beds. In one of these she saw quite distinctly a sick person, whose distorted features betokened the approach of death.

"Around this bed were standing several people, amongst whom she

[1] Divination by means of pictures, which are delineated in the water before the eyes of the seer [*i.e.* a species of crystal-gazing].

could distinguish a young woman and two children, all three dressed in black.

"Being much astonished at this vision, and not knowing with what to connect it, we asked the experimenter if these persons were known to her. She replied at once that the dying man seemed to her to be a friend of ours, M. X., an employee in a government office, and that the three persons dressed in black must be his wife and his two sons.

"Although this appeared very strange, we did not attach much importance to the matter, for M. X. had a strong constitution, and at that time was in good health.

"However, about three months ago—that is to say, about nine months after the vision of which we have given an account—M. X. was suddenly attacked by acute bronchitis and congestion of the lungs."

M. X. died a month after this letter was sent. It was read by us in the presence of MM. le Baron du Potet, Petit d'Ormoy, and Morin, who, after having considered all the circumstances, and having verified the date of the postmark, December 11th, certified that the details therein contained were absolutely accurate. §

I pass on to a small group of cases which form a curious transition from these communications *inter vivos* to communications which I shall class as coming from the dead. These are cases where the message professes to come from a deceased person, but shows internal evidence of having come, telepathically, from the mind of some one present. I shall begin with a case such as is often cited as proof (insufficient proof, I think) that a deceased person is communicating.

Our informant, Mr. Lewis, a man of business in Cincinnati, states that an automatist to whom his (Mr. Lewis's) family were absolutely unknown wrote a message, with true name, purporting to come from an infant sister long deceased. Mr. Lewis, naturally enough, accepts this message, as similar messages have often been accepted, as an indication of his sister's actual presence. The account is quoted from *Proceedings* S.P.R., vol. ix. p. 64.

§ Mr. S. Lewis, 347 Baymiller Avenue, Cincinnati, Ohio writes that on January 28, 1888 he called at the home of some friends (none of whom knew anything about his family or his background), and during the evening there was some planchette writing. Mr. Lewis had a sister who had died before his birth, whose name was Angeline. The message which came to him that evening was: "Mr. Lewis, I am his sister, I am glad you came here tonight; come again (signed) Angeline."

Mr. Lewis wonders how ideas or thoughts about this little sister Angeline and himself could originate in the mind of the medium. He says: "I had not for years past even thought of her until the name was written on the evening spoken of." §

Now let us consider a similar message, which might have produced a similar belief in another informant's mind. But here it so happened that he tested the alleged fact of death; and found that the supposed spirit was still alive at the time of the message. The correspondent, Mr. G. E. Long, is known to Dr. Hodgson. From *Proceedings* S.P.R., vol. ix. p. 65.

§ Mr. George E. Long says that once about two years before he had an experience with an unpaid nonprofessional medium which was a most convincing test of spirit-return—convincing to all except himself.

When I asked for the name of the "spirit" it spelt out "George (my name), you ought to know me as I am Jim." But I didn't, and said so. Then, without my looking at the board, it spelt out "Long Island, Jim Rowe," and "Don't you remember I used to carry you when you were a little fellow," or words to that effect. I had to acknowledge the truth of it. I must own I was puzzled for the moment. To make sure of his power I asked that he count the pickets in the fence outside of the house and I would go out and confirm his statement. Somehow he couldn't agree to this, and even the medium objected. As a last resort I asked how long he had been in the spirit land and the answer came, between thirteen and fourteen years.

Now to the sequel. First it occurred to me a day or two after, that . . . the name should have been given as ROE instead of Rowe. Second, I was upon Long Island this summer, and the matter coming to my mind I inquired how long Jim Roe had been dead, and was informed he died last winter; so when I received this test so convincing to the believers *the man was not dead.* Yours truly,

GEO. E. LONG §

Thus much for the present with regard to communications from the living, and as to the danger that a message purporting to come from a deceased person may in reality emanate from the mind of one of the living persons present, or, indeed, from some living person at a distance. But this, although a real risk, is by no means the only risk of deception which such messages involve. The communication may conceivably come from some unembodied spirit indeed, but not from the spirit who is claimed as its author. Have we any way of guarding against this deception—any hints which may even help us to conceive the nature of a danger which lies so entirely outside our terrene experience?

The answer to this question cannot be brief, and must for the present be delayed. I can best, perhaps, introduce the reader to this new range of problems by quoting at this point some extracts from a record of the varied experiences of automatic writing which have been intermingled with Miss A.'s crystal-visions, etc. already narrated. Such account as can here be produced is, from various causes, very incomplete. It contains, however, specimens of several of the problems of which mention has already been made. I may remind the reader that this is a case with which I am intimately acquainted, having carefully watched the progress of the phenomena for some years. The statements refer largely to facts within my own knowledge, and these are given without exaggeration.

I should add that the phenomena have continued, whenever invited, up to the present date (December, 1900), and that they have developed in the direction of recognized identities. I have myself lately had through Miss A. what appear to me convincing messages, given by raps, on private matters from departed friends. That this element exists amid these confused communications, I feel sure; but the recognized spirits are seldom able to explain much beyond their own actual message, nor to throw light on the strange anonymity in which most of the writings are shrouded. There is now no case that I have watched longer than Miss A.'s—none where I have more absolute assurance of the scrupulous probity of the principal sensitive herself and of the group who share the experiments—but none also which leaves me more often baffled as to the unseen source of the information given. There is a knowledge both of the past and of the future, which seems capriciously limited, and is mingled with mistakes, yet on the other hand is of a nature which it is difficult to refer to any individual human mind, incarnate or discarnate. We meet here some of the first indications of a possibility of which more must be said in a later chapter (IX), that discarnate spirits communicating with us have occasional access to certain sources of knowledge which even to themselves are inscrutably remote and obscure.

The following account of Miss A.'s experiences is quoted from *Proceedings* S.P.R., vol. ix. (1893) pp. 73–92.

§ *Statement of Miss A. as to her Automatic Writing*

Origin of the Writing—About eight years ago we first heard that people could sometimes write without knowing what they wrote; and that it was supposed that departed friends could communicate in this way. We determined to try whether any of us could write thus. We tried first with a planchette, and when my mother's hand and my hand were upon it we got writing easily. We did not at first get any message professing to come from any spirit known to us.

Mode of Writing—We soon ceased to use the planchette, and I was able to write alone. I can now generally, but not always, write when I sit quiet with a pencil in my hand. The writing often comes extremely fast; at a much faster rate than I could keep up by voluntary effort for so long a time. I have to turn over the pages of the large paper which I generally use, and to guard the lines of writing from running into each other, but except for this there is no need for me to look at the paper, as I can talk on other subjects while the writing is going on. I can always stop the writing by a distinct effort of will. One curious thing is that my hand is never in the least tired by automatic writing.

Character of the Script—I get various handwritings; I may have had a dozen altogether. . . .

Medical Advice has often been given by a control calling himself "Semirus," and this has been often successful; which is strange, since I am quite ignorant of medicine, and often do not know the names either of diseases or of drugs mentioned. Of course I cannot be quite sure that I have never *read* the words, but certainly when I have written them I have often not known what they meant.

Clairvoyance—I sometimes get messages which perhaps may be called clairvoyant, telling me, for instance, where lost objects are, or warning me of some danger at hand. Thus about September 20th, 1888 my sister M. and I had just finished dressing for dinner in the dressing-rooms leading from a large bedroom. The maid had left the room. M. had left her dressing-room, and was standing in the bedroom, when suddenly she called to me: "Get a bit of paper; there are some raps." I came in and took an envelope and pencil, and at once the words came, by raps: "Look to the candle or the house will be on fire." We saw that it was not the candle in the bedroom, so we went into M.'s dressing-room, and found that her candle was so close to a cardboard pocket depending from the looking-glass that it would have been on fire in a moment. It was already smoking. No servant would have come in for some time.

But the most puzzling cases are those where the message professes to be from some departed person, and tells some true things, but perhaps mixes up some mistakes with them. . . . But sometimes I do think that the message really comes from the person who professes to communicate.

Another frequent writer is a strange person to have come to us, as I knew nothing about him, and should not have thought that we had anything in common. That is Lord Chancellor Hardwicke. He—or whatever it is that takes that name—has become a sort of family friend. He has a distinct character of his own, which is not quite what I should have expected in a Lord Chancellor, for he is full of jokes and very bluff and outspoken. He has given a number of facts about himself, names of friends, and laws about marriage that he had made.

One reason which makes me think that the messages come from outside myself is the feeling which I have sometimes of rivalry or even conflict between them. When I am writing there will occasionally be sudden changes, as if some new personality had been able to get hold of the pencil. . . .

Again, if I see figures and then have writing which professes to come from those figures, it seems to me natural to suppose that it does so come. §

I will now give some examples of motor messages, by writing and raps, given through Miss A.

The first message which I shall quote is evidentially interesting, on account of the mere chance by which its truth was verified. It should be premised that Miss A. has never been to Blankney, and is not acquainted with the Chaplin family.

Lady Radnor writes under date January 15th, 1893:

§ The following case has always struck me as particularly curious.

About eight years ago, when Miss A.'s powers had only quite recently shown themselves, her automatic writing told me that I had two *guides,* "Estelle" and "Silvo"—Spirits who accompanied me and took an interest in my welfare. I did not think of this at first as a thing which could be either proved or disproved. But one day, when a question was mooted as to whether "spirit guides" had ever lived on earth, I asked whether mine had done so, and was told that *Estelle* had. I asked for her earth-name; and as we were then getting answers by *raps* (through Miss A.'s power) it was rapped out "Loved voices called me Anne." I asked for the surname. C—H—A was rapped out. As my maiden name was Chaplin I at once jumped to the conclusion that that was the name meant. But the raps said decidedly No, and rapped out *Chambers.* I had no associations with this name. I asked if connected with my family? "Yes." Any portrait? "Yes." At Blankney? (my brother's place). "Yes."

Now I had spent much of my childhood at Blankney, and I had been particularly fond of one picture there, representing a lady whose name I did not know. It used to hang in the morning room, and then on the staircase, and represented a lady in a red velvet gown with a basket of cherries in her hand. As a child I used to sit and talk to this picture, and make a friend of the lady with the cherries.

So when I heard that the picture of my "guide" was at Blankney, I hoped it might be this lady, and asked, "Is it the lady with the cherries?" "Yes," was eagerly rapped out. I at once wrote to my old nurse who was still at Blankney, and who knew a good deal about the pictures, and asked her to get the picture examined for any name which might be on it. She got the picture taken down and carefully examined, but there was no clue. She told me, however, that she thought she had heard a Mrs. S.—a connection of the family, who knew the pictures better than any one—say that the lady with the cherries was a Miss *Taylor.* This disheartened me; but I wrote to a friend at the College of Heralds to ask whether the name Chambers occurred anywhere in the Chaplin pedigree. He wrote back that there was no such name in the pedigree.

The same day that I got his letter I happened to meet Mrs. S. (whom I had not seen for many years) in a shop in London. I knew that she had once made a catalogue (which I had never seen) of the Blankney pictures; so I felt that here was my last chance. I asked her if she knew who the lady with the cherries was. "Oh, that is Lady Exeter," she said, "whose daughter, Lady Betty Chaplin, married an ancestor of yours." "Do you know what Lady Exeter's maiden name was?" "It was Mellish." I now lost all hope, but I just asked: "Has the name *Chambers* any association for you?" "How stupid I am!" she exclaimed, "Lady Exeter was a Miss Chambers, of Mellish!" My friend at the Heralds' College then looked in the *Exeter* pedigree, and, sure enough, the lady with the cherries was *Hannah Chambers.*

H. M. RADNOR

I was cognizant of all this, and attest the accuracy of the account.

RADNOR

The following writing was given at Longford, February 27th, 1890, avowedly by "Estelle":

"You ask me whom I see in this habitation. I see so many shades and several spirits. I see also a good many reflections. Can you tell me if there was a child died upstairs? Was there an infant who died rather suddenly? [Why?] Because I continually see the shadow of an infant upstairs, near to the room where you dress. [A *shadow?*] Yes, it is only a shadow. [What do you mean?] A shadow is when any one thinks so continually of a person that they imprint their shadow or memory on the surrounding atmosphere. In fact they make a form; and I myself am inclined to think that so-called ghosts, of those who have been murdered, or who have died suddenly, are more often shadows than earthbound spirits; for the reason that they are ever in the thoughts of the murderer, and so he creates, as it were, their shadow or image; for it would be sad if the poor souls suffered, being killed through no fault of their own—that they should be earthbound; though, remember, they very often are earthbound too."

With reference to the above communication I may say that an infant brother of mine died of convulsions in a nursery which then occupied the part of the house where the figure of the baby was said to have appeared. I do not see any way in which Miss A. could have known either of the death of my infant brother or of the fact that that part of the house had previously been a nursery.

RADNOR §

I pass on to a series of messages which afford an interesting field for the discussion of the rival hypotheses of "cryptomnesia" and spirit-control. The automatist, who must here be called Mrs. R., is a lady well known to me for some years, and to whom I was first introduced by the late Mr. Hensleigh Wedgwood (the cousin and brother-in-law of Charles Darwin, and himself a well-known *savant*), who reported certain messages obtained in his presence, and partly through his cooperation.

The first case which I shall give is in the words of Mr. Wedgwood, in the *Journal* S.P.R. for December, 1889 vol. iv. p. 174.

§ Whenever I have an opportunity, perhaps once or twice a year, I sit at planchette-writing with my friend, whom I will call Mrs. R., a most observant witness in whom I have entire confidence. We sit opposite each other at a small table, each resting the fingers of one hand lightly upon the board, and when the board begins to move, allow our hand to follow the movement freely without interfering with it in any way.

The following account of our last sitting, on June 26th, is from the journal of Mrs. R., written the same evening, transcribing the part of planchette from the actual writing, and filling in our share of the investigation from immediate memory.

Extract from journal of Wednesday, June 26th, 1889, and copy of planchette-writing with Mr. Wedgwood:

"A spirit is here today who we think will be able to write through the medium. Hold very steady, and he will try first to draw."

We turned the page and a sketch was made, rudely enough of course, but with much apparent care.

"Very sorry can't do better. Was meant for test. Must write for you instead.—J. G."

We do not fully understand the first drawing, taking it for two arms and hands clasped, one coming down from above. Mr. Wedgwood asked the spirit of J. G. to try again, which he did.

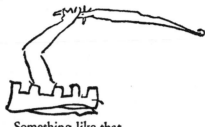

Something like that.

Below the drawing he wrote: "Now look." We did, and this time comprehended the arm and sword.

"Now I will write for you if you like."

Mr. W.: "What did the drawing represent?"

"Something that was given me."

I said: "Are you a man or a woman?"

"Man. John G."

Mr. W.: "How was it given to you?"

"On paper and other things. . . . My head is bad from the old wound I got there when I try to write through mediums."

Mr. W.: "We don't know J. G. Have you anything to do with us?"

"No connection."

Mr. W. said he knew a J. Giffard, and wondered if that was the name.

"Not Giffard. Gurwood."

Mr. W. suggested that he had been killed in storming some fort.

"I killed myself on Christmas Day, years ago. I wish I had died fighting."

"Were you a soldier?"

"I was in the army."

"Can you say what rank?"

"No. . . . It was the pen did for me, and not the sword." . . .

We suggested that he was an author who had failed, or had been maligned.

"I did not fail. I was not slandered. Too much for me after . . . pen was too much for me after the wound."

"Where were you wounded, and when did you die?" . . .

"I was wounded in the head in Peninsula. It will be forty-four years next Christmas Day since I killed myself. Oh, my head. . . . I killed myself. John Gurwood."

"Where did you die?"

"I had my wound in 1810. I cannot tell you more about myself. The drawing was a test." . . .

The only person besides ourselves present at the sitting was Miss H., an aunt of Mrs. R.'s, and none of us knew anything of Colonel Gurwood beyond the fact of his having edited the dispatches of the Duke of Wellington, not even that his name was John. It is possible that I might have heard of his suicide at the time that it occurred, without its making any impression on me, but I am sure I did not read such an obituary notice as would be published in the *Times,* and when my attention was directed to his editorial work eighteen or twenty years afterwards I did not know whether he was alive or dead, and was entirely ignorant of his military career. I never read any history of the Peninsula War, and am perfectly certain that I never had an opportunity of seeing Gurwood's crest, or knowing anything about it.

When I came to verify the message of planchette I speedily found that Colonel Gurwood, the editor of the Duke's dispatches, led the forlorn hope at the storming of Ciudad Rodrigo, in 1812 [note error in date], "and received a wound in the skull from a musket ball which affected him for the remainder of his life."—*Annual Register,* 1845. In recognition of the bravery shown on that occasion he received a grant of arms in 1812, registered in the College of Arms as having been passed "upon the narrative that he (Captain G.) had led the forlorn hope at Ciudad Rodrigo, and that, after the storming of the fortress, the Earl of Wellington presented him with the sword of the Governor, who had been taken prisoner by Captain Gurwood."

The services thus specified were symbolized in the crest, "Out of a mural coronet, a castle ruined in the center, and therefrom an arm in armor embowed, holding a scimitar."

In accordance with the assertion of planchette, Colonel Gurwood killed himself on Christmas Day, 1845, and the *Annual Register* of that year, after narrating the suicide, continues: "It is thought that this laborious undertaking (the editing the dispatches) produced a relaxation of the nervous system and consequent depression of spirits. In a fit of despondency the unfortunate gentleman terminated his life." Compare planchette: "——Pen was too much for me after the wound." . . . §

The following is another case of planchette-writing communicated by Mr. Hensleigh Wedgwood, the operators being himself and Mrs. R. The account is quoted from the *Journal* S.P.R., vol. iv. p. 319 (*November,* 1890).

§ *Extract from Mrs. R.'s Journal*

October 10th, [1890,] Friday, at ——, Mr. Wedgwood and I sitting. The board moved after a short pause and one preliminary circling.

"David—David—David—dead 143 years."

The butler at this moment announced lunch, and Mr. Wedgwood said to the spirit, "Will you go on for us afterwards, as we must break off now?"

"I will try."

During lunch Mr. Wedgwood was reckoning up the date indicated as 1747, and conjecturing that the control was perhaps David Hume, who he thought had died about then. On our beginning again to sit, the following was volunteered:

"I am not Hume. I have come with [Mrs. V., Mrs. R.'s sister]. I was attracted to her during her life in America. My work was in that land, and my earthly toil was cut short early, as hers has been. I died at thirty years old. I toiled five years, carrying forward the lamp of God's truth as I knew it."

Mr. Wedgwood remarked that he must have been a missionary.

"*Yes,* in Susquehannah and other places."

"Can you give any name besides David?"

"David Bra—David Bra—David Brain—David Braine—David Brain."

Mr. W.: "Do you mean that your name is Braine?"

"Very nearly right."

Mr. W.: "Try again."

"David Braine. Not quite all the name; right so far as it goes . . . I was born in 1717."

Mr. W.: "Were you a native of America?"

"(Illegible) My native land. The Indians knew many things. They heard me, and my work prospered. In some things they were wise."

Mr. W.: "Are you an American?"

"America I hold to be my country as we consider things. I worked at ——" (sentence ends with a line of D.'s).

Here Mr. Wedgwood felt tired, and Miss Hughes proposed that she and I should go for a walk while he rested. When we came in Mr. Wedgwood said he thought it had come into his head who our control was. He had some recollection that in the eighteenth century a man named David Brainard was missionary to the North American Indians. We sat again, and the following was written:

"I am glad you know me. I had not power to complete name or give more details."

Mr. Wedgwood said the writing was so faint he thought power was failing.

"Yes, nearly gone. I wrote during my five years of work. It kept my heart alive." §

Mr. Wedgwood writes:

§ I could not think at first where I had ever heard of Brainard, but I learn from my daughter in London that my sister-in-law, who lived with me forty or fifty years ago, was a great admirer of Brainard, and seemed to have an account of his life, but I am quite certain that I never opened the book and knew nothing of the dates, which are all correct, as well as his having been a missionary to the Susquehannahs. . . .

I see the name is Brainerd, not ard, as I had supposed, and this removes a difficulty in the writing. Planchette had written Braine, and said that was right as far as it went, which it would not have been if the name had been Brainard. My daughter has sent me extracts from his life, stating that he was born in 1718, and not 1717 as planchette wrote. But Mrs. R.'s *Biographical Dictionary* says that he died in 1747, aged 30.

[Mrs. R. writes that she had no knowledge whatever of David Brainerd before this.

Extract from *Biographical Dictionary* sent by Mr. Wedgwood:]

Brainerd, David. A celebrated American missionary, who signalized himself by his successful endeavors to convert the Indians on the Susquehanna, Delaware, etc. Died, aged 30, 1747. §

It is perhaps noteworthy in connection with the last sentence of the planchette-writing that in the life of Brainerd by Jonathan Edwards extracts given from his journal show that he wrote a good deal, *e.g.* "Feb. 3, 1744. Could not but write as well as meditate," etc. "Feb. 15, 1745. Was engaged in writing almost all the day." He invariably speaks of comfort in connection with writing.

Finally, a few months before his death, I received from Hensleigh Wedgwood a third retrocognitive case, which is printed in full in *Proceedings* S.P.R., vol. ix. pp. 99–104. It relates to the execution of Alice Grimbold—a maidservant at an inn at Leicester—who was condemned to be burnt alive for complicity in the murder of her mistress in 1605. A number of names and details were given, all of which were afterwards verified in a History of Leicester. The automatists were confident that they had never heard of any of the facts before.

I have given these cases in succession, so that the reader may see the kind of growing difficulty which the theory of forgotten memories here involves.

From these remote historical narratives I go on to certain messages avowedly coming from persons more recently departed, and into which something more of definite personality seems to enter. One element of this kind is *handwriting;* and in the next case it will be seen that resemblance of handwriting is one of the evidential points alleged. Now proof of identity from resemblance of handwriting may conceivably be very strong. But in estimating it we must bear two points in mind. The first is that (like the resemblances of so-called "spirit-photographs" to deceased friends) it is often very loosely asserted. One needs, if not an expert's opinion, at least a careful personal scrutiny of the three scripts— the automatist's voluntary and his automatic script, and the deceased person's script—before one can feel sure that the resemblance is in more than some general scrawliness. This refers to the cases where the automatist has probably never seen the deceased person's handwriting. Where he *has* seen that handwriting, we have to remember (in the second place) that a hypnotized subject can frequently imitate any known handwriting far more closely than in his waking state; and that consequently we are bound to credit the subliminal self with a mimetic faculty which may come out of these messages without any supraliminal guidance whatever on the automatist's part. I give below an abridged account of a series of experiments by Professor Rossi-Pagnoni at Pesaro, into which the question of handwriting enters. The full account illustrates automatic utterance as well as other forms of motor automatism, and possibly also telekinetic phenomena. The critical discussion of the evidence by Mr. H. Babington Smith, to whom we are indebted for the account, shows with what complex considerations we have to deal in the questions now before us.

I give extracts from the report on these experiments by Mr. H. Babington Smith, C.S.I.—a member of the Council of the S.P.R.—published in *Proceedings* S.P.R., vol. v. pp. 549–65.

Professor Rossi-Pagnoni is Director of the Public School at Pesaro, Italy. In the year 1871 he was led to take an interest in spiritualism, and began daily to practice automatic writing under the advice and direction of a friend who had frequently obtained communications from spirits, as he believed, by that means. He held a lead pencil in his hand, allowing its point to rest on a sheet of paper, but not touching the table with his arm, and waited for results. For the first forty-three days the movements of the pencil were incoherent and unintelligible. On the forty-fourth a name was written; and from that time onwards the facility and distinctness of the writing increased, and communications of considerable length were often obtained.

The following are some of the cases of automatic writing:

§ In April, 1872 a friend asked Rossi to evoke the spirit of a relation, formerly living near Modena, who had been dead about two years. "I had never known her," says Rossi, "and my friend told me what I was to ask her on his account. I did as I was asked, and after the answer was obtained, to my great astonishment (for a similar thing had never happened before) I felt my hand impelled to draw, one after the other, two flowers, with their little leaves. After this *addio* was written, and the movement ceased. The following day I took the answer to my friend and told him of the curious drawings. 'Do not be surprised,' said he. 'Know that she was very fond of drawing, and also every time that she writes by my hand, she makes me draw something.' "

This account is confirmed by a document dated December 28th, 1888, and signed by Cesare Perseguiti, barrister, who states that he is the friend mentioned by Rossi, and that the account of the incident is perfectly true in all particulars.

[The following letter was addressed to Professor Rossi:]

I have a lively recollection of having come sometimes to your house in 1873, to take part in spiritualistic experiments with the table and with writing. One evening, after some experiments with the table, I asked you to summon my dear writing-master, Luigi Brunetti, to write. He had at that time been dead for some years. . . . You set yourself to try the experiment, the pencil resting vertically upon the paper, and your wrist and elbow raised. When the motion of the hand, which you assured us was spontaneous, began, there appeared, after the signature of Brunetti, some lines of writing of various sizes. The first was extremely small—so that a magnifying glass was necessary to read it and to see its great precision. The following lines were of middle size, and the last large. This, I recollect, was a beautiful verse. I remember that I immediately bore witness to those present—in accordance with the truth—that, specially in the larger character, the manner of writing and the hand of my dear master were clearly to be seen.

So much for the truth, which now, also, I willingly confirm.

CLETO MASINI,
Professor of Writing and Book-keeping at the Royal
Technical School of Pesaro

[In the following case a message, apparently telepathic, was received by means of raps and automatic writing.]

(*Letter to Mamiani*, p. 143):

On November 21st, 1873, about half-past ten in the evening, Rossi was in his study. He had been correcting proofs for more than an hour, and was tired and rather cold. In consequence he intended, when his work was finished, not to go to the *café*, as was then his custom almost every evening about eleven, but to warm himself a little with a walk through the streets. He then perceived two slight but very distinct raps close to him on a side door opening into an inner room in which there was no one. He paid no attention to these, trying to persuade himself that they were due to natural causes. Half-an-hour afterwards he had finished his work and was going out; but at the moment when he had his hand upon the door of his rooms, to shut it after him, he heard a loud knock upon it as if given with the fist. He had no doubt that this was spiritualistic in character, and returning at once to his room, sat down to write. He fully expected to receive a warning against going out that evening for fear of some dangerous encounter. Instead, however, of any such warning the following message appeared: "My sincere friendship leads me to warn you that you are desired by Stanislao Cecchi: go, therefore, to see him." This message was signed with the name of a dead person in whose name messages had been obtained on other occasions. Rossi considered it extremely improbable that Cecchi (an acquaintance with whom he was not then intimate) would wish to see him; but went at once to the *café* where he was generally to be found at that hour. As he approached, he saw Stanislao and some friends coming out of the *café*. "He had no sooner seen me," continues Rossi, "than he came to meet me, and said he had need of a certain favor from me. Knowing from some conversations which I had had with him that he was a disbeliever (in spiritualism), I caught at the opportunity and answered that I would willingly do him the service, on condition that he would at once accompany me to my house. . . . We went to my house together, we entered into the room together, and I showed him on my table the message which had caused me to go in search of him. . . . He subsequently gave an account of the occurrence to some friends, though without adopting my explanation, and, so far as he was able, loyally bore witness to its truth." §

Stanislao Cecchi is now dead, and therefore direct confirmation of this account cannot be obtained; but in a letter written in 1889, a friend of his —Carlo Cinelli—at Professor Rossi's request gives his recollections of what he had heard from Cecchi at the time, and these correspond with Professor Rossi's account.

The case of Mrs. Underwood next to be quoted contains several points of interest besides the alleged resemblance of handwriting. It shows once more, for instance, the great similarity of ways in which this writing takes its rise with automatists all over the world, and the recurrence of the same puzzles with observers of many different types, and may thus serve as an introduction to the groups of cases which follow. It is taken from *Proceedings* S.P.R., vol. ix. p. 107, being there quoted from an article in the *Arena* for August, 1891, entitled "Psychic Experiences," by Sara A. Underwood.

§ A gentleman of this city whom I will call John Smith, with whom Mr. Underwood had been acquainted many years, but of whose family relations he knew little, died here more than a year ago. Mr. Underwood had met him but once in the year previous to his death, he having been away on account of failing health, staying, we understood, with a daughter recently married, whose home was in Florida. The first name of this married daughter, or of any of Mr. Smith's daughters except one, was unknown to Mr. Underwood. I had met one of his daughters whose name I knew to be Jennie. I also knew that there was another named Violet. I was not sure, however, whether this was the name of the married one, or of another unmarried, but had the impression that Violet was unmarried. One evening, while waiting for automatic writing with no thought of Mr. Smith in my mind, and Mr. Underwood sitting near me at the table with his thoughts concentrated on an article he was preparing, this was written: "John Smith will now enter into conversation with B. F. Underwood." I read this to Mr. Underwood, who laid aside his pen, and in order to test the matter, asked if Mr. Smith remembered the last time they met, soon after his return from the South, and a short time previous to his death. There was some delay in the answer, but soon reply came, "On Madison Street." "Whereabouts on Madison?" was asked. "Near Washington." "At what hour?" "About 10 A.M., raining." As it was rarely that Mr. Underwood was in that part of the city at so early an hour, and especially on a rainy day, I doubted the correctness of this reply, but Mr. Underwood recalled to my mind the unusual circumstance which made it necessary for him to be in that vicinity on the day and at the hour named, on which he and Mr. Smith, he distinctly remembered, last met. Only a few words passed between them on account of the rain.

After this, writing, purporting to be from Mr. Smith, came frequently. Very soon something was written which induced Mr. Underwood half sportively to inquire whether there was anything which troubled Mr. Smith, anything which he wished he had done, but had omitted, before his death. The answer came, "One thing—change deeds on Violet's account.

None of my wife's are at my daughter's disposal. All in her own disposal."
Mr. Underwood asked if it was meant that he had not left his property—
for he was a man of some wealth—as he now wished he had. "You are
right," was written, "want all my girls to share alike." "Which daughter do
you refer to?" was asked. "Went away from her in Florida—Violet," was
the answer. I remarked, "Why, I thought Violet was one of the unmarried
girls, but it must be that that is the name of the married daughter." Then
Mr. Underwood was strongly urged to call on Mr. Smith's married son,
James, with whom Mr. Underwood had a slight acquaintance, and tell him
of this communication. "Clearly state my desire that my daughter Violet
share equally with her sisters." Of course this was utterly out of the question. At that time we had no intention of informing any one of our psychic
experience, and if we had, Mr. James Smith would have thought us insane
or impertinent to come to him with so ridiculous a story, the truth of which
we ourselves strongly doubted. Pages were, however, written concerning
the matter in so earnest and pleading a manner that I came to feel con-
science-stricken at refusing to do what was asked, and to shrink from seeing Mr. Smith's name appear. Once was written, "Say to James that in my
new position, and with my new views of life, I feel that I did wrong to treat
his sister Violet as I did. She was not to blame for following out her own
convictions, when I had inculcated independent thought and action for
all." This and other sentences of the kind seemed to convey the idea that
Violet had in some way incurred his displeasure by doing according to her
own will in opposition to his. This was puzzling to us, as we knew that in
her marriage, at least, the daughter we thought to be Violet had followed
her father's wishes.

A few weeks later, however, came an unlooked-for verification of Mr.
Smith's messages. In a conversation between Mr. Underwood and a business friend of Mr. Smith, who was well acquainted with all his affairs,
regret was expressed that so wealthy a man had left so little for a certain
purpose. Mr. Underwood then inquired as to what disposition had been
made of his property, and was told that he had left it mainly to his wife and
children—so much to this one, and that. "But Violet," continued Mr. Underwood's informant, "was left only a small amount, as Mr. Smith was
angry because she married against his wishes." "Why," remarked Mr. Underwood, "I understood that he approved of the match, and the fact that he
accompanied herself and husband to Florida, and remained with them
some time, would seem to indicate that." "Oh, you are thinking of Lucy,
the eldest girl; her marriage was all right, but Violet, one of the younger
daughters, going to Florida with her [Lucy's] husband, fell in love with a
young man of whom her father did not approve, so she made a runaway

marriage, and on account of his displeasure, Mr. Smith left her only a small sum." The intelligence writing was aware of facts unknown to either Mr. Underwood or myself, and no other persons were in the room when these communications were given.

[In the *Arena* for June, 1892, Mr. Underwood writes:]

One morning a message purporting to be from a young man recently deceased was received. Neither Mrs. Underwood nor I had ever seen his handwriting. We knew his name only as William S. The message was signed "Z. W. S." At the time I remarked that I did not believe there was any Z in his name, and in this opinion Mrs. Underwood concurred. A few days afterwards we met the father and the mother of the young man, who were so impressed with the resemblance between the handwriting and that of their son that they wished to take the writing with them. There was a Z in the name, but it was the initial of his second name, and not of the first, as it was written. In the presence of the young man's mother, Mrs. Underwood's hand was moved to write, and the lady asked if her father would give a test by writing his name. The first name, Solomon, was written slowly; and after a pause, the surname was written very quickly. Mrs. Underwood did not know and never had known the name, which was written correctly; and Mr. S., who is a lawyer and a man of critical and discriminating mind, and his wife both declared that the signature closely resembled that of the old gentleman.

Later Mr. S. referred to the message purporting to be from his son, thus: "I have compared it with signatures of our boy. As I told you in Chicago at the time, the writing bears a *very* strong resemblance to his writing. Mrs. Underwood did not, in my opinion, either consciously or unconsciously, have any knowledge of Will's full name. The writing, while quite similar to Will's, is very different from Mrs. Underwood's. My wife's father's name had not been mentioned at all. Never had been in Mrs. Underwood's presence. I don't think she had ever met a member of Mrs. S.'s family by that name, yet she certainly wrote the name of Mrs. S.'s father, Solomon M., very plainly. This writing was also *very, very* similar to the handwriting of the old gentleman."

Fully aware that incidents long forgotten may be recalled, that possibly no lapse of memory is irrevocable, and that under certain conditions from the submerged self may be sent up memories which cannot be distinguished from newly-acquired knowledge, still, I am confident that Mrs. Underwood's hand has written names and statements of facts not only once, but several times, which were not and never had been any part of her conscious knowledge. §

I now cite a few cases where the point of central interest is the announcement of a death unknown to the sitters.

The first is a case which we received from Dr. Liébeault, of Nancy, and which was first published in *Phantasms of the Living* (vol. i. p. 293), where it was regarded as an example of a spontaneous telepathic impulse proceeding directly from a dying person. I now regard it as more probably due to the action of the spirit after bodily death. The translation of Dr. Liébault's narrative is as follows:

§ I hasten to write to you as to that case of thought-transference of which I spoke to you when you were present at my hypnotic séances at Nancy. The incident occurred in a French family from New Orleans, who had come to stay for some time at Nancy for business reasons. I had become acquainted with this family from the fact that M. G., its head, had brought to me his niece, Mlle B., to be treated by hypnotism. She suffered from slight anæmia and from a nervous cough, contracted at Coblentz, in a High School where she was a teacher. I easily induced somnambulism, and she was cured in two sittings. The production of this hypnotic state suggested to the G. family (Mrs. G. was a spirit medium) and to Mlle B. herself that she might easily become a medium. She set herself to the evocation of spirits (in which she firmly believed) by the aid of her pen, and at the end of two months she had become a remarkable writing medium. I have myself seen her rapidly writing page after page of what she called "messages" —all in well-chosen language and with no erasures, while at the same time she maintained conversation with the people near her. An odd thing was that she had no knowledge whatever of what she was writing. "It must be a spirit," she would say, "which guides my hand; it is certainly not I."

One day she felt a kind of need, an impulse which prompted her to write; and she rushed off at once to her large note-book, where she wrote in pencil, with feverish haste, certain undecipherable words. She wrote the same words again and again on the pages which followed, and at last, as her agitation diminished, it was possible to read that a person called Marguérite was thus announcing her death. The family at once assumed that a young lady of that name, a friend of Mlle B.'s and her companion and colleague in the Coblentz High School, must have just expired. They all came immediately to me, Mlle B. among them, and we decided to verify the announcement of death that very day. Mlle B. wrote to a young English lady who was also a teacher in that same school. She gave some other reason for writing—taking care not to reveal the true motive of the letter. By return of post we received an answer in English, of which they copied for me the essential part. It expressed the surprise of the English lady at the receipt of

Mlle B.'s unexpected and apparently motiveless letter. But at the same time the English correspondent made haste to announce to Mlle B. that their common friend, Marguérite, had died on February 7th, at about 8 A.M. Moreover, the letter contained a little square piece of printed paper—the announcement of death sent round to friends.

I need not say that I examined the envelope, and that the letter appeared to me to have veritably come from Coblentz. Yet I have since felt a certain regret. In the interests of science I ought to have asked the G. family to allow me to go with them to the telegraph office to inquire whether they had received a telegram early on February 7th. Science should feel no shame; truth does not dread exposure. My proof of the fact is ultimately a moral one: the honor of the G. family which has always appeared to me to be absolutely above suspicion.

A. A. LIÉBEAULT §

Upon these last sentences Gurney remarks that, apart from the improbability that the whole family would join in a conspiracy to deceive their friend, the nature of the answer received from Coblentz shows that the writer of it cannot have been aware that any telegraphic announcement had been sent. And it is in itself unlikely that the authorities of the school would have felt it necessary instantly to communicate the news to Mlle. B.

I shall next give a case of curious complexity received from M. Aksakoff —an automatic message written by a Mlle. Stramm, informing her of the death of a M. Duvanel. The principal incidents may here be disentangled as follows:

§ Duvanel dies by his own hand on January 15th, 1887, in a Swiss village, where he lives alone, having no relations except a brother living at a distance, whom Mlle. Stramm had never seen (as the principal witness, M. Kaigorodoff, informs us in a letter of May, 1890).

Mlle. Stramm's father does not hear of Duvanel's death till two days later, and sends her the news in a letter dated January 18th, 1887.

Five hours after Duvanel's death an automatic message announcing it is written at the house of M. Kaigorodoff, at Wilna in Russia, by Mlle. Stramm, who had certainly at that time received no news of the event.

From what mind are we to suppose that this information came?

(1) We may suppose that the telepathic message came from the dying man, but did not rise into consciousness until an opportunity was afforded by Mlle. Stramm's sitting down to write automatically.

But to this interpretation there is an objection of a very curious kind. The message written by Mlle. Stramm was not precisely accurate. Instead of ascribing Duvanel's death to suicide, it ascribed it to a stoppage of blood, "un engorgement de sang."

And when M. Stramm, three days after the death, wrote to his daughter in Russia to tell her of it, he also used the same expression, "un engorgement de sang," thus disguising the actual truth in order to spare the feelings of his daughter, who had formerly refused to marry Duvanel, and who (as her father feared) might receive a painful shock if she learnt the tragic nature of his end. There was, therefore, a singular coincidence between the automatic and the normally-written message as to the death; a coincidence which looks as though the same mind had been at work in each instance. But that mind cannot have been M. Stramm's ordinary mind, as he was not supraliminally aware of Duvanel's death at the time when the first message was written. It may, however, be supposed that his subliminal self had received the information of the death telepathically, had transmitted it in a deliberately modified form to his daughter, while it remained latent in himself, and had afterwards influenced his supraliminal self to modify the information in the same way when writing to her.

(2) But we must also consider the explanation of the coincidence given by the intelligence which controlled the automatic writing. That intelligence asserted itself to be a brother of Mlle. Stramm's, who died some years before. And this "Louis" further asserted that he had himself influenced M. Stramm to make use of the same euphemistic phrase, with the object of avoiding a shock to Mlle. Stramm; for which purpose it was needful that the two messages should agree in ascribing the death to the same form of sudden illness.

Now if this be true, and the message did indeed come from the deceased "Louis," we have an indication of continued existence, and continued knowledge of earthly affairs, on the part of a person long dead.

But if we consider that the case, as presented to us, contains no proof of "Louis'" identity, so that "Louis" may be merely one of those arbitrary names which the automatist's subliminal intelligence seems so prone to assume; then we must suppose that Duvanel was actually operative on two occasions after death, first inspiring in Mlle. Stramm the automatic message, and then modifying in M. Stramm the message which the father might otherwise have sent. §

I next give a case where certain telekinetic phenomena seem to have been connected with the announcement of a recent death. From *Proceedings* S.P.R., vol. vi. pp. 355–57. For this case also I am indebted to M. Aksakoff.

§ THE PÉRÉLIGUINE CASE

Document I. Copy of report of séance held November 18th, 1887, in the house of M. Nartzeff, at Tambof, Russia.

Present: M. A. Nartzeff [landed proprietor, belonging to the Russian nobility, in the Government of Tambof]; Madame A. Slepzof [aunt of M. Nartzeff]; Madame Ivanof [M. Nartzeff's housekeeper]; M. N. Touloucheff [official physician of the municipality of Tambof].

The sitting began at 10 P.M. at a table placed in the middle of the room, by the light of a night-light placed on the mantelpiece. All doors closed. The left hand of each was placed on the right hand of his neighbor, and each foot touched the neighbor's foot, so that during the whole of the sitting all hands and feet were under control. Sharp raps were heard in the floor, and afterwards in the wall and the ceiling, after which the blows sounded immediately in the middle of the table, as if some one had struck it from above with his fist; and with such violence, and so often, that the table trembled the whole time.

M. Nartzeff asked: "Can you answer rationally, giving three raps for yes, one for no?" "Yes." "Do you wish to answer by using the alphabet?" "Yes." "Spell your name." The alphabet was repeated, and the letters indicated by three raps—"Anastasie Péréliguine." "I beg you to say now why you have come and what you desire." "I am a wretched woman. Pray for me. Yesterday, during the day, I died at the hospital. The day before yesterday I poisoned myself with matches." "Give us some details about yourself. How old were you? Give a rap for each year." Seventeen raps. "Who were you?" "I was a housemaid. I poisoned myself with matches." "Why did you poison yourself?" "I will not say. I will say nothing more."

After this a heavy table which was near the wall, outside the chain of hands, came up rapidly three times, towards the table round which the chain was made, and each time it was pushed backwards, no one knew by what means. Seven raps (the signal agreed upon for the close of the sitting) were now heard in the wall; and at 11:20 P.M. the séance came to an end.

(Signed) A. SLEPZOF, N. TOULOUCHEFF, A. NARTZEFF, A. IVANOF

I certify that this copy is in complete accordance with the original.

A. NARTZEFF

Document II. The undersigned, having been present at the séance of November 18th, 1887, at the house of M. A. N. Nartzeff, hereby certify that they had no previous knowledge of the existence or the death of Anastasie Péréliguine, and that they heard her name for the first time at the above-mentioned séance.

N. P. TOULOUCHEFF, ALEXIS NARTZEFF, A. SLEPZOF, A. IVANOF TAMBOF, *April 6th,* 1890

Document III. Letter of Dr. Touloucheff to M. A. Aksakoff

TAMBOF, *rue du Séminaire, April* 15*th,* 1890.

SIR,—At the sitting held at M. Nartzeff's house, November 18th, 1887, we received a communication from an intelligence giving the name of Anastasie Péréliguine. She asked us to pray for her; and said that she had poisoned herself with lucifer matches, and had died on the 17th of that month. At the first moment I did not believe this; for in my capacity as physician of the municipality I am at once informed by the police of all cases of suicide. But since Péréliguine had added that her death had taken place at the hospital; and since at Tambof we have only one hospital, that of the "Institutions de Bienfaisance," which is in no way within my official survey, and whose authorities, in such cases as this, themselves send for the police or the magistrate—I sent a letter to my colleague, Dr. Sundblatt, the head physician of this hospital. Without explaining my reason, I simply asked him to inform me whether there had been any recent case of suicide at the hospital, and, if so, to give me the name and particulars. I have already sent you a copy of his reply, certified by Dr. Sundblatt's own signature. The original is at M. Nartzeff's house, with the protocols of the séances.

N. TOULOUCHEFF

Document IV. Copy of Dr. Th. Sundblatt's letter to Dr. Touloucheff

November 19*th,* 1887.

MY DEAR COLLEAGUE, On the 16th of this month I was on duty; and on that day two patients were admitted to the hospital, who had poisoned themselves with phosphorus. The first, Vera Kosovitch, aged thirty-eight, wife of a clerk in the public service ... was taken in at 8 P.M.; the second, a servant in the insane ward [a part of the hospital], Anastasie Péréliguine, aged seventeen, was taken in at 10 P.M. This second patient had swallowed, besides an infusion of boxes of matches, a glass of kerosine, and at the time of her admission was already very ill. She died at 1 P.M. on the 17th, and the post-mortem examination has been made today. Kosovitch died yesterday, and the post mortem is fixed for tomorrow. Kosovitch said that she had taken the phosphorus in an excess of melancholy, but Péréliguine did not state her reason for poisoning herself.

TH. SUNDBLATT

Copy of letter certified by Th. Sundblatt and Alexis Nartzeff

Document V. Letter of M. A. Nartzeff to M. Aksakoff, May 16th, 1890

[M. Nartzeff writes a letter in English and one in French, which I abridge and combine.]

In answer to your letter I inform you that my aunt's housekeeper is not a housekeeper strictly speaking, but rather a friend of the family, having been nearly fifteen years with us, and possessing our entire confidence. She could not have already learnt the fact of the suicide, as she has no relations or friends in Tambof, and never leaves the house.

The hospital in question is situated at the other end of the town, about five versts from my house. Dr. Sundblatt informs me, on the authority of the *Procès verbal* of the inquest, that Péréliguine was able to read and write. [This in answer to M. Aksakoff's inquiry whether the deceased could have understood alphabetic communication.]

Sittings were held at Tambof, April, 1885—October, 1889, but in no other instance were irrefutable proofs obtained. Generally the manifestations were of a trivial character. Twice or thrice we received communications apparently serious, but on inquiry these were found to be untrue. §

It is remarkable that this veridical message should have stood alone, but its correctness obviously was not due to chance.

I next give two cases where the supposed communicators had been dead some time, the deaths being known to the automatists, but certain details of the deaths were correctly given, in opposition to the beliefs of the automatists.

The following is part of an account which was printed in the *Journal* S.P.R., vol. iii. pp. 216–19 (February, 1888), having been furnished to me at that time by Mrs. FitzGerald of 19 Cambridge Street, Hyde Park Square, London, W., and her son Mr. Desmond FitzGerald, at one time a member of the Council of the S.P.R. Mrs. FitzGerald revised the abstract of her papers before they were printed in the *Journal*.

§ Mrs. FitzGerald and her daughter-in-law, Mrs. Desmond FitzGerald, have been for some years in the habit of sitting quietly together to receive messages by slight tilts of a table. Mr. FitzGerald has occasionally joined the group, but strangers have rarely been admitted, and the communications have been throughout of a very private kind. . . .

[I cite a case in connection with a Mr. E.—an intimate friend of Mrs. FitzGerald's—whose true name has been communicated to me.]

Mr. E., when on his deathbed, sent for Mrs. FitzGerald to come and see him. She visited him in his chambers in the Albany and said farewell, he being then past hope, and his death expected at any moment. He blessed her and promised to watch over her. Afterwards his spirit was one of the habitual and most trusted communicants, and Mrs. F. believed herself able to feel sure of his identity when he came. After many such messages, she alluded one day to his death in the Albany. "I did not die in the Albany," was tilted out. Shocked at what seemed the intrusion of some lying spirit in the friend's name, Mrs. F. solemnly repeated the question, "You died in the Albany, did you not?" The answer was an emphatic No. This was repeated several times, and then Mrs. F. was so pained and bewildered at the breakdown of her cherished belief in this spirit's identity and trustworthiness that for a considerable time she sought no further communication. She had no thought of testing the truth of the message, as she considered that she absolutely *knew* that Mr. E. had died in his chambers. It was not till some months later that a common friend accidentally mentioned that Mr. E. had been removed from the Albany at his own wish, when almost at the point of death, with the idea that he would be better nursed in a private house.

It is deeply to be regretted that Mrs. F. did not inquire from the communicating spirit *where* he had died. If the address had been given the test would have been excellent. No further facts, it appears, can now be got from Mr. E.'s spirit. The coincidence is therefore reduced to a single fact; but that one fact is a striking one, and cannot be said to have been in Mrs. FitzGerald's mind. §

The following case was printed in the *Journal* S.P.R., for May, 1899 vol. ix. pp. 65–8, having been sent to us by Mr. Michael Petrovo-Solovovo, of St. Petersburg, now Hon. Secretary for Russia to the S.P.R. Mr. Solovovo writes:

§ In the following pages I have endeavored to present all the evidence obtainable concerning an instance of an automatic message, which appears at first sight to be due to some other cause than "unconscious cerebration."

The amount of information unknown contained in the following message is certainly very slight, but still the unexpectedness of the fact that it was in the sea and not in a river that the soldier was drowned may be considered entitled to some weight. The most interesting feature of the case, however, appears to me to have been the circumstance that the mediums did not see the letters of the alphabet. This is stated by both of them as well as by the third person present at the sitting. . . On Jan. 22, 1898 Lieut. Col. N. Starck and his wife and daughter sat at a table for the purpose of making an effort at communication. M. Starck wrote down the alphabet, placed upon it a saucer with a pointer, the women put their hands upon it—and the writing began. He put questions, aloud or in writing, and copied down the answers, which he frequently did not expect and which he found very mystifying. He bandaged his wife's and daughter's eyes, but the writing continued, and it seemed to make sense. Then suddenly they got: "I have the honor to present myself, Your High Nobility—Skrytnikoff." This was completely unexpected. Skrytnikoff was a soldier who had served in the Col.'s regiment in Caucasia, and was drowned in Pzezuappe river a year before, according to reports. The saucer then wrote: "I was drowned in the sea, far away." M. Starck was perplexed, because he had been told the man had been drowned in the river. The name of the local chief of district was then given by the saucer —"Doubovik. Go to him."

The next morning M. Starck went to Doubovik, without saying what the matter was, and asked about the man Skrytnikoff. The secretary in this office then found an official paper which referred to the subject, with no new information except this one sentence: "The horse swam out, but Skrytnikoff was carried into the sea." M. Starck then realized that the river, which is generally shallow, but swift and deep during high water, must have carried him into the sea. §

I know not in what light I should have regarded the next had I seen it only in a book bearing the somewhat alarming title of *The Holy Truth.* But the aggressiveness of religious conviction with which Mr. Hugh Junor Browne's experiences have inspired him does not prevent his being, as I have heard from the Hon. Sir W. G. Windeyer, Judge of Supreme Court, Sydney, and have found on personal acquaintance, a man of high standing as to both character and practical capacity. He is a prosperous man of business at Melbourne, and the elder of the two daughters with whose automatism we have to deal is married to one of the foremost men of the Colony of Victoria. I regard him, therefore, as a witness whose strong opinions, indeed, might help a fraudulent medium to deceive him, but who is fully to be trusted as regards easily observed events occurring in his own family circle. I discussed this case with him and Mrs. Browne on October 3rd, 1891. Mrs. Browne seemed to me a good witness, and corroborated the facts so far as immediately known to her.

From *Proceedings* S.P.R., vol. ix. pp. 124–27, quoted from *The Holy Truth,* by Hugh Junor Browne, pp. 63–71.

§ In automatic writing we were unsuccessful, until it came to the turn of my eldest daughter, a girl of eleven years of age, to take the pencil in hand. Immediately on her doing so her hand was influenced to write, causing her to be considerably alarmed. She called out, "Oh, mamma! I am so frightened, my hand is moving." We all pacified her as much as possible, and on taking up the paper we found her hand had written on it quite legibly, though in rather tremulous characters, quite different from her ordinary writing, the following sentence: "Helen Grace Browne, I am come to see you. Your beloved aunt. You will," etc. The remainder of the writing was too faint to decipher. The name written above is that of my second daughter, between five and six years of age, who is called after two of her aunts, my sisters, one of whom . . . passed away many years ago. . . .

We had a number of communications through the same source that evening from different spirit-friends, and since that time, whenever my eldest girl sits down for the purpose of communicating with our spirit-friends, her hand is almost immediately influenced to write. Her hand has written as many as forty pages of large notepaper within half-an-hour, which in her ordinary handwriting would take her several hours to copy.

My daughter is quite unaware of what she is writing and describes the sensation of the influence as though electricity were running down her arm from the shoulder. This is what is termed mechanical writing mediumship. She often writes far beyond her own powers of comprehension on subjects of which she has not the least conception, spelling words correctly which she does not understand, and of which, when read over, she inquires the meaning—such words as clairvoyantly, physically, etc. She has written in French, of which language she knows but the rudiments; she has written in Chinese characters, and also in the Kaffir language, of neither of which does she understand a word. She has written in blank verse, which, though it would not stand the scrutiny of a critic, is decidedly beyond her powers in this line, she being more of a romp than a student.

My daughter has frequently been influenced to write messages to strangers from their spirit-friends, giving them particulars about things of which she could not possibly know anything, and signing correctly the names of their spirit-friends in spirit-life of whom she had never before heard. Her mother and I have thought of a question to put to one of our spirit-friends when she was not present, and calling her into the room have given her a pencil and paper, and she has written a correct reply to the question mentally asked, and signed the name of the spirit-friend of whom we thought. She can write either looking away from or on to the paper. . . . I have seen her write the letters upside down, backwards, left-handed, and in various ways quite impossible for the child to do herself.

[Once] in reply to a query by me on some deep theological matter, through my daughter's hand it was written, "How can you expect an answer to such a question through a child's organization?" I have several reams of paper filled with communications received through my daughter's hand. §

From *Proceedings* S.P.R., vol. ix. pp. 122–24. The following case came to Dr. Hodgson from a group of persons who may not be very critical, but who are plainly sincere. The phenomenon alleged, however surprising, involves but a simple act of observation, and should have been easy to note and remember.

§ A little child of four named Etta, niece of the recently deceased Emma, was sitting with a group of older Sunday School pupils and was given a slate and pencil to keep her quiet. Although she had no knowledge of her letters, she wrote the word "Emma" on the slate. The next day she was given a paper and pencil and "Your Aunt Emma" was written several times in perfect handwriting.

This is to certify that we were present and witnessed the writing of little Etta, as described in the foregoing statement, and know that neither Etta nor any other pupil present at the time could have written the messages of their own abilities.

LAURA HEMPSTEAD
L. A. K.

I am the mother of little Etta, and know she had not been taught the alphabet, or how to hold her pencil.

MRS. B. W. TERRY §

I now quote a general account of his experiences in automatic writing by Mr. W., a lawyer. Dr. Hodgson visited and had long talks with him, and formed the highest impression of his ability and care. Some of the automatic messages are perhaps best explicable on the hypothesis of subliminal clairvoyance, others by telepathy from living minds, while others are at least *primâ facie* referable to a source in the mind of a departed person, from whom they professed to come. Whether there are in reality so many different origins of a series of messages given to one automatist, or whether any one explanation can be made to cover them all, is a matter to which we shall have to return in the next chapter. From *Proceedings S.P.R.*, vol. viii. pp. 242–48.

§ N.Y., *November 15th*, 1891.

DR. RICHARD HODGSON—DEAR SIR, Recently I learned that you are the Secretary of the American Branch of the Society for Psychical Research. Being interested in the subject, I concluded to write to you, offering a statement of my own experience. As so-called spiritual manifestations are viewed unfavorably *here,* and as it would be much to my detriment if my connection with the subject were to become known, I ask that my name be withheld from the public.

For the past five years I have been a so-called writing medium. The writing is involuntary on my part, and the thoughts expressed are not mine—that is, as far as I know they are not mine.

I am anxious to find a satisfactory explanation of this, and I hope the Society may yet be able to furnish one.

As an indication of the trend of my thoughts, I will add that for the past thirteen or fourteen years I have been a student of the works of Herbert Spencer and other great men of liberal views, and that I am an evolutionist, so called.

[In answer to Dr. Hodgson's letter showing interest, he writes:]

Five years ago I was in Vermont on business, and while there made a visit at the home of a relative. In the evening, for amusement, a planchette was produced and operated. Pretty soon it was written that I was a writing medium, and I was requested to try with a pencil. I took a pencil in my hand and to my surprise I found I could write some in the "automatic" manner. The writing was not very good and was accompanied with more or less breaks and difficulties. It was written that practice would make it much freer and better. This I found to be so. Persons in the room asked as to dates on pieces of money and other similar tests, and the answers were generally correct. After that I wrote some almost daily for some time and soon became quite a ready writer in this manner.

On one occasion, not long after, a friend, of whose life I had known nothing until about that time, proposed to ask some questions mentally and see if the answers written would be correct. It was written that the spirit of his wife was present. I inquired (mentally) for her name. In reply her name was written out in full, correctly. I did not know her name: I knew that he was a widower, and I knew no more of his wife or the matters inquired about. My friend then asked (mentally) where she died and when? The answers were correct. He then asked, "What was the cause of her death?" The answer, "Heart disease," was correct. He then asked for the circumstances of her death. It was written that she died suddenly, at night, by the side of him, in bed, and that the first thing he knew of her death was when he found her dead in the morning. This was correct. He asked for her age, size, and for any particular mark by which she could be identified.' The answer was correct as to age and size, and as to identification it was written that she had a large scar near the knee, caused by a burn. This was also correct.

Many other questions were asked and answered; and whether he asked the questions aloud, or mentally to himself, the answers were strictly correct in almost every instance. There was no one but us two present. . . .

In May, 1887, while looking for authorities on an obscure point in a case I was then preparing for trial, it was written in substance: "I know where the authority is that you need." Q.: "Where?" A.: "In 'Wendell's Reports,' vol.—, page—." Q.: "Who are you?" A.: "I am A. B." The volume and page, as well as the name, were given in full; the name was that of an old lawyer that I had known well. The case cited was just what I needed. I had never seen or heard of the case before to my best knowledge. There are twenty-six volumes of "Wendell's Reports," of about 700 pages each.

In a contested case over a certain clause or bequest in the will of C. we had been defeated and were about to appeal to the Court of Appeals, our highest court. It was my opinion, also my partner's, that we would win on the appeal; but upon inquiry it was written that we should be beaten, and this opinion was expressed on several occasions, with very good reasons assigned. We were advised not to appeal. We brought the appeal and were defeated.

I have made many inquiries as to whether certain sick persons would recover or die. The answers have been very correct, generally. Writing touching the future is generally stated to be but an opinion, based on known facts, and fallibility is freely admitted. When opinions are written the reasons assigned are very frequently not only new to me, or unthought of, but are generally good reasons.

I have had a good deal of experience and made a good many tests. Those I have given are a fair sample, I think, of the writing that proved to be true. Many statements made were false and many predictions made proved untrue; of these I have given no illustration, but could if necessary. I have done most of my writing when no one was present. Perhaps I should state that it has been repeatedly written not to believe any writing or statement unless my own good judgment approved of it. I have written a good deal touching a future state, political and philosophical matters. Of all this I have not spoken, as it does not seem of much importance for our present purposes. In passing I will say that much of it was apparently very good, and quite reasonable.

December 28th

On Christmas Eve there was, as you are probably aware, a railway accident near Hastings, a little way out from New York City, in which twelve persons were killed and another has since died from injuries received. This last-mentioned person resided near me. The news of the injury to this person reached me on Christmas Day. Telegrams in the afternoon were favorable, and indicated a recovery. I made inquiry as to the matter, and it was written in substance that the person would not recover. I suggested that telegrams indicated a recovery. The answer was: "Yes; but we have made an examination, and are of opinion that no recovery will take place." Telegrams the second day were still more favorable, but my writing did not change in opinion. The party died at nine o'clock on the evening of the 26th. . . . §

Mr. W. tells of a case he investigated in which a woman who had just died was said to have had $700 on her person, but the money could not be found. Through automatic writing he learned that the woman's sister who was with her at the time of her death had stolen the money. This was later proved to be true.

He also tells of his aunt, who had a cancer removed from her breast, and who was then said by the doctor to be out of danger. When she began to fail in a few months, he learned by automatic writing that she was dying of the cancer and would live only one month longer. She died in just thirty days.

The following experience of Mr. W's. is told in *Proceedings* S.P.R. vol. xi. p. 463:

§ One afternoon he was riding on the N.Y.C. and H.R. road toward Schenectady, N.Y. where he was to change for a train to Troy. At Troy he would get a train on the Fitchburgh and Hoosac Tunnel Road. After he was on the first train he asked the conductor whether he would be able to make good connections, and was informed that he would at Schenectady but not at Troy, because he would arrive at Troy five minutes after the departure of the train on the F. & H.T. The conductor was not able to suggest any way that it would be possible for him to make his train at Troy. He was discouraged because he would have to lay over Sunday in Troy, and he took a paper and pencil, but did not try to write.

He said to himself, "Well, I'm very sorry I won't get through tonight." Immediately his pencil wrote, "You will reach the place you are bound for tonight." "Why, it's impossible," he exclaimed, but he continually got the message that he would complete his trip that evening.

As it turned out, when he got on the train for Troy, the conductor told him how he could jump off the train as it stopped before it reached the depot in Troy, and run across and jump on his other train as it was leaving. This he was able to do.

He says:

"When seated in the car I gave the pencil one more chance, and it was written: 'I see you are on board all right; don't you think I knew what I was telling you?'

"I had no further trouble in reaching the desired place that night.

"I will say that I was not aware of any of the material facts prior to their appearing as I have stated them. I had not consulted any time-table or otherwise learned as to the times on which these trains were to arrive or depart: and *I knew nothing* of the train *stopping outside the Troy Depôt* or of the possibility of getting from it and running up the street and catching the train I wished to take. . . .

"I think this experience is quite unique. Perhaps some one can explain it."

W.

It is plain that if we admit that departed spirits can still see and judge of earthly matters, and can impress their knowledge on incarnate minds, we should have a single explanation which would cover all Mr. W.'s experiences as here recorded. It is to be noted, moreover, that the premonitions, of which he gives several instances, are such as might fall within the scope of a discarnate spirit, with intelligence comparable with our own, but able to examine certain diseased organisms more thoroughly than any earthly physician could do. §

I next quote a case which illustrates the continued terrene knowledge on the part of the dead of which other instances were given in the last chapter.

From *Proceedings* S.P.R., vol. vi. pp. 349–53. The narrative is a translation from an article in *Psychische Studien,* December, 1889, pp. 572–77, by the Editor, the Hon. Alexander Aksakoff.

§ The case belongs not to the category of *facts which are known only to the deceased,* but to the category of those which *could only be imparted by the deceased,* for it relates to a political secret concerning a living person, which was revealed by an intimate friend of that living person for the purpose of saving him. I shall set forth this case in all possible detail, because I consider it a most convincing one in support of the spiritualistic hypothesis. I will even express myself still more strongly. I consider that it affords as absolute a proof of identity as it is possible for evidence of this kind to present.

[Mrs. A. von Wiesler, the writer's sister-in-law, and her only daughter, Sophie, who at the time of those séances was completing her studies, found that they were able to get messages when they sat with an alphabet and saucer. These usually purported to come from Andreas.] This was quite natural, for Andreas was the name of Sophie's father, the deceased husband of Mrs. von Wiesler. The communication presented nothing remarkable, but it was nevertheless resolved to continue the séances once a week, on every Tuesday. For three weeks the character of the communications remained unchanged. The name Andreas was continually repeated.

But on the fourth Tuesday—January 22nd—in place of the customary name, Andreas, the name "Schura" was spelt out, to the great astonishment of both sitters. Then, by quick and precise movements of the pointer, these words were added:

"It is given to thee to save Nikolaus."

"What does this mean?" asked the astonished ladies.

"He is compromised as Michael was, and will like him go to ruin. A band of good-for-nothing fellows are leading him astray."

"What can be done to counteract it?"

"Thou must go to the Technological Institute before three o'clock, let Nikolaus be called out, and make an appointment with him at his house."

This being all addressed to the young lady, Sophie, she replied that it would be difficult for her to carry out these directions on account of the slight acquaintanceship which existed between her and Nikolaus' family.

"Absurd ideas of propriety!" was Schura's indignant reply.

"But in what way shall I be able to influence him?" asked Sophie.

"Thou wilt speak to him in my name."

"Then your convictions no longer remain the same?"

"Revolting error!" was the reply.

I must now explain the meaning of this mysterious communication. "Schura" is the Russian pet name for Alexandrine. Nikolaus and Michael were her cousins. Michael, quite a young man, had unfortunately allowed himself to become entangled by the revolutionary ideas of our Anarchists or Socialists. He was arrested, tried, and condemned to imprisonment at a distance from St. Petersburg, where he lost his life in an attempt to escape. Schura loved him dearly, and fully sympathized with his political convictions, making no secret of it. After his death, which occurred in September, 1884, she was discouraged in her revolutionary aspirations, and ended her life by poison, at the age of seventeen, on the 15th of January, 1885, just one week before the séance above described. Nikolaus, Michael's brother, was then a student at the Technological Institute.

Mrs. von Wiesler and her daughter were aware of these circumstances, for they had long been acquainted with Schura's parents, and with those of her cousins, who belong to the best society of St. Petersburg.

Naturally, neither Mrs. von Wiesler nor her daughter knew anything as to the views or secret conduct of Nikolaus. The communication was just as unexpected as it was important. It involved a great responsibility. Sophie's position was a very difficult one. The literal carrying out of Schura's demands was, for a young lady, simply impossible, merely from considerations of social propriety. What right could she have, on the ground of simple acquaintanceship, to interfere in family affairs of so delicate a character? Besides, it might not be true; or, quite simply and most probably, Nikolaus might deny it. What position would she then find herself in? Mrs. von Wiesler knew only too well, from the séances she had taken part in with me, how little dependence can be placed on spiritualistic communications.

Many details, which I have passed over, tended to convince Sophie of the reality of Schura's identity, yet she could not bring herself to carry out that which Schura desired her to do. She therefore proposed as a suitable compromise that she should acquaint Nikolaus' parents with what had occurred.

This proposal aroused Schura's strongest displeasure, expressed by violent movements of the saucer, and by the sentence:

"That will lead to nothing"; after which disparaging epithets followed, impossible to repeat here, especially applicable to persons of weak and irresolute character, with whom the energetic and decisive Schura had no patience—epithets which are not found in dictionaries, but which were expressions used by Schura in her lifetime, and characteristic of her. This was confirmed in the sequel.

Nevertheless Sophie continued to hesitate, and at each successive séance Schura insisted more and more imperatively that Sophie must act at once. This is very important to notice, as we shall see later.

How great was the astonishment and consternation of the ladies, when at the séance on the 26th of February the first words were:

"It is too late. Thou wilt repent it bitterly. The pangs of remorse will follow thee. Expect his arrest!"

These were Schura's last words. From this time she was silent. A séance was attempted on the following Tuesday, but there was no result. The séances of Mrs. von Wiesler and her daughter were from that time entirely given up.

Some time after they had ceased Mrs. von Wiesler, to satisfy her own conscience and to comfort her daughter, resolved to communicate the whole episode to the parents of Nikolaus. They paid no attention to it. The family were quite satisfied in regard to Nikolaus' conduct. But it is important to bear in mind the fact that these spiritualistic communications were made known to the parents before the final issue. When during the remainder of the year everything went on happily, Sophie became fully convinced that all the communications were only lies, and formed a resolution that she would never again occupy herself with spiritualistic séances.

Another year passed without any special event. But on the 9th of March, 1887, the secret police suddenly searched Nikolaus' rooms. He was arrested in his own house, and within twenty-four hours was exiled from St. Petersburg. It came out later that his crime was taking part in anarchical assemblies—assemblies which were held in the months of January and February, 1885, exactly corresponding with the time when Schura was insisting that steps should *then* be taken to dissuade Nikolaus from taking part in such meetings. Only now were the communications of Schura estimated at their true value. The notes which Mrs. von Wiesler had made were read again and again by the families both of Schura and of Nikolaus. Schura's identity in all those manifestations was recognized as incontestably demonstrated, in the first place, by the main fact in relation to Nikolaus, by other intimate particulars, and also by the totality of the features which characterized her personality. This mournful occurrence fell like a fresh thunderclap on Nikolaus' family, and they had only to thank God that the errors of the young man were not followed by fatal results. §

I now give a case which in one respect stands alone. It narrates the success of a direct experiment—a test-message planned before death, and communicated after death, by a man who held that the hope of an assurance of continued presence was worth at least a resolute effort, whatever its result might be. His tests, indeed, were two, and both were successful. One was the revealing of the place where, before death, he hid a piece of brick marked and broken for special recognition, and the other was the communication of the contents of a short letter which he wrote and sealed before death. We may say that the information was certainly not possessed supraliminally by any living person.

It purports to be the successful accomplishment of an experiment which every one may make—which every one *ought* to make; for, small as may be the chances of success, a few score of distinct successes would establish a presumption of man's survival which the common sense of mankind would refuse to explain away. If accepted, the incident shows a continued perception on the part of the deceased of the efforts made by friends to communicate with him. (From *Proceedings* S.P.R., vol. viii. pp. 248–51.)

§ Mrs. William A. Finney of Rockland, Mass. writes to Mr. Hodgson to tell him of her experience. She says that her brother Benja had conversed with her freely for some months before his death on the subject of spirit communion and such matters, and one morning he requested her to bring him a piece of brick, and also pen and ink. He made two marks on one side of the brick and one on the other with ink. He then broke it into two pieces, retaining a piece weighing one and a half ounces, and handing the other piece, weighing about two and a quarter ounces, to his sister. He told her to take care of it, that he would hide his piece of brick and then after his death he would try to tell her where it was hidden. He said that she could then compare them together and it would be a test that he could return and communicate. She could be sure her own mind could not have any influence in the matter, as she would not know where he had put it.

For months after his death Mrs. Finney and her mother anticipated a message from Benja, but got nothing satisfactory. Then they began sitting at a small table at home, and at last it began tipping. It spelled out where they could find the piece of brick he had hidden, and also the contents of a letter he had written. By their repeating the alphabet, and the table tipping when they got to certain letters, the following message was given: "You will find that piece of brick in the cabinet under the toma-hawk—Benja."

Mrs. Finney went to a cabinet in which her brother had kept souvenirs. It had not been touched since his death. She unlocked it and looked on the shelf directly under the tomahawk. There she found a Triton shell about 10 inches long, lying so that its opening was entirely concealed. Deep in the recess of the shell, wrapped in folds of soft paper, and held in by gummed tape, was Benja's piece of brick.

At the time they made their pact, her brother had also given Mrs.

Finney a sealed letter, saying he would try to tell her its contents from the spirit world. When she received the directions for finding the brick, she also was told that the contents of the letter were: "Julia! do right and be happy—Benja." When she opened the letter she found that this indeed was the message written therein.

Since Mrs. Finney's mother and other witnesses to this event had died, she appended a character witness from the Rev. C. Y. deNormandie of Kingston, Canada. She sent the pieces of brick and the shell to Dr. Hodgson. §

From *Proceedings* S.P.R., vol. viii. pp. 238–42. The following case of a communication indicating the whereabouts of a missing note of hand was sent to Dr. Hodgson by Judge W. D. Harden, of Savannah, Georgia, who is well known to him:

§ Judge HARDEN—In compliance with your request I will state: After my honored husband Major Lucius B.'s departure from this life, I was in distress of mind that none could understand but one surrounded by similar circumstances. Of his business transactions I knew but little. After a week or two of stunning agony, I aroused myself to look into our financial condition. I was aware that he had in his keeping a note given by Judge H. W. Hopkins to some several hundred which was due, and I searched all the nooks and corners of his secretaire, manuscript, letters, memorandum-books, read several hundred letters; but all for naught. For two months I spent most of the time going over and over, but with the same result. I finally asked him at a séance about the note.

Q. "Have you deposited the note anywhere?" A. "I have."
Q. "Where?" No answer.

Finally I wrote to Judge H. (who had written me about it): "I had as well tell you the note has not been found. I cannot imagine where it is." This was on Friday. The following Sunday, about four o'clock, my daughter Nina, who possesses some singular power, proposed we try if we could not get a communication from our loved ones. While she went to get a little arrangement (a rod that worked on a board upon which the letters of the alphabet were printed) I sat in my room alone, thinking, if it were possible for Major B. to see the heart filled to overflowing with anguish, and added to this the mind distressed by business cares, would he not communicate with me and try to give some consolation or assistance.

But I did not express my thoughts to any one. Nina returned, and after a little conversation we put our hands on the *rod* and it *promptly* spelt

"Look in my long drawer and find Willie." I became excited, ran to the bureau and pulled out the bottom drawer, turned the contents upon the floor, and commenced to search. Under all the things was a vest; in its little breast pocket was the note.

Major B. was in the habit of calling the bottom drawer, where only his under-garments were kept, "My long drawer," to designate it from several small drawers set aside for his use. The vest was the only garment, other than underwear, in the drawer. The vest was the one taken off him when he first became ill. He was unconscious during the first day of his illness. The vest was put in the drawer after or during his illness by my friend, I think, who assisted in caring for him while sick.

The drawer had not been opened that we knew of after he left us until the note was discovered.

As soon as the rod spelt "Look in my long drawer and find Willie," I was perfectly electrified with the knowledge that Willie H.'s note was in that drawer, although I never would have thought of looking in such a place for a valuable paper.

Major B. and myself always spoke to and of Judge H. as "Willie," he being a relation of mine and a favorite of Major B. from Willie's child-hood.

I have just read the above to my daughter, and she says she will en-dorse the statement as being correct. I am, very respectfully,

> Mrs. E. F. B. B., widow of the
> late Major Lucius C. B.
> N. H. B.

[Dr. Louis Knorr writes:]

In answer to No. 5 of Dr. H.'s questions ("Is Mrs. B. certain that neither she nor her daughter put the vest away?") I have to state that I have the repeated assurance of both the ladies that they feel sure that they did not put the vest away, nor that they had the least suspicion that there could have been so valuable a paper in that vest-pocket, or else they would have hunted for the vest in that drawer, among others where cloth-ing might have been stowed away, and thus should have discovered what they hunted for. . . . §

I think it very desirable that as many persons as possible should pro-vide a decisive test of their own identity, in case they should find them-selves able to communicate through any sensitive after their bodily death. The simplest plan is to write down some sentence embodying an idea or a name which you feel it probable that you will remember, if you remember anything, and then to seal this sentence up in an envelope, without communicating it to any person whatever. Then label the envelope "Posthumous letter," and leave it with your attorney or the executor of your estate. If, then, the writer (it may be many years afterwards) finds himself capable of sending a message from the other world, let him mention this test sentence, and try to reproduce it. The sealed envelope can then be opened; and if the spirit's message should be found to coincide with the words therein written, there will be as good a proof as we can get that that message has at any rate not emanated from any living mind; and has emanated, therefore, from some unlimited source of knowledge, or—which will seem to most persons more probable—from the surviving mind of the original writer.

I may add the remark that it is to experiment with automatic writing, crystal-vision, etc. rather than to spontaneous apparitions, that we must look for any real information as to the degree in which departed spirits retain their knowledge of the things of earth.

Once more I must express my astonishment and regret that amongst some tens—perhaps hundreds—of thousands of persons, scattered over many countries, who already believe that the road of communication between the two worlds is open, there should be so very few who can or will make any serious effort to obtain fresh evidence of so important a fact. But, quite apart from the spiritist camp, there are now many inquirers who know that automatic writing is a real fact in nature, and who are willing to discuss with an open mind the origin of any message which may thus be given. Let these set themselves to the task, and the result of organized and intelligent effort will soon, as I believe, be made plain.

For aught that we can tell, there may be—I believe that there are—collaborators elsewhere who only await our appeal. Why should not every death-bed be made the starting-point of a long experiment? And why should not every friend who sails forth into the unknown sea endeavor to send us news from there?

Here, then, let us pause and consider to what point the evidence contained in this chapter has gradually led us. We shall perceive that the motor phenomena have confirmed, and have also greatly extended, the results to which the sensory phenomena had already pointed. We have already noted, in each of the two states of sleep and of waking, the variously expanding capacities of the subliminal self. We have watched intensification of ordinary faculty leading up to clairvoyance, and to telepathy from the living and from the departed.

This now reminds us of the great mass of vague tradition and belief to the effect that spirits of the departed may exercise possession or control over the living. To those ancient and vague beliefs it will be our task in the next chapter to give a form as exact and stable as we can. And observe with how entirely novel a preparation of mind we now enter on that task. The examination of "possession" is no longer to us, as to the ordinary civilized inquirer, a merely antiquarian or anthropological research into forms of superstition lying wholly apart from any valid or systematic thought. On the contrary, it is an inquiry directly growing out of previous evidence; directly needed for the full comprehension of known facts as well as for the discovery of facts unknown. We are now aware that we are obliged to seek for certain definite phenomena in the spiritual world in order to explain certain definite phenomena of the world of matter.

Chapter Nine

TRANCE, POSSESSION AND ECSTASY

The appearance of this book has been delayed for several years by several causes. What *evil* may have resulted from the long deferment it is not for the author to say. What counterbalancing *good* there may have accrued ought to be manifest in the following chapter. For it is in this chapter that the main difference lies between what I should have written ten years ago, and what it seems to me not only permissible, but even urgently necessary to write today. It is in what must needs be said about Possession that the great change has come.

Possession is a more developed form of motor automatism in which the automatist's own personality does for the time altogether disappear, while there is a more or less complete *substitution* of personality; writing or speech being given by a spirit through the entranced organism. The change which has come over this branch of evidence since the present work was first projected, in 1888, is most significant. There existed at that date a good deal of evidence which pointed in this direction, but for various reasons most of that evidence was still possibly explicable in other ways. Even the phenomena of Mr. W. S. Moses left it possible to argue that the main "controls" under which he wrote or spoke when entranced were self-suggestions of his own mind, or phases of his own deeper personality. I had not then had the opportunity, which the kindness of his executors after his death afforded to me, of studying the whole series of his original note-books, and forming at first-hand my present conviction that spiritual agency was an actual and important element in that long sequence of communications. On the whole, I did not then anticipate that the theory of possession could be presented as more than a plausible speculation, or as a supplement to other lines of proof of man's survival of death.

The position of things has in the last decade undergone a complete change. The trance-phenomena of Mrs. Piper, and more recently other series of trance-phenomena with other mediums have added materially to the evidence. The result broadly is that these phenomena of possession are now the most amply attested, as well as intrinsically the most advanced, in our whole repertory.

The claim, then, is that the automatist falls into a trance, during which his spirit partially "quits his body": enters at any rate into a state in which the spiritual world is more or less open to its perception; and in which also—and this is the novelty—it so far ceases to occupy the organism as to leave room for an invading spirit to use it in somewhat the same fashion as its owner is accustomed to use it.

The brain being thus left temporarily and partially uncontrolled, a disembodied spirit sometimes, but not always, succeeds in occupying it; and occupies it with varying degrees of control. In some cases (Mrs. Piper) two or more spirits may simultaneously control different portions of the same organism.

The controlling spirit proves his identity mainly by reproducing, in speech or writing, facts which belong to *his* memory and not to the automatist's memory. He may also give evidence of supernormal perception of other kinds.

His manifestations may differ very considerably from the automatist's normal personality. Yet in one sense it is a process of selection rather than of addition; the spirit selects what parts of the brain-machinery he will use, but he cannot get out of that machinery more than it is constructed to perform. The spirit can indeed produce facts and names unknown to the automatist; but they must be, as a rule, such facts and names as the automatist could easily have repeated, had they been known to him: not, for instance, mathematical formulæ or Chinese sentences, if the automatist is ignorant of mathematics or of Chinese.

After a time the control gives way, and the automatist's spirit returns. The automatist, awaking, may or may not remember his experiences in the spiritual world during the trance. In some cases (Swedenborg) there is this memory of the spiritual world, but no possession of the organism by an external spirit. In others (Cahagnet's subject) there is utterance during the trance as to what is being discerned by the automatist, yet no memory thereof on waking. In others (Mrs. Piper) there is neither utterance as a rule, or at least no prolonged utterance, by the automatist's own spirit, nor subsequent memory; but there is writing or utterance during the trance by controlling spirits.

Now this seems a strange doctrine to have reached after so much disputation. For it simply brings us back to the creeds of the Stone Age. We have come round again to the primitive practices of the shaman and the medicine-man; to a doctrine of spiritual intercourse which was once universal, but has now taken refuge in African swamps and Siberian tundras and the snow-clad wastes of the Red Indian and the Esquimaux. If, as is sometimes advised, we judge of the worth of ideas by tracing their *origins,* no conception could start from a lower level of humanity. It might be put out of court at once as unworthy of civilized men.

Fortunately, however, our previous discussions have supplied us with a somewhat more searching criterion. Instead of asking in what age a doctrine originated—with the implied assumption that the more recent it is, the better—we can now ask how far it is in accord or in discord with a great mass of actual recent evidence which comes into contact, in one way or another, with nearly every belief as to an unseen world which has been held at least by western men. Submitted to this test, the theory of possession gives a remarkable result. It cannot be said to be inconsistent with any of our proved facts. We know absolutely nothing which negatives its possibility.

Nay, more than this. The theory of possession actually supplies us with a powerful method of coordinating and explaining many earlier groups of phenomena, if only we will consent to explain them in a way which at first sight seemed extreme in its assumptions—seemed unduly prodigal of the marvelous. Yet as to that difficulty we have learned by this time that no explanation of psychical phenomena is really simple, and that our best clue is to get hold of some group which seems to admit of one interpretation only, and then to use that group as a starting point from which to attack more complex problems.

Now I think that the Moses-Piper group of trance-phenomena cannot be intelligently explained on any theory except that of possession. And I therefore think it important to consider in what way earlier phenomena have led up to possession, and in what way the facts of possession, in their turn, affect our view of these earlier phenomena.

If we analyze our observations of possession, we find two main factors —the control by a spirit of the sensitive's organism and the partial and temporary desertion of that organism by the percipient's own spirit.

Let us consider first how far this withdrawal of the living man's spirit from his organism has been rendered conceivable by evidence already obtained.

First of all, the splits, and substitutions of phases of personality with which our second chapter made us familiar have great significance for *possession* also.

We have there seen some secondary personality, beginning with slight and isolated sensory and motor manifestations, yet going on gradually to complete predominance—complete control of all supraliminal manifestation.

The mere collection and description of such phenomena has up till now savored of a certain boldness. The idea of tracing the possible mechanism involved in these transitions has scarcely arisen.

Yet it is manifest that there must be a complex set of laws concerned with such alternating use of brain-centers—developments, one may suppose, of those unknown physical laws underlying ordinary memory, of which no one has formed as yet even a first rough conception.

An ordinary case of ecmnesia may present problems as insoluble in their way as those offered by spirit-possession itself. There may be in ecmnesia periods of life absolutely and permanently extruded from memory; and there may be also periods which are only temporarily thus extruded. Thus on Wednesday and Thursday I may be unaware of what I learned and did on Monday and Tuesday; and then on Friday I may recover Monday's and Tuesday's knowledge, as well as retaining Wednesday's and Thursday's, so that my brain-cells have taken on, so to say, two separate lines of education since Sunday—that which began on Monday, and that which began on Wednesday. These intercurrent educations may have been naturally discordant, and may be fused in all kinds of ways in the ultimate synthesis.

These processes are completely obscure; and all that can be said is that their mechanism probably belongs to the same unknown series of operations which ultimately lead to that completest break in the history of the brain-cells which consists in their occupation by an external spirit.

Passing on to *genius,* which I discussed in my third chapter, it is noticeable that there also there is a certain degree of temporary substitution of one control for another over important brain-centers. We must here regard the subliminal self as an entity partially distinct from the supraliminal, and its occupation of these brain-centers habitually devoted to supraliminal work is a kind of possession. The highest genius would thus be the completest *self-possession*—the occupation and dominance of the whole organism by those profoundest elements of the self which act from the fullest knowledge, and in the wisest way.

The next main subject which fell under our description was *sleep.* And this state—the normal state which most resembles trance—has long ago suggested the question which first hints at the possibility of ecstasy, namely, What becomes of the soul during sleep? I think that our evidence has shown that sometimes during apparent ordinary sleep the spirit may travel away from the body, and may bring back a memory, more or less confused, of what it has seen in this clairvoyant excursion. This may indeed happen for brief flashes during waking moments also. But ordinary sleep seems to help the process; and deeper states of sleep—spontaneous or induced—seem still further to facilitate it. In the coma preceding death, or during that "suspended animation" which is sometimes taken for death, this travelling faculty has seemed to reach its highest point.

I have spoken of deeper states of sleep, "spontaneous or induced," and here the reader will naturally recall much that has been said of ordinary somnambulism, much that has been said of hypnotic trance. Hypnotic trance has created for us, with perfect facility, situations externally indistinguishable from what I shall presently claim as true possession. A quasi-personality, arbitrarily created, may occupy the organism, responding to speech or sign in some characteristic fashion, although without producing any fresh verifiable facts as evidence to the alleged identity. Nay sometimes there may be indications that something of a new personality is there. And on the other hand, the sensitive's own spirit often claims to have been absent elsewhere, much in the fashion in which it sometimes imagines itself to have been absent during ordinary sleep, but with greater persistence and lucidity.

Cases like these do of course apparently support that primitive doctrine of the spirit's actual wandering in space. On the other hand, this notion has become unwelcome to modern thought, which is less unwilling to believe in some telepathic intercourse between mind and mind in which space is not involved. For my own part, I have already explained that I think that the evidence to an at least apparent movement of some kind in space must outweigh any mere speculative presumption against it. And I hold that these new experiences of possession fall on this controversy with decisive force. It is so strongly claimed, in every instance of possession, that the sensitive's own spirit must in some sense *vacate* the organism, in order to allow another spirit to enter—and the evidence for the reality of possession is at the same time so strong—that I think that we must argue back from this spatial change as a relatively certain fact, and must place a corresponding interpretation on earlier phenomena.

This matter of psychical excursion from the organism ultimately involves the extremest claim to novel faculty which has ever been advanced for men. For it involves, as we shall see, the claim to *ecstasy:* to a wandering vision which is not confined to this earth or this material world alone, but introduces the seer into the spiritual world and among communities higher than any which this planet knows.

Among the cases of trance discussed in this chapter, we discover intimately interwoven with the phenomena of possession many instances of its correlative—ecstasy. Mrs. Piper's fragmentary utterances and visions during her passage from trance to waking life—utterances and visions that fade away and leave no remembrance in her waking self; Moses' occasional visions, his journeys in the "spirit world" which he recorded on returning to his ordinary consciousness; Home's entrancement and converse with the various controls whose messages he gave—all these suggest actual excursions of the incarnate spirit from its organism. The theoretical importance of these spiritual excursions is, of course, very great. It is, indeed, so great that most men will hesitate to accept a thesis which carries us straight into the inmost sanctuary of mysticism; which preaches "a precursory entrance into the most holy place, as by divine transportation."

Yet I think that this belief, although extreme, is not, at the point to which our evidence has carried us, in any real way improbable. To put the matter briefly, if a spirit from outside can enter the organism, the spirit from inside can go out, can change its center of perception and action, in a way less complete and irrevocable than the change of death. Ecstasy would thus be simply the complementary or correlative aspect of spirit-control.

In the meantime, however, the fact that this kind of communion of ecstasy has been, in preliminary fashion, rendered probable is of the highest importance for our whole inquiry. We thus come directly into relation with the highest form which the various religions known to men have assumed in the past.

It is hardly a paradox to say that the evidence for ecstasy is stronger than the evidence for any other religious belief. Of all the subjective experiences of religion, ecstasy is that which has been most urgently, perhaps to the psychologist most convincingly, asserted; and it is not confined to any one religion. From a psychological point of view, one main indication of the importance of a subjective phenomenon found in religious experience will be the fact that it is common to all religions. I doubt whether there is any phenomenon, except ecstasy, of which this can be said. From the medicine-man of the lowest savages up to St. John, St. Peter, St. Paul, with Buddha and Mahomet on the way, we find records which, though morally and intellectually much differing, are in psychological essence the same.

At all stages alike we find that the spirit is conceived as quitting the body; or, if not quitting it, at least as greatly expanding its range of perception in some state resembling trance. Observe, moreover, that on this view all genuine recorded forms of ecstasy are akin, and all of them represent a real fact.

We thus show continuity and reality among phenomena which have seldom been either correlated with each other or even intelligibly conceived in separation. With our new insight we may correlate the highest and the lowest ecstatic phenomena with no injury whatever to the highest. The shaman, the medicine-man—when he is not a mere imposter—enters as truly into the spiritual world as St. Peter or St. Paul. Only he enters a different region thereof; a confused and darkened picture terrifies instead of exalting him. For us, however, the very fact that we believe in *his* vision gives a new reality to strengthen and aid our belief in the apostle's vision of "the seventh heaven."

We need not deny the transcendental ecstasy to any of the strong souls who have claimed to feel it—to Elijah or to Isaiah, to Plato or to Plotinus, to St. John or to St. Paul, to Buddha or Mahomet, to Virgil or Dante, to St. Theresa or to Joan of Arc, to Kant or to Swedenborg, to Wordsworth or to Tennyson. Through many ages that insight and that memory have wrought their work in many ways. The remembrance of ecstasy has inspired religions, has founded philosophies, has lifted into stainless heroism a simple girl. Yet religions and philosophies—as these have hitherto been known—are but balloon-flights which have carried separate groups up to the mountain summit, whither science at last must make her road for all men clear.

The following is a case of ecstasy, which was reported to us along with a series of incidents suggesting an unseen protection or guidance. The narrator, Mr. J. W. Skilton, was a railway engineer, residing at Jacksonville, Florida, U.S.A., who had several times had veridical dreams or impressions, which in some cases saved himself and his train from serious accidents. One of these—a premonition of an accident—was published in *Proceedings* S.P.R., vol. v. p. 333, and further cases in vol. xi, pp. 559–567. I quote from vol. xi. p. 560. Mr. Skilton's narrative is dated November 10th, 1890.

§ I have been engaged a great part of my life as a locomotive engineer, and this happened while in that business. I was engaged with two other men one day about two o'clock P.M. in taking out some evergreen trees from a box car to take home and set out; they were large and heavy. . . . Just at that instant I saw a medium-sized person standing at my right hand clothed in white with a bright countenance, beaming with intelligence. I knew what he wanted in an instant, although he put his hand on my shoulder and said, "Come with me." We moved upward, and a little to the south-east, with the speed of lightning, as it were; I could see the hills, trees, buildings, and roads as we went up side by side till they vanished out of our sight. As we passed on, this glorious being that was with me told me he was going to show me that bright heavenly world. We soon came to a world of light and beauty, many thousand times larger than this earth, with at least four times as much light. The beauties of this place were beyond any human being to describe. I was seated by the tree of life on a square bunch of what appared to be a green velvet moss, about eighteen inches high; there I saw many thousand spirits clothed in white, and singing heavenly music —the sweetest song I have ever heard. I here told my attendant that it was the first time I had ever been perfectly at rest in my life. They did not converse by sound, but each knew the other's thoughts at the instant, and conversation was carried on in that way, and also with me.

After viewing the wonderful beauties of the place for some time, and the thousands of spirits, robed in spotless white, passing through the air, for they did not confine themselves to the surface, but went every direction as they pleased, I wanted to see my dear mother, two sisters, and a child of mine that had died some time before this. The request was granted at once, but I was not allowed to converse with them. They were standing in a row in front of me, and I looked at them and estimated the distance we were apart at thirty feet, and wondered how these things could be. They seemed very much pleased to see me, and I shall never forget how they welcomed me when I first saw them, although no conversation passed. About this time my attendant told me we must go back; I wished to stay, but he told me my time had not come yet, but would in due time, and that I should wait with patience. At this we started back, and were soon out of sight of that heavenly land. When we came in sight of this world, I saw everything as it looked from a great height, such as trees, buildings, hills, roads, and streams, as natural as could be, till we came to the car that I had opened the door of, and I found myself there in the body, and he vanished out of my sight. I spoke then (just as I opened my watch and found it had been just twenty-six minutes that I had been engaged with that mysterious one), and said I thought I had left this world for good. One of the men said, "There is something the matter with you ever since you opened the car door; we have not been able to get a word out of you," and that I had done all the work of taking out everything and putting it back into the car, and one item was eight barrels of flour I had taken off the ground alone and put back in the car, three feet and a half high, with all the ease of a giant. I told them where I had been and what I had seen, but they had seen no one.

This I count the brightest day of my life, and what I saw is worth a lifetime of hardship and toil. Being in good health, and in my right mind in mid-day, while busy about my work, and my mind not more than ordinarily engaged on the great subject of eternal life, I consider this a most extraordinary incident. I was told by this mysterious person that if we are counted worthy at death, we shall be accompanied to that bright world by one of those glorious beings, and this is my firm belief. §

Mr. Skilton writes to me that he has never had any trance save this.

As I have said, I incline to believe that ecstasy is the highest condition into which a spirit still incarnate can pass.

Frau Frederica Hauffe, better known as the "Seeress of Prevorst," was one of the most noted of the group of somnambules who flourished in Germany in the early part of the nineteenth century. A history of her trances was published soon after her death by Justinus Kerner, a well-known poet and physician to whom she had come for "magnetic" treatment.

It was claimed that the Seeress possessed supernormal powers of vision, both of distant scenes and of the future; she was supposed to see and converse with discarnate spirits, who gave her information on their affairs and family history, and physical phenomena were observed in her presence. The evidence, however, for her supernormal powers was what would now be considered quite inadequate. She excited even greater interest by her supposed revelations of things spiritual.

We now pass on to Emmanuel Swedenborg, and the mere subject-matter of his trance-revelations was enough to claim respectful attention. For my own part I regard him, not, assuredly, as an inspired teacher, nor even as a trustworthy interpreter of his own experiences, but yet as a true and early precursor of that great inquiry which it is our present object to advance.

And here I meet with a kind of difficulty which is sure to present itself sooner or later to all persons who endeavor to present to the world what they regard as novel and important truths. There is sure to be some embarrassing likeness or travesty of that truth in the world already. There are sure to be sects or persons, past or present, holding something like the same beliefs on different grounds—on grounds which one may find it equally difficult to endorse and to disavow.

I have indeed already been able to admit without reluctance that the "humble thinkers" of the Stone Age, the believers in Witchcraft, in Shamanism, have been my true precursors in many of the ideas upheld in this book. But these spiritual ancestors are remote and unobtrusive; and it may be easier to admit that one is descended from an ape than that one is own brother to a madman. Swedenborg is, in fact, a madman in most men's view, and this judgment has much to support it. The great bulk of his teaching—almost the whole content of *Arcana Cœlestia*—has undergone a singularly unfortunate downfall. A seer, a mystic, cannot often be *disproved;* his visions may fall out of favor, but they still record one man's subjective outlook on the universe. Swedenborg's wildnesses, on the other hand, were based upon a definite foundation which has definitely crumbled away. No one now regards the Old Testament as a homogeneous and verbally inspired whole; and unless it be so, the spiritual meaning which Swedenborg draws from its every word by his doctrine of Correspondences is not only a futile fancy, but a tissue of gross and demonstrable errors. And yet, on the face of it, was not all this error more amply accredited than any of the utterances of possession or the recollections of ecstasy which I shall be able to cite from modern sensitives? Swedenborg was one of the leading *savants* of Europe; it would be absurd to place any of our sensitives on the same intellectual level. If *his* celestial revelations turn out to have been nonsense, what are Mrs. Piper's likely to be?

I might, of course, save myself from this dilemma by repudiating Swedenborg's seership altogether. The *evidential* matter which he has left behind him is singularly scanty in comparison with his pretensions to a communion of many years with so many spirits of the departed. I do not, however, accept this means of escape from the difficulty. I think that the half-dozen "evidential cases" scattered through the memoirs of Swedenborg are stamped with the impress of truth, and I think, also, that without some true experience of the spiritual world Swedenborg could not have entered into that atmosphere of truth in which even his worst errors are held in solution. Swedenborg's writings on the world of spirits fall in the main into two classes, albeit classes not easily divided. There are *experiential* writings and there are *dogmatic* writings. The first of these classes contains accounts of what he saw and felt in that world, and of such inferences with regard to its laws as his actual experience suggested. Now, speaking broadly, all this mass of matter, covering some hundreds of propositions, is in substantial accord with what has been given through the most trustworthy sensitives since Swedenborg's time. It is indeed usual to suppose that they had all been influenced by Swedenborg; and although I feel sure that this was not so in any direct manner in the case of the sensitives best known to myself, it is probable that Swedenborg's alleged experiences have affected modern thought more deeply than most modern thinkers know.

On the other hand, the *second* or purely *dogmatic* class of Swedenborg's writings—the records of instruction alleged to have been given to him by spirits on the inner meaning of the Scriptures, etc.—these have more and more appeared to be mere arbitrary fancies—mere projections and repercussions of his own preconceived ideas.

On the whole, then, with some stretching, yet no contravention, of conclusions independently reached, I may say that Swedenborg's story—one of the strangest lives yet lived by mortal men—is corroborative rather than destructive of the slowly rising fabric of knowledge of which he was the uniquely gifted, but uniquely dangerous, precursor.

It seemed desirable here to refer thus briefly to the doctrinal teachings of Swedenborg, but I shall deal later with the general question how much or how little of the statements of "sensitives" about the spiritual world—whether based on their own visions or on the allegations of their "controlling spirits"—are worthy of credence. In the case of Swedenborg there was at least some evidence, of the kind to which we can here appeal, of his actual communication with discarnate spirits.

For Kant's evidence in regard to the supernormal powers of Swedenborg, see *Dreams of a Spirit Seer,* by Immanuel Kant, translated by E. F. Goerwitz; edited by Frank Sewall (London: Swan Sonnenschein & Co.; New York: The Macmillan Company, 1900).

The three most famous cases are: (1) Swedenborg's communication to the Queen of Sweden of some secret information, which she had asked him for, and believed that no living human being could have told him. (2) The widow of the Dutch Ambassador at Stockholm was called upon by a goldsmith to pay for a silver service which her husband had purchased. She believed that it had been paid for, but could not find the receipt; so she begged Swedenborg to ask her husband where it was. Three days later he came to her house and informed her in the presence of some visitors that he had conversed with her husband, and had learnt from him that the debt had been paid, and the receipt was in a bureau in an upstairs room. The spirit had said that after pulling out the left-hand drawer a board would appear, and on drawing out this a secret compartment would be disclosed, containing his private Dutch correspondence and the receipt. The whole company went upstairs and the papers were found, as described, in the secret compartment, of which no one had known before.

(3) In September, 1759, at four o'clock on a Saturday afternoon, Swedenborg arrived at Gottenburg from England, and was invited by a friend to his house. Two hours after he went out and then came back and informed the company that a dangerous fire had just broken out in Stockholm (which is about fifty German miles from Gottenburg), and that it was spreading fast. He was restless and went out often. He said that the house of one of his friends, whom he named, was already in ashes, and that his own was in danger. At eight o'clock, after he had been out again, he declared that the fire was extinguished at the third door from his house. This news occasioned great commotion throughout the whole city, and was announced to the Governor the same evening. On Sunday morning Swedenborg was summoned to the Governor, who questioned him about the disaster. He described the fire precisely, how it had begun and in what manner it had ceased, and how long it had continued. On Monday evening a messenger arrived at Gottenburg, who had been despatched by the Board of Trade during the time of the fire. In the letters brough by him, the fire was described precisely as stated by Swedenborg, and next morning the news was further confirmed by information brought to the Governor by the Royal Courier. As Swedenborg had said, the fire had been extinguished at eight o'clock.

Continuing, now, our analysis of the idea of possession, we come to its specific feature—the occupation by a spiritual agency of the entranced and partially vacated organism.

We first thought of telepathy as of a communication between two minds, whereas what we have here looks more like a communication between a mind and a body—an external mind, in place of the mind which is accustomed to rule that particular body. The phenomena of possession seem to indicate that the extraneous spirit acts on a man's organism in very much the same way as the man's own spirit habitually acts on it. One must thus practically regard the body as an instrument upon which a spirit plays—an ancient metaphor which now seems actually our nearest approximation to truth.

We must not allow ourselves to ascribe to spirit-control cases where no new knowledge is shown in the trance state. And this rule has at once an important consequence—a consequence which profoundly modifies the antique idea of possession. I know of no evidence, reaching in any way our habitual standard, either for angelic, for diabolical, or for hostile possession.

And here comes the question: What attitude are we to assume to savage cases of possession? Are we to accept as genuine the possession of the Esquimaux, the Chinaman—nay, of the Hebrew of old days?

A devil is not a creature whose existence is independently known to science; and the accounts of the behavior of the invading devils seems due to mere self-suggestion. With uncivilized races, even more than among our own friends, we are bound to insist on the rule that there must be some supernormal knowledge shown before we may assume an external influence. It may of course be replied that the character shown by the "devils" was fiendish and actually *hostile* to the possessed person. Can we suppose that the tormentor was actually a fraction of the tormented?

I reply that such a supposition, so far from being absurd, is supported by well-known phenomena both in insanity and in mere hysteria.

Temporary control of the organism by a widely divergent fragment of the personality, self-suggested in some dream-like manner into hostility to the main mass of the personality, and perhaps better able than that normal personality to reach and manipulate certain stored impressions, or even certain supernormal influences, such will be the formula to which we shall reduce the invading Chinese devils, the devils with terrifying names which possessed Soeur Angélique of Loudun in the Middle Ages, and *probably* the great majority of supposed devil-possessions of similar type.

The great majority, no doubt, but perhaps not *all*. It would indeed be matter for surprise if such trance-phenomena as those of Mrs. Piper and other modern cases had appeared in the world without previous parallel. Much more probable is it that similar phenomena have occurred sporadically from the earliest times, although men have not had enough of training to analyze them.

And, in fact, among the endless descriptions of trance-phenomena with which travellers furnish us, there are many which include points so concordant with our recent observations that we cannot but attach some weight to coincidences so wholly undesigned.[1] The belief in devils has played an enormous part in almost all human creeds, and it was undoubtedly strong in the minds of many of the persons with whom communication has been held. Unhappy figures have been seen; regret and remorse have been expressed. But of evil spirits other than human there is no news whatever.

The possibility of being dominated by some unwelcome spirit was naturally regarded by Mr. Moses with fear and dislike. His guides admitted it as a real, but not as an alarming, danger. Such spiritual infections, they said in effect, take root only in a congenial soil. The healthy medium can repel their attack, much as the healthy organism destroys the germs which are perpetually seeking lodgment within it.

The foregoing remarks may, I hope, have prepared the reader to consider the problems of possession with the same open-mindedness which has been needed for the study of previous problems attacked in the present work. And yet I shall next feel bound to utter an earnest warning against the fraud and folly which have made of spiritualism a kind of by-word in scientific circles as a credulous sect, preyed upon by a specially repulsive group of impostors. I do not say that the public interest in this has been a very wide one. It has been wide enough to foster and support a particularly detestable group of charlatans; but it has not been wide enough, or earnest enough, to compile any considerable mass of careful experiment. I have conjectured that not a hundred men, at the ordinary professional level, had up till now made the study of the phenomena of hypnotism the main intellectual business of their lives. If for hypnotism we substitute these

---

[1] One important point of similarity is the concurrence in some savage ceremonies of utterance through an invading spirit and travelling clairvoyance exercised meantime by the man whose organism is thus invaded. The uncouth spirit shouts and bellows, presumably with the lungs of the medicine-man, hidden from view in profound slumber. Then the medicine-man awakes, and tells the listening tribe the news which his sleep-wanderings, among gods or men, have won.

If this indeed be thus, it fits in strangely with the experiences of our modern seers, with the spiritual interchange which takes place when a discarnate intelligence occupies the organism and meantime the incarnate intelligence, temporarily freed, awakes to wider percipience—in this or in another world.

"phenomena of spiritualism" the list of serious students might probably be reduced to fifty.

It is well to point out the scantiness of efficient investigators of these problems, in view of the objection often made to the lack of progress in the difficult task.

It will be best, to consider first some of the more rudimentary cases before going on to our own special instances of possession—those of Mr. Stainton Moses or Mrs. Piper.

I have reason to believe, both from what I have witnessed myself and from the reports of others, that occasional phenomena of ecstasy or possession are not infrequent in some family circles or groups of intimate friends.

The persons concerned, however, generally do not realize the importance of accurate records; in some cases the manifestations are sporadic in character and scarcely susceptible of any detailed investigation; and often the very occurrence of the phenomena has been sedulously concealed from all outside the circle. Sometimes the sacredness of the manifestations has been pleaded as a sufficient reason for their concealment, or the tendency to trance on the part of the "sensitive" has been regarded as a calamity, to be checked and prohibited as though it were a distressing disease.

A family-group case from *Proceedings* S.P.R., vol. ix. p. 119 follows. The phenomena described were various, but consisted mainly of automatic writing and speech. Some of the writings evinced a knowledge greater than the automatist possessed. Especially two lines from Homer were correctly written in response to a request for some Greek, although the writer was certainly quite ignorant even of the Greek alphabet. Some indications of identity were also given.

I first heard Mr. O.'s narrative from himself by word of mouth on November 20th, 1889, while the events were still fresh in his memory. I regard him as an excellent witness. Mr. O. writes in 1890:

§ In the winter of '88–9 I began, along with a few intimate friends, to investigate the phenomena commonly called spiritualistic. None of the company was at all anxious for any specific communication from another sphere, but partly for the gratification of an invalid brother, and partly for the sake of satisfying ourselves as to the possibility of some things we had read, we attempted a sitting. The results far exceeded our expectation. We were favored with phenomena somewhat startling to novices in the art . . . but their interesting nature soon overcame our natural diffidence, and before the end of the winter we were on quite familiar terms with our unsubstantial visitants. . . . We had all our sittings in our own home, the circle was confined to personal friends in whom we had full confidence, so that there was neither motive nor opportunity for deception. . . . Our sittings were all in the dark. Our medium was, in most cases, Mr. Andrew . . . I mentioned an invalid brother. He suffered from a heart affection known as presystolic murmur. At one sitting we consulted a medical man, who called himself Dr. Snobinski of Russia. This gentleman not only prescribed for my brother, but also furnished us with a diagram of the human heart, and put a special mark to indicate the valve diseased in my brother's case. How this diagram was actually drawn by a person ignorant of human physiology, and how the diseased valve was shown and explained by one ignorant of pathology, was more than I could account for. . . .

Still more inexplicable was the evidential sign given to a doubting acquaintance. This gentleman requested permission to be present at one of the sittings, but his general behavior there indicated that he regarded a sitting as a kind of farce. He brought with him another gentleman of equally skeptical temper. The first remark from the medium that evening was, "There are strangers present tonight." This remark seemed to our friend so commonplace that he requested evidence of the presence of a spirit. On being asked what evidence he would like, he jokingly said, "Bring a candle!"—an idea probably suggested by sitting in the dark. The wish had scarcely been expressed when a candle was placed on the table before him, with the request that he should immediately quit the company. The candle was found to be warm, a circumstance explained by the fact that it had been used in the next room only a few minutes before. My brother immediately went to the next room and asked for a candle. The good lady was much surprised to find that while the candlestick was still standing where she had placed it shortly before, the candle itself was gone. My brother then showed her the candle which he held in his hand, and this she identified as the one she had used a few minutes before—indeed there could not be two opinions, as there was only one candle in the house. This was regarded by the circle as the most wonderful result yet obtained.

During that winter we obtained many interesting phenomena. The spirits (?) would strike any note we asked on a violin or harmonium which stood by. The notes requested would sound forth distinctly, though no visible hand was near; and this was done both in the dark and in the light, though more often in the dark. §

There are further occasional cases of the frankly "mediumistic" type, one of which is given below. But the problems involved are so complicated, and the main question—that of the agency of discarnate spirits in the matter—is so difficult of determination, that no collection of such fragmentary material could be of much service to us in our present inquiry unless per-

haps to indicate that the fully-developed cases belong, after all, to a not uncommon type.

The case of Miss White comes from America, and is specially interesting both in the apparent fulfillment of the promise made by the alleged
discarnate spirit control to appear to the narrator's sick wife, and in the apparent knowledge shown of the immediate approach of death. From *Proceedings* S.P.R., vol. viii. p. 227.

§ *January* 28*th,* 1891.

About eleven years ago, I was much distressed owing to the illness of
my wife, who suffered from cancer in the stomach. I heard about a medium,
Miss Susie Nickerson White, who was said to have given some remarkable
tests, and I called on her as a stranger and requested a sitting. My wife's
sister purported to "control," giving her name, Maria, and mentioning
facts about my family which were correct. She also called my wife by her
name, Eliza Anne, described her sickness, and said that she would pass
over, but not for some months. I said, "What do you call this? Is it psychology, or mesmerism, or what?" Maria said, "I knew you were going to
ask that; I saw it in your mind." I said, "Do you get all the things out of my
mind?" She replied, "No. I'll tell you some things that are not in your
mind. Within three days Eliza Anne will say that she has seen me and
mother, too." (My wife's mother had died about forty-five years previously, and my wife's sister had been dead from six to eight years.)

I kept these circumstances to myself, but within three days the nurse
who was in attendance upon my wife came running to me and said that my
wife was worse, and was going out of her mind; that she had called upon
Maria and mother, and had sprung out of bed and ran towards the door
crying, "Stop, Maria! Stop, mother! Don't go yet!"

I soon consulted Miss White again, and Maria purported to control.
My wife had been unable for some days to retain any food in her stomach,
could not keep even water or milk, and was very weak and also unable to
sleep.

Maria told me to give her some hot, very strong coffee, with plenty of
cream and sugar and some cream toast. This prescription amazed me, but
it was prepared. My wife ate and drank with relish, and slept soundly afterwards. She lived upon this food for some days, but gradually became unable even to take this.

I consulted Miss White again, and Maria told me to get some limes, and
to give my wife some pure juice of the lime several times a day; she said
that this would give her an appetite and enable her to retain food. The prescription was a success; but gradually my wife failed and I consulted Miss

White again, and asked Maria how long my wife would continue to suffer. She said she could not tell exactly when she would pass away, but would give me a warning—"The next time she says she has seen me, don't leave her afterwards."

Some days later, as I was relieving the nurse about three or four in the morning, the nurse said, "Mammie" (meaning my wife) "says she has seen Maria again." In a few minutes my wife said, "I must go." And she expired.

E. PAIGE

[I have had long interviews with Mr. Paige. He seems to be a shrewd and careful witness—RICHARD HODGSON.] §

The first step in possession apparently is the abeyance of the supraliminal self and the dominance of the subliminal self, which may lead in rare cases to a form of trance (or of what we have hitherto called secondary personality) where the whole body of the automatist is controlled by his own subliminal self, or incarnate spirit, but where there is no indication of any relation with discarnate spirits. The next form of trance is where the incarnate spirit, whether or not maintaining control of the whole body, makes excursions into or holds telepathic intercourse with the spirit world. And, lastly, there is the trance of possession by another, a discarnate spirit. We cannot, of course, always distinguish between these three main types of trance—which, as we shall see later, themselves admit of different degrees and varieties.

The most striking case known to me of the first form of trance—possession by the subliminal self—is that of the Rev. C. B. Sanders, whose trance-personality has always called itself by the name of "$X + Y = Z$." What little explanation is offered seems to be in singular harmony with one of the main tenets advanced in this book, since the claim made by "$X + Y = Z$" is obviously that he represents the incarnate spirit of Mr. Sanders exercising the higher faculties which naturally pertain to it, but which can be manifested to the full only when it is freed from its fleshly barriers. This frequently occurs, he says, in dying persons, who describe scenes in the spiritual world, and in his own experience when "his casket" (as he called his supraliminal self) is similarly affected, and the bodily obstructions to spiritual vision are removed.

An account of the experiences of the Rev. C. B. Sanders was published in a book entitled $X + Y = Z$; or, The Sleeping Preacher of North Alabama. Containing an account of most wonderful mysterious mental phenomena, fully authenticated by living witnesses. By Rev. G. W. Mitchell. (New York: W. C. Smith, 65 John Street. 1876.) The book includes statements by numerous witnesses of the supernormal manifestations of Mr. Sanders, and additional corroborations were obtained by Professor James and Dr. Hodgson in reply to inquiries about the case. From these sources of information the following brief sketch is made.

§ From his early childhood Constantine Blackmon Sanders was much interested in the subject of preaching the gospel. He would preach juvenile funeral sermons over dead chickens, pigs, etc. and baptize his playmates. On this account he was familiarly called "The Preacher." When he was twenty years old he attended a revival meeting; and presented himself as a candidate for the ministry under the care of the Presbytery of Tennessee, was licensed to preach in 1855, and ordained in 1862. At the time he joined the Presbytery, when he was 21 years old, he could scarcely read and write.

In the spring of 1854, when studying at school in Elkton, Tennessee he had attacks of sickness, described by Mrs. Harlow, with whose family he was living, as follows:

"On one occasion he said: 'My head feels like it has opened.' Taking my hand with his, he placed it on his head, when, to my astonishment, I found what appeared to be a separation of the bone, nearly wide enough to bury my little finger, ranging from above his eyes near the center of his forehead to the top of his head, and from the top down towards and near to each ear. The opening increased in width as it reached the top of the head. This condition of his head I saw frequently. When the paroxysms would subside, the openings would nearly close up." §

He had many similar attacks during the next five years, accompanied by much physical suffering. In the meantime, in 1856, he married, and over the years he and his wife had six healthy children. After an unusually severe convulsion in 1859, the convulsions stopped, but he still suffered much, as appears from the following statement made by Dr. W. T. Thach in 1876:

§ I have been acquainted with him about sixteen years. He has complained ever since my acquaintance with him, and he says, for a number of years previous, with a continuous headache, though differing in severity at different times, often becoming excruciating. . . .

With these paroxysms of suffering there is almost always a peculiar condition, to me inexplicable, and which I know not what to denominate, which those acquainted with him generally call "sleep," merely from the fact that, when recovered from this condition, he is totally ignorant of any and everything that has occurred while in this state (even the length of time that has elapsed, not knowing whether an hour or a week). Hence the name of the "Sleeping Preacher." And yet, at the time, he seems conscious of everything that is going on around him; and not only so, but of what is transpiring at any point to which his attention is directed, regardless of distance. The length of these paroxysms is quite variable, extending from a moment to hours and days, during which time he gets no natural sleep; the mind to all appearance being much more active than when in a normal condition; being all the time engaged in conversation or writing (of which he does a great deal), or some other active mental exercise. . . .

In all of his notes, letters, and writing of every kind, while in this condition, he ignores the name of "Sanders." His signature is "X + Y = Z."

While in these sleeps, if left to himself, his thoughts are confined mostly to theology or medicine. And though never having studied medicine, he seems, while in this mental state, to be very conversant with it; using the technical names, giving the properties, uses, etc., thereof. He always examines the sick who may happen to be about him when in this state, without coming in contact with the patient; making in writing a diagnosis and prescription, which he will usually give, if requested. And I could mention a great many who have been relieved by his directions. I have frequently had him to give me the exact condition of patients whom he had never seen, and who were miles distant. His prescriptions frequently contain medicines which cannot be procured in this country; which he makes arrangements to import; showing his comprehensive view of Materia Medica in this preternatural way. §

The normal Mr. Sanders had no recollection of anything occurring in his sleep state, "but X + Y = Z seems to have had entire consciousness of Mr. Sanders, or of his 'casket,' as he always called him."

Various cases are described of Mr. Sanders' finding lost articles—such as dollar-bills, coins, a watch chain, a bunch of keys—or specifying correctly where they would be found. I give an instance. Mr. Bentley writes:

§ . . . Sometime during the summer a bunch of keys was lost. After a lapse of about one week I requested Mr. William White to ask the Sleeping Preacher to tell me where my keys were. He said my keys were under the steps at the west door of my dwelling. They were found under the door-step just as Mr. Sanders had said, and somewhat rusty. They must have been thrown there a week before by a little child that played about the house.

I add that I know Mr. Sanders had not been in my house nor on the place for at least twelve months before that time.

A. J. BENTLEY §

Several cases are also recorded of his knowledge that a distant person was just dying or dead. I quote one of these:

§ One day our attention was attracted by manifestations of sympathy, sadness, and distress from Mr. Sanders, accompanied by such expressions as "Poor fellow! What a pity!" Then he said, "He is gone! gone! gone!" closing in a solemn whisper. I asked the cause of these manifestations. We were quite shocked on hearing his reply that "Lieutenant McClure has just died suddenly from an internal hemorrhage, near Clarkesville, Tennessee."

We append the following facts: Lieutenant Robert McClure, a new bridegroom, had a few days before this gone on a visit to his father near Clarkesville, Tennessee. On the next morning after Mr. Sanders' above comments, a telegram was received from Clarkesville bringing to his young bride the unexpected and melancholy news of her husband's sudden death. It confirmed in every circumstance what Mr. Sanders had stated the night before.

A recent letter, from a lady who was present, states that Lieutenant McClure died on Wednesday night, between eight and nine o'clock, the 2nd of November, 1866. He was sitting in her room, reading aloud a book; had a paroxysm of coughing, and remarked to her that it was blood that he spit out. She put her babe down, which she was nursing, and assisted him in sitting down, for he had arisen to his feet. She thinks he did not breathe after being seated. . . .

G. W. MITCHELL §

The suggestion which I made in the case of Anna Winsor—that the intelligence controlling her sane right arm was her own subliminal self —may now perhaps appear less strange than it did at the outset of our inquiry; but whereas in that case the supraliminal self was only partially in abeyance, the supraliminal self of Mr. Sanders seems to become completely dormant during his trances.

In this case then the subliminal self seems to take complete control of the organism, exercising its own powers of telepathy and clairvoyance but showing no evidence of direct communication with discarnate spirits.

The second volume of Alphonse Cahagnet's *Arcanes de la vie future devoilés* reporting his sittings with Adèle Maginot was published at Paris in 1849. This medium had been long known to him; she had been a natural somnambulist from her childhood, and he had "magnetized" her to put a stop to the spontaneous attacks which were impairing her health. He found her an excellent clairvoyant, especially for the diagnosis and cure of diseases. Later, she was chiefly consulted by persons who wished for interviews with deceased friends. It appears that Cahagnet took great care to report the communications, and to obtain signed attestations from witnesses, so that the case stands on a much higher evidential level than most early records of clairvoyants. An account of Cahagnet's work, quoting the records of some of the best cases, is given in an article by Mr. F. Podmore in *Proceedings* S.P.R., vol. xiv. p. 50, and I give below some extracts.

§ M. Petiet asks for M. Jérôme Petiet. . . . Adèle sees a young man, about twenty-four or twenty-six years of age (he was thirty), not so tall as his brother now present; auburn hair, rather long; open forehead, arched and very pronounced eyebrows; brown and rather sunken eyes; nose rather long, pretty well formed; complexion fresh, skin very white and delicate; medium-sized mouth, round dimpled chin. "He was weak in the chest; he would have been very strong had it not been for this. He wears a rough grey vest, buttons with a shank and eye such as are no longer worn. I do not think they are brass ones, nor of the same stuff as the vest. They don't look to me very bright. His pantaloons are of a dark color, and he wears low quartered shoes without any instep.

"This man was of a stubborn disposition, selfish, without any fine feelings, had a sinister look, was not very communicative, devoid of candor, and had but little affection for any one. He had suffered with his heart. His death was natural, but sudden. He died of suffocation." Adèle chokes as this man choked, and coughed as he did. She says that "he must have had moxas or a plaster applied to his back, and this accounts for the sore I see there. He had no disease, however, in that part. The spine was sound. Those who applied this remedy did not know the seat of the disease. He holds himself badly. His back is round without being humped."

M. Petiet finds nothing to alter in these details, which are very exact, and confirm him in his belief that the application of this plaster, advised by a man who was not a doctor, brought on his brother's death, which was almost sudden.

Signed the present report as very exact.

PETIET,
19 Rue Neuve-Coquenard

M. du Potet [a well-known writer on Animal Magnetism] wishes to call up Dr. Dubois, a friend who had been dead about fifteen months.

Adèle said: "I see a grey-headed man, he has very little hair on the front of his head; his forehead is bare and prominent at the temples, making his head appear square. He may be about sixty years of age. He has two wrinkles on either side of his cheeks, a crease under his chin, making it look double; he is short-necked and stumpy; has small eyes, a thick nose, a rather large mouth, a flat chin, and small thin hands. He does not look to me quite so tall as M. du Potet; if he is not stouter, he is more broad-shouldered. He wears a brown frock-coat with side pockets. I see him draw a snuff-box out of one of them and take a pinch. He has a very funny walk, he does not carry himself well, and has weak legs; he must have suffered from them. He has rather short trousers. Ah! he does not clean his shoes every day, for they are covered with mud. Taking it altogether, he is not well dressed. He has asthma, for he breathes with difficulty. I see, too, that he has a swelling in the abdomen, he has something to support it. I have told him that it is M. du Potet who asked for him. He talks to me of magnetism with incredible volubility; he talks of everything at once; he mixes everything up; I cannot understand any of it; it makes him sputter saliva."

M. du Potet asks that the apparition may be asked why he has not appeared to him before as he had promised. He answers: "Wait till I find out my whereabouts; I have only just arrived, I am studying everything I see. I want to tell you all about it when I appear, and I shall have many things to tell you."

"Which day did you promise me you would do so?" "On a Wednesday." Adèle adds: "This man must be forgetful; I am sure that he was very absent-minded." M. du Potet asks further: "When will you appear to me?" "I cannot fix the time; I shall try to do so in six weeks." "Ask him if he was fond of the Jesuits." At this name he gives such a leap in the air, stretching out his arms, and crying "The Jesuits," that Adèle draws back quickly, and is so startled that she does not venture to speak to him again.

M. du Potet declares that all these details are very accurate, that he cannot alter a syllable. He says that this man's powers of conversation were inexhaustible; he mixed up all the sciences to which he was devoted, and spoke with such volubility that, as the clairvoyant says, he sputtered in consequence. He took little pains with his appearance; he was so absent-minded that he sometimes forgot to eat. When any one mentioned the Jesuits to him he jumped as Adèle has described. He was always covered with mud like a spaniel. It is not surprising that the clairvoyant should see him with muddy shoes. He had, in fact, promised M. du Potet that he would appear to him on a Wednesday or a Saturday. M. du Potet has acknowledged the accuracy of this apparition in No. 75 of the *Journal du Magnétisme.* §

In some cases, with the express object of excluding thought-transference, the sitter came armed with the name of some dead person of whom he knew nothing—as in the following case:

§ Pastor Rostan desired. . . . to obtain an apparition. . . . He asked his maidservant to give him a name of one of her acquaintances who had been dead some time; he came armed with this name, and asked for Jeannette Jex. Adèle replied: "I see a woman who is not tall, she may be between thirty and forty years of age; if she is not hump-backed she must be crook-backed, for she carries herself very badly. I cannot make her turn round. Her hair is auburn, approaching to red; she has small grey eyes, a thick nose. She is not good-looking. She has a prominent chin, a receding mouth, thin lips; her dress is countrified. I see that she has a cap with two flat bands, rounded over the ears. She must have suffered from a flow of blood to the head, she had had indigestion. I see she has a swelling in the abdomen on the left side and in the glands of one breast. She has been ill a long time."

M. Rostan handed over the report to his servant, and gave it back to me after adding his signature and the following remarks:

"This is correct as regards stature, age, dress, carriage, the disease and deformed figure."

J. J. ROSTAN §

The next case to be considered, and one of the most important, is that of D. D. Home. But, although I attribute much value to what evidence exists in the case of Home, it cannot but be deplored that the inestimable chance for experiment and record which this man afforded was almost entirely thrown away by the scientific world. Unfortunately the record is especially inadequate in reference to Home's trances and the evidence for the personal identity of the communicating spirits. His name is known to the world chiefly in connection with the telekinetic phenomena which are said to have occurred in his presence, and the best accounts of which we owe to Sir William Crookes.

Just as Swedenborg was the first leading man of science who distinctly conceived of the spiritual world as a world of law, so was the celebrated physicist and chemist, Sir W. Crookes the first leading man of science who

seriously endeavored to test the alleged mutual influence and interpene-
tration of the spiritual world and our own by experiments of scientific precision. It is not my intention, as I have already explained, to deal with
these, but it must be understood that they form an integral part of the
manifestations in this case. For detailed accounts of them the reader
should consult the history of Home's life and experiences.

In Home's case it is especially important to consider the question of
fraud, since various charges of fraud have been brought against him—
some, however, without any evidence at all, and others on second-hand
statements only, while the most serious one—that connected with the
famous Lyon case—related rather to his character than to the real nature
of his powers. A detailed discussion, by Professor Barrett and myself, of
the question of fraud, was printed in the *Journal* S.P.R. I give an abridgement of it now:

§ There is thus a considerable body of evidence as to Home, which enables us to discuss the three questions: (1) Was he ever convicted of
fraud? (2) Did he satisfy any trained observer in a series of experiments
selected by the observer and not by himself? (3) Were the phenomena
entirely beyond the known scope of the conjurer's art?

With regard to (1), Mr. Robert Browning told us the circumstances
which mainly led to the opinion of Home which he expressed in *Mr.
Sludge the Medium*. A lady had repeated to him a statement made to her
by a lady and gentleman that they had found Home experimenting with
phosphorus on the production of "spirit-lights." This evidence, then,
came to us at third-hand; the incident had occurred nearly forty years before, and it was impossible to learn more of it, since all the witnesses were
dead and had left no written record.

We received one first-hand account, from a gentleman of character
and ability, of a séance given in very poor light, where a small "spirit
hand"—visible to all the sitters—appeared, and moved about. It seemed
to him that he could see slight movements in the shoulder or upper part
of Home's arm corresponding with the movements of the "spirit hand."
Afterwards, "the movements of both plainly corresponded, and at length
. . . I saw continuous connection in the upper outline of Home's arm
and the thing, whatever it was, that supported the 'spirit hand.' " The
sitting took place in 1855, but the account was not written until 1889.

There is also a frequently repeated story that Home was found in
France to be using a stuffed hand; our inquiries into this tended to show
that the story was a fabrication.

The most serious blot on Home's character was that revealed by the

Lyon case. He had sittings with Mrs. Lyon, at which communications were given purporting to come from her deceased husband, and urging her to adopt Home as her son and give him £700 a year. An admitted letter from her to Home, in which she said that she presented him with £24,000 "as an entirely free gift," was stated by her at the trial to have been written at Home's dictation and under "magnetic influence." The strongest evidence against Home was furnished by memorandum books, in his own writing, containing accounts of his experiences with her, and communications in the form of a dialogue between her and her husband, in which Home was alluded to as "our beloved son." Of Mrs. Lyon, the judge observed that "Reliance cannot be placed on her testimony"; but there was much evidence besides hers to show that Home worked on her mind by spiritualistic devices, especially by suggesting communications from her husband, and the Court held that such transactions as those in question could not be upheld "unless the Court is quite satisfied that they are acts of pure volition uninfluenced." Such proof not being forthcoming, the case was decided against Home.

We must observe, however, that the Lyon case, however discreditable to Home personally, has no clear bearing on the reality of his powers, since there seems to have been no assertion that any of the phenomena were produced by fraudulent means.

(2) With regard to our second question—whether his powers were tested by competent observers—Home in this respect stands pre-eminent; since we have the evidence of Sir William Crookes corroborated by the testimony of the Master of Lindsay (now Earl of Crawford and Balcarres) himself a *savant* of some distinction, and the privately printed series of careful observations by the present and the late Lords Dunraven.

(3) As to our third question—whether the phenomena could have been produced by conjuring—many of them, especially the "fire tests" and the movements of large untouched objects in good light, seem inexplicable by this supposition. The hypothesis of collective hallucination on the part of the sitters seems very improbable, because in most cases all those present saw the same thing;[1] and often without receiving from Home any audible suggestion as to what was about to happen.

[1] The famous case of Home floating out at one window and in at another, related by Lords Lindsay and Adare, as witnessed by them, was quoted by Dr. Carpenter in the *Contemporary Review* for January, 1876, as an instance of believers affirming that they saw the phenomenon, "while a single honest skeptic declares that Mr. Home was sitting in his chair all the time." In reply to this, the only other person who was present at the time, Captain Wynne, wrote a letter (seen by the present writer and printed in Home's *Life*) stating that he also on that occasion had seen Home go out of one window and in at the other.

The telekinetic phenomena observed in Home's case were those which attracted most attention; but the communications given at his sittings purporting to come from deceased persons are also noteworthy, though the records of them are unfortunately very inadequate. From a brief abstract of thirty-five cases of "recognition" taken from Madame Home's work, omitting those which rest on Home's uncorroborated testimony, we give the following.

These cases are of very different evidential value. But many are first-hand accounts, volunteered by independent witnesses, of messages closely affecting themselves, and sometimes involving incidents which can hardly have been known to servants or dependents.

Mr. S. B. Brittan's testimony: Home suddenly becomes entranced; says "Hannah Brittan is here"—a relative long since dead, and whose existence, as Mr. Brittan believes, was not known to any one "in all that region." Home, entranced, acts as though a melancholic in terror of hell; Hannah Brittan "became insane from believing in the doctrine of endless punishment."

Mrs. Senior's evidence: At their first meeting Mr. Home describes Mr. Senior and adds, "You forgot to wind his watch, and how miserable it made you." "Now this was a fact known to no living being but myself. I had wound the watch the night I lost my husband and resolved never to let it go down again. I forgot to wind it one night, and my agony was great when I discovered it in the morning, but I never mentioned it even to my husband's sister, who was in the house with me." Home also mentions "Mary," Mr. Senior's mother.

Mr. B. Coleman's evidence: At his first séance messages are given by raps as from his aunts Elizabeth and Hannah. "I did not recognize the names. I had never known of my aunts of those names," but he learns that sisters of his father, thus named, died before he was born.

Lord Lindsay's testimony: Lord Lindsay misses train at Norwood, sleeps on sofa in Home's room; sees female figure standing near Home's bed, which fades away; recognizes face among other photographs next morning; it was Home's deceased wife.

Mrs. Peck's testimony: "By permission I put several *mental* questions, each of which was promptly and correctly answered, with the full names of friends and relatives deceased, and circumstances which could not have been known to any of those present; all, as I have stated, having been previous to the past twenty-four hours strangers to me." (Mrs. Peck was an American, staying at a hotel in Geneva.)

Home says: "There is a portrait of *his* mother." "I made no reply; but my thought was, 'There is *no* portrait of her.'" Home insists that there is, "with an open Bible upon her knee." There was, in fact, a daguerreotype thirty years old, which Mrs. Peck had forgotten, in attitude described—with indistinct book on knee, which was, in fact, a Bible. §

In brief, the study of such records as are available of Home's psychical phenomena leaves me with the conviction that—apart altogether from the telekinetic phenomena with which they were associated—his trance-utterances belong to the same natural order as those, for instance, of Mr. Moses and Mrs. Piper.

It was on May 9th, 1874, that Edmund Gurney and I met Stainton Moses for the first time, through the kindness of Lady Mount-Temple, who knew that we had become interested in psychical problems, and wished to introduce us to a man of honor who had recently experienced phenomena, due wholly to some gift of his own, which had profoundly changed his conception of life.

That evening was epoch-making in Gurney's life and mine. Standing as we were in the attitude natural at the commencement of such inquiries, under such conditions as were then attainable, an attitude of curiosity tempered by a vivid perception of difficulty and drawback, we now met a man of university education, of manifest sanity and probity, who vouched to us for a series of phenomena—occurring to himself, and with no doubtful or venal aid—which seemed at least to prove, in confusedly intermingled form, three main theses unknown to science. These were (1) the existence in the human spirit of hidden powers of insight and of communication; (2) the personal survival and near presence of the departed; and (3) interference, due to unknown agencies, with the ponderable world. He spoke frankly and fully; he showed his notebooks; he referred us to his friends; he inspired a belief which was at once sufficient, and which is still sufficient, to prompt to action.

The experiences which Stainton Moses had undergone had changed his views, but not his character. He was already set in the mold of the hard-working, conscientious, dogmatic clergyman, with a strong desire to do good, and a strong belief in preaching as the best way to do it. For himself the essential part of what I have called his "message" lay in the actual words automatically uttered or written—not in the accompanying phenomena which really gave their uniqueness and importance to the automatic processes. In a book called *Spirit Teachings* he collected what he regarded as the real fruits of those years of mysterious listening in the vestibule of a world unknown.

And much as we may regret this too exclusive ethical preoccupation in a region where the establishment of actual fact is still the one thing needful, it must be admitted that at that time the scientific importance of these phenomena had hardly dawned on any mind. Among all the witnesses of Home's marvels Sir William Crookes was almost the only man who made any attempt to treat them as reasonable men treat all the facts of nature. Most of the witnesses, though fully believing in the genuineness of the wonders, appear to have regarded them as a kind of uncanny diversion. The more serious sought for assurance that their beloved dead were still near them, and straitly charged Home to tell no man of the proofs which they said had brought to themselves unspeakable joy. An attempt made, in 1875, by Serjeant Cox and a few others (among whom were Stainton Moses and myself) to get these phenomena more seriously discussed in a "Psychological Society," languished for want of suitable coadjutors, and on the death of Serjeant Cox (in 1879) the Society was dissolved. During these important years, therefore, while his experiences were fresh in Stainton Moses' mind, and while they were to some extent still recurring, he had little encouragement to deal with them from a scientific point of view.

When, however, in 1882, Professor Barrett consulted him as to the possibility of founding a new society, under better auspices, he warmly welcomed the plan. Edmund Gurney and I were asked to join, but made it a condition that the consent of Professor Sidgwick (with whom we had already been working) to act as our President should first be obtained.[1] Under his guidance the Society for Psychical Research assumed a more cautious and critical attitude than was congenial to Stainton Moses' warm heart, strong convictions, and impulsive temper, and in 1886 he left the Society, in consequence of the publication in the *Proceedings* of certain comments on phenomena occurring through the agency of the so-called "medium" Eglinton.

From this time he frankly confessed himself disgusted with our attempts at scientific method, and as main contributor to *Light,* and afterwards editor until his death, he practically reverted to "spiritualism as a religion," as opposed to psychical research as a scientific duty. And assuredly the religious implications of all these phenomena are worthy of any man's most serious thought. But those who most feel the importance of the ethical superstructure are at the same time most plainly bound to treat the establishment of the facts at the foundation as no mere personal search for a faith, to be dropped when private conviction has been attained, but as a serious, a continuous, a public duty. And the more convinced

[1] The Society for Psychical Research was founded in 1882, Professor W. F. Barrett taking a leading part in its promotion. Henry Sidgwick was its first President, and Edmund Gurney was its first Honorary Secretary—he and I being joint Honorary Secretaries of its Literary Committee, whose business was the collection of evidence.

they are that their faith is sound, the more ready should they be to face distrust and aversion.

Stainton Moses was ill-fitted for this patient, uphill toil. In the first place he lacked—and he readily and repeatedly admitted to me that he lacked—all vestige of scientific, or even of legal instinct. The very words "first-hand evidence," "contemporary record," "corroborative testimony," were to him as a weariness to the flesh. His attitude was that of the preacher who is already so thoroughly persuaded in his own mind that he treats any alleged fact which falls in with his views as the uncriticized text for fresh exhortation. And in the second place, though this was a minor matter, his natural sensitiveness was sometimes exaggerated by gout and other wearing ailments into an irritability which he scarcely felt compelled to conceal in a journal circulating mainly among attached disciples.

The reason for noticing these defects is that they constitute the only ground on which Stainton Moses' trustworthiness as a witness to his own phenomena could possibly be impugned. I mention them in order that I may say that, having read, I think, all that he has printed, and having watched his conduct at critical moments, I see much ground for impugning his judgment, but no ground whatever for doubting that he has narrated with absolute good faith the story of his own experience. He allowed me, before he left the Society, to examine almost the whole series of his automatic writings—those especially which contain the evidence on which *Spirit Identity* is based; and in no instance did I find that the printed statement of any case went beyond the warrant of the manuscript.

My original impressions were strengthened by the opportunity which I had of examining the unpublished manuscripts of Mr. Moses after his death on September 5th, 1892. These consist of thirty-one note-books —twenty-four of automatic script, four of records of physical phenomena, and three of retrospect and summary. In addition to these, the material available for a knowledge of Mr. Moses' experiences consists of his own printed works, and the written and printed statements of witnesses to his phenomena.

With the even tenor of this straightforward and reputable life was inwoven a chain of mysteries which, in whatever way they be explained, make that life one of the most extraordinary which our century has seen.

From *Proceedings* S.P.R., vol. xi. pp. 106–7. I will now give the account of "Rector"—one of the alleged spirits who wrote through Mr. Moses' hand, among them "Doctor, the Teacher," "Imperator," etc.—as to a quotation from a closed and unknown book.

§ *Q.* I am told you can read. Is that so? Can you read a book?

A. "Yes, friend, with difficulty."

Q. Will you write for me the last line of the first book of the Æneid?

A. "Wait——*Omnibus errantem terris et fluctibus æstas.*"

[This was right.]

Q. Quite so. But I might have known it. Can you go to the book-case, take the last book but one on the second shelf, and read me the last paragraph of the ninety-fourth page? I have not seen it, and do not even know its name.

A. "I will curtly prove by a short historical narrative, that Popery is a novelty, and has gradually arisen or grown up since the primitive and pure time of Christianity, not only since the apostolic age, but even since the lamentable union of kirk and the state by Constantine."

[The book on examination proved to be a queer one called "*Roger's Antipopopriestian,* an attempt to liberate and purify Christianity from Popery, Politikirkality, and Priestrule." The extract given above was accurate, but the word "narrative" was substituted for "account."]

Q. How came I to pitch upon so appropriate a sentence?

A. "I know not, my friend. It was by coincidence. The word was changed by error. I knew it when it was done, but would not change."

Q. How do you read? You wrote more slowly, and by fits and starts.

A. "I wrote what I remembered, and then I went for more. It is a special effort to read, and useful only as a test. Your friend was right last night; we can read, but only when conditions are very good. We will read once again, and write and then impress you of the book: 'Pope is the last great writer of that school of poetry, the poetry of the intellect, or rather of the intellect mingled with the fancy.' That is truly written. Go and take the eleventh book on the same shelf. [I took a book called *Poetry, Romance, and Rhetoric.*] It will open at the page for you. Take it and read, and recognize our power, and the permission which the great and good God gives us, to show you of our power over matter. To Him be glory. Amen."

The book opened at page 145, and there was the quotation perfectly true. I had not seen the book before: certainly had no idea of its contents. [These books were in Dr. Carleton Speer's library.—F. W. H. M.] §

[Abridged from *Proceedings* S.P.R., vol. xi. pp. 69–93.] In his little book on "Spirit Identity" (1879), Mr. Moses had collected some of the most impressive cases of identity, and added some interesting matter as to the subjective side of his experiences. From this paper I cite the following instances:

§ Dr. and Mrs. Speer and I were then sitting regularly almost every evening. A friend of Mrs. Speer's, of whom I had never heard, came and wrote through my hand her name," "A. P. Kirkland." Dr. Speer said, "Is that our old friend?" Then I wrote. "Yes. I came to tell you that I am happy, but I can't impress our friend tonight." The handwriting then changed, and there came communications from others.

With regard to these communications, they were distinct in style, and it is of importance to notice that the handwriting of Miss Kirkland was very similar to her own, which I had never seen.

On an evening in the month of January, 1874, I repeatedly said to Mrs. Speer, "Who is Emily C——.? Her name keeps sounding in my ear." Mrs. Speer replied that she did not know any one of that name. "Yes," I said very emphatically, "there is some one of that name passed over to the world of spirit." She could give me no information, and I was disturbed, in the way in which I always am when such things take place. When the evening paper came in we looked (as we frequently did) at the obituary. I may say that our minds were set on this subject of identity. At our daily sittings fact on fact was given to prove it and to remove any doubts. It became a regular thing for us to receive a message giving such facts as an obituary notice would contain. We therefore looked for them, and we found an announcement of the death of "Emily, widow of the late Captain C—— C——." On a subsequent evening she returned again. Dr. Speer and I had gone out for a walk in the afternoon—I was then staying with him at Dudley Villa, Shanklin, Isle of Wight—and at our séance in the evening came "Emily C—— C——." I inquired what brought her, and her answer was rapped out on the table, "You passed my grave." Here I should explain that at this time I never went near a graveyard but I attracted some spirit, identified afterwards as one whose body lay there. I said, "No, that is impossible; we have been near no graveyard," and Dr. Speer confirmed my impression. The communication, however, was persistent, and we agreed that we would take the same walk the next day. We did so, and at a certain place I had an impulse to climb up and look over a wall, which quite shut out from the view of the ordinary passer-by what was behind it. I climbed up and looked over, and my eye fell at once on the grave of "Emily C—— C——," and on the dates and particulars given to us, all exactly accurate.

Another instance similar in kind—though this is of a personal friend of Mrs. Speer's—is the case of Cecilia Feilden. (See "Spirit Identity," p. 58.) We were then at Shanklin, sitting regularly every evening, when on January 1st, 1874, there came a fresh sound, a little ticking sound in the air, close to Mrs. Speer. We inquired what it might represent, and were told that it indicated the presence of Cecilia Feilden, who had died 17 years ago. We asked why she came, and were told that she had been attracted to her old friend, Mrs. Speer, through me, and in consequence of Dr. Speer's and my presence at her grave at Bonchurch that afternoon. She answered many questions, and finally rapped out, "I must now depart. Adieu." This word Miss Feilden always used at the end of her letters. Mrs. Speer tells me that she seldom concluded a letter otherwise. I had never known her, or heard of her until Dr. Speer pointed out her grave. When we rose from the table we found that a piece of marked paper, which we had put down under the table, had written upon it the words, "passed 17 years."

Again, there is the case of Henry Spratley. We were then the same circle, sitting in the same way, on January 2nd, 1874, and I can aver that not one of us had ever heard of this person. He had lately departed (December, 1873), and it was alleged that he had been brought by the controlling spirit, "Imperator," for purposes of evidence, and in pursuance of a plan intended to break down my persistent skepticism. We had from him messages of the usual type, saying simply who he was, when he was born, and when he died. We found it difficult, I remember, to verify the facts, but in the end Mrs. Speer succeeded in doing so by writing (1) to the Post Office, making a general inquiry, to which no answer came; (2) to the vicar of Maidenhead, with no reply (we afterwards discovered that he was on his holiday); (3) to the "present occupant of Moor Cottage," the address given to us by the spirit; (4) to his nearest surviving representative, who wrote back with some surprise to say that all things were quite true. "My father lived here till he died on December 24th."

Out of a profusion of cases here is one of a different kind. In the year 1880, one Thursday afternoon (date unknown), Dr. and Mrs. Speer and I had dined together, and the party included a lady who had been visiting a connection of Dr. Speer's family in that spring. There she had seen, and been much attracted to, a lovely little girl about seven months old. The child used to be brought in after dinner, and the lady in question grew very fond of her. Between the time of leaving her friends and coming to London the child passed away. It is important to notice that none of these points had ever been mentioned to, or were known by, myself. On the occasion to which I refer, this lady had risen from her seat and was about to place herself in another chair, when I suddenly called out, "Don't sit down on it, don't sit down on it. Little Baby Timmins." None of us knew its first name, and they asked me. I said "Marian; the grandmother has brought it." I then suddenly came out of the trance in which I had been, and in my own natural voice—so different to the voice in which I had been speaking—said, "Mrs. Speer, will you have some coffee?" quite ignorant of all that had passed. We wrote, and then found out a fact unknown to any of us—that the child's name was Marian. I do not put this forth as a complete piece of evidence, for the lady may have heard and forgotten the name.

[Mrs. Speer has described to me this incident, which is remarkable as the only *observed* case where Mr. Moses had a sudden access of unconsciousness during ordinary life, although he himself mentions others.— F. W. H. M.] §

I add a case not included by Mr. Moses in his paper on "The Identity of Spirit." (From *Proceedings* S.P.R., vol. xi. p. 100.) This is a communication made, not by the departed spirit itself, but by friends.

§ *September* 20th, 1881, 10 A.M.—This morning, on waking at 5:54 A.M., I was aware of a spirit who desired to communicate. It turned out to be Mentor, with him B. Franklin, [Epes] Sargent and others. They told me in effect "President [Garfield] is gone. We were with him to the last. He died suddenly, and all our efforts to keep him were unavailing. We labored hard, for his life was of incalculable value to our country. He would have done more to rescue it from shame than any one now left." I asked why it had been deemed necessary to come to me with the news. It was replied that a period of great activity in the spirit world was now being renewed, and that my sympathies with him and with his work, and their own knowledge of me, had inclined them to bring the news. The *Daily News* contained no tidings, though the bulletins were bad. It seemed, on the contrary, that the news of the previous night which they contained was a little more favorable. I walked down to the station feeling convinced that the news would come, but up to 11:30 A.M. could not hear of it. About 12:37 I again went and found that a rumor had reached Bedford. The evening papers—*Globe* and *Echo*—which I purchased at 4:30 P.M. gave me the first mundane information of the event. It is now stated that he died at 10:50 P.M. on the 19th (yesterday). That in English time is 3:50 A.M. of this day (20th) or two hours before I woke and got the message.

I have since learned that the death was sudden, and the remarkable fluctuations are not inconsistent with efforts such as described.

September 21st.—The latest reports fix 10:35, not 10:50 P.M. [or 3:35 A.M. English time] as the exact time of death. §

The instance which I now proceed to recount (from my article in *Proceedings* S.P.R., vol. xi. pp. *96 et seq.*) is in some ways the most remarkable of all, from the series of chances which have been needful in order to establish its veracity. The spirit in question is that of a lady known to me, whom Mr. Moses had met, I believe, once only, and whom I shall call Blanche Abercromby. The publication of the true name was forbidden by the spirit herself.

This lady died on a Sunday afternoon, about twenty-five years ago, at a country house about 200 miles from London. Her death, which was regarded as an event of public interest, was at once telegraphed to London, and appeared in Monday's *Times;* but, of course, on Sunday evening no one in London, save the Press and perhaps the immediate family, was cognizant of the fact. It will be seen that on that evening, near midnight, a communication, purporting to come from her, was made to Mr. Moses at his secluded lodgings in the north of London. The identity was some days later corroborated by a few lines purporting to come directly from her, and to be in her handwriting. There is no reason to suppose that Mr. Moses had ever seen this handwriting. His one known meeting with this lady and her husband had been at a séance—not, of course, of his own—where he had been offended by the strongly expressed disbelief of the husband in the possibility of any such phenomena.

On receiving these messages Mr. Moses seems to have mentioned them to no one, and simply gummed down the pages in his MS. book, marking the book outside "Private Matter." The book when placed in my hands was still thus gummed down. I opened the pages (as instructed by the executors), and was surprised to find a brief letter which, though containing no definite facts, was entirely characteristic of the Blanche Abercromby whom I had known. But although I had received letters from her in life, I had no recollection of her handwriting. I happened to know a son of hers sufficiently well to be able to ask his aid—aid which, I may add, he would have been most unlikely to afford to a stranger. He lent me a letter for comparison. The strong resemblance was at once obvious, but the A. of the surname was made in the letter in a way quite different from that adopted in the automatic script. The son then allowed me to study a long series of letters, reaching down till almost the date of her death. From these it appeared that during the last year of her life she had taken to writing the A (as her husband had always done) in the way in which it was written in the automatic script.

The resemblance of handwriting appeared both to the son and to myself to be incontestable; but as we desired an experienced opinion he allowed me to submit the note book and two letters to Dr. Hodgson.

Readers of the *Proceedings* S.P.R. vol. iii. pp. 201–401, may remember that Dr. Hodgson succeeded in tracing the authorship of the "Koot Hoomi" letters to Madame Blavatsky and to Damodar, by evidence based on a minute analysis of handwriting. As regards the present matter, Dr. Hodgson reported as follows:

§ I have no doubt whatever that the person who wrote the note book writing intended to reproduce the writing of Blanche Abercromby.

RICHARD HODGSON §

The case of Mrs. Piper differs in two important respects from that of W. Stainton Moses or D. D. Home. In the first place no telekinetic phenomena have occurred in connection with her trance-manifestations; and in the second place her supraliminal self shows no traces of any supernormal faculty whatsoever. She passes into a trance, during which her organs of speech or writing are "controlled" by other personalities than the normal waking one. Occasionally either just before or just after the trance, the subliminal self appears to take some control of the organism for a brief interval; but with this exception the personalities that speak or write during her trance claim to be discarnate spirits.

Mrs. Piper's trances may be divided into three stages: (1) Where the dominant controlling personality was known as "Dr. Phinuit" and used the vocal organs almost exclusively, communicating by *trance-utterance*, 1884–91.

(2) Where the communications were made chiefly by automatic writing in the trance under the supervision more particularly of the control known as "George Pelham," or "G. P.," although "Dr. Phinuit" usually communicated also by speech during this period, 1892–96.

(3) Where supervision is alleged to be exercised by Imperator, Doctor, Rector, and others already mentioned in connection with the experiences of Mr. Moses, and where the communications have been mainly by writing, but occasionally also by speech. This last stage began early in 1897.

I proceed now to indicate in further detail the nature of the evidence and the character of the manifestations themselves, and begin by quoting Dr. Hodgson (*Proceedings* S.P.R., vol. xiii. pp. 367–68) a brief statement of some of the historical facts for the case:

§ Mrs. Piper has been giving sittings for a period extending over thirteen [now. 1901, seventeen] years. Very early in her trance history she came under the attention of Professor James, who sent many persons to her as strangers, in most cases making the appointments himself, and in no case giving their names. She came to some extent under my own supervision in 1887, and I also sent many persons to her, in many cases accompanying them and recording the statements made at their sittings, and taking all the care that I could to prevent Mrs. Piper's obtaining any knowledge beforehand of who the sitters were to be. In 1889–90 Mrs. Piper gave a series of sittings in England under the supervision of Dr. Walter Leaf and Mr. Myers and Professor Oliver Lodge, where also the most careful precautions possible were taken to ensure that the sitters went as strangers to Mrs. Piper. Further sittings were supervised by myself in 1890–91 after Mrs. Piper's return to America. Many persons who had sittings in the course of these earlier investigations were convinced that they were actually receiving communications from their "deceased" friends through Mrs. Piper's trance, but although the special investigators were satisfied, from their study of the trance-phenomena themselves and a careful analysis of the detailed records of the sittings, that some supernormal power was involved, there was no definite agreement as to their precise significance. And to myself it seemed that any hypothesis that was offered presented formidable difficulties in the way of its acceptance. In the course of these earlier investigations the communications were given almost entirely through the speech-utterance of the trance-personality known as Phinuit, and even the best of them were apt to include much matter that was irrelevant and unlike the alleged communicators, while there were many indications that Phinuit himself was far from being the kind of person in whom we should be disposed to place implicit credence.

During the years 1892–96 inclusive, I exercised a yet closer supervision of Mrs. Piper's trances than I had done in previous years, continuing to take all the precautions that I could as regards the introduction of persons as strangers. This period was marked by a notable evolution in the quality of the trance results, beginning early in 1892. The character of the manifestations changed with the development of automatic writing in the trance, and with what was alleged to be the continual rendering of active assistance by the communicator whom I have called G. P. [George Pelham]. As a result of this it appeared that communicators were able to express their thoughts directly through the writing by Mrs. Piper's hand, instead of conveying them more dimly and partially through Phinuit as intermediary; and the advice and guidance which they, apparently, received from G. P. enabled them to avoid much of the confusion and irrelevancy so characteristic of the earlier manifestations. §

The following passages are quoted from the report by Professor William James (*Proceedings* S.P.R., vol. vi. pp. 651–59:

§ I made Mrs. Piper's acquaintance in the autumn of 1885. My wife's mother, Mrs. Gibbens, had been told of her by a friend, during the previous summer, and never having seen a medium before, had paid her a visit out of curiosity. She returned with the statement that Mrs. P. had given her a long string of names of members of the family, mostly Christian names, together with facts about the persons mentioned and their relations to each other, the knowledge of which on her part was incomprehensible without supernormal powers. My sister-in-law went the next day, with still better results, as she related them. Amongst other things, the medium had accurately described the circumstances of the writer of a letter which she held against her forehead, after Miss G. had given it to her. The letter was in Italian, and its writer was known to but two persons in this country.

[I may add that on a later occasion my wife and I took another letter from this same person to Mrs. P., who went on to speak of him in a way which identified him unmistakably again. On a third occasion, two years later, my sister-in-law and I being again with Mrs. P., she reverted in her trance to these letters, and then gave us the writer's name, which she said she had not been able to get on the former occasion.]

But to revert to the beginning. I remember playing the *esprit fort* on that occasion before my feminine relatives, and seeking to explain by simple considerations the marvelous character of the facts which they brought back. This did not, however, prevent me from going myself a few days later, in company with my wife, to get a direct personal impression. The names of none of us up to this meeting had been announced to Mrs. P., and Mrs. J. and I were, of course, careful to make no reference to our relatives who had preceded. The medium, however, when entranced, repeated most of the names of "spirits" whom she had announced on the two former occasions and added others. The names came with difficulty, and were only gradually made perfect. My wife's father's name of Gibbens was announced first as Niblin, then as Giblin. A child Herman (whom we had lost the previous year) had his name spelt out as Herrin. I think that in no case were both Christian and surnames given on this visit. But the *facts predicated* of the persons named made it in many instances impossible not to recognize the particular individuals who were talked about. We took particular pains on this occasion to give the Phinuit control no help over his difficulties and to ask no leading questions. In the light of subsequent experience I believe this not to be the best policy. For it often happens, if you give this trance-personage a name or some small fact for the lack of which he is brought to a standstill, that he will then start off with a copious flow of additional talk, containing in itself an abundance of "tests."

My impression after this first visit was, that Mrs. P. was either possessed of supernormal powers, or knew the members of my wife's family by sight and had by some lucky coincidence become acquainted with such a multitude of their domestic circumstances as to produce the startling impression which she did. My later knowledge of her sittings and personal acquaintance with her has led me absolutely to reject the latter explanation, and to believe that she has supernormal powers.

I visited her a dozen times that winter, sometimes alone, sometimes with my wife, once in company with the Rev. M. J. Savage. I sent a large number of persons to her, wishing to get the result of as many *first* sittings as possible. I made appointments myself for most of these people, whose names were in no instance announced to the medium ... My own conviction is not evidence, but it seems fitting to record it. I am persuaded of the medium's honesty, and of the genuineness of her trance; and although at first disposed to think that the 'hits' she made were either lucky coincidences, or the result of knowledge on her part of who the sitter was and of his or her family affairs, I now believe her to be in possession of a power as yet unexplained.

As for the explanation of her trance-phenomena, I have none to offer. The *primâ facie* theory, which is that of spirit-control, is hard to reconcile with the extreme triviality of most of the communications. What real spirit, at last able to revisit his wife on this earth, but would find something better to say than that she had changed the place of his photograph? And yet that is the sort of remark to which the spirits introduced by the mysterious Phinuit are apt to confine themselves. I must admit, however, that Phinuit has other moods. He has several times, when my wife and myself were sitting together with him, suddenly started off on long lectures to us about our inward defects and outward shortcomings, which were very earnest, as well as subtle morally and psychologically, and impressive in a high degree. These discourses, though given in Phinuit's own person, were very different in style from his more usual talk, and probably superior to anything that the medium could produce in the same line in her natural state....

The most remarkable thing about the Phinuit personality seems to me the extraordinary tenacity and minuteness of his memory. The medium has been visited by many hundreds of sitters, half of them, perhaps, being strangers who have come but once. To each Phinuit gives an hourful of disconnected fragments of talk about persons living, dead, or imaginary, and events past, future, or unreal. What normal waking memory could keep this chaotic mass of stuff together? Yet Phinuit does so; for the chances seem to be that if a sitter should go back after years of interval, the medium, when once entranced, would recall the minutest incidents of the earlier interview, and begin by recapitulating much of what had been said. So far as I can discover, Mrs. Piper's waking memory is not remarkable, and the whole constitution of her trance-memory is something which I am at a loss to understand. §

The next passage I quote from the Introduction by myself—*Proceedings* S.P.R., vol. vi. pp. 436–442, to the records of sittings given by Mrs. Piper in England, 1889–90:

§ Mrs. Piper's case has been more or less continuously observed by Professor James and others almost from the date of the first sudden inception of the trance, some five years ago. Mr. Hodgson has been in the habit of bringing acquaintances of his own to Mrs. Piper, without giving their names; and many of these have heard from the trance-utterance facts about their dead relations, which they feel sure that Mrs. Piper could not have known. Mr. Hodgson also had Mr. and Mrs. Piper watched or "shadowed" by private detectives for some weeks, with the view of discovering whether Mr. Piper (who is employed in a large store in Boston), went about inquiring into the affairs of possible "sitters," or whether Mrs. Piper received letters from friends or agents conveying information. This inquiry was pushed pretty closely, but absolutely nothing was discovered which could throw suspicion on Mrs. Piper—who is now aware of the procedure, but has the good sense to recognize the legitimacy—I may say the scientific necessity—of this kind of probation.

It was thus shown that Mrs. Piper made no discoverable attempt to acquire knowledge even about persons whose coming she had reason to expect. Still less could she have been aware of the private concerns of persons brought anonymously to her house at Mr. Hodgson's choice. And a yet further obstacle to such clandestine knowledge was introduced by her removal to England—at our request—in November, 1889. Professor Lodge met her on the Liverpool landing-stage, November 19th, and conducted her to a hotel, where I joined her on November 20th, and escorted her and her children to Cambridge. She stayed first in my house; and I am convinced that she brought with her a very slender knowledge of English affairs or English people. The servant who attended on her and on her two young children was chosen by myself, and was a young woman from a country village whom I had full reason to believe to be both trustworthy and also quite ignorant of my own or my friends' affairs. For the most part I had myself not determined upon the persons whom I would invite to sit with her. I chose these sitters in great measure by chance; several of them were not resident in Cambridge; and (except in one or two cases where anonymity would have been hard to preserve) I brought them to her under false names, sometimes introducing them only when the trance had already begun.

Mrs. Piper while in England was twice in Cambridge, twice in London, and twice in Liverpool, at dates arranged by ourselves; her sitters (almost always introduced under false names) belonged to several quite different social groups, and were frequently unacquainted with each other. Her correspondence was addressed to my care, and I believe that almost every letter which she received was shown to one or other of us. When in London she stayed in lodgings which we selected; when at Liverpool, in Professor Lodge's house; and when at Cambridge, in Professor Sidgwick's or my own. No one of her hosts, or of her hosts' wives, detected any suspicious act or word.

We took great pains to avoid giving information in talk; and a more complete security is to be found in the fact that we were ourselves ignorant of many of the facts given as to our friends' relations, etc. As regards my own affairs, I have not thought it worth while to cite *in extenso* such statements as might possibly have been got up beforehand; since Mrs. Piper of course knew that I should be one of her sitters. Such facts as that I once had an aunt, "Cordelia Marshall, more commonly called Corrie," might have been learnt—though I do not think that they were learnt—from printed or other sources. But I do not think that any larger proportion of such accessible facts was given to me than to an average sitter, previously unknown; nor were there any of those subtler points which could so easily have been made by dint of scrutiny of my books or papers. On the other hand, in my case, as in the case of several other sitters, there were messages purporting to come from a friend who had been dead many years, and mentioning circumstances which I believe that it would have been quite impossible for Mrs. Piper to have discovered.

I am also acquainted with some of the facts given to other sitters, and suppressed as too intimate, or as involving secrets not the property of the sitter alone. I may say that, so far as my own personal conviction goes, the utterance of one or two of these facts is even more conclusive of supernormal knowledge than the correct statement of dozens of names of relations, etc., which the sitter had no personal motive for concealing.

On the whole, I believe that all observers, both in America and in

England, who have seen enough of Mrs. Piper in both states to be able to form a judgment, will agree in affirming (1) that many of the facts given could not have been learned even by a skilled detective; (2) that to learn others of them, although possible, would have needed an expenditure of money as well as of time which it seems impossible to suppose that Mrs. Piper could have met; and (3) that her conduct has never given any ground whatever for supposing her capable of fraud or trickery. Few persons have been so long and so carefully observed; and she has left on all observers the impression of thorough uprightness, candor, and honesty. §

More important, as regards the question of personal identity, is the series of sittings which formed the second stage of Mrs. Piper's trance history, in the years 1892–96, of which a detailed account is given in *Proceedings* S.P.R., vol. xiii. pp. 284–582 and vol. xiv. pp. 6–49, where the chief communicator or intermediary was G. P. This G. P., whose name (although, of course, well known to many persons) has been altered for publication into "George Pelham," was a young man of great ability, mainly occupied in literary pursuits. Although born an American citizen, he was a member of a noble English family. I never met him, but I have the good fortune to include a number of his friends among my own, and with several of these I have been privileged to hold intimate conversation on the nature of the communications which they received. I have thus heard of many significant utterances of G. P.'s, which are held too private for print; and I have myself been present at sittings where G. P. manifested. [The following account is quoted from the beginning of the "History of the G. P. Communications," given by Dr. Hodgson in *Proceedings* S.P.R., vol. xiii. pp. 295–335.]

§ G. P. met his death accidentally, and probably instantaneously, by a fall in New York in February, 1892, at the age of thirty-two years. He was a lawyer by training, but had devoted himself chiefly to literature and philosophy, and had published two books which received the highest praise from competent authorities. He had resided for many years in Boston or its vicinity, but for three years preceding his death had been living in New York in bachelor apartments. He was an Associate of our Society, his interest in which was explicable rather by an intellectual openness and fearlessness characteristic of him than by any tendency to believe in supernormal phenomena. He was in a sense well known to me personally, but chiefly on this intellectual side; the bond between us was not that of an old, intimate, and if I may so speak, emotional friendship. We had several long talks together on philosophic subjects, and one very long discussion, probably at least two years before his death, on the possibility of a "future life." In this he maintained that in accordance with a fundamental philosophic theory which we both accepted, a "future life" was not only incredible, but inconceivable; and I maintained that it was at least conceivable. At the conclusion of the discussion he admitted that a future life was conceivable, but he did not accept its credibility, and vowed that if he should die before I did, and found himself "still existing," he would "make things lively" in the effort to reveal the fact of his continued existence.

I knew of G. P.'s death within a day or two of its occurrence, and was present at several sittings with Mrs. Piper in the course of the following few weeks, but no allusion was made to G. P. On March 22nd, 1892, between four and five weeks after G. P.'s death, I accompanied Mr. John Hart [not the real name], who had been an old intimate friend of his, to a sitting.[1] I understood from Mr. Hart that he had some articles with him to be used as tests, but he gave me no further information than this, though I surmised that the articles might have belonged to G. P. The appointment for the sitting was made by myself, and of course Mr. Hart's real name was not mentioned to Mrs. Piper.

[Questions from the sitters are written in parentheses].

The sitting began by some remarks of Phinuit concerning the sitter, . . . The influences are confusing. (I have something else here) [giving watch]. Yes. George. Ha . . . Har . . . Hart. [All correct. The name of my uncle George is in the back of the watch. When he died, my uncle Albert wore it. I did not remember that the name was engraved on the inner case of the watch.—J. H.]

L a l . . . lal . . . Albert . . . is that the way you pronounce it? He is very fond of you. He says he is not d e d . . . d e a d. He will see you again. He is glad to see you. He is very fond of you. [Lal was a pet name my father sometimes called my uncle Albert.—J. H.] . . . There is another George

[1] Owing to the personal character of many of the incidents referred to in the G. P. communications, I have in nearly all cases substituted other names for the real ones. It has been suggested that the important witnesses in connection with the G. P. evidence may have been in collusion with Mrs. Piper. The absurdity of this suggestion would be at once apparent if their real names were given, but since the only real full names given of actual sitters with G. P. are those of Professors C. Eliot Norton and James M. Peirce, of Harvard University, who are referred to chiefly as cases of being recognized by the communicating G. P. as personally known to him, I state concerning the others that I know personally all but two of the G. P. sitters, and most of them intimately, that they belong to the most cultivated and responsible class in the United States, and that it would be as absurd to suppose any collusion between them and Mrs. Piper as to suppose that the members of the Council of the S.P.R. were in collusion with her. Many of them are also known personally to Mr. Myers—R. H.

who wants to speak to you. How many Georges are there about you any way?

The rest of the sitting, until almost the close, was occupied by statements from G. P., Phinuit acting as intermediary. George Pelham's real name was given in full, also the names, both Christian and surname, of several of his most intimate friends, including the name of the sitter.

Moreover, incidents were referred to which were unknown to the sitter or myself.

One of the pair of studs which J. H. was wearing was given to Phinuit. . . . "(Who gave them to me?) That's mine. I gave you that part of it. I sent that to you. (When?) Before I came here. That's mine. Mother gave you that. (No.) Well, father then, father and mother together. You got those after I passed out. Mother took them. Gave them to father, and father gave them to you. I want you to keep them. I will them to you." Mr. Hart notes: "The studs were sent to me by Mr. Pelham as a remembrance of his son. I knew at the time that they had been taken from G.'s body, and afterwards ascertained that his step-mother had taken them from the body and suggested that they would do to send to me, I having previously written to ask that some little memento be sent to me."

James and Mary [Mr. and Mrs.] Howard were mentioned with strongly personal specific references, and in connection with Mrs. Howard came the name Katharine. "Tell her, she'll know. I will solve the problems, Katharine." Mr. Hart notes: "This had no special significance for me at the time, though I was aware that Katharine, the daughter of Jim Howard, was known to George, who used to live with the Howards. On the day following the sitting I gave Mr. Howard a detailed account of the sitting. These words, 'I will solve the problems, Katharine,' impressed him more than anything else, and at the close of my account he related that George, when he had last stayed with them, had talked frequently with Katharine (a girl of fifteen years of age) upon such subjects as Time, Space, God, Eternity, and pointed out to her how unsatisfactory the commonly accepted solutions were. He added that some time he would solve the problems, and let her know, using almost the very words of the communication made at the sitting." Mr. Hart added that he was entirely unaware of these circumstances. I was myself unaware of them, and was not at that time acquainted with the Howards, and in fact nearly every statement made at the sitting, during which I was the note-taker, concerned matters of which I was absolutely ignorant.

[Dr. Hodgson's Report continues as follows:]

It so happened that appointments had been made for other sitters, and it was nearly three weeks before a special opportunity was given for further communication from G. P., at a sitting when Mr. and Mrs. James Howard were present alone. [Mr. Howard, who is, by the way, a well-known and able man of professorial status, was a definite disbeliever in a future life until G. P. convinced him.]

The following passages are from Mr. Howard's notes taken during the sitting, and may serve to suggest to some extent the freedom with which the conversation was carried on. All the references to persons and incidents are correct.

G. P.: Jim, is that you? Speak to me quick. I am not dead. Don't think me dead. I'm awfully glad to see you. Can't you see me? Don't you hear me? Give my love to my father and tell him I want to see him. I am happy here, and more so since I find I can communicate with you. I pity those people who can't speak . . . I want you to know I think of you still. I spoke to John about some letters. I left things terribly mixed, my books and my papers; you will forgive me for this, won't you? . . .

(What do you do, George, where you are?)

I am scarcely able to do anything yet; I am just awakened to the reality of life after death. It was like darkness, I could not distingush anything at first. Darkest hours just before dawn, you know that, Jim. I was puzzled, confused. Shall have an occupation soon. Now I can see you, my friends. I can hear you speak. Your voice, Jim, I can distinguish with your accent and articulation, but it sounds like a big bass drum. Mine would sound to you like the faintest whisper.

(Our conversation then is something like telephoning?)

Yes.

(By long distance telephone.)

[G. P. laughs.]

(Were you not surprised to find yourself living?)

Perfectly so. Greatly surprised. I did not believe in a future life. It was beyond my reasoning powers. Now it is as clear to me as daylight. We have an astral facsimile of the material body. . . . Jim, what are you writing now?

[G. P. when living would probably have jeered at the associations of the word "astral."—R. H.]

(Nothing of any importance.)

Why don't you write about this?

(I should like to, but the expression of my opinions would be nothing. I must have facts.)

These I will give to you and to Hodgson if he is still interested in these things.

(Will people know about this possibility of communication?)

They are sure to in the end. It is only a question of time when people in the material body will know all about it, and every one will be able to communicate. . . . I want all the fellows to know about me. . . . §

The following is from Dr. Hodgson's report in *Proceedings* S.P.R., vol. xiii. pp. 353–57.

§ I close this section of my Report by a brief account of the case of the friend whom I have called Mr. John Hart, to whom in the first instance G. P. manifested, and who himself died in Naples on May 2nd, 1895. I had not been having regular series of sittings at this time, and heard incidentally on May 3rd that a cablegram had been received by a relative announcing the death of Hart. My assistant, Miss Edmunds, went out to Mrs. Piper at my request to arrange a sitting for me the next day, May 4th, and to say that it was extremely important that I must have the sitting. I did not tell Miss Edmunds the reason, and she made a totally erroneous conjecture concerning it. The anouncement of the death, how-ever, with the place and cause of death (inflammation of the heart), appeared in a Boston evening paper on May 3rd. At the sitting on May 4th, after a few words from Phinuit, G. P. wrote and gave several mes-sages from friends, and then asked what he could do for me. I replied that I had something for him to do, but could not tell him what it was. He made a brief reference to his father and mother, and then to a friend of my own, and then came the following: [Dr. Hodgson is referred to as "H"]

Hold, H. See all of these people bringing a gentleman. . . .

I think I knew him. Come here and listen, H. He has been here before and I have seen him since I passed out. (Who is it?) John. "Do you see me, H.?" He says this. (No.) "What about my health? Oh, George, I am here, do not go away from me," . . . not to you, H., to me. (Yes, I understand.) "I thought I should see you once more before I came here." (What is the full name?) John H. (Give me the second name in full.) Did you speak? (Write the second name in full.) Hart. (That's right, Hart, old fellow.) "Will you listen to me, Hodg . . . [Much excitement in hand, and letters jumbled over. G. P. writing throughout, but at times apparently much perturbation introduced.] George knew I was here and met me, but I was too weak to come here and talk, H." . . . Yes, H., but the dear old fellow is short-breathed. . . . "I expected to see you before I came here, H. (Yes, I hoped to have met you in the body again) but you see I was failing. How are you?" . . . Will they send my body on to New York? (I don't know.) I hope they will. They are now talking about it."

[I learned later that the desirability of taking the body to America was discussed.]

When I asked, "Why didn't George tell me to begin with?" he replied, "Because I told him to let me come and tell myself." This was like Hart, and so was the statement quoted above that it was he who brought G. P. first.

At this sitting, and several also in the following week, during which the confusion continued, a knowledge was shown of various matters known to me which were specially suggestive of Hart, references to friends and relatives, presents which he had given to me, jokes about cigars, magazines which he had entrusted to me just before he went to Europe three years previously, etc., but of course I was anxious to obtain information concerning events in Europe of which I was entirely ignorant, especially any that occurred just before his death; and have such on record, but have not yet succeeded in discovering how much correct statement they include. Between the first and second sitting it occurred to me that the announcement of his being there to communicate was "led up to" by G. P., and at the second sitting, when Hart wrote part of the time himself, I said, "I suppose last time you thought I took your coming very coolly." The hand wrote excitedly: "You seemed very inconsiderate to what you used to do." I explained that I had heard of his death by a cablegram which had been received by his brother-in-law. He then wrote the name of the brother of his sister's husband. I said no, "your wife's brother." . . .

In June and July a friend of mine was having a series of sittings, and Hart sent a message to me through him; he was becoming clearer, and wished to communicate. There were no opportunities for any further series of sittings, however, and Mrs. Piper stopped sitting for her summer rest, and I visited England later. Few sittings were given in the winter of 1895–6 owing to Mrs. Piper's ill-health. Hart gave brief messages on several occasions; said that he wanted to follow in "G. P.'s tracks," and seemed somewhat aggrieved, so to speak, because he did not have the same opportunity as had been afforded to G. P. Thus, on January 22nd, 1896:

. . . What in the world is the reason you never call for me? I am not sleeping. I wish to help you in identifying myself . . . I am a good deal better now. (You were confused at first.) Very, but I did not really understand how confused I was. It is more so, I am more so when I try to speak to you. I understand now why George spelled his words to me. [Several sentences, even of ordinary words, were spelt out by Phinuit from G. P. at his first appearance, to Hart.]

He became clearer later on, and purported to take part in an inquiry I was making concerning a person's whereabouts in Mexico. It was during this time that Miss Warner had her two sittings, January 6th and 7th, 1897. She remarked to me during the sitting of January 7th that Hart knew one of her brothers, Charlie, and that they went to the Azores together. [She knew nothing more about their trip than that the boat was driven on the rocks and they watched her break up.] I asked Phinuit if he or G. P. could get Hart. Shortly afterwards G. P. wrote, and after a short conversation with the sitter came the following:

Did you have a brother Jack, Hart asks. (Yes.)

[For Hart.] I am here. George, tell her I see her and I long to ask her brother if he recalls the storm we experienced.

(I know he does. I've heard him speak of it.)

Good, and ask him if he still has the stick like mine. Take the pipe, old chap, I do not wish it. Hear you? (R. H.: Yes, it may be the one he gave me) and I have it in my mind. A memento. He ought to have it. [Hart gave me a pipe. It is not clear whether the reference is to this, or to one connected with sitter's brother. R. H.]

We went to a queer little hotel, at a little hotel together. Charlie had a headache from hunger. We were almost starved when we got there, the food was bad, the food was so bad, poor. I am content here, quite. Do you ever see me as I really am? (No. I don't see you at all.) Not at all. I do, H. Hear Hart say have a smoke, anything for relief. Ask him [Charlie] about this for me. Hungry. (R. H.: He's still talking about Charlie and their experiences together?) Yes, H. He is.

(Tell some more.) We went up to the hotel and ask him if he recalls the laugh we had after we got up to our room. Give him my love.

(What did you laugh about?) because of the dirt, etc. ... very amusing. ... Give [Charles] my love and do not forget about the stick."

Charley Warner was then in California, and in reply to inquiries he wrote on February 2nd, 1897:

J. H. and myself once were hove to on the North Atlantic for about three days during a severe storm. At another time we were at Horta, Fayal Island, and watched our vessel drag ashore and break up on account of a very bad storm, or hurricane. J. H. had a very serviceable stick. As I remember it, a stout little blade dropped out of the ferrule. I never had one like it that I can remember. He thought highly of it and advised me to get one like it. I don't remember anything about a pipe. What he says about the queer little hotel is all true; I don't remember that I had a headache, but we were hungry. J. H. was extremely amused about something at that hotel and we had a hearty laugh. It was connected with dirt. §

Not least important as regards the question of identity are some of the communications purporting to come from young children. I give first a synopsis of the chief points in connection with the twin children, Margaret and Ruthie, of Dr. A. B. Thaw. From Dr. Hodgson's report in *Proceedings* S.P.R., vol. xiii. pp. 384–5.

§ ... One of these, Margaret, died a year before their first sitting at the age of six months, and the other, Ruthie, died three months before their first sitting at the age of fifteen months. The communications concerning these children were given almost entirely by Phinuit, who had, however, some difficulty with the names. At the first sitting several attempts were made before the name Margaret was given clearly. Trouble with teeth was mentioned in connection with the children. . . . Margaret was teething when she died. Phinuit also said that one of the children wanted baby's beads. Margaret used to play with a necklace of beads belonging to her older sister living. And referring to Margaret, Phinuit said that she had some flowers in her hand, that "she liked them and took them with her." Mrs. Thaw had placed three little flowers in Margaret's hand after her death. Phinuit got much more in connection with Ruthie, whose first appearance seemed to be accompanied by a recurrence of associations connected with the trouble that caused her death, dysentery and sore throat. Phinuit indicated the locality and the distress, and Ruthie's dislike of "the powder." Bismuth was given through the entire illness of two weeks and was always given with trouble. Phinuit spoke of Ruthie as having light golden hair, afterwards adding curly—correct—but called her a boy. The living Ruthie was very generally mistaken for a boy, but not, of course, by the Thaws. Yet Phinuit had much difficulty in getting the name, and failed to get nearer than Ethie, and the sitters told him it began with R. Phinuit said that she had not learned to talk, but later on he got the name Ruth-ie correctly. He remarked that she only said papa and mamma. Other words that the living Ruthie said were given in later sittings. Phinuit described her as wanting to see the stars. For two or three months before her death Ruthie was fond of pointing at the stars through the window. At the beginning of the sitting Phinuit said she put her hand on Dr. Thaw's head, and afterwards described her as wanting to pat his face, actions which were characteristic of the living Ruthie towards Dr. Thaw. Similarly she wanted to hear the tick tick (watch) in connection with her uncle Alack, and it was he who chiefly used to hold the watch for her to hear it. And another characteristic action was reproduced in connection with Mr. Melvin W.; Phinuit said she wanted him to wave the hand in a certain way to Mr. W., and the living

Ruthie waved her hand in that way to Mr. W., and to him only. Reference was also made to her picture, and Mrs. Thaw was painting a picture of Ruthie when she was taken ill. In later sittings Phinuit described her as saying other words, *baby, pretty, Bettie,* and *pussie,* with the accent used by Ruthie when living. These were the only words besides the *papa* and *mamma* mentioned before, used by Ruthie when living. The first time Mrs. Thaw wore fur at a sitting, the hand stroked it, and Phinuit whispered "pussie" as Ruthie living used to do. Two or three times there seemed to be a direct control of the voice by Ruthie who took the place of Phinuit. The first time she whispered *pttee* and *pssee* (pretty and pussie) and the second time *pttee* only, the words being many times repeated. This second occasion was connected with rather a striking incident. Mrs. Piper was visiting the Thaws in New York, and they took her up the river Hudson to their country house and had a sitting on the afternoon of the day of their arrival. I was taking notes, sitting slightly to one side and partly behind Mrs. Piper, while Dr. and Mrs. Thaw were sitting in front of her, with their heads somewhat bowed. Phinuit apparently "left" and his place was taken by Ruthie, who began whispering *pttee pttee.* The hand rose and turned somewhat diagonally and extended the forefinger and pointed towards a picture on the far side of the room. The Thaws did not see this action until I drew their attention to it, when they looked up, and followed the direction of the pointing. The hand then trembled and sank. Dr. Thaw noted: "During the last month of Ruthie's life it was a regular morning custom to bring her to the room in which this sitting was held—our bedroom—and she would always point, as hand did in sitting, with *one* finger (unusual with a baby) and say 'pt-tee, pt-tee,' just as in sitting. This little incident had not been in either sitter's conscious mind since baby's death six months before. Mrs. Piper had never been in that room until the actual time of sitting. There were many other pictures in the room, two of which Mrs. Piper's hand could have pointed at more easily than the particular one always noticed by the baby." §

I quote here an account of communications coming from the child of Mrs. Katherine Paine Sutton. From *Proceedings* S.P.R., vol. xiii. pp. 386–9.

§ In the two sittings which Mrs. Sutton had in December, 1893 she had articles which had been used by her recently deceased little girl Katherine. Katherine had "lovely curls," mentioned by Phinuit, and also called for the "tick-tick," but Phinuit added correctly that she called it "the clock," and the word *babee* was given correctly, as Ruthie also used to pronounce it. Apparently the only incorrect statement purporting to come from the child was that she called a lady (Mrs. C., a friend of Mrs. Sutton, who purported to be present in "spirit," bringing the child, and whose Christian name and surname were given correctly by Phinuit) *Auntie*. The lady was not her aunt. The statements made came through Phinuit. Concerning a silver medal it was said that she wanted to bite it, and concerning a string of buttons that she wanted to put them in her mouth. both correct. Phinuit said that she had no sore throat any more, and that she kept showing him her tongue. Katherine living had sore throat and her tongue was paralyzed. She gave correctly the name by which she called herself, *Kakie*, the name *Dodo* by which she called her brother George, the name *Bagie* by which she called a living sister, Margaret, and the name Eleanor, of another living sister for whom she called much in her last illness. She also asked for Dinah, this being the name of an old rag-doll. She said truly that Dodo used to march with her, "He put me way up." She wanted to go to "wide horsey"—as the living Katherine had pleaded all through her illness, and to be taken "to see the mooley-cow," the name by which the living Katherine called the cow, which she was taken almost daily to see. She said she had "the pretty white flowers you put on me," and Phinuit described lilies of the valley, which were the flowers that had been placed in the casket. She said she was happy with grandma—Mrs. Sutton's mother had been dead many years—and later on wanted to send her love to her grandma and also apparently to her great grandma who was referred to as *Marmie*. She had a grandmother and also a great-grandmother then living, and *Marmie* was the name by which Mr. and Mrs. Sutton spoke of the great-grandmother, but Katherine always called her *Grammie*. She also referred to two songs she used to sing: "Bye-bye, O baby bye," and "Row Row, my song." This "Row Row" song was sung frequently by Katherine during her illness, and was the last sung by her when living, and she asked Mr. and Mrs. Sutton to sing it at the sitting. They sang the first four lines, and the voice—presumably still "controlled" by Phinuit in imitation of Katherine—sang with them. Phinuit then hushed the sitters, and the voice sang the remaining four lines [alone]. It is, of course, a familiar child's song. At the second sitting a fortnight later, the voice sang all eight lines alone, then asked Mrs. Sutton to sing it with her, as she did, and then at Mrs. Sutton's request also sang with her the other song "Bye-bye," precisely, according to Mrs. Sutton, as the living Katherine sang it. Mr. Sutton, who was present at the first sitting, did not attend the second sitting, and he was asked for immediately after this singing, which came at the beginning of the sitting. "Kakie wants papa." This was a very characteristic expression. There were indications suggesting a knowledge of what was going on in Mrs. Sutton's family. At the first sitting Katherine said she went "to see horsey" every day. The sitters had been staying in the country with Mr. Sutton's parents and had been driving frequently. Margaret, a living sister, was still there, and driving daily. Mrs. Sutton, who has had many psychical experiences herself in seeing the "apparitions" of "deceased" persons (see p. 484) had "seen Kakie" during that visit to Mr. Sutton's parents. At the second sitting Katherine said that she saw Bagie with grandma, and that she played with Eleanor every day and liked the little bed. A lady had recently lent Eleanor a doll's bed, but Mrs. Sutton had not associated this with Kakie. There were incidents at both sittings which showed associations that seemed to be in the mind of the child, which did not awaken the corresponding associations in the minds of the sitters even when the contemporary notes to the sittings were made. Thus in the first sitting she asked for "horsey." Mrs. Sutton gave a little toy horse with which the child had played during her illness. But the child said "big horsey, not this little one," and Mrs. Sutton surmised that she referred to another toy cart-horse that she used to like. At the second sitting came "Kakie wants the horse," and the little horse was again given.

"No, that is not the one. The big horse—so big. [Phinuit shows how large.] Eleanor's horse. Eleanor used to put it in Kakie's lap. She loved that horsey."

These additional particulars, which were true, then reminded Mrs. Sutton of the horse referred to, which was packed away in another city, and which had not occurred to the mind of Mrs. Sutton in connection with Kakie. Similarly at the first sitting she asked two or three times for "the little book." The sitter noted that she liked a linen picture-book. But the remarks made at her second sitting suggest that the little book in the child's mind was not this one. "Kakie wants the little bit of a book mamma read by her bedside, with the pretty bright things hanging from it—mamma put it in her hands—the last thing she remembers." Mrs. Sutton states that this was a little prayer-book with a cross and other symbols in silver attached to ribbons for marking the places, and that it was sent to her by a friend after Kakie had ceased to know any one except perhaps for a passing moment. Mrs. Sutton read it when Kakie seemed unconscious, and *after Kakie's death* placed it in her hands to prevent the blood settling in the nails. She adds later that Mrs. Piper's hands, when the book was asked for at the sitting, were put into the same position as Kakie's.

Another book was mentioned at the second sitting which apparently was the one *Mrs. Sutton* thought of at the first sitting. "Kakie wants the book with red letters and pictures of animals." Correct description.

On one occasion Mrs. Sutton "saw her for a moment standing at the table trying to reach a spool" of silk; and at the same moment Phinuit reached for it, saying: "She wants that, she and Eleanor used to play with. She calls it Eleanor's." This was all true, but the sitter "had not connected it with Eleanor in her thoughts." Another incident I quote here just as it is given in the detailed report of the sitting.

[Kakie asks for her ball. I gave it to Phinuit, who tries to find what she wants to do with it.]

"Bite it? Toss it? Roll it? Throw it?"

[No, she wants a string. Mrs. H. gave him a string. He tries to tie it around the ball.] [A little red wooden ball with a hole through it. The ball had a string through it when she used to play with it.]

"No, that is not right—through it."

"There, there, be a good little girl. Don't cry. Don't be impatient. You want your mamma to see how you do it, so she will know it is you, don't you, dear? Old man will do it for her."

[He put the string through, held it up, and hit it with the finger, making it swing.]

"That is it, is it not, darling? Nice little girl as ever was."

[While she was sick it was her great delight to have me hold the string and let her hit the little red ball with her finger or spoon. She made the motions as if doing it, after she became unconscious.] §

I now cite a few instances of prophecies given through Mrs. Piper.

The following is from Miss W.'s report (made from contemporary notes) of sittings with Mrs. Piper, *Proceedings* S.P.R., val. viii. p. 34.

§ In the spring of 1888, an acquaintance, S., was suffering torturing disease. There was no hope of relief, and only distant prospect of release. A consultation of physicians predicted continued physical suffering and probably mental decay, continuing perhaps through a series of years. S.'s daughter, worn with anxiety and care, was in danger of breaking in health. "How can I get her away for a little rest?" I asked Dr. Phinuit, May 24, 1888. "She will not leave her father," was his reply, "but his suffering is not for long. The doctors are wrong about that. There will be a change soon, and he will pass out of the body before the summer is over." His death occurred in June, 1888.

E. G. W. §

See *Proceedings* S.P.R., vol. xiii. pp. 447–449.

At a sitting with Mrs. Piper on March 7, 1892, the death of her uncle David was foretold to Miss Macleod. Her contemporary note of the statement was: "David will die soon."

She wrote on March 27, 1893:

"My uncle David, whose death Mrs. Piper predicted at the sitting which I had with her on March 7, 1892, died at Chicago on last Tuesday, the 21st of March. As far as I know, his health was perfectly good at the time of the sitting."

From Dr. Hodgson's account of the sittings of Dr. A. B. Thaw with Mrs. Piper, *Proceedings* S.P.R., vol. xiii. p. 352.

§ Several minor prophecies proved correct; one important prophecy concerning the success of certain machines was wrong as to time, as well as other circumstances connected with them; but another concerning the death of a brother, who was never present at a sitting, was right. This brother was a chronic invalid with asthma. At the sitting of May 10th, 1892, Phinuit said that his kidneys were out of order, and it was discovered for the first time that he had kidney disease on a careful medical examination made two weeks later. At the same sitting Phinuit said that he would die "within six months or a year," and, in reply to the question how, said, "He's going to sleep, and when he wakes he'll be in the spirit. Heart will stop." On May 22nd, the time was given as "six months or a little less." He died in sleep, of heart failure, on the 3rd of the following September. §

The accounts here quoted are perhaps sufficient to illustrate that theory of possession which seems especially to apply to the case of Mrs. Piper, according to which her bodily organism is controlled by discarnate spirits who attempt to prove their identity by reproducing recollections of their earthly lives.

In the case of Mr. Moses the control of the mind or body by discarnate spirits seemed to vary in degree at different times, and the medium's own preconceptions seemed to form an important factor in the communications he received, and it is obvious that in Mrs. Piper's case also the control must be limited by the idiosyncrasies of the medium. But we must continually bear in mind the impossibility of distinguishing the different elements that may enter into so complex a phenomenon. I have spoken of parallel series of manifestations indicating on the one hand the powers of the subliminal self, which culminate in ecstasy, and on the other the agency of discarnate spirits, leading on to possession. But the phenomena are not, in fact, so simply arranged. It seems probable that when a spirit can control a sensitive's organism, the sensitive's own subliminal self may be able to do the same. The transparency which renders the one possession possible facilitates also the other. This may be one reason for the admixture seen in most trance utterances of elements which come from the sensitive's own mind with elements inspired from without. To this source of confusion must be added the influence of the sensitive's supraliminal self also, whose habits of thought and turns of speech must needs appear whenever use is made of the brain centers which that supraliminal self habitually controls. Further, we cannot draw a clear line between the influence of the organism itself—as already moulded by its own indwelling spirit—and the continuing influence of that spirit, not altogether separated from the organism. That is to say, the sensitive's own previous ideas may go on developing themselves during the trance, which may thus be incomplete. The result may be a kind of mixed telepathy between the sitter, the sensitive's spirit, and the extraneous spirit. I believe that sometimes during one and the same access of trance all these elements are in turn apparent; and a long familiarity with the sensitive will be needed if we would disentangle the intermingled threads.

There is much additional evidence yet to be published that has come through Mrs. Piper during the last few years in support of the claim that recently deceased persons are communicating, besides instances of failures and confusion which we must doubtless continue to expect under the conditions apparently involved in the communications. It seems from our experience thus far that the most valuable evidence we can hope to obtain of personal identity is likely to come from spirits who have recently passed over with all their inexperience of that other world, but it may be that these are aided in their task by more remote spirits whose identity we can neither prove nor disprove. It is perhaps more reasonable to suppose that there is such supervision—if we are in actual communication with a spiritual world at all—than to think that the great spirits of the past take no abiding interest in the communication of that spiritual world with ours.

We must now try to form some more definite idea—based not on preconceived theories but on our actual observation of trances—of the processes of possession; though it is hardly necessary to say that the most adequate conception that we can reach at present must be restricted and distorted by the limitations of our own material existence, and can only be expressed by the help of crude analogies.

Let us try to realize what kind of feat it is which we are expecting the disembodied spirit to achieve. Such language, I know, again suggests the medicine-man's wigwam rather than the study of the white philosopher.

In dealing with matters which lie outside human experience, our only clue is some attempt at *continuity* with what we already know. We cannot, for instance, form independently a reliable conception of life in an unseen world. That conception has never yet been fairly faced from the standpoint of our modern ideas of continuity, conservation, evolution. The main notions that have been framed of such survival have been framed first by savages and then by philosophers. To the man of science the question has never yet assumed enough of actuality to induce him to consider it with scientific care. He has contented himself, like the mass of mankind, with some traditional theory, some emotional preference for some such picture as seems to him satisfying and exalted. Yet he knows well that this subjective principle of choice has led in history to the acceptance of many a dogma which to more civilized perceptions seems in the last degree blasphemous and cruel.

The savage, I say, made his own picture first. And he at any rate dimly felt after a principle of continuity; although he applied it in crudest fashion. Yet the happy hunting-ground and the faithful dog were conceptions not more arbitrary and unscientific than that eternal and unimaginable worship *in vacuo* which more accredited teachers have proclaimed. And, passing on to modern philosophic conceptions, one may say that where the savage assumed *too little* difference between the material and the spiritual world the philosopher has assumed *too much*. He has regarded the gulf as too unbridgeable; he has taken for granted too clean a sweep of earthly modes of thought. Trying to shake off time, space, and definite form, he has attempted to transport himself too magically to what may be in reality an immensely distant goal.

Have we new philosophical conceptions solid enough to withstand the impact of even a small mass of actual evidence? Have our notions of the dignified and undignified in nature—the steady, circular motion of the planets, for instance, as opposed to the irregular and elliptical—guided us in the discovery of truth? Would not Aristotle, divinizing the fixed stars by reason of their very remoteness, have thought it undignified to suppose them compacted of the same elements as the stones under his feet? May not disembodied souls, like stars, be of a make rather closer to our own than we have been wont to imagine?

What, then, is to be our conception of identity prolonged beyond the tomb? In earth-life the actual body, in itself but a subordinate element in our thought of our friend, did yet by its physical continuity override as a symbol of identity all lapses of memory, all changes of the character within. Yet it was memory and character, the stored impressions upon which he reacted, and his specific mode of reaction, which made our veritable friend. How much of memory, how much of character, must he preserve for our recognition?

Do we ask that either he or we should remember always, or should remember all? Do we ask that his memory should be expanded into omniscience and his character elevated into divinity? And, whatever heights he may attain, do we demand that he should reveal to us? Are the limitations of our material world no barrier to him?

It is safest to fall back for the present upon the few points which these communications do seem to indicate. The spirit, then, is holding converse with a living man, located in a certain place at a certain moment, and animated by certain thoughts and emotions. The spirit (to which I must give a neuter pronoun for greater clearness) in some cases can find and follow the man as it pleases. It is therefore in some way cognizant of space, although not conditioned by space. Its mastery of space may perhaps bear somewhat the same relation to our eyesight as our eyesight bears to the gropings of the blind. Similarly, the spirit appears to be partly cognizant of our *time,* although not wholly conditioned thereby. It is apt to see as *present* both certain things which appear to us as past and certain things which appear to us as future.

Once more, the spirit is at least partly conscious of the thought and emotions of its earthly friend, so far as directed towards itself; and this not only when the friend is in the presence of the sensitive, but also (as G. P. has repeatedly shown) when the friend is at home and living his ordinary life.

Lastly, it seems as though the spirit had some occasional glimpses of material fact upon the earth (as the contents of drawers and the like), not manifestly proceeding through any living mind. I do not, however, recall any clear evidence of a spirit's perception of material facts which provably have never been known to any incarnate mind whatever.

Accepting this, then, for argument's sake, as the normal condition of a spirit in reference to human things, what process must it attempt if it wishes to communicate with living men? That it *will* wish to communicate seems probable enough, if it retains not only memory of the loves of earth, but actual fresh consciousness of loving emotion directed towards it after death.

Seeking then for some open avenue, it discerns something which corresponds (in G. P.'s phrase) to a *light*—a glimmer of translucency in the confused darkness of our material world. This "light" indicates a *sensitive* —a human organism so constituted that a spirit can temporarily *inform* or *control* it, not necessarily interrupting the stream of the sensitive's ordinary consciousness; perhaps using a hand only, or perhaps, as in Mrs. Piper's case, using voice as well as hand, and occupying all the sensitive's channels of self-manifestation. The difficulties which must be inherent in such an act of control are thus described by Dr. Hodgson:

"If, indeed, each one of us is a spirit that survives the death of the fleshly organism, there are certain suppositions that I think we may not unreasonably make concerning the ability of the discarnate spirit to communicate with those yet incarnate. Even under the best of conditions for communication—which I am supposing for the nonce to be possible—it may be that the aptitude for communicating clearly may be as rare as the gifts that make a great artist, or a great mathematician, or a great philosopher. Again, it may well be that, owing to the change connected with death itself, the spirit may at first be much confused, and such confusion may last for a long time; and even after the spirit has become accustomed to its new environment, it is not an unreasonable supposition that if it came into some such relation to another living human organism as it once maintained with its own former organism, it would find itself confused by that relation. The state might be like that of awakening from a prolonged period of unconsciousness into strange surroundings. If my own ordinary body could be preserved in its present state, and I could absent myself from it for days or months or years, and continue my existence under another set of conditions altogether, and if I could then return to my own body, it might well be that I should be very confused and incoherent at first in my manifestations by means of it. How much more would this be the case were I to return to *another* human body. I might be troubled with various forms of aphasia and agraphia, might be particularly liable to failures of inhibition, might find the conditions oppressive and exhausting, and my state of mind would probably be of an automatic and dreamlike character. Now, the communicators through Mrs. Piper's trance exhibit precisely the kind of confusion and incoherence which it seems to me we have some reason to expect if they are actually what they claim to be."

G. P. himself appears to be well aware of the dream-like character of the communications, which, indeed, his own style often exemplifies. Thus he wrote on February 15th, 1894:

"Remember we share and always shall have our friends in the dream-life, *i.e.* your life so to speak, which will attract us for ever and ever, and so long as we have any friends *sleeping* in the material world; you to us are more like as we understand sleep, you look shut up as one in prison, and in order for us to get into communication with you, we have to enter into your sphere, as one like yourself, asleep. This is just why we make mistakes, as you call them, or get confused and muddled."

Yet even this very difficulty and fragmentariness of communication ought in the end to be for us full of an instruction of its own. We are here actually witnessing the central mystery of human life, unrolling itself under novel conditions, and open to closer observation than ever before. We are seeing a mind use a brain. The human brain is in its last analysis an arrangement of matter expressly adapted to being acted upon by a spirit; but so long as the accustomed spirit acts upon it the working is generally too smooth to allow us a glimpse of the mechanism. *Now,* however, we can watch an unaccustomed spirit, new to the instrument, installing itself and feeling its way. The lessons thus learned are likely to be more penetrating than any which mere morbid interruptions of the accustomed spirit's work can teach us. In aphasia, for instance, we can watch with instruction special difficulties of utterance, supervening on special injuries to the brain. But in *possession* we perceive the controlling spirit actually engaged in overcoming somewhat similar difficulties—writing or uttering the wrong word and then getting hold of the right one—and sometimes even finding power to explain to us something of the minute verbal mechanism through whose blocking or dislocation the mistake has arisen.

We may hope, indeed, that as our investigations proceed, and as we on this side of the fateful gulf, and the discarnate spirits on the other, learn more of the conditions necessary for perfect control of the brain and nervous system of intermediaries, the communications will grow fuller and more coherent, and reach a higher level of unitary consciousness. Many the difficulties may be, but is there to be no difficulty in linking flesh with spirit —in opening to man, from his prisoning planet, a first glimpse into cosmic things? If in such speech as this there be any reality, it is not stumblings or stammerings that should stop us. Nay, already on certain occasions there has been no stumble or stammer—when some experienced communicator has poured out an intimate message under strong emotion.

In this way we may explain certain facts as to the mode of communication which are likely to be at first misinterpreted, and to create an impression of pain or strangeness where, in my view, there is nothing beyond wholesome effort in the normal course of evolution among both incarnate and discarnate men. One touch of pathos, indeed—though not of tragedy —stands out to my recollection from the trances which I have watched— this is the thronging multitude of the departed pressing to the glimpse of light. Eager, but untrained, they interject their uncomprehended cries; vainly they call the names which no man answers; like birds that have beaten against a lighthouse, they pass in disappointment away. At first this confusion interfered with coherent messages, through Mrs. Piper, but during the second and third stages of her trances, under the care apparently of supervising spirits, it has tended more and more to disappear.

All this must needs be so; yet I, at least, had not realized beforehand that the pressure from *that* side was likely to be more urgent than from *this*. Naturally; since often on this side something of inevitable doubt—of shuddering prejudice and causeless fear—curdles the stream of love; while for them the imperishable affection flows on unchecked and full. They yearn to tell of their bliss, to promise their welcome at the destined hour. A needless scruple, indeed, which dreads to call or to constrain them! We can bind them by no bonds but of love; they are more ready to hear than we to pray; of their own act and grace they visit our spirits in prison.

We must now remember that this series of incidents does not stand alone. This case of Mrs. Piper is, indeed, one of the most instructive in our collection, on account of its length and complexity and the care with which it has been observed. But it is led up to by all our previous evidences, and I will here briefly state what facts they are which our recorded apparitions, intimations, messages of the departing and the departed, have, to my mind, actually proved.

(*a*) In the first place, they prove survival pure and simple; the persistence of the spirit's life as a structural law of the universe; the inalienable heritage of each several soul.

(*b*) In the second place, they prove that between the spiritual and the material worlds an avenue of communication does in fact exist; that which we call the dispatch and the receipt of telepathic messages, or the utterance and the answer of prayer and supplication.

(*c*) In the third place, they prove that the surviving spirit retains, at least in some measure, the memories and the loves of earth. Without this persistence of love and memory should we be in truth the *same?* To what extent has any philosophy or any revelation assured us hereof till now?

The above points, I think, are certain, if the apparitions and messages proceed in reality from the *sources* which they claim. On a lower evidential level comes the thesis drawn from the *contents* of the longer messages, which contents may of course be influenced in unknown degree by the expectation of the recipients or by some such infusion of dream-like matter as I have already mentioned. That thesis is as follows; I offer it for what it may be worth: Every element of individual wisdom, virtue, love, develops in infinite evolution toward an ever-highering hope; toward "Him who is at once thine innermost Self, and thine ever unattainable Desire."

There is, however, one feeling which has done much to deter inquiry in these directions. To many minds there seems to be a want of *dignity* in this mode of acquiring knowledge of an unseen world. It is felt that even as there is something grand and noble in the object, there ought to be something correspondingly exalted in the means employed. This has, it is thought, been the case with all former revelations which have made any serious claim on the attention of mankind. Religions have been supported by tradition, by miracle, by the deep personal emotion which they have been able to generate. There is something paltry or even repugnant in the notion of establishing a new faith upon a series of experiments dealing mainly with certain kinds of physical sensibility which seem at best to be scattered at random among mankind.

There is real force in such an objection. It is not fanciful to demand something of manifest congruity between means and end; not fanciful, at any rate, to distrust any powers merely of the flesh as explaining to us the powers of the spirit.

And yet, on a wider view, we shall perceive that what is missing in this new inquiry lies merely in such elements of impressiveness as befit the mere childhood of the world; while, on the other hand, we are gaining for the quest of spiritual truth that truer dignity which Science has given to man's scattered knowledge; the dignity of universal cogency and of unarrested progressiveness. Science, as we know, will not rest with complacency in presence of the exceptional, the catastrophic, the miraclous. Such qualities constitute for her not a claim to reverence but a challenge to explanation. She finds a truer grandeur in the colligation of startling phenomena under some comprehensive generalization. Her highest ideal is cosmic law; and she begins to suspect that any law which is truly cosmic is also in some sense evolutionary.

·   ·   ·   ·   ·   ·   ·

We have reached at last a position very remote from that from which we started. Yet it will not be easy to say exactly at what point we could have paused in our gradual sequence of evidence. In the first place, it now seems clear that a serious inquiry, whenever undertaken, was destined to afford ample proof of the inadequacy of the current material synthesis; to demonstrate the existence of faculties and operations which imply a spiritual environment, acted upon by a spirit in man. Telepathy and clairvoyance, as we now see, indisputably imply this enlarged conception of the universe as intelligible by man; and so soon as man is steadily conceived as dwelling in this wider range of powers, his survival of death becomes an almost inevitable corollary. With this survival his field of view broadens again. If we once admit discarnate spirits as actors in human affairs, we must expect them to act in some ways with greater scope and freedom than is possible to the incarnate spirits which we already know.

We cannot simply admit the existence of discarnate spirits as inert or subsidiary phenomena; we must expect to have to deal with them as agents on their own account—agents in unexpected ways, and with novel capacities. If they are concerned with us at all, the part which they will play is not likely to be a subordinate one.

We are standing then at a crisis of enormous importance in the history of life on earth. The spiritual world is just beginning to act systematically upon the material world. Action of the spiritual world upon our own there must always have been; action both profound, universal, and automatic, and very probably also irregular action with specific moral purport, such as has been assumed to accompany the rise of religions.

But a change seems to be impending, and the kind of action which now seems likely to be transmitted from the one world to the other is of a type which in the natural course of historic evolution has scarcely been likely to show itself until now. For it depends on the attainment of a certain scientific level by spirits incarnate and excarnate alike.

A few words will suffice to sum up broadly the general situation as it at present seems to me to stand. The dwellers on this earth, themselves spirits, are an object of love and care to spirits higher than they. The most important boon that can possibly be bestowed on them is knowledge as to their position in the universe, the assurance that their existence is a cosmic and not merely a planetary, a spiritual and not merely a corporeal, phenomenon. I conceive that this knowledge has in effect been apprehended from time to time by embodied spirits of high inward perceptive power, and has also been communicated by higher spirits, either affecting individual minds or even (as is believed especially of Jesus Christ) voluntarily incarnating themselves on earth for the purpose of teaching what they could recollect of that spiritual world from which they came. In those ages it would have been useless to attempt a scientific basis for such teaching. What could best be done was to enforce some few great truths—as the soul's long upward progress, or the Fatherhood of God—in such revelations as East and West could understand. Gradually Science arose, uniting the beliefs of all peoples in one scheme of organized truth, and suggesting that religion must be the spirit's subjective reaction to all the truths we know.

But when once this point was reached it must have become plain to wise spirits that the communications from their world which hitherto had had somewhat the character of inspirations of genius ought now to be based upon something of organized and definite observation, something which would work in with the great structure of Truth which observation has already established. Here, then, new difficulties must have arisen, just as they arise on earth when we endeavor to reduce to rules practicable for the many the results achieved by the extraordinary gifts of the few. Now it is that we are forced on both sides of the gulf to recognize how rare and specific is that capacity for intercommunication on which our messages must depend. Now it is that we feel the difficulty of being definite without being trivial; how little of earthly memory persists; how little of heavenly experience can be expressed in terms of earth; how long and arduous must be the way, how many must be the experiments, and how many the failures, before any systematized body of new truth can be established. But a sound beginning has been made, and whatever may be possible hereafter need not be wasted on a fresh start; it may be added to a growing structure of extra-terrene verities such as our race has never known till now.

It is not we who are in reality the discoverers here. The experiments which are being made are not the work of earthly skill. All that we can contribute to the new result is an attitude of patience, attention, care; an honest readiness to receive and weigh whatever may be given into our keeping by intelligences beyond our own. Experiments there are, probably experiments of a complexity and difficulty which surpass our imagination; but they are made from the other side of the gulf, by the efforts of spirits who discern pathways and possibilities which for us are impenetrably dark. We should not be going beyond the truth if we described our sensitives as merely the instruments, our researchers as merely the registrars, of a movement which we neither initiated nor can in any degree comprehend.

The true discoverers, however, show no wish to be thus sharply distinguished from ourselves. Their aim is a collaboration with us as close as may be possible. Some of them were on earth our own familiar friends; we have spoken with them in old days of this great enterprise; they have promised that they would call to us, if it were possible, with the message of their undying love. It may be that the most useful thing that some of us have done on earth has been to interest in this inquiry some spirit more potent than himself, who has passed into that world of unguessed adventure, not forgetful of his friend.

The very faintness and incoherence of such a spirit's message, besides being a kind of indication that we are dealing with the imperfections of actual reality rather than with the smoothly finished products of mere imagination, does also in itself constitute a strong appeal to our gratitude and reverence. Not easily and carelessly do these spirits come to us, but after strenuous preparation, and with difficult fulfillment of desire. So came Tennyson's *Persephone:*

> "Faint as a climate-changing bird that flies
> All night across the darkness, and at dawn
> Falls on the threshold of her native land,
> And can no more. . . ."

They commune with us, like Persephone, willing and eager, but "dazed and dumb with passing through at once from state to state." They cannot satisfy themselves with their trammeled utterance; they complain of the strange brain, the alien voice. What they are doing, indeed, they *desire* to do—this is their willing contribution to that universal scheme by which the higher helps the lower, and the stronger the weaker, through all the ideal relationships of the world of Life. But we on our part ought to remember that there may be a dignity in this very confusion, a proof of persistent strong affection in the very hesitancies and bewilderments of some well-loved soul.

"After the tempest a still small voice." One may have listened perhaps, to the echoing pomp of some Œcumenical Council, thundering its damnations *Urbi et Orbi* from an Infallible Chair; and yet one may find a more Christlike sanctity in the fragmentary whisper of one true soul, descending painfully from unimaginable brightness to bring strength and hope to kindred souls still prisoned in the flesh.

Beyond us still is mystery; but it is mystery lit and mellowed with an infinite hope. We ride in darkness at the haven's mouth; but sometimes through rifted clouds we see the desires and needs of many generations floating and melting upwards into a distant glow, "up through the light of the seas by the moon's long-silvering ray."

The high possibilities that lie before us should be grasped once for all, in order that the dignity of the quest may help to carry the inquirer through many disappointments, deceptions, delays. But he must remember that this inquiry must be extended over many generations; nor must he allow himself to be persuaded that there are byways to mastery. I will not say that there cannot possibly be any such thing as occult wisdom, or dominion over the secrets of nature ascetically or magically acquired. But I will say that every claim of this kind which my colleagues or I have been able to examine has proved deserving of complete mistrust; and that we have no confidence here any more than elsewhere in any methods except the open, candid, straightforward methods which the spirit of modern science demands.

All omens point towards the steady continuance of just such labor as has already taught us all we know. Perhaps, indeed, in this complex of interpenetrating spirits our own effort is no individual, no transitory thing. That which lies at the root of each of us lies at the root of the Cosmos too. Our struggle is the struggle of the Universe itself; and the very Godhead finds fulfillment through our upward-striving souls.

INDEX

A CATALOG OF SELECTED
DOVER BOOKS
IN ALL FIELDS OF INTEREST

A CATALOG OF SELECTED DOVER
BOOKS IN ALL FIELDS OF INTEREST

CONCERNING THE SPIRITUAL IN ART, Wassily Kandinsky. Pioneering work by father of abstract art. Thoughts on color theory, nature of art. Analysis of earlier masters. 12 illustrations. 80pp. of text. 5⅜ x 8½.   23411-8

ANIMALS: 1,419 Copyright-Free Illustrations of Mammals, Birds, Fish, Insects, etc., Jim Harter (ed.). Clear wood engravings present, in extremely lifelike poses, over 1,000 species of animals. One of the most extensive pictorial sourcebooks of its kind. Captions. Index. 284pp. 9 x 12.   23766-4

CELTIC ART: The Methods of Construction, George Bain. Simple geometric techniques for making Celtic interlacements, spirals, Kells-type initials, animals, humans, etc. Over 500 illustrations. 160pp. 9 x 12. (Available in U.S. only.)   22923-8

AN ATLAS OF ANATOMY FOR ARTISTS, Fritz Schider. Most thorough reference work on art anatomy in the world. Hundreds of illustrations, including selections from works by Vesalius, Leonardo, Goya, Ingres, Michelangelo, others. 593 illustrations. 192pp. 7⅛ x 10¼.   20241-0

CELTIC HAND STROKE-BY-STROKE (Irish Half-Uncial from "The Book of Kells"): An Arthur Baker Calligraphy Manual, Arthur Baker. Complete guide to creating each letter of the alphabet in distinctive Celtic manner. Covers hand position, strokes, pens, inks, paper, more. Illustrated. 48pp. 8¼ x 11.   24336-2

EASY ORIGAMI, John Montroll. Charming collection of 32 projects (hat, cup, pelican, piano, swan, many more) specially designed for the novice origami hobbyist. Clearly illustrated easy-to-follow instructions insure that even beginning papercrafters will achieve successful results. 48pp. 8¼ x 11.   27298-2

THE COMPLETE BOOK OF BIRDHOUSE CONSTRUCTION FOR WOODWORKERS, Scott D. Campbell. Detailed instructions, illustrations, tables. Also data on bird habitat and instinct patterns. Bibliography. 3 tables. 63 illustrations in 15 figures. 48pp. 5¼ x 8½.   24407-5

BLOOMINGDALE'S ILLUSTRATED 1886 CATALOG: Fashions, Dry Goods and Housewares, Bloomingdale Brothers. Famed merchants' extremely rare catalog depicting about 1,700 products: clothing, housewares, firearms, dry goods, jewelry, more. Invaluable for dating, identifying vintage items. Also, copyright-free graphics for artists, designers. Co-published with Henry Ford Museum & Greenfield Village. 160pp. 8¼ x 11.   25780-0

HISTORIC COSTUME IN PICTURES, Braun & Schneider. Over 1,450 costumed figures in clearly detailed engravings—from dawn of civilization to end of 19th century. Captions. Many folk costumes. 256pp. 8⅜ x 11¾.   23150-X

CATALOG OF DOVER BOOKS

STICKLEY CRAFTSMAN FURNITURE CATALOGS, Gustav Stickley and L. & J. G. Stickley. Beautiful, functional furniture in two authentic catalogs from 1910. 594 illustrations, including 277 photos, show settles, rockers, armchairs, reclining chairs, bookcases, desks, tables. 183pp. 6½ x 9¼.   23838-5

AMERICAN LOCOMOTIVES IN HISTORIC PHOTOGRAPHS: 1858 to 1949, Ron Ziel (ed.). A rare collection of 126 meticulously detailed official photographs, called "builder portraits," of American locomotives that majestically chronicle the rise of steam locomotive power in America. Introduction. Detailed captions. xi+129pp. 9 x 12.   27393-8

AMERICA'S LIGHTHOUSES: An Illustrated History, Francis Ross Holland, Jr. Delightfully written, profusely illustrated fact-filled survey of over 200 American lighthouses since 1716. History, anecdotes, technological advances, more. 240pp. 8 x 10¾.
25576-X

TOWARDS A NEW ARCHITECTURE, Le Corbusier. Pioneering manifesto by founder of "International School." Technical and aesthetic theories, views of industry, economics, relation of form to function, "mass-production split" and much more. Profusely illustrated. 320pp. 6⅛ x 9¼. (Available in U.S. only.)   25023-7

HOW THE OTHER HALF LIVES, Jacob Riis. Famous journalistic record, exposing poverty and degradation of New York slums around 1900, by major social reformer. 100 striking and influential photographs. 233pp. 10 x 7⅞.   22012-5

FRUIT KEY AND TWIG KEY TO TREES AND SHRUBS, William M. Harlow. One of the handiest and most widely used identification aids. Fruit key covers 120 deciduous and evergreen species; twig key 160 deciduous species. Easily used. Over 300 photographs. 126pp. 5⅜ x 8½.   20511-8

COMMON BIRD SONGS, Dr. Donald J. Borror. Songs of 60 most common U.S. birds: robins, sparrows, cardinals, bluejays, finches, more—arranged in order of increasing complexity. Up to 9 variations of songs of each species.
Cassette and manual 99911-4

ORCHIDS AS HOUSE PLANTS, Rebecca Tyson Northen. Grow cattleyas and many other kinds of orchids—in a window, in a case, or under artificial light. 63 illustrations. 148pp. 5⅜ x 8½.   23261-1

MONSTER MAZES, Dave Phillips. Masterful mazes at four levels of difficulty. Avoid deadly perils and evil creatures to find magical treasures. Solutions for all 32 exciting illustrated puzzles. 48pp. 8¼ x 11.   26005-4

MOZART'S DON GIOVANNI (DOVER OPERA LIBRETTO SERIES), Wolfgang Amadeus Mozart. Introduced and translated by Ellen H. Bleiler. Standard Italian libretto, with complete English translation. Convenient and thoroughly portable—an ideal companion for reading along with a recording or the performance itself. Introduction. List of characters. Plot summary. 121pp. 5¼ x 8½.   24944-1

TECHNICAL MANUAL AND DICTIONARY OF CLASSICAL BALLET, Gail Grant. Defines, explains, comments on steps, movements, poses and concepts. 15-page pictorial section. Basic book for student, viewer. 127pp. 5⅜ x 8½.   21843-0

THE CLARINET AND CLARINET PLAYING, David Pino. Lively, comprehensive work features suggestions about technique, musicianship, and musical interpretation, as well as guidelines for teaching, making your own reeds, and preparing for public performance. Includes an intriguing look at clarinet history. "A godsend," *The Clarinet,* Journal of the International Clarinet Society. Appendixes. 7 illus. 320pp. 5⅜ x 8½. 40270-3

HOLLYWOOD GLAMOR PORTRAITS, John Kobal (ed.). 145 photos from 1926-49. Harlow, Gable, Bogart, Bacall; 94 stars in all. Full background on photographers, technical aspects. 160pp. 8⅜ x 11¼. 23352-9

THE ANNOTATED CASEY AT THE BAT: A Collection of Ballads about the Mighty Casey/Third, Revised Edition, Martin Gardner (ed.). Amusing sequels and parodies of one of America's best-loved poems: Casey's Revenge, Why Casey Whiffed, Casey's Sister at the Bat, others. 256pp. 5⅜ x 8½. 28598-7

THE RAVEN AND OTHER FAVORITE POEMS, Edgar Allan Poe. Over 40 of the author's most memorable poems: "The Bells," "Ulalume," "Israfel," "To Helen," "The Conqueror Worm," "Eldorado," "Annabel Lee," many more. Alphabetic lists of titles and first lines. 64pp. 5 3/16 x 8¼. 26685-0

PERSONAL MEMOIRS OF U. S. GRANT, Ulysses Simpson Grant. Intelligent, deeply moving firsthand account of Civil War campaigns, considered by many the finest military memoirs ever written. Includes letters, historic photographs, maps and more. 528pp. 6⅛ x 9¼. 28587-1

ANCIENT EGYPTIAN MATERIALS AND INDUSTRIES, A. Lucas and J. Harris. Fascinating, comprehensive, thoroughly documented text describes this ancient civilization's vast resources and the processes that incorporated them in daily life, including the use of animal products, building materials, cosmetics, perfumes and incense, fibers, glazed ware, glass and its manufacture, materials used in the mummification process, and much more. 544pp. 6⅛ x 9¼. (Available in U.S. only.) 40446-3

RUSSIAN STORIES/RUSSKIE RASSKAZY: A Dual-Language Book, edited by Gleb Struve. Twelve tales by such masters as Chekhov, Tolstoy, Dostoevsky, Pushkin, others. Excellent word-for-word English translations on facing pages, plus teaching and study aids, Russian/English vocabulary, biographical/critical introductions, more. 416pp. 5⅜ x 8½. 26244-8

PHILADELPHIA THEN AND NOW: 60 Sites Photographed in the Past and Present, Kenneth Finkel and Susan Oyama. Rare photographs of City Hall, Logan Square, Independence Hall, Betsy Ross House, other landmarks juxtaposed with contemporary views. Captures changing face of historic city. Introduction. Captions. 128pp. 8¼ x 11. 25790-8

AIA ARCHITECTURAL GUIDE TO NASSAU AND SUFFOLK COUNTIES, LONG ISLAND, The American Institute of Architects, Long Island Chapter, and the Society for the Preservation of Long Island Antiquities. Comprehensive, well-researched and generously illustrated volume brings to life over three centuries of Long Island's great architectural heritage. More than 240 photographs with authoritative, extensively detailed captions. 176pp. 8¼ x 11. 26946-9

NORTH AMERICAN INDIAN LIFE: Customs and Traditions of 23 Tribes, Elsie Clews Parsons (ed.). 27 fictionalized essays by noted anthropologists examine religion, customs, government, additional facets of life among the Winnebago, Crow, Zuni, Eskimo, other tribes. 480pp. 6⅛ x 9¼. 27377-6

FRANK LLOYD WRIGHT'S DANA HOUSE, Donald Hoffmann. Pictorial essay of residential masterpiece with over 160 interior and exterior photos, plans, elevations, sketches and studies. 128pp. 9¼ x 10¾. 29120-0

THE MALE AND FEMALE FIGURE IN MOTION: 60 Classic Photographic Sequences, Eadweard Muybridge. 60 true-action photographs of men and women walking, running, climbing, bending, turning, etc., reproduced from rare 19th-century masterpiece. vi + 121pp. 9 x 12. 24745-7

1001 QUESTIONS ANSWERED ABOUT THE SEASHORE, N. J. Berrill and Jacquelyn Berrill. Queries answered about dolphins, sea snails, sponges, starfish, fishes, shore birds, many others. Covers appearance, breeding, growth, feeding, much more. 305pp. 5¼ x 8¼. 23366-9

ATTRACTING BIRDS TO YOUR YARD, William J. Weber. Easy-to-follow guide offers advice on how to attract the greatest diversity of birds: birdhouses, feeders, water and waterers, much more. 96pp. 5³⁄₁₆ x 8¼. 28927-3

MEDICINAL AND OTHER USES OF NORTH AMERICAN PLANTS: A Historical Survey with Special Reference to the Eastern Indian Tribes, Charlotte Erichsen-Brown. Chronological historical citations document 500 years of usage of plants, trees, shrubs native to eastern Canada, northeastern U.S. Also complete identifying information. 343 illustrations. 544pp. 6½ x 9¼. 25951-X

STORYBOOK MAZES, Dave Phillips. 23 stories and mazes on two-page spreads: Wizard of Oz, Treasure Island, Robin Hood, etc. Solutions. 64pp. 8¼ x 11. 23628-5

AMERICAN NEGRO SONGS: 230 Folk Songs and Spirituals, Religious and Secular, John W. Work. This authoritative study traces the African influences of songs sung and played by black Americans at work, in church, and as entertainment. The author discusses the lyric significance of such songs as "Swing Low, Sweet Chariot," "John Henry," and others and offers the words and music for 230 songs. Bibliography. Index of Song Titles. 272pp. 6½ x 9¼. 40271-1

MOVIE-STAR PORTRAITS OF THE FORTIES, John Kobal (ed.). 163 glamor, studio photos of 106 stars of the 1940s: Rita Hayworth, Ava Gardner, Marlon Brando, Clark Gable, many more. 176pp. 8⅜ x 11¼. 23546-7

BENCHLEY LOST AND FOUND, Robert Benchley. Finest humor from early 30s, about pet peeves, child psychologists, post office and others. Mostly unavailable elsewhere. 73 illustrations by Peter Arno and others. 183pp. 5⅜ x 8½. 22410-4

YEKL and THE IMPORTED BRIDEGROOM AND OTHER STORIES OF YIDDISH NEW YORK, Abraham Cahan. Film Hester Street based on *Yekl* (1896). Novel, other stories among first about Jewish immigrants on N.Y.'s East Side. 240pp. 5⅜ x 8½. 22427-9

SELECTED POEMS, Walt Whitman. Generous sampling from *Leaves of Grass*. Twenty-four poems include "I Hear America Singing," "Song of the Open Road," "I Sing the Body Electric," "When Lilacs Last in the Dooryard Bloom'd," "O Captain! My Captain!"—all reprinted from an authoritative edition. Lists of titles and first lines. 128pp. 5³⁄₁₆ x 8¼. 26878-0

THE BEST TALES OF HOFFMANN, E. T. A. Hoffmann. 10 of Hoffmann's most important stories: "Nutcracker and the King of Mice," "The Golden Flowerpot," etc. 458pp. 5⅜ x 8½. 21793-0

FROM FETISH TO GOD IN ANCIENT EGYPT, E. A. Wallis Budge. Rich detailed survey of Egyptian conception of "God" and gods, magic, cult of animals, Osiris, more. Also, superb English translations of hymns and legends. 240 illustrations. 545pp. 5⅜ x 8½. 25803-3

FRENCH STORIES/CONTES FRANÇAIS: A Dual-Language Book, Wallace Fowlie. Ten stories by French masters, Voltaire to Camus: "Micromegas" by Voltaire; "The Atheist's Mass" by Balzac; "Minuet" by de Maupassant; "The Guest" by Camus, six more. Excellent English translations on facing pages. Also French-English vocabulary list, exercises, more. 352pp. 5⅜ x 8½. 26443-2

CHICAGO AT THE TURN OF THE CENTURY IN PHOTOGRAPHS: 122 Historic Views from the Collections of the Chicago Historical Society, Larry A. Viskochil. Rare large-format prints offer detailed views of City Hall, State Street, the Loop, Hull House, Union Station, many other landmarks, circa 1904-1913. Introduction. Captions. Maps. 144pp. 9⅜ x 12¼. 24656-6

OLD BROOKLYN IN EARLY PHOTOGRAPHS, 1865-1929, William Lee Younger. Luna Park, Gravesend race track, construction of Grand Army Plaza, moving of Hotel Brighton, etc. 157 previously unpublished photographs. 165pp. 8⅞ x 11¾. 23587-4

THE MYTHS OF THE NORTH AMERICAN INDIANS, Lewis Spence. Rich anthology of the myths and legends of the Algonquins, Iroquois, Pawnees and Sioux, prefaced by an extensive historical and ethnological commentary. 36 illustrations. 480pp. 5⅜ x 8½. 25967-6

AN ENCYCLOPEDIA OF BATTLES: Accounts of Over 1,560 Battles from 1479 B.C. to the Present, David Eggenberger. Essential details of every major battle in recorded history from the first battle of Megiddo in 1479 B.C. to Grenada in 1984. List of Battle Maps. New Appendix covering the years 1967-1984. Index. 99 illustrations. 544pp. 6½ x 9¼. 24913-1

SAILING ALONE AROUND THE WORLD, Captain Joshua Slocum. First man to sail around the world, alone, in small boat. One of great feats of seamanship told in delightful manner. 67 illustrations. 294pp. 5⅜ x 8½. 20326-3

ANARCHISM AND OTHER ESSAYS, Emma Goldman. Powerful, penetrating, prophetic essays on direct action, role of minorities, prison reform, puritan hypocrisy, violence, etc. 271pp. 5⅜ x 8½. 22484-8

MYTHS OF THE HINDUS AND BUDDHISTS, Ananda K. Coomaraswamy and Sister Nivedita. Great stories of the epics; deeds of Krishna, Shiva, taken from puranas, Vedas, folk tales; etc. 32 illustrations. 400pp. 5⅜ x 8½. 21759-0

THE TRAUMA OF BIRTH, Otto Rank. Rank's controversial thesis that anxiety neurosis is caused by profound psychological trauma which occurs at birth. 256pp. 5⅜ x 8½. 27974-X

A THEOLOGICO-POLITICAL TREATISE, Benedict Spinoza. Also contains unfinished Political Treatise. Great classic on religious liberty, theory of government on common consent. R. Elwes translation. Total of 421pp. 5⅜ x 8½. 20249-6

MY BONDAGE AND MY FREEDOM, Frederick Douglass. Born a slave, Douglass became outspoken force in antislavery movement. The best of Douglass' autobiographies. Graphic description of slave life. 464pp. 5⅜ x 8½.   22457-0

FOLLOWING THE EQUATOR: A Journey Around the World, Mark Twain. Fascinating humorous account of 1897 voyage to Hawaii, Australia, India, New Zealand, etc. Ironic, bemused reports on peoples, customs, climate, flora and fauna, politics, much more. 197 illustrations. 720pp. 5⅜ x 8½.   26113-1

THE PEOPLE CALLED SHAKERS, Edward D. Andrews. Definitive study of Shakers: origins, beliefs, practices, dances, social organization, furniture and crafts, etc. 33 illustrations. 351pp. 5⅜ x 8½.   21081-2

THE MYTHS OF GREECE AND ROME, H. A. Guerber. A classic of mythology, generously illustrated, long prized for its simple, graphic, accurate retelling of the principal myths of Greece and Rome, and for its commentary on their origins and significance. With 64 illustrations by Michelangelo, Raphael, Titian, Rubens, Canova, Bernini and others. 480pp. 5⅜ x 8½.   27584-1

PSYCHOLOGY OF MUSIC, Carl E. Seashore. Classic work discusses music as a medium from psychological viewpoint. Clear treatment of physical acoustics, auditory apparatus, sound perception, development of musical skills, nature of musical feeling, host of other topics. 88 figures. 408pp. 5⅜ x 8½.   21851-1

THE PHILOSOPHY OF HISTORY, Georg W. Hegel. Great classic of Western thought develops concept that history is not chance but rational process, the evolution of freedom. 457pp. 5⅜ x 8½.   20112-0

THE BOOK OF TEA, Kakuzo Okakura. Minor classic of the Orient: entertaining, charming explanation, interpretation of traditional Japanese culture in terms of tea ceremony. 94pp. 5⅜ x 8½.   20070-1

LIFE IN ANCIENT EGYPT, Adolf Erman. Fullest, most thorough, detailed older account with much not in more recent books, domestic life, religion, magic, medicine, commerce, much more. Many illustrations reproduce tomb paintings, carvings, hieroglyphs, etc. 597pp. 5⅜ x 8½.   22632-8

SUNDIALS, Their Theory and Construction, Albert Waugh. Far and away the best, most thorough coverage of ideas, mathematics concerned, types, construction, adjusting anywhere. Simple, nontechnical treatment allows even children to build several of these dials. Over 100 illustrations. 230pp. 5⅜ x 8½.   22947-5

THEORETICAL HYDRODYNAMICS, L. M. Milne-Thomson. Classic exposition of the mathematical theory of fluid motion, applicable to both hydrodynamics and aerodynamics. Over 600 exercises. 768pp. 6⅛ x 9¼.   68970-0

SONGS OF EXPERIENCE: Facsimile Reproduction with 26 Plates in Full Color, William Blake. 26 full-color plates from a rare 1826 edition. Includes "The Tyger," "London," "Holy Thursday," and other poems. Printed text of poems. 48pp. 5¼ x 7.   24636-1

OLD-TIME VIGNETTES IN FULL COLOR, Carol Belanger Grafton (ed.). Over 390 charming, often sentimental illustrations, selected from archives of Victorian graphics—pretty women posing, children playing, food, flowers, kittens and puppies, smiling cherubs, birds and butterflies, much more. All copyright-free. 48pp. 9¼ x 12¼.   27269-9

PERSPECTIVE FOR ARTISTS, Rex Vicat Cole. Depth, perspective of sky and sea, shadows, much more, not usually covered. 391 diagrams, 81 reproductions of drawings and paintings. 279pp. 5⅜ x 8½. 22487-2

DRAWING THE LIVING FIGURE, Joseph Sheppard. Innovative approach to artistic anatomy focuses on specifics of surface anatomy, rather than muscles and bones. Over 170 drawings of live models in front, back and side views, and in widely varying poses. Accompanying diagrams. 177 illustrations. Introduction. Index. 144pp. 8⅜ x11¼. 26723-7

GOTHIC AND OLD ENGLISH ALPHABETS: 100 Complete Fonts, Dan X. Solo. Add power, elegance to posters, signs, other graphics with 100 stunning copyright-free alphabets: Blackstone, Dolbey, Germania, 97 more—including many lower-case, numerals, punctuation marks. 104pp. 8⅛ x 11. 24695-7

HOW TO DO BEADWORK, Mary White. Fundamental book on craft from simple projects to five-bead chains and woven works. 106 illustrations. 142pp. 5⅜ x 8.
20697-1

THE BOOK OF WOOD CARVING, Charles Marshall Sayers. Finest book for beginners discusses fundamentals and offers 34 designs. "Absolutely first rate . . . well thought out and well executed."–E. J. Tangerman. 118pp. 7¾ x 10⅝. 23654-4

ILLUSTRATED CATALOG OF CIVIL WAR MILITARY GOODS: Union Army Weapons, Insignia, Uniform Accessories, and Other Equipment, Schuyler, Hartley, and Graham. Rare, profusely illustrated 1846 catalog includes Union Army uniform and dress regulations, arms and ammunition, coats, insignia, flags, swords, rifles, etc. 226 illustrations. 160pp. 9 x 12. 24939-5

WOMEN'S FASHIONS OF THE EARLY 1900s: An Unabridged Republication of "New York Fashions, 1909," National Cloak & Suit Co. Rare catalog of mail-order fashions documents women's and children's clothing styles shortly after the turn of the century. Captions offer full descriptions, prices. Invaluable resource for fashion, costume historians. Approximately 725 illustrations. 128pp. 8⅜ x 11¼. 27276-1

THE 1912 AND 1915 GUSTAV STICKLEY FURNITURE CATALOGS, Gustav Stickley. With over 200 detailed illustrations and descriptions, these two catalogs are essential reading and reference materials and identification guides for Stickley furniture. Captions cite materials, dimensions and prices. 112pp. 6½ x 9¼. 26676-1

EARLY AMERICAN LOCOMOTIVES, John H. White, Jr. Finest locomotive engravings from early 19th century: historical (1804–74), main-line (after 1870), special, foreign, etc. 147 plates. 142pp. 11⅜ x 8¼. 22772-3

THE TALL SHIPS OF TODAY IN PHOTOGRAPHS, Frank O. Braynard. Lavishly illustrated tribute to nearly 100 majestic contemporary sailing vessels: Amerigo Vespucci, Clearwater, Constitution, Eagle, Mayflower, Sea Cloud, Victory, many more. Authoritative captions provide statistics, background on each ship. 190 black-and-white photographs and illustrations. Introduction. 128pp. 8⅞ x 11¾.
27163-3

LITTLE BOOK OF EARLY AMERICAN CRAFTS AND TRADES, Peter Stockham (ed.). 1807 children's book explains crafts and trades: baker, hatter, cooper, potter, and many others. 23 copperplate illustrations. 140pp. 4⅝ x 6.   23336-7

VICTORIAN FASHIONS AND COSTUMES FROM HARPER'S BAZAR, 1867–1898, Stella Blum (ed.). Day costumes, evening wear, sports clothes, shoes, hats, other accessories in over 1,000 detailed engravings. 320pp. 9⅜ x 12¼.   22990-4

GUSTAV STICKLEY, THE CRAFTSMAN, Mary Ann Smith. Superb study surveys broad scope of Stickley's achievement, especially in architecture. Design philosophy, rise and fall of the Craftsman empire, descriptions and floor plans for many Craftsman houses, more. 86 black-and-white halftones. 31 line illustrations. Introduction 208pp. 6½ x 9¼.   27210-9

THE LONG ISLAND RAIL ROAD IN EARLY PHOTOGRAPHS, Ron Ziel. Over 220 rare photos, informative text document origin (1844) and development of rail service on Long Island. Vintage views of early trains, locomotives, stations, passengers, crews, much more. Captions. 8⅞ x 11¾.   26301-0

VOYAGE OF THE LIBERDADE, Joshua Slocum. Great 19th-century mariner's thrilling, first-hand account of the wreck of his ship off South America, the 35-foot boat he built from the wreckage, and its remarkable voyage home. 128pp. 5⅜ x 8½.   40022-0

TEN BOOKS ON ARCHITECTURE, Vitruvius. The most important book ever written on architecture. Early Roman aesthetics, technology, classical orders, site selection, all other aspects. Morgan translation. 331pp. 5⅜ x 8½.   20645-9

THE HUMAN FIGURE IN MOTION, Eadweard Muybridge. More than 4,500 stopped-action photos, in action series, showing undraped men, women, children jumping, lying down, throwing, sitting, wrestling, carrying, etc. 390pp. 7⅞ x 10⅝.   20204-6 Clothbd.

TREES OF THE EASTERN AND CENTRAL UNITED STATES AND CANADA, William M. Harlow. Best one-volume guide to 140 trees. Full descriptions, woodlore, range, etc. Over 600 illustrations. Handy size. 288pp. 4½ x 6⅜.   20395-6

SONGS OF WESTERN BIRDS, Dr. Donald J. Borror. Complete song and call repertoire of 60 western species, including flycatchers, juncoes, cactus wrens, many more—includes fully illustrated booklet.   Cassette and manual 99913-0

GROWING AND USING HERBS AND SPICES, Milo Miloradovich. Versatile handbook provides all the information needed for cultivation and use of all the herbs and spices available in North America. 4 illustrations. Index. Glossary. 236pp. 5⅜ x 8½.   25058-X

BIG BOOK OF MAZES AND LABYRINTHS, Walter Shepherd. 50 mazes and labyrinths in all—classical, solid, ripple, and more—in one great volume. Perfect inexpensive puzzler for clever youngsters. Full solutions. 112pp. 8⅛ x 11.   22951-3

PIANO TUNING, J. Cree Fischer. Clearest, best book for beginner, amateur. Simple repairs, raising dropped notes, tuning by easy method of flattened fifths. No previous skills needed. 4 illustrations. 201pp. 5⅜ x 8½. 23267-0

HINTS TO SINGERS, Lillian Nordica. Selecting the right teacher, developing confidence, overcoming stage fright, and many other important skills receive thoughtful discussion in this indispensible guide, written by a world-famous diva of four decades' experience. 96pp. 5⅜ x 8½. 40094-8

THE COMPLETE NONSENSE OF EDWARD LEAR, Edward Lear. All nonsense limericks, zany alphabets, Owl and Pussycat, songs, nonsense botany, etc., illustrated by Lear. Total of 320pp. 5⅜ x 8½. (Available in U.S. only.) 20167-8

VICTORIAN PARLOUR POETRY: An Annotated Anthology, Michael R. Turner. 117 gems by Longfellow, Tennyson, Browning, many lesser-known poets. "The Village Blacksmith," "Curfew Must Not Ring Tonight," "Only a Baby Small," dozens more, often difficult to find elsewhere. Index of poets, titles, first lines. xxiii + 325pp. 5⅝ x 8¼. 27044-0

DUBLINERS, James Joyce. Fifteen stories offer vivid, tightly focused observations of the lives of Dublin's poorer classes. At least one, "The Dead," is considered a masterpiece. Reprinted complete and unabridged from standard edition. 160pp. 5$\frac{3}{16}$ x 8¼. 26870-5

GREAT WEIRD TALES: 14 Stories by Lovecraft, Blackwood, Machen and Others, S. T. Joshi (ed.). 14 spellbinding tales, including "The Sin Eater," by Fiona McLeod, "The Eye Above the Mantel," by Frank Belknap Long, as well as renowned works by R. H. Barlow, Lord Dunsany, Arthur Machen, W. C. Morrow and eight other masters of the genre. 256pp. 5⅜ x 8½. (Available in U.S. only.) 40436-6

THE BOOK OF THE SACRED MAGIC OF ABRAMELIN THE MAGE, translated by S. MacGregor Mathers. Medieval manuscript of ceremonial magic. Basic document in Aleister Crowley, Golden Dawn groups. 268pp. 5⅜ x 8½. 23211-5

NEW RUSSIAN-ENGLISH AND ENGLISH-RUSSIAN DICTIONARY, M. A. O'Brien. This is a remarkably handy Russian dictionary, containing a surprising amount of information, including over 70,000 entries. 366pp. 4½ x 6⅛. 20208-9

HISTORIC HOMES OF THE AMERICAN PRESIDENTS, Second, Revised Edition, Irvin Haas. A traveler's guide to American Presidential homes, most open to the public, depicting and describing homes occupied by every American President from George Washington to George Bush. With visiting hours, admission charges, travel routes. 175 photographs. Index. 160pp. 8¼ x 11. 26751-2

NEW YORK IN THE FORTIES, Andreas Feininger. 162 brilliant photographs by the well-known photographer, formerly with *Life* magazine. Commuters, shoppers, Times Square at night, much else from city at its peak. Captions by John von Hartz. 181pp. 9¼ x 10¾. 23585-8

INDIAN SIGN LANGUAGE, William Tomkins. Over 525 signs developed by Sioux and other tribes. Written instructions and diagrams. Also 290 pictographs. 111pp. 6⅛ x 9¼. 22029-X

ANATOMY: A Complete Guide for Artists, Joseph Sheppard. A master of figure drawing shows artists how to render human anatomy convincingly. Over 460 illustrations. 224pp. 8⅜ x 11¼. 27279-6

MEDIEVAL CALLIGRAPHY: Its History and Technique, Marc Drogin. Spirited history, comprehensive instruction manual covers 13 styles (ca. 4th century through 15th). Excellent photographs; directions for duplicating medieval techniques with modern tools. 224pp. 8⅜ x 11¼. 26142-5

DRIED FLOWERS: How to Prepare Them, Sarah Whitlock and Martha Rankin. Complete instructions on how to use silica gel, meal and borax, perlite aggregate, sand and borax, glycerine and water to create attractive permanent flower arrangements. 12 illustrations. 32pp. 5⅜ x 8½. 21802-3

EASY-TO-MAKE BIRD FEEDERS FOR WOODWORKERS, Scott D. Campbell. Detailed, simple-to-use guide for designing, constructing, caring for and using feeders. Text, illustrations for 12 classic and contemporary designs. 96pp. 5⅜ x 8½. 25847-5

SCOTTISH WONDER TALES FROM MYTH AND LEGEND, Donald A. Mackenzie. 16 lively tales tell of giants rumbling down mountainsides, of a magic wand that turns stone pillars into warriors, of gods and goddesses, evil hags, powerful forces and more. 240pp. 5⅜ x 8½. 29677-6

THE HISTORY OF UNDERCLOTHES, C. Willett Cunnington and Phyllis Cunnington. Fascinating, well-documented survey covering six centuries of English undergarments, enhanced with over 100 illustrations: 12th-century laced-up bodice, footed long drawers (1795), 19th-century bustles, 19th-century corsets for men, Victorian "bust improvers," much more. 272pp. 5⅜ x 8¼. 27124-2

ARTS AND CRAFTS FURNITURE: The Complete Brooks Catalog of 1912, Brooks Manufacturing Co. Photos and detailed descriptions of more than 150 now very collectible furniture designs from the Arts and Crafts movement depict davenports, settees, buffets, desks, tables, chairs, bedsteads, dressers and more, all built of solid, quarter-sawed oak. Invaluable for students and enthusiasts of antiques, Americana and the decorative arts. 80pp. 6½ x 9¼. 27471-3

WILBUR AND ORVILLE: A Biography of the Wright Brothers, Fred Howard. Definitive, crisply written study tells the full story of the brothers' lives and work. A vividly written biography, unparalleled in scope and color, that also captures the spirit of an extraordinary era. 560pp. 6⅛ x 9¼. 40297-5

THE ARTS OF THE SAILOR: Knotting, Splicing and Ropework, Hervey Garrett Smith. Indispensable shipboard reference covers tools, basic knots and useful hitches; handsewing and canvas work, more. Over 100 illustrations. Delightful reading for sea lovers. 256pp. 5⅜ x 8½. 26440-8

FRANK LLOYD WRIGHT'S FALLINGWATER: The House and Its History, Second, Revised Edition, Donald Hoffmann. A total revision–both in text and illustrations–of the standard document on Fallingwater, the boldest, most personal architectural statement of Wright's mature years, updated with valuable new material from the recently opened Frank Lloyd Wright Archives. "Fascinating"–*The New York Times*. 116 illustrations. 128pp. 9¼ x 10¾. 27430-6

CATALOG OF DOVER BOOKS

PHOTOGRAPHIC SKETCHBOOK OF THE CIVIL WAR, Alexander Gardner. 100 photos taken on field during the Civil War. Famous shots of Manassas Harper's Ferry, Lincoln, Richmond, slave pens, etc. 244pp. 10⅞ x 8¼.   22731-6

FIVE ACRES AND INDEPENDENCE, Maurice G. Kains. Great back-to-the-land classic explains basics of self-sufficient farming. The one book to get. 95 illustrations. 397pp. 5⅜ x 8½.   20974-1

SONGS OF EASTERN BIRDS, Dr. Donald J. Borror. Songs and calls of 60 species most common to eastern U.S.: warblers, woodpeckers, flycatchers, thrushes, larks, many more in high-quality recording.   Cassette and manual 99912-2

A MODERN HERBAL, Margaret Grieve. Much the fullest, most exact, most useful compilation of herbal material. Gigantic alphabetical encyclopedia, from aconite to zedoary, gives botanical information, medical properties, folklore, economic uses, much else. Indispensable to serious reader. 161 illustrations. 888pp. 6½ x 9¼. 2-vol. set. (Available in U.S. only.)   Vol. I: 22798-7
                    Vol. II: 22799-5

HIDDEN TREASURE MAZE BOOK, Dave Phillips. Solve 34 challenging mazes accompanied by heroic tales of adventure. Evil dragons, people-eating plants, blood-thirsty giants, many more dangerous adversaries lurk at every twist and turn. 34 mazes, stories, solutions. 48pp. 8¼ x 11.   24566-7

LETTERS OF W. A. MOZART, Wolfgang A. Mozart. Remarkable letters show bawdy wit, humor, imagination, musical insights, contemporary musical world; includes some letters from Leopold Mozart. 276pp. 5⅜ x 8½.   22859-2

BASIC PRINCIPLES OF CLASSICAL BALLET, Agrippina Vaganova. Great Russian theoretician, teacher explains methods for teaching classical ballet. 118 illustrations. 175pp. 5⅜ x 8½.   22036-2

THE JUMPING FROG, Mark Twain. Revenge edition. The original story of The Celebrated Jumping Frog of Calaveras County, a hapless French translation, and Twain's hilarious "retranslation" from the French. 12 illustrations. 66pp. 5⅜ x 8½.   22686-7

BEST REMEMBERED POEMS, Martin Gardner (ed.). The 126 poems in this superb collection of 19th- and 20th-century British and American verse range from Shelley's "To a Skylark" to the impassioned "Renascence" of Edna St. Vincent Millay and to Edward Lear's whimsical "The Owl and the Pussycat." 224pp. 5⅜ x 8½.   27165-X

COMPLETE SONNETS, William Shakespeare. Over 150 exquisite poems deal with love, friendship, the tyranny of time, beauty's evanescence, death and other themes in language of remarkable power, precision and beauty. Glossary of archaic terms. 80pp. 5³⁄₁₆ x 8¼.   26686-9

THE BATTLES THAT CHANGED HISTORY, Fletcher Pratt. Eminent historian profiles 16 crucial conflicts, ancient to modern, that changed the course of civilization. 352pp. 5⅜ x 8½.   41129-X

THE WIT AND HUMOR OF OSCAR WILDE, Alvin Redman (ed.). More than 1,000 ripostes, paradoxes, wisecracks: Work is the curse of the drinking classes; I can resist everything except temptation; etc. 258pp. 5⅜ x 8½. 20602-5

SHAKESPEARE LEXICON AND QUOTATION DICTIONARY, Alexander Schmidt. Full definitions, locations, shades of meaning in every word in plays and poems. More than 50,000 exact quotations. 1,485pp. 6½ x 9¼. 2-vol. set.
Vol. 1: 22726-X
Vol. 2: 22727-8

SELECTED POEMS, Emily Dickinson. Over 100 best-known, best-loved poems by one of America's foremost poets, reprinted from authoritative early editions. No comparable edition at this price. Index of first lines. 64pp. 5 3/16 x 8¼. 26466-1

THE INSIDIOUS DR. FU-MANCHU, Sax Rohmer. The first of the popular mystery series introduces a pair of English detectives to their archnemesis, the diabolical Dr. Fu-Manchu. Flavorful atmosphere, fast-paced action, and colorful characters enliven this classic of the genre. 208pp. 5 3/16 x 8¼. 29898-1

THE MALLEUS MALEFICARUM OF KRAMER AND SPRENGER, translated by Montague Summers. Full text of most important witchhunter's "bible," used by both Catholics and Protestants. 278pp. 6⅝ x 10. 22802-9

SPANISH STORIES/CUENTOS ESPAÑOLES: A Dual-Language Book, Angel Flores (ed.). Unique format offers 13 great stories in Spanish by Cervantes, Borges, others. Faithful English translations on facing pages. 352pp. 5⅜ x 8½. 25399-6

GARDEN CITY, LONG ISLAND, IN EARLY PHOTOGRAPHS, 1869–1919, Mildred H. Smith. Handsome treasury of 118 vintage pictures, accompanied by carefully researched captions, document the Garden City Hotel fire (1899), the Vanderbilt Cup Race (1908), the first airmail flight departing from the Nassau Boulevard Aerodrome (1911), and much more. 96pp. 8⅞ x 11¾. 40669-5

OLD QUEENS, N.Y., IN EARLY PHOTOGRAPHS, Vincent F. Seyfried and William Asadorian. Over 160 rare photographs of Maspeth, Jamaica, Jackson Heights, and other areas. Vintage views of DeWitt Clinton mansion, 1939 World's Fair and more. Captions. 192pp. 8⅞ x 11. 26358-4

CAPTURED BY THE INDIANS: 15 Firsthand Accounts, 1750-1870, Frederick Drimmer. Astounding true historical accounts of grisly torture, bloody conflicts, relentless pursuits, miraculous escapes and more, by people who lived to tell the tale. 384pp. 5⅜ x 8½. 24901-8

THE WORLD'S GREAT SPEECHES (Fourth Enlarged Edition), Lewis Copeland, Lawrence W. Lamm, and Stephen J. McKenna. Nearly 300 speeches provide public speakers with a wealth of updated quotes and inspiration–from Pericles' funeral oration and William Jennings Bryan's "Cross of Gold Speech" to Malcolm X's powerful words on the Black Revolution and Earl of Spenser's tribute to his sister, Diana, Princess of Wales. 944pp. 5⅜ x 8⅜. 40903-1

THE BOOK OF THE SWORD, Sir Richard F. Burton. Great Victorian scholar/adventurer's eloquent, erudite history of the "queen of weapons"–from prehistory to early Roman Empire. Evolution and development of early swords, variations (sabre, broadsword, cutlass, scimitar, etc.), much more. 336pp. 6⅛ x 9¼.
25434-8

AUTOBIOGRAPHY: The Story of My Experiments with Truth, Mohandas K. Gandhi. Boyhood, legal studies, purification, the growth of the Satyagraha (nonviolent protest) movement. Critical, inspiring work of the man responsible for the freedom of India. 480pp. 5⅜ x 8½. (Available in U.S. only.) 24593-4

CELTIC MYTHS AND LEGENDS, T. W. Rolleston. Masterful retelling of Irish and Welsh stories and tales. Cuchulain, King Arthur, Deirdre, the Grail, many more. First paperback edition. 58 full-page illustrations. 512pp. 5⅜ x 8½. 26507-2

THE PRINCIPLES OF PSYCHOLOGY, William James. Famous long course complete, unabridged. Stream of thought, time perception, memory, experimental methods; great work decades ahead of its time. 94 figures. 1,391pp. 5⅜ x 8½. 2-vol. set. Vol. I: 20381-6 Vol. II: 20382-4

THE WORLD AS WILL AND REPRESENTATION, Arthur Schopenhauer. Definitive English translation of Schopenhauer's life work, correcting more than 1,000 errors, omissions in earlier translations. Translated by E. F. J. Payne. Total of 1,269pp. 5⅜ x 8½. 2-vol. set. Vol. 1: 21761-2 Vol. 2: 21762-0

MAGIC AND MYSTERY IN TIBET, Madame Alexandra David-Neel. Experiences among lamas, magicians, sages, sorcerers, Bonpa wizards. A true psychic discovery. 32 illustrations. 321pp. 5⅜ x 8½. (Available in U.S. only.) 22682-4

THE EGYPTIAN BOOK OF THE DEAD, E. A. Wallis Budge. Complete reproduction of Ani's papyrus, finest ever found. Full hieroglyphic text, interlinear transliteration, word-for-word translation, smooth translation. 533pp. 6½ x 9¼. 21866-X

MATHEMATICS FOR THE NONMATHEMATICIAN, Morris Kline. Detailed, college-level treatment of mathematics in cultural and historical context, with numerous exercises. Recommended Reading Lists. Tables. Numerous figures. 641pp. 5⅜ x 8½. 24823-2

PROBABILISTIC METHODS IN THE THEORY OF STRUCTURES, Isaac Elishakoff. Well-written introduction covers the elements of the theory of probability from two or more random variables, the reliability of such multivariable structures, the theory of random function, Monte Carlo methods of treating problems incapable of exact solution, and more. Examples. 502pp. 5⅜ x 8½. 40691-1

THE RIME OF THE ANCIENT MARINER, Gustave Doré, S. T. Coleridge. Doré's finest work; 34 plates capture moods, subtleties of poem. Flawless full-size reproductions printed on facing pages with authoritative text of poem. "Beautiful. Simply beautiful."–*Publisher's Weekly*. 77pp. 9¼ x 12. 22305-1

NORTH AMERICAN INDIAN DESIGNS FOR ARTISTS AND CRAFTSPEOPLE, Eva Wilson. Over 360 authentic copyright-free designs adapted from Navajo blankets, Hopi pottery, Sioux buffalo hides, more. Geometrics, symbolic figures, plant and animal motifs, etc. 128pp. 8⅜ x 11. (Not for sale in the United Kingdom.) 25341-4

SCULPTURE: Principles and Practice, Louis Slobodkin. Step-by-step approach to clay, plaster, metals, stone; classical and modern. 253 drawings, photos. 255pp. 8⅛ x 11. 22960-2

THE INFLUENCE OF SEA POWER UPON HISTORY, 1660–1783, A. T. Mahan. Influential classic of naval history and tactics still used as text in war colleges. First paperback edition. 4 maps. 24 battle plans. 640pp. 5⅜ x 8½. 25509-3

CATALOG OF DOVER BOOKS

THE STORY OF THE TITANIC AS TOLD BY ITS SURVIVORS, Jack Winocour (ed.). What it was really like. Panic, despair, shocking inefficiency, and a little heroism. More thrilling than any fictional account. 26 illustrations. 320pp. 5⅜ x 8½. 20610-6

FAIRY AND FOLK TALES OF THE IRISH PEASANTRY, William Butler Yeats (ed.). Treasury of 64 tales from the twilight world of Celtic myth and legend: "The Soul Cages," "The Kildare Pooka," "King O'Toole and his Goose," many more. Introduction and Notes by W. B. Yeats. 352pp. 5⅜ x 8½. 26941-8

BUDDHIST MAHAYANA TEXTS, E. B. Cowell and others (eds.). Superb, accurate translations of basic documents in Mahayana Buddhism, highly important in history of religions. The Buddha-karita of Asvaghosha, Larger Sukhavativyuha, more. 448pp. 5⅜ x 8½. 25552-2

ONE TWO THREE . . . INFINITY: Facts and Speculations of Science, George Gamow. Great physicist's fascinating, readable overview of contemporary science: number theory, relativity, fourth dimension, entropy, genes, atomic structure, much more. 128 illustrations. Index. 352pp. 5⅜ x 8½. 25664-2

EXPERIMENTATION AND MEASUREMENT, W. J. Youden. Introductory manual explains laws of measurement in simple terms and offers tips for achieving accuracy and minimizing errors. Mathematics of measurement, use of instruments, experimenting with machines. 1994 edition. Foreword. Preface. Introduction. Epilogue. Selected Readings. Glossary. Index. Tables and figures. 128pp. 5⅜ x 8½. 40451-X

DALÍ ON MODERN ART: The Cuckolds of Antiquated Modern Art, Salvador Dalí. Influential painter skewers modern art and its practitioners. Outrageous evaluations of Picasso, Cézanne, Turner, more. 15 renderings of paintings discussed. 44 calligraphic decorations by Dalí. 96pp. 5⅜ x 8½. (Available in U.S. only.) 29220-7

ANTIQUE PLAYING CARDS: A Pictorial History, Henry René D'Allemagne. Over 900 elaborate, decorative images from rare playing cards (14th–20th centuries): Bacchus, death, dancing dogs, hunting scenes, royal coats of arms, players cheating, much more. 96pp. 9¼ x 12¼. 29265-7

MAKING FURNITURE MASTERPIECES: 30 Projects with Measured Drawings, Franklin H. Gottshall. Step-by-step instructions, illustrations for constructing handsome, useful pieces, among them a Sheraton desk, Chippendale chair, Spanish desk, Queen Anne table and a William and Mary dressing mirror. 224pp. 8⅛ x 11¼. 29338-6

THE FOSSIL BOOK: A Record of Prehistoric Life, Patricia V. Rich et al. Profusely illustrated definitive guide covers everything from single-celled organisms and dinosaurs to birds and mammals and the interplay between climate and man. Over 1,500 illustrations. 760pp. 7½ x 10⅛. 29371-8

Paperbound unless otherwise indicated. Available at your book dealer, online at **www.doverpublications.com**, or by writing to Dept. GI, Dover Publications, Inc., 31 East 2nd Street, Mineola, NY 11501. For current price information or for free catalogues (please indicate field of interest), write to Dover Publications or log on to **www.doverpublications.com** and see every Dover book in print. Dover publishes more than 500 books each year on science, elementary and advanced mathematics, biology, music, art, literary history, social sciences, and other areas.